THE EVOLUTION
OF REGIONAL ECONOMIES

THE
EVOLUTION
OF REGIONAL
ECONOMIES

Entrepreneurship
and Macroeconomic Change

LUIS SUAREZ-VILLA

PRAEGER

New York
Westport, Connecticut
London

Library of Congress Cataloging-in-Publication Data

Suarez-Villa, Luis.
 The evolution of regional economies : entrepreneurship and
macroeconomic change / Luis Suarez-Villa.
  p. cm.
 Bibliography: p.
 Includes index.
 .ISBN 0–275–93198–6 (alk. paper)
  1. Entrepreneurship. 2. Regional economics. I. Title.
HB615.S89 1989
338'.04—dc19   89–3762

Library of Congress Catalog Card Number: 89–3762
ISBN: 0–275–93198–6

First published in 1989

Praeger Publishers, One Madison Avenue, New York, NY 10010
A division of Greenwood Press, Inc.

Printed in the United States of America

The paper used in this book complies with the
Permanent Paper Standard issued by the National
Information Standards Organization (Z39.48–1984).

10 9 8 7 6 5 4 3 2 1

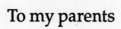

To my parents

Contents

Tables

Figures

Preface

Writing a work that deals with both entrepreneurship and long term regional economic change is a difficult task. From a broad multidisciplinary perspective, the entrepreneur is less well understood than many social scientists would acknowledge. Whether seen from a micro or a macro perspective, the driving forces, roles, and outcomes of entrepreneurship are often analyzed, critiqued, or exalted without considering the broader historical view of the processes and changes that entrepreneurial action sets in motion. At the same time, the data required to test any of the assumptions connected with this perspective, at both the micro and macro levels, are always incomplete, at best. It is therefore hardly surprising that most studies of entrepreneurship tend to focus on the micro aspects of entrepreneurial activity, neglecting its broader implications. Equally difficult is the fact that most macro studies of socioeconomic change tend to ignore the entrepreneur's roles completely, or implicitly assume some automatic functions that either yield preaccepted outcomes, or unrealistically tend to narrow down the range of possibilities considerably.

In this problematic context, the aim of this book would seem overly ambitious. Still, the topic of entrepreneurship and long-term regional change must be broached, even if its treatment is less complete than might be desired, or more elusive to capture empirically with the universe of historical data that is available. Relating entrepreneurship, and the historical emergence of its various socioeconomic roles, to the process of long-term regional change will therefore be the central concern of this work. It is by no means an exhaustive treatment of the subject, nor of the relationships involved. No models with easily specifiable variables or parameters are provided. These, and the consideration of the microanalytic details of the relationships involved, remain tasks for future research. It is in this context that the subject matter of this work was approached. It should be up to the reader to decide the ultimate value of this treatment, and its motivational value for future research agendas in this area.

An adequate consideration of the emergence of the various entrepreneurial roles driving major socioeconomic and spatial transformations requires deeper insights into the classical works than would normally be necessary in a study of long-term change. This approach is essential to the definition of the various roles, inasmuch as those works provide the seminal perspectives on their original conceptualization. The impacts of the classic spatial works considered are also found today in virtually all of the treatments of regional economic change found in our field, whether adequately acknowledged or not. Thus, a consideration of the classical contributions of the past two hundred years is crucial to the definition of the entrepreneurial roles. Needless to say, this effort would have been incomplete, at best, without that perspective.

The emphasis placed on the innovative aspects of each entrepreneurial role unquestionably owes much to the Schumpeterian approach. Each entrepreneurial role is therefore viewed as an innovative agent of change. The emergence of these roles since the time of the Industrial Revolution becomes a central concern of the historical focus and the various stages that are conceptualized, linking each role to the sectoral and the spatial transformations. Thus, the emergence of each role invariably leads to a consideration of historical periods and stages, as they shape the space economy through sectoral transformations that influence the spatial distribution of employment and population. A great deal of documentation on the ideas and discussions of Chapters 2 and 3 will be found in the chapter notes. Readers may indeed find these as important as the text, in grounding and deepening the textual discussions and materials.

The empirical analyses of Chapters 4 and 5 provide insights on the sectoral transformations promoted by the historical emergence of each entrepreneurial role. The measurement of long-term change with U.S. data for the ninety-four year (1889–1983) period helps place two of the historical stages conceptualized in an earlier chapter in perspective. Chapter 4 then considers national trends, while Chapter 5 focuses on the regional changes. Much of the cited data, although published, still required substantial archival research to determine the compatibility of information among the various years. The data limitations involved in the coverage of such a long period, including the paucity of information for the earlier years, are unfortunately too difficult to allow a more sophisticated statistical analysis of the macro relationships involved. Still, the empirical chapters yield insightful perspectives on the sectoral changes and transformations that were previously conceptualized. The importance of the entrepreneur in shaping the empirical outcomes is inescapable, given the nature of our market economy, the institutional mechanisms supporting entrepreneurial action, and the limitations placed on government intervention in the workings of the market, or even in the long-term formulation and implementation of major policies.

The apparent correspondence of some of the historical periods with those hypothesized for long waves by some authors may prompt readers to wonder whether an analysis of long-wave dynamics might not have been appropriate for the empirical chapters. Such an effort, though doubtlessly interesting, would have been beyond the scope of this work. Most long-wave analyses are primarily concerned with measurement issues rather than with the historical processes in which the entrepreneur is the explicit determinant of long-term change. The consideration of innovative entrepreneurship and the emergence of various historical roles could nevertheless provide the essential conceptual ground for the occurrence of long-wave phenomena. Unfortunately, long-wave analyses usually use outcomes as the starting point, attempting to work backward insofar as any causal linkages are concerned. In such an approach, the crucial roles played by entrepreneurs and their organizations are usually lost, while the analytical focus shifts toward macro variables and market trends as the immediate determinants of change.

It is my hope that this contribution will inspire others to pursue further research on this topic. Indeed, the spatial literature is conspicuous for its lack of explicit treatments of entrepreneurship and its impact on the urban and regional transformations that are of greatest interest to our field.

Acknowledgments

Much is owed to those who have helped in the production of this work. I am particularly indebted to those in my field of research who provided thoughtful comments, insights, and encouragement at various stages in the preparation of the manuscript. I am grateful to Bill Alonso, Ben Chinitz, Art Getis, Lay Gibson, Niles Hansen, Leo Klaassen, Peter Nijkamp, Harry Richardson, and Morgan Thomas for their feedback and encouragement. I would also like to express my gratitude to William Baumol, Alfred Chandler, William Glade, Harvey Leibenstein, Richard Nelson, Walter Rostow, and Raymond Vernon for their comments and suggestions at various stages in the preparation of the manuscript or on related papers. Special appreciation is owed to Barclay Jones, who enriched my historical appreciation and perspectives during my years as a graduate student at Cornell, and to Walter Isard for introducing me to regional analysis and regional science.

The financial assistance provided by a University of California Faculty Career Development Grant, and research grants awarded by the Academic Senate of the University of California at Irvine are acknowledged and appreciated. My colleagues Joseph DiMento and Carol Whalen supported my research by allowing periods of sabbatical leave during their tenure as directors of the Program in Social Ecology. I am also indebted to all of my Social Ecology colleagues at Irvine, who provided moral support and a good measure of collegiality throughout the preparation of this work. Julia Gelfand was especially supportive in providing access to bibliographical materials at Irvine, and funding the acquisition of many works related to this project. Peter Johnson provided access to the Firestone Library at Princeton; his thoughtful comments on various aspects of the production of this work are also appreciated. Louise Mahoney, Warren Boyd, and Roger Der provided much needed assistance in the preparation of the computer-generated graphs at the Irvine computing facility. The staff of the Social Ecology manuscript processing unit and, in particular, Fran Doty, Jill Vidas, Dianne Christianson, and Carol Wyatt, were especially helpful in processing the numerous tables and the manuscript. I thank our secretary, Cathy Reynolds, for preparing correspondence related to the production and submission of this manuscript.

THE EVOLUTION
OF REGIONAL ECONOMIES

Economic Change as a Process

The study of economic change presents both enormous potentialities and dismal obstacles. It is difficult to find any other topic in the social sciences that has consistently attracted more attention over the years. The social scientist's fascination with questions of economic change has indeed been evident in most classical and seminal works throughout history, where the study of this topic and its fundamental causes has been a major concern. Similarly, economic change has been a major interest in the literature on contemporary issues, reflecting our perplexity at its accelerating pace and its positive and negative impacts.

Virtually every major socioeconomic issue of concern today deals with the question of change. Most of these issues have, furthermore, longer term implications and impacts that are seldom fully understood. Thus, for example, questions on the international competitiveness of American goods and services have a major bearing on this nation's long-term ability to survive as a source of innovation and economic initiative. Domestically, the unprecedented shifts in economic and population growth toward the Sunbelt states have raised major questions on the nation's long-term regional division of labor. The restructuring of farming in the traditional agricultural regions has, for example, raised concerns about the future of family farming and the long-term impacts of major agribusiness corporations in this sector. In manufacturing, the increasing internationalization of many industries has placed substantial pressure on this nation's long-term ability to provide innovative breakthroughs as a means of remaining competitive.

Despite the enormous relevance of long-term economic change to current issues, the study of this topic faces some very substantial obstacles. The most significant obstacle to the study of economic change arises primarily from the limited, discipline-oriented perspectives that have been typical of the social sciences since their inception. Social scientists have shown a remarkable inability to pool the knowledge stocks of each field, to study a topic that would be inadequately approached in any but a multidisciplinary way. Thus, significant advances in the study of socioeconomic change by economic historians have remained virtually unknown to many social and behavioral scientists. Similarly, strides made by behavioral scientists in the study of many microbehavioral aspects bearing on economic change, have remained unknown to many economists, geographers, and regional scientists.

The dismal character of the obstacles to an analysis of long-term change is enlarged only by the uncertainties and complexities of the variables affecting it, especially over the long term. Far from dealing with clean-cut, laboratory-type conditions, the study of economic change must attempt to analyze phenomena that are quite "open" to external disturbances and distortions. Also, all too often, analytical efforts attempting to study the process of change have suffered from a considerable lack of perspective on the deeper factors and elements that affect it. Thus, even the best of efforts at modeling long-term change are bound to suffer from the constraints imposed by the lack of overarching theoretical perspectives, and by the limitations of discipline-focused approaches.

THE ELEMENTS OF ECONOMIC CHANGE

A fruitful approach to the study of economic change must consider those elements that most significantly affect its deeper structure. The most important of these undoubtedly is innovation. Innovation, be it organizational or technological, is at the very core of the process of economic change. In this respect, virtually every single major breakthrough that has contributed to economic change in any significant way can be traced to the development and diffusion of innovations.

The emphasis placed on technological innovation over the past few decades has overshadowed another equally important, but less well-known form. Organizational innovations involve a restructuring of productive and decision-making tasks where the application of scientific inventions is not a central aspect of the process. Thus, new forms of organizational structuring that result in more efficient communication and better ways of achieving results are one of the most common examples of this form of innovation. Technological innovation, on the other hand, involves the application of new scientific inventions to the production of a good or service. Many technological innovations undoubtedly also involve organizational innovations, as human organization and behavior are adjusted to deal with new technology in more effective ways.

Innovations do not occur through some mysterious volition or in a "black box," where their nature, scope, and applications are automatically decided. The entrepreneur is, rather, the agent through which economic innovations occur. Innovative entrepreneurship, in all its various roles, is therefore at the core of innovation diffusion in every walk of economic life.

Innovation diffusion through entrepreneurship is the single most important factor underlying regional economic change. There is not a single activity in the space-economy that is not ultimately affected by the diffusion of entrepreneurial innovations. In this respect, a significant aspect of our era is that the spatial diffusion process has not only accelerated, but that the very mechanisms of diffusion have themselves been innovated upon. The development of communications and transportation technology, organization, and infrastructure has made it feasible for manufacturing and service activities to decentralize to the nation's less developed areas and regions. Thus, the so-called "information economy" has become an important reality of our times, with significant impacts on the interregional distribution of economic activities and population.

The crucial importance of entrepreneurship in this process becomes all the more obvious when the various roles of the entrepreneurial function are defined and understood. There, the learning and decision-making aspects of each role can be better related to economic change from a process-oriented perspective. Thus, a differentiation of the various entrepreneurial roles should serve as a logical starting point for deeper analysis. This should help avoid the fairly common practice of using entrepreneurship as a vague, "catch-all" term whenever economic behavior and decision making are not fully understood or cannot be readily quantified.[1]

As an agent of innovation diffusion and economic change, the entrepreneurial function responds to the population's wants and needs. Indeed, the most important and deeper causes of entrepreneurial innovation are the changes that occur in those wants. Market demand mechanisms then translate those changes into signals of opportunity that entrepreneurs can explore and exploit. Thus, the learning process aspect of innovative entrepreneurship starts from a reactive condition where perception, timely decision making, and action play a crucial role.

At an aggregate macroeconomic level, the impact of entrepreneurial innovation is felt in the restructurings that occur in the various economic sectors. Thus, the sum of entrepreneurial actions and decisions occurring individually, or through groups, organizations, or the state, has a major impact on the national and regional macroeconomies. Changes in manufacturing toward advanced technology industries have revolutionized not only this sector, but also many related activities in services and agriculture. The introduction of biotechnology, and of advanced chemicals and machinery in agriculture, has had major qualitative and quantitative impacts on this sector's output trends. In services, where a substantial proportion of the nation's growth has occurred, new organizational forms and technology have changed this sector's role, making it more "basic" than anyone could have foreseen a few decades before. The macroeconomic changes that these sectoral restructurings, driven by innovative entrepreneurship, have induced in the space-economy's growth, productivity, and employment patterns have been historically unprecedented.

ECONOMIC PROCESS AND THEORY

Conceptualizing the process of regional change requires an incorporation of the various elements of the process in a general framework. Thus, the many limited observations, hypotheses, and empirical evidence found on each element and their interrelationships must be consolidated in a meaningful way. An excessively focused or a much too general perspective would provide incomplete results, and compromise the objectives of this effort.[2]

A theory of economic change also requires an understanding of how the basic concepts are underlain by human behavior. For this purpose, a realistic treatment of this aspect is imperative. Any socioscientific conceptualization that deals with the microbehavioral underpinnings of economic change in a simplistic way would, at best, be inadequate. Unfortunately, the main economic paradigms, Neoclassical and Marxian, are of little help in this respect. Their usually narrow, highly simplified treatment of the behavioral underpinnings of entrepreneurial action and decision making makes either of these paradigms unsuitable for this purpose.[3]

The set of relationships specified for the various elements of the theory must lead to definite conclusions. Such conclusions must then lead to sufficiently specified parameters that can be falsified by the facts. At the same time, a direction of change must become explicit in the structuring of the relationships involved. This is particularly important to any form of theorizing on long-term economic change, for, to be valid, the direction of change must also be falsifiable by previous events.

A high degree of theoretical consistency with past experience and events will therefore be essential for its validity. This implies that the phenomena observed were not so significantly affected by changes in the contextual parameters that they can be assumed to have been determined by the hypothetical relationships.[4] Obviously, the analysis of past events is particularly important for any theorizing on long-term change. Thus, an appropriate historical frame of reference will be essential to any conceptualization of long-term change. Without it, long-term change theorizing would be reduced to a mere manipulation of variables.

Here, it should be useful to distinguish model building from the elaboration of theory. Modeling usually considers a more limited range of phenomena and possibilities than does a theory. More restrictive parameters are therefore adopted in modeling, in an effort to test some aspects of a broader body of concepts, and to provide didactic illustrations. A conceptualization of long-term change will therefore have much broader perspectives, and will incorporate the set of models that are consistent with its assumptions.

Finally, the importance of explanation as a major theoretical objective in the analysis of long-term change must be addressed. In the social sciences, and especially in economics, prediction has been favored over explanation as a more important objective of theory-building. Prediction is, however, a product of good explanatory power. Without explanation, prediction would be virtually useless. Achieving significant explanatory power is especially important for this study, since a conceptualization of long term change must, more than other analytical efforts, be based on the explanation of past historical events and phenomena.

Explanation is also more suitable to a process-oriented focus than is prediction. The nature of prediction, in fact, usually favors outcomes over process. In prediction, if the process through which the outcomes occur is considered at all, it is usually a very secondary or accessory aspect of the effort. Outcomes must nevertheless be considered in an evaluation of a concept's consistency with past experience. The difference in emphasis given to process over outcomes in this study will therefore be a matter of degree, with greater emphasis on the former.

THE STRUCTURE OF LONG-TERM CHANGE

The theoretical perspective of this study will relate the various elements of long-term change in a general conceptual framework. This approach will require, first, some analysis of the microbehavioral underpinnings of economic change, based on insights and evidence found in the behavioral science literature. A second component will then provide definitions of the entrepreneurial function and its various innovative roles. The neglect endured by broad-based studies on entrepreneurship, especially in the spatial literature, should alone make this a worthwhile undertaking.

A typology of innovative entrepreneurship would, at best, be incomplete without an adequate consideration of the historical emergence of each role, and their place and function in the process of long-term change. An interpretation of economic history, and the contributions provided by various fields, will be required for this purpose. A multidisciplinary perspective therefore becomes essential to this effort, assembling evidence from major contributions and interrelating their insights in the conceptual perspective of this study. This is especially important to the spatial perspective, since any theory building effort on this topic must look beyond the boundaries of the fields dealing with the space-economy, drawing from the knowledge resources of numerous disciplines.

The importance of the historical perspective becomes all the more obvious when the impact of each entrepreneurial role on the sectoral macroeconomy is analyzed. Clearly, the emergence of each role is a product of the economic conditions of a historical period, and the structural and functional deepening of each economic sector, based on the previous development of innovations and on changes in the population's wants and needs. This definition implies that the emergence of any given role, far from being a random event, is greatly determined by the economic conditions and the demands placed on each sector to satisfy new wants. Differences in the level of demand between sectors in any historical period will therefore determine which entrepreneurial role emerges, and the function that any new role must fulfill.

Organizational and technological innovations are a product of this historical process, and will undoubtedly have a crucial influence on the impact of each entrepreneurial role in the sectoral macroeconomy—partly because the appearance of new organizational forms is inseparable from the emergence of a given entrepreneurial role. The causal relationship between entrepreneurship in any given role and new organizations is therefore a major link in the sequence of impacts on the various economic sectors. Similarly, new technologies are also specific to the historical emergence of any given role, responding to the pressures and opportunities to satisfy new wants faced by entrepreneurs and the economic sectors in which they operate. The differential impact of these innovations on any given sector will determine how the growth leadership of its activities is established. The spatial preferences and tendencies of a new leading sector will then, in turn, determine the changing structure of the space-economy. Regional population redistribution, sectoral employment reallocation, and the emergence of some regions as sources of new economic growth will be among its more important impacts.

The innovative impacts of the entrepreneurial function are not restricted to individual sectors and the spatial changes that result. The pattern of intersectoral changes and linkages promoted by the historical emergence of a new entrepreneurial role will be as important as the impacts felt by any given sector. Organizational and technological innovations have a crucial impact on such interrelations, particularly as the diffusion process advances from the sector where an innovation originates to another sector favored by the new wants. Changes in intersectoral relations are therefore logically traceable to the emergence of each entrepreneurial role and to the innovations that they generate.

A study of the structure of long-term change could never be complete without an empirical evaluation of past events and the central variables that affect the process of change. Clearly, the most important impacts of entrepreneurial innovation and sectoral restructuring on regional change are best analyzed at the level of the macroeconomy. There, the interplay between growth, employment, and productivity shapes the various trends, revealing the process through which regions grow, stagnate, or decline. The impact of these variables on spatial population redistribution has promoted the most historically significant changes in regional settlement structure, through urbanization and the differential growth of some city sizes over others. Indeed, the very process of change in urban hierarchies and regional settlement systems can be traced to the historical evolution of the sectoral macroeconomy, brought about by the emergence of entrepreneurial roles and their innovations.

Among its most significant aspects, this study will therefore attempt to explore the broader relationships between the "micro" and "macro" underpinnings of the process of long term regional change.[5] This approach will require a unified treatment of sectoral and regional change as the macroeconomic outcomes of entrepreneurial action, where organizational and technological innovations have a crucial impact. An historical perspective will be essential in developing the various linkages and interrelationships between the various elements of the conceptual framework. Without it, much contextual sense and meaning would be lost. Finally, greater analytical emphasis on process rather than outcomes, and on explanation, will also be important aspects of this effort. Such emphasis will support the combination of conceptual and empirical perspectives underlying this study's approach.

The Entrepreneurial Question

The social science literature has so far been unable to yield a general, comprehensive perspective on entrepreneurship. The neglect of broad treatments of this topic is astonishing, given the importance of entrepreneurship in the processes of economic and social change. Most of the issues, concepts, and theories developed in the social sciences are substantially underscored by assumptions regarding entrepreneurial behavior and its economic, social, and cultural roles. Entrepreneurial action and behavior are, furthermore, at the root of virtually all the current spatial and temporal concerns in the social sciences, ranging from issues related to very broad phenomena, such as the processes of industrial and demographic change, to more narrow and specific questions about the way in which individual decisions are made.

Neglect of entrepreneurship as a topic of scholarly research can best be explained by a set of historical, disciplinary, and methodological influences that have conditioned both the spatial and the social science literature. Perhaps the most important factor has been the fact that a broad perspective on entrepreneurship is beyond the reach of any given field. Most attempts to deal with this topic in any of the social science disciplines have so far produced piecemeal, though often very significant, perspectives on various aspects, such as decision making, risk, or the motivational factors that are involved. At the same time, qualitative aspects that defy easy quantification have been a serious obstacle to broader considerations of the entrepreneurial function in empirical and conceptual analyses.

In the field of economics, where significant discussion of this topic has occurred, the onset of Keynesian and static Walrasian perspectives over the past five decades has drawn much attention away from the interests relevant to entrepreneurship, and has confined these to the residual category of market imperfections. At the same time, the methodological tools used by these approaches are not well suited to the analysis of the dynamic phenomena that are essential to the study of entrepreneurial processes. As these conceptual and methodological perspectives became entrenched as orthodox dogma, the possibility of adequately considering entrepreneurship in mainstream economics diminished considerably. The resulting neglect prompted William Baumol (1968, p. 66), years ago, to note: "Look for [the entrepreneur] in the index of some of the most noted of recent writings on value theory, in neoclassical or activity analysis models of the firm. The references are scanty and more often they are totally absent. The theoretical firm is entrepreneurless—the Prince of Denmark has been expunged from the discussion of *Hamlet*."

Even in the area of economic development, where this topic has received relatively greater attention, very limited treatments have emerged over the years. Leibenstein's (1985, p. 6) survey of twenty-five general works on economic development, many of them textbooks, is particularly revealing in this respect. While several of these works had either a section or a chapter on entrepreneurship, the ideas developed in those sections were not applied elsewhere in the text. Their analyses therefore implicitly disregarded entrepreneurship, despite the fact that significant attention had been devoted to this topic in other sections. Similarly, Leibenstein's discussions with economists who teach development courses reflected a parallel neglect of the topic.[1]

The treatment of entrepreneurship in regional economic research has not fared any better than that in mainstream economic literature. In many respects, the neglect of this topic has been much more conspicuous in this field, partly because of the widespread adoption and application of orthodox economic concepts and techniques.[2] Our modeling efforts, which have served us well in providing many important insights on the nature of spatial economic processes, have therefore, at the same time, contributed to the neglect of the entrepreneurial function. Major emphasis on such assumptions as optimization, perfect knowledge, and equilibrium has often prevented a consideration of even some limited aspects of entrepreneurial processes, such as decision making and risk analysis. At the same time, stressing outcomes over *process*-oriented considerations has also prevented the development of general perspectives on entrepreneurship in the process of regional economic change.

Recent general overviews of the spatial economic literature have confirmed this neglect. Nijkamp's (1985) survey of research topics in regional science over a twenty-five year period, for example, revealed no broad or explicit consideration of entrepreneurship, even though most of the interests that were specified had a direct connection to entrepreneurial activities.[3] Similarly, previous general surveys of the regional economics literature by Richardson (1978b) and Meyer (1963) offered little evidence of entrepreneurship as a significant research interest, despite the fact that it was explicitly discussed in several major works, and had significant bearing on all of the research topics discussed.[4]

Economic geographers have fared no better than economists in providing general perspectives on entrepreneurship. An emphasis on the case study approach has provided many significant facts and evidence about various activities and processes that can be directly related to the entrepreneurial function. The fragmented nature of this approach has, however, produced benefits usually at the expense of a substantial neglect of theory. At the same time, the lack of a "macro" perspective that can bring the various currents of research together has been a serious obstacle to geographical inquiry on entrepreneurial processes.[5]

A review of the various research topics covered in the spatial economic literature suggests not only that a consideration of entrepreneurship can add significantly to the themes that have attracted attention over the years, but also that it is essential for a complete and coherent account of spatial macroeconomic change. In this sense, a broad and comprehensive treatment of entrepreneurship can provide the "micro" basis of regional macroeconomic change. This is based on the assumption that its consideration as a central component of spatial economic change can lead to better explanations of short- and long-term change processes than can the traditional "economic man" constructs.[6]

The consideration of entrepreneurship is also especially important if a more realistic account of economic processes is to occur. An understanding of the general entrepreneurial roles must then be complemented by more specific insights on such aspects as the innovative capabilities, motivational contexts, decision processes, risk perceptions, and organizational environments. The realization that most entrepreneurial roles and their qualities, and in many cases their quantity as well, are a scarce resource is essential to this argument.[7] Scarcity constraints can then be expected to influence the pace of regional growth and change, their interregional differences, and the levels of development.

Thus, a broad and comprehensive account of the entrepreneurial function must necessarily rely on multidisciplinary perspectives if a significant contribution to spatial economic research is to be made. The valuable contributions of economic historians, psychologists, sociologists, economists, anthropologists, economic geographers, and management specialists, among others, must be gathered and molded to provide as complete a perspective on the various roles of the entrepreneurial function and their spatial implications as can possibly be obtained. The difficulty of this approach is compounded by the fact that emphases and interests in the study of entrepreneurship have been strongly conditioned by each scholar's field.[8] In this respect, economic historians have provided significantly broader interdisciplinary accounts of the entrepreneurial function over the years. Gras' (1922) very significant early effort to study the historical role of the entrepreneur, for example, provided an excellent evidence of this approach, as it contributed a general perspective on its importance in the economic structure of societies.[9]

The definitions of the entrepreneurial function provided in this chapter will therefore rely heavily on the contributions of economic historians over the years. In this sense, entrepreneurship is generally defined as the making or implementing of decisions on the coordination and utilization of scarce resources in the space economy, that result in new long-term outcomes or in "new ways of doing things."[10] The making of such decisions requires qualities and quantities of skills and incentives that are spatially distributed. Risk taking, calculation, and uncertainty are intrinsic components of this definition of entrepreneurship, corresponding with Cantillon's (1931) early nineteenth century view on entrepreneurship as the bearing of noninsurable risk.

Most important, the definitions provided in this chapter also correspond closely with Schumpeterian views on entrepreneurship as innovation, or the carrying out of "new combinations" in any economic endeavor. Schumpeter's (1934) broad definition included such activities as the introduction of a new product or method of production, the opening up of new markets or sources of supply, or the carrying out of a new organization within an industry.[11] All of these examples have spatial dimensions and enormous significance for long term spatial economic change. The decisions made in executing these tasks often also result in new spatial distributions of economic activities, with significant new flows and spatial interactions.[12]

The entrepreneurial definitions, roles, and motivations to be explored in this chapter are common to all modern economic systems, be they of the free market, mixed, or centrally planned structure. What does vary among these systems are the agents through which the various roles are exercised. In Western-style market economies, for example, individuals, alone or working through private organizations, typically exercise the various entrepreneurial roles to be discussed in this chapter. In centrally planned economies, on the other hand, the entrepreneurial roles are usually executed by government technocrats acting with directives from superiors, on the basis of a temporal economic plan, or sometimes on their own initiative.

The next sections of this chapter will explore the motivational bases of innovation, risk taking, and the entrepreneurial ethos, in general.

The discussion on entrepreneurial motivation will be applicable to entrepreneurship carried out both individually and within structured organizations. A comprehensive, multidisciplinary review of the major roles found in the historical and social science literature will then follow, providing the microanalytic roots of the process of long-term spatial economic change.

ENTREPRENEURIAL INITIATIVE: THE MOTIVATIONAL ASPECT

The Major Paradigms: Assumptions and Shortcomings

Much of the social science literature has traditionally provided very simple and convenient abstractions of the factors motivating entrepreneurship. The two major currents of economic thought, the Neoclassical, where "economic man" assumptions are central, and the Marxian (including both the Marxist and the less dogmatic Neo-Marxist), are surprisingly similar in their assumptions regarding entrepreneurial motivation and behavior. Their central assumptions provide inadequate explanations of the complexity and range of factors that motivate entrepreneurship.

These two approaches generally view profits as the sole motivator of entrepreneurial action.[13] They therefore advance what is basically a very incomplete heuristic as the behavioral foundation of their theoretical constructs. Purely hedonic behavior is at the root of their assumptions, providing a very convenient and quick way to simplify what is in fact a complex reality and behavior. To a great extent, the lack of insights on human behavior of these two paradigms reflects the undeveloped state of behavioral science, at the time when the historically most significant contributions to both of these approaches were made.

This exclusive concern with profits has produced an interpretation of entrepreneurial action that is almost completely focused on capital accumulation, to the neglect of all the other, and in many cases more significant, entrepreneurial roles and activities. Other significant motivations of entrepreneurial behavior, such as achievement needs and altruism, cannot therefore be adequately considered by either of these two approaches. As an ultimate measure, profits are not, furthermore, good indicators of entrepreneurial efficiency. A given level of profit may reflect lower costs, lower prices, or a manipulated context that results in higher costs and prices. At the same time, profit levels, by themselves, do not normally reflect the various internal tradeoffs that are made within organizations in order to cope with endogenous and exogenous pressures, and which are very much a part of entrepreneurial decision making.[14]

Both the Neoclassical and Marxian approaches view entrepreneurial roles and activities as being basically automatic and always perfectly available. To a great extent, this assumption follows on, and extends, the profit assumption, since it assumes that whenever and wherever profits are to be made, entrepreneurial skills and ability will be ubiquitously available. This assumption also implies perfect foresight and largely ignores the element of risk in pursuing most economic actions.

Viewing entrepreneurship as automatic, the Neoclassical and Marxian perspectives also reduce entrepreneurial decision making to the level of a trivial endeavor. It is implicitly assumed that all entrepreneurs operate the same way, regardless of the entrepreneurial role, the industry, sector, economic activity, organizational size, level of development, or the nation, region, and locality where the entrepreneurial action is undertaken. This supposition is further reinforced in the Neoclassical construct by optimization assumptions that require perfect knowledge of the context, and ignore individual tolerance in overcoming difficulties, and differences in individual satisfaction with the outcomes obtained.[15]

Both the Neoclassical and Marxian constructs are based on comparative statics, the latter being only marginally less so. For the Neoclassical paradigm, the Walrasian influence provided an aesthetic that substantially limited its realism and, in the minds of many critics, was greatly responsible for turning much of mainstream economics into a circumscribed, puzzle-solving exercise. On the Marxian approach, recent Neo-Marxist views have done little to loosen up what is basically a static perspective on entrepreneurial action and social change.

Major differences between the Neoclassical and Marxian approaches are also of little help in providing realistic insights on entrepreneurial motivation and behavior. In the Marxian ethos, its uppermost concern is the question of social justice, particularly in connection with problems arising from the exercise of entrepreneurial roles and activities.[16] In this context, profits, regarded as the sole motivator of entrepreneurship, are evil, and entrepreneurial decision making and action become the mechanism through which the labor force is exploited. Issues of control of labor, and of potential and actual conflict between management and the labor force and between different social groups, are obsessively focused upon, to the exclusion of most other considerations in the entrepreneurial decision-making process.

The Marxian approach further elevates conflict, assumed to be the result of entrepreneurial action and of the injustices and inequalities it creates, as the supreme medium for socioeconomic change. Such conflict arises from the opposed interests of the various social classes and the socioeconomic imbalances created by substantial economic expansion and entrepreneurial action. The intended outcomes, greater equality and social justice, are usually achieved in Marxian praxis by turning over to the state the prerogatives of entrepreneurial decision making and action. It is a reflection of the Marxian lack of understanding of entrepreneurial motivation and behavior, however, that greater equality in the new social structure of Marxist societies is usually traded off with a substantial lack of innovative and productive motivation, and the widespread emergence of underground entrepreneurial activities.[17]

Besides the Neoclassical and Marxian perspectives, a third current of economic thought, the Managerialist perspective, may also be considered. In many ways, the assumptions of this approach are similar to those of the Neoclassical perspective, particularly with respect to the role of profits as a motivator of entrepreneurship. Profit levels therefore become the major indicator of the quality of operation of any enterprise. All assumptions regarding decision making are considered solely with respect to their eventual effects on profits. Other entrepreneurial motivations, priorities, and organizational characteristics are ignored as indicators of performance or are subordinated to the profit "bottom line."

A fourth significant perspective that has attracted much interest in recent years can be traced to Alchian's (1950) consideration of economic evolution. A notable aspect of this approach has been its concern over the difficulty of extending orthodox microeconomic concepts in order to consider uncertainty. Unfortunately, this approach overlooked the fact that quite different methods from those of the orthodox paradigm would have to be introduced if this "evolutionary approach" and the very significant impact of uncertainty on economic action were to become formalized. This paradigm also basically assumed that evolutionary mechanisms would confirm the expectations of orthodox theory on optimizing behavior and equilibrium conditions, despite the fact that these assumptions become untenable whenever uncertainty is considered in economic decision processes. The biological analogy of this approach, based on natural selection, is basically ahistorical, and in many ways, is also detached from socioeconomic reality, at least insofar as a strict application of biological natural selection is concerned. Although it represents an intellectually valuable exercise, an explicit consideration of entrepreneurship in all its roles and functions in the process of long-term economic change was missing from this approach, as it sought to focus more on the application of the biological analogy, than on understanding the process of long-term economic change and the functional role of the entrepreneur.

A consideration of these currents of economic thought unfortunately provides little help in accounting for the other major motivational mechanisms of entrepreneurship. At the same time, it must be acknowledged that behavioral science has not advanced enough to be able to provide conclusive or complete evidence on the factors motivating entrepreneurial behavior. Profits and material rewards do motivate entrepreneurship and are significant factors, but they are nevertheless incomplete explanations of entrepreneurial behavior. Other factors must necessarily be considered, therefore, for a better explanation of entrepreneurial motivation and behavior.

A central assumption of the forthcoming discussion on entrepreneurial motivation will therefore be that nonmaterial aspects and rewards are at least as important as profits or material motives in promoting entrepreneurial action. Indeed, if the significant work of various psychologists and behavior specialists over the past four decades is carefully considered, such aspects and motives may actually be more significant than material motivations. This view will be further reflected upon later in the discussion of the various entrepreneurial roles.

Achievement Motivation

Much psychological research has traditionally been oriented toward identifying basic human needs, and the attitudinal and behavior patterns that these generate. The need for affiliation with other human beings and the development of a sense of "belonging," the need for control over one's environment, and the need for achievement, whether of a materialistic nature or not, have been identified as three major human psychological wants.[18]

Of these, the need for achievement provides the greatest insights on entrepreneurial motivation and behavior. Entrepreneurial achievement need is, at the individual level, a variable element. It is precisely this variable aspect, and the need to account for it in any explanation of either micro- or macroeconomic performance, that creates the greatest problem in incorporating achievement motives in the "economic man" construct. At the same time, it is not entirely clear whether achievement motives can be assumed to be purely hedonic, in a materialistic sense. Much evidence gleaned from the psychological literature indicates that achievement motivation may in fact not be significantly oriented toward material rewards.[19]

David McClelland's work, and its subsequent development by various authors, has been significant in articulating and documenting the entrepreneurial achievement motive.[20] His "n-Achievement" (need for achievement) concept provided a "micro" basis for a broad, macrocultural theory of socioeconomic change. McClelland's (1961) seminal contribution linked human psychological needs with the process of economic development, by isolating psychological factors dealing with individual achievement tendencies, and attempted to demonstrate quantitatively their importance in the development process.

The causal sequence of McClelland's construct first links cultural values with the process of educational socialization in middle childhood, by assuming the latter to reflect society's central beliefs and tendencies regarding economic achievement.[21] More directly, such reflection is obvious in, and occurs through, the various learning tools used in primary education.

This socialization process then leads on to achievement learning, in various degrees, and eventually to the formation of achievement motives. Entrepreneurial achievement in adulthood can then be traced to earlier achievement learning provided by the educational system and, to some extent, the family context. The aggregation of individual achievement motives and performances in society would provide an indication of macroeconomic performance, over the long term, once a given generation reaches sufficient maturity to exercise socioeconomic and political leadership.[22]

Risk taking becomes a central component of entrepreneurial achievement motivation, but it is generally assumed that individuals with high "n-Achievement" mostly engage in activities carrying moderate risk that can be reduced by increased effort or skill. Such individuals then work harder at tasks that pose a real challenge, involving a moderate degree of risk, rather than at any task per se. The abilities to set priorities, plan actions accordingly, and make timely decisions are significant skills that can also promote rapid learning in individuals with high "n-Achievement" characteristics. Other significant characteristics often cited in the literature are a high need for autonomy, order, and a sense that allows apparently chaotic phenomena to be viewed as being part of a system that is conceptually comprehensible.

McClelland's empirical verification focused on content analyses of widely used, primary school books of twenty-five nations, searching for indicators of achievement learning. These were then related to the economic growth rate performances of each nation twenty-five years later, and a significant, positive relationship was found between educational systems containing higher achievement content in their primary school materials, and their respective nation's economic growth performance. The empirical approach, although not without problems, nevertheless convincingly showed an important relationship that had not previously been explored.[23]

Subsequent work on the "n-Achievement" construct, by McClelland and Winter (1969), McClelland and Steel (1972), and Miron and McClelland (1979), adopted a "micro" perspective and has attempted to show that achievement motivation can be learned, thereby changing the quality of an individual's socioeconomic contribution. Unfortunately, orthodox economics so undervalues the returns to education that these significant experiments have been virtually unnoticed in the mainstream literature.[24] The significance of the "n-Achievement" concept is therefore not restricted to its interpretation of reality and the causal linkages involved, but also in its approach to changing that reality through achievement motivation training.

The "n-Achievement" concept can also be related to Schumpeterian views on innovation. It is not difficult to visualize high "n-Achievement" as an essential prerequisite to innovative entrepreneurship, whether in actions that are carried out within a structured decision-making or productive process, or in those that change the process itself. Schumpeterian innovative entrepreneurship therefore gains a significant microbehavioral base in the "need for achievement" concept, as it potentially explains a major cause of long-term economic change and societal evolution.

It is unfortunate that the implications of international and interregional differences in "n-Achievement" have been completely ignored in the spatial economic literature. At a "micro" level, for example, many significant questions on the relationship between the level of entrepreneurial "n-Achievement" and the quality or success of locational decision making could be asked. Similarly, the "macro" aspects of differences in economic performance and social structure between more and less developed regions, as reflected in their educational and achievement motivation structures, could provide significant insights on the process of long-term spatial economic development.

Status

The analysis of social status has for many years been central to sociological inquiry on factors affecting entrepreneurial motivation. Research in this area can best be categorized into two main currents of thought. One of these has viewed entrepreneurs as modal personalities representative of the prevailing social structure. Entrepreneurial motivation therefore becomes a function of the search for status preservation by dominant social groups and can be readily influenced by changing economic and social incentives. Policy intervention then acquires significant importance in this scheme, as a means either to motivate or to limit the participation of any social group.[25]

A second major current of thought has focused on the search for social status of marginal social groups, usually either ethnic or religious, or both, through innovative entrepreneurship. In this case, the withdrawal of status by the larger society, or its inaccessibility to such groups, is assumed to trigger the motivation to overcome a disadvantaged position. Entrepreneurial activities then often become the most attractive of all possible alternatives in the search for social status. Four major events usually associated with such search are forced displacement, prohibition or denigration of valued symbols or customs by the larger society, the lack of correspondence between social status and economic power (especially if the group has achieved the latter but not the former), and difficulty of integration and acceptance in the new social structure after migration occurs.[26]

From this perspective, innovative entrepreneurs are seen as marginal men, lacking acceptance by the predominant social structure. Their ambiguous position, from a social and cultural viewpoint, allows them to make creative adjustments that result in significant innovations. From a Schumpeterian perspective, such entrepreneurship is more likely to result in actions oriented toward process change, rather than a willingness to work within existing, structured processes.

The implications of status search and marginal groups in entrepreneurial activities have remained vastly underresearched in the spatial economic literature. Most often, studies have been undertaken in the historical literature through case study research on specific localities, individuals, or groups. Little effort has also been made to relate these phenomena to the process of interregional migration, although its potential implications for long-term spatial economic change would appear to be very significant.

Structural and Institutional Incentives

Much concern has been aroused in recent years about the role of government in promoting or impeding entrepreneurial activities and innovation. This concern has focused primarily on the market, institutional, and policy structures and their effects on entrepreneurial innovation and investment through the mechanisms they create, such as the tax structure, regulatory practices, and the state's participation in the economy, as an entrepreneur in its own right. Arguments, pro and con, have been raised from all sides and ideological persuasions, attempting to prove the beneficial or detrimental effects of any number of policies or government actions.[27] The treatment of this topic, difficult as it may be, nevertheless merits discussion in this review of factors affecting entrepreneurial motivation.

Structural and institutional incentives for entrepreneurship are only partial motivational factors affecting entrepreneurial development. Others, such as achievement motives, material rewards, and social status issues, are just as important, and can manage to overcome significant impediments in the institutional, policy, and market structure arenas over time. Institutional and policy incentives for entrepreneurship can nevertheless be a powerful motivational force when they support and work in concert with the other motivational factors.

From a social perspective, institutional and policy structures are often not free of bias, in terms of eventual outcomes and effects; these results are sometimes independent of processes designed to ensure a certain degree of impartiality or objectivity in achieving their proposed objectives. The entrepreneurial motivation, roles, and skills they affect are highly differentiated, especially with respect to a given industry or industries, and specific groups or individuals. Furthermore, as students of the space economy well know, they seldom affect all regions or localities in the same manner, and their spatial effects on such areas can linger for years or decades.

These institutional and structural incentives usually affect entrepreneurial motivation and supply by lowering the opportunity costs to innovative entrepreneurs, based on the alternatives that are available.[28] Very often, possibilities for innovative entrepreneurship have to be identified, they are simply not obvious or readily available. These steps require varying degrees of skill and persistence, such as a sense for concentration, attention, and striving or, in other words, the "drive" to conceive and sustain a given entrepreneurial activity.

A number of perceived pecuniary advantages can come into play in motivating this process such as, for example, a choice of self-employment that is thought to be superior to other alternatives, or the possibility of gaining substantial material rewards if the enterprise grows large.[29] Nonpecuniary advantages can also play an important motivating role, such as the autonomy to organize one's own working environment through self-employment, or the possibility of creating market imperfections that allow the enterprise to gain additional market share, thereby increasing the entrepreneur's social status or political influence.

The value placed by institutional mechanisms on innovative entrepreneurship can reflect broader societal attitudes toward such activities, at least in some socioeconomic systems. Often, however, a tradeoff has been perceived between institutional incentives for entrepreneurship, and the achievement of greater socioeconomic equity in such areas as the distribution of wealth, availability of opportunities, or the production of social goods.[30] To a great extent, this perception seems unjustified from a long-term, evolutionary perspective, inasmuch as many entrepreneurial innovations, documented in much of the historical literature, have actually produced results that promote greater social equity and well-being for the majority of the population. The discovery and development of many medical breakthroughs by scientist-entrepreneurs, and the invention and production of new communication and transportation technologies by engineer-entrepreneurs are examples of this development.

These possibilities are not independent of the structural and institutional incentives for entrepreneurship found in any given sociopolitical structure, however. Such mechanisms as patents, property, and ownership rights act as powerful incentives for individual entrepreneurial innovation. Although recent experience has shown that some research and development can be carried out bureaucratically, through government institutions, even there the development of such inventions can usually be linked to a reward structure that provides benefits similar in many ways to those of the individual patent or property right system.[31]

A TYPOLOGY OF ENTREPRENEURIAL ROLES

The historical development of definitions of entrepreneurship reflects many scholars' preoccupations with issues of entrepreneurial supply spanning more than two centuries. In some cases, scholarly attention to a specific role has closely reflected pressing practical concerns and issues of their times, as in some of the classical works related to capital accumulation and investment. In others, significant scholarly interest developed only long after the specific role had appeared and become formally institutionalized. Scholarly publications on concepts and methods related to intermarket linkage, productive coordination, or strategic planning, for example, did not appear until decades after these roles had been formally established in practice. In some cases, scholarly attention to these roles surfaced only after significant innovations were introduced in their day-to-day activities, providing an incentive for reflection on their effects in the broader economy or society. In many cases, significant interest in the spatial economic literature did not appear until after the broader theoretical concerns and societal implications had been seminally considered in the social science literature.

Creating a typology of any human activity is a difficult task in almost any circumstance. Developing a typology of entrepreneurial roles is more troublesome, however, because many entrepreneurial activities defy easy classification into a handful of neat or easily defined categories. Overlaps exist between some of the major entrepreneurial roles that are not easy to resolve. Some of these roles are also highly interrelated, making it difficult to disentangle their individual rationale and characteristics. Furthermore, some major scholarly works, providing significant insights on more than one role, have made it more difficult to assess their significance in terms of a single function. In such cases, the more innovative treatment of a given entrepreneurial role received greater priority in the contribution's consideration. This would not prevent, however, its additional consideration regarding any other entrepreneurial role to which it contributed significantly. Finally, a lack of scholarly contributions on some entrepreneurial roles, particularly in the spatial economic literature, has made the task of constructing a typological framework doubly difficult.

One significant problem, in searching for definitions of the entrepreneurial function in the contemporary orthodox economic literature, is the tendency to include entrepreneurial roles and activities in "catch-all" residual categories, such as those assumed to result in "technological change." Invariably, these are roles and activities that, as was discussed previously in this chapter, the orthodox paradigm is not well equipped to handle. A consideration of entrepreneurial motivation, decision making, risk, and uncertainty would have either invalidated or seriously contradicted precepts that are essential to the orthodox paradigm, such as the assumption of perfect knowledge and foresight, perfect optimizing behavior, or the existence of equilibrium conditions.[32]

Technological change is, no doubt, an outcome of entrepreneurial action, and research and models dealing with this factor have made significant contributions to our knowledge of entrepreneurship. The entrepreneurial function must, however, be seen in broader terms. It encompasses other roles and activities that are just as significant as those commonly identified with technological change.

Ironically, it was the work on the Neoclassical production function that uncovered some significant empirical evidence on the importance of entrepreneurship in long-term economic change.[33] Production function specifications have traditionally considered two major factors: capital and labor. Longitudinal empirical tests have focused on changes in the proportions of labor and capital (or allocative efficiency) as the major determinants of output change. As a convenient simplification and, also, because of the conceptual shortcomings of the Neoclassical approach, any proportion of output change not explained by changes in the allocation of either labor or capital has been treated as a residual, and assumed to be the combined effects of "technological change." Most Neoclassical models have usually treated such residuals as "exogenous" elements influencing economic change.

A major contribution, in this respect, was Solow's (1957) test of a Neoclassical production function specification with U.S. data for a forty-year period (1909–49). Gross output per man-hour doubled over this period, with 87.5 percent of this increase being left unexplained by changes in the allocation of either labor or capital.[34] Allocative efficiency could therefore explain only a very small proportion of economic change over this period of time.

The residual found in this and other empirical tests prompted a significant reformulation of the factors affecting output and productivity change. Thus, Leibenstein's (1966) important formulation of the "X-Efficiency" concept focused on the effects of managerial and worker motivation in production, as a way of explaining the residual left unaccounted for in Solow's and in subsequent empirical analyses.

Accounting adequately for such residuals or, for that matter, long-term economic change and performance, does require a broader view than that provided by either the conventional "technological efficiency" residual or the unorthodox "X-Efficiency" concept. Indeed, even allocative efficiency is itself a product of entrepreneurial action. It therefore seems that a better way to account for long-term economic change is to consider the entrepreneurial function broadly and comprehensively, in all its myriad roles. The subsequent sections of this chapter should therefore be seen as a start in this direction.

The implications of this approach for the way we presently analyze spatial economic change will be quite substantial, inasmuch as our view of the factors affecting long-term processes of change is much too limited, and has been greatly influenced by the orthodox economic paradigm. Innovation will be stressed in all of the entrepreneurial roles considered in the following sections of this chapter, reflecting a broader interpretation of this activity than has so far been possible. Thus, technological innovation will be treated as one of the various important byproducts of innovative entrepreneurship, rather than as its sole outcome.

Investment: A Classic Role

As an entrepreneurial role, investment is of special importance because its performance is crucial to the development of all other roles. Negative feedback on investment in the decision process can prevent action in any other role, with the possible exception of invention, insofar as any specific venture is concerned. The historical importance attached to this role is reflected in the Classical economic literature, where it received earlier and more significant attention than any other entrepreneurial role.

The earliest scholarly interest in this role can be traced to Richard Cantillon's (1931) contribution in the middle of the eighteenth century, a time that coincides with the emergence of industrialization in England and shortly thereafter in parts of continental Europe. Cantillon's perspective was mercantilist, reflecting the dominant tendencies of economic thought at the time. He viewed entrepreneurship primarily as a process of capital investment and accumulation, and the bearing of noninsurable risk.[35]

Decades later, Adam Smith's general definition of entrepreneurship as the provision and accumulation of capital would once again be influenced by the weight of historical precedent. In his view, the modern entrepreneur was little more than the equivalent of the seventeenth-century merchant-capitalist. This narrow view of entrepreneurship would be later enshrined in much of the Classical, Neoclassical, and Marxian literature, leading to a major historical misunderstanding of the nature and scope of the entrepreneurial function. This definition would also be adopted and developed by Marx, in his critique of the capitalist process and the negative effects of entrepreneurial action. As Redlich (1966) noted years ago, this legacy would prove difficult to modify, and is thought to have prevented an adequate consideration of entrepreneurship in much of the subsequent economic literature, up to our own time.

The Smithian definition had other significant shortcomings that would not become apparent until much later, as the industrial age developed in Europe and North America. His definition totally ignored innovation as an essential aspect of entrepreneurship. Its absence is evident in his use of the terms "merchant," "master," and "undertaker" to describe the incipient industrial entrepreneur.[36] Another shortcoming was the lack of insight on the question of risk; in Smith's view, risk was implicitly assumed to be solely a function of capital investment and accumulation. The consideration of other entrepreneurial roles by subsequent authors would later provide additional perspectives on the many facets of risk-taking behavior.

Almost half a century after Smith, Jean Baptiste Say (1803) located risk bearing as a central characteristic of entrepreneurial action. His definition was significant because it explicitly differentiated between risk bearing occurring through investment, and that which occurs through other potential roles. John Stuart Mill (1848) would later add to this definition by making an explicit distinction between entrepreneurship per se and the provision of investment capital. This conceptual distinction coincided with the rapid development of capital markets as major institutions in their own right, in the advanced industrial economies of the middle and late nineteenth century. The establishment of these institutions would have enormous significance for the development of this role as a major component of entrepreneurship in modern society, inasmuch as they institutionalized this very important activity.

Schumpeter's views on the investment role would be significantly influenced by his focus on innovation as the most important aspect of entrepreneurship. He and, to some extent, Max Weber assumed entrepreneurial initiative and risk taking to be distinct from capital accumulation. Investment and capital accumulation could then be seen as two different types of activities; the former being an important role if it contributes to innovative entrepreneurship, while the latter is merely a byproduct of entrepreneurship in all its various roles.[37] In the Schumpeterian view, any innovative entrepreneurial role, including investment, would then undergo a learning process in its development, regardless of whether a given venture became successful or not by the yardsticks of capital accumulation.

So far, it has been made obvious in this review that risk was viewed as an integral component of the investment role. However, this aspect was not dealt with in depth until Knight's (1921) seminal contribution related entrepreneurial decision making to risk, uncertainty, and the availability of information. Until Knight's contribution, none of these aspects had been fully or adequately considered in the literature. Although it has substantial implications for the investment role, his work nevertheless focused more on market processes than on investment per se. This accent would prove to be very helpful later on to Austrian school economists such as Hayek (1945) and Kirzner (1979), especially as they related market processes to the perception of investment opportunities.

The onset of the Keynesian era after the 1930s and the emergence of the Neoclassical paradigm, unable to account for uncertainty and, to a great extent, risk in entrepreneurial decision making, unfortunately overshadowed efforts to provide more realistic insights on the entrepreneurial investment role. The first Neoclassical model of investment behavior, provided by Tinbergen (1939), was then based on the theory of optimal capital accumulation, yielding significant insights on the potential explanatory variables of short- and medium-term economic change. Since then, many highly sophisticated models have provided significant insights on various aspects of the investment function, but from a Neoclassical perspective.[38]

Various criticisms of the Neoclassical investment function have emerged in the literature. Cyert and Simon's (1983) work is particularly noteworthy, because of its incisive questioning of the validity of the Neoclassical paradigm on the investment role. Most arguments in favor of the Neoclassical investment function have relied on the success of empirical curve fitting between the hypothesized and the actual results. Cyert and Simon cast serious doubts on these analyses, because of the large degrees of freedom (five to seven, usually) employed, and the brevity of the time series to which the hypothetical functions are usually fitted.[39] Curve-fitting procedures have also failed to yield reasonable estimates for the capital coefficient in Cobb-Douglas production functions, according to Cyert and Simon (1983, p. 103). In their view, the "desired capital" terms, assuming they can be adequately foreseen by entrepreneurs, normally explain only approximately 10 percent of the magnitude that one would expect from the theory.

Fitting such functions to the data to estimate the parameters of an investment, *after the fact*, is relatively easy when compared to the entrepreneur's purported estimation of those parameters *before* the activity actually occurs, if the Neoclassical assumptions are to be applied. Neoclassical decision rules in such situations are particularly artificial, considering that the entrepreneur would have to estimate the parameters based on other data, with perfect foresight, uncertainty notwithstanding. For the Neoclassical assumptions to hold, the entrepreneur would furthermore have to estimate the aggregate marginal productivity of capital for each investment decision, from data actually available.

Another significant shortcoming of the Neoclassical approach in this respect is that profit maximization under uncertainty, related to investment or any other entrepreneurial role, becomes extremely vague, partly because of the lack of uniqueness of any maximizing approach under these conditions. Years ago, Alchian (1950) noted that any action chosen with the objective of maximizing under uncertainty has to be identified with a potential, rather than a unique, set of outcomes. The maximizing task then becomes one of selecting an action whose potential distribution of outcomes is preferable. A maximizing distribution cannot exist in such cases because the decision maker is forced to choose actions with a perceived, nonunique optimum distribution, thereby axiomatically contradicting the very purpose of maximization and its theoretical underpinnings.

A rational approach to entrepreneurial decision making with respect to the investment role or, for that matter, any of the other roles, must take into account the imperfect foresight of the entrepreneur, or the entrepreneur's organization, and that individual's limitations on experience and information, capacity for computation, understanding of theory (Neoclassical or otherwise), and the possibility of applying it practically. As Cyert and Simon (1983, p. 104) have pointed out, the exercise of this form of rationality leads to the use of simple heuristics (rules of thumb) to guide investment decisions when faced with uncertainty.[40] Satisficing, as postulated by Simon (1955b), is one such heuristic. At the same time, the use of these behavioral rules often introduces biases in the decision process, because of the nature and availability of information, as demonstrated by Tversky and Kahneman (1982).[41]

The spatial economic literature's treatment of this role and the decision processes involved has been very sparse indeed. Most often, the investment role has only been considered marginally, in connection with spatial production functions, adopting all the Neoclassical assumptions intrinsic to that approach. In the few cases where investment activities have been addressed, it is rather the spatial effects of investment that have been considered, instead of the nature of spatial entrepreneurship in this role.[42] A unifying conceptual framework, outside of the Neoclassical paradigm, has unfortunately been missing from these studies. The types of decision-making processes applied in spatial investment activities, the heuristics involved, the types and motivations of entrepreneurs, the magnitude of their ventures, the interrelations between these factors, and the policies that influence them have been completely ignored.

The significance of this role for long-term spatial economic change is paramount, and poses many interesting research questions, particularly in view of the globalization and rapid expansion of capital markets and their outreach to even the least developed nations and regions. Where serious supply limitations in the investment role occur, secular stagnation is a likely outcome, with excessive specialization in agriculture or the traditional manufacturing activities.[43] Often, the effective supply of this role depends on the development of capital markets and communications infrastructure that are essential for a more efficient allocation of investment risk across the population. Alternatively, the stimulation of foreign or extraregional domestic investment has often been sought as a means to overcome local supply limitations in this role.

Intermarket Linkage and the Need for Integration

At the level of the spatial macroeconomy, intermarket linkage is one of the most important entrepreneurial roles. It has also been significant historically in the development of industrialization since its earliest stages, because of the need to link together sources of supply and raw material inputs with productive activities. Surprisingly, however, explicit scholarly interest in this role did not develop until well into the present century.

In its various forms, intermarket linkage involves the opening up and coordination of sources of inputs to any entrepreneurial activity. It ensures, for example, the reliability of input sources, decides on whether, and how, to use alternative suppliers, arranges the vertical integration of related activities and firms, and coordinates input and product linkages among the various activities of the vertically integrated units. At another level, this role also arranges and coordinates linkages between horizontally integrated units of the same enterprise.

Although the intermarket linkage role was implicitly introduced in various classical economic works throughout the eighteenth and nineteenth centuries, it was not made explicit until Schumpeter's (1934) recognition of the "opening up of new sources of inputs" as an important innovative entrepreneurial endeavor. Although its treatment in Schumpeter's work was rather fleeting and general, its significance for long-term economic evolution is undoubtedly a major one, particularly because of its importance in the restructuring process that occurs as industries grow, mature, and decline.

These implications, and their significance in the long-term process of development, were made most forcefully and explicit in Albert Hirschman's (1958) seminal contribution. Entrepreneurship was viewed there as the "filling in" of missing linkages in the supply chain from extractive activities to the provision of final demand goods. Hirschman's definition of backward and forward linkages was central to this conceptualization, providing a means of operationalizing and testing it. Later on, this would be reflected in the vast popularity the concept acquired among development scholars and, particularly, with respect to import substitution policies in less developed economies. The enormous implications of Hirschman's work for spatial economic analysis would also become obvious in later years, as linkage research gained substantial importance in the geographical and regional science literature.

Another significant contribution toward the identification of this entrepreneurial role was in Harvey Leibenstein's (1968, 1979a) definition of "gap filling" in the "X-Efficiency" paradigm. Gap filling arises primarily because many needs and skills are simply not marketed as specific services or products, and therefore have to be fulfilled through entrepreneurial ability and resourcefulness. Another consideration driving this definition is that some inputs, such as leadership, trust, and the organizational ability to solve crises or maintain supply relationships, are vague and their results are usually indeterminate. In other cases, as with new industries, input markets will not even exist, and will have to be created if a venture will exist at all.

The spatial literature was unfortunately rather late in recognizing this role and its spatial manifestations explicitly. Alfred Weber (1929, pp. 201–206) had implicitly acknowledged its existence, through his static location analysis, where input linkages were a major component. Later, Edgar Hoover (1948, pp. 116–123) explicitly conceptualized input linkage structures by relating the process of spatial industrial concentration to the vertical integration of complementary activities. In Hoover's view, the benefits (localization and agglomeration economies) derived from such concentration would induce enterprises to agglomerate, and to rationalize their operations by sharing and consolidating their input linkages.

Vertical integration can be a major outcome of linkage filling as industrialization advances. Viewing it broadly, Cyert and March (1963) believed this process to be part of a need for uncertainty reduction at the enterprise level. More specifically, uncertainty reduction would involve such objectives as reducing costs or increasing revenues through price discrimination, or by ensuring the reliability of supply sources.

Citing Adam Smith's theorem, Stigler (1968, p. 135) earlier viewed vertical integration as being more typical of mature or declining industries, occurring through mergers, acquisitions of existing firms, or the creation of new firms and subsidiaries that can become sources of new inputs. Significant vertical integration is often the result of monopoly and oligopoly, given that firms cannot practice price discrimination in input markets where they do not operate. The effects of such restructuring on input markets would therefore be to lower prices when conditions are more competitive with, say, other input markets elsewhere and, conversely, to raise prices when they are not.

One of the more significant impacts of vertical integration on organizational structure is the internal differentiation that results when different units of the same enterprise respond to different external pressures, such as market competition and regulation. The outcome of such situations is usually a greater delegation of authority to the various units.[44] The spatial implications of this can be, first, greater decentralization of locational decision making, resulting in greater autonomy in selecting locations such as, for example, following managerial preferences on quality of life issues rather than on strict operational efficiency considerations. Second, greater dispersion of productive locations can result, as each unit approaches location decisions based on its own operational objectives rather than those of the overall enterprise. Thus, for example, greater dispersion than is favorable for the parent firm may be finally chosen, if it is perceived to be more appropriate for the unit, regardless of its broader implications for company welfare. Third, lower probability of locational changes, such as plant closings or relocations, to meet interregional competitive challenges, may occur than for firms in more competitive markets or with less vertical integration.

Different degrees of vertical integration can also be expected between enterprises located in more and in less developed regions. Greater vertical integration is more likely in the latter, because monopoly or oligopoly is more likely to occur there.[45] The intermarket linkage role is also more likely to be in greater demand in less developed regions, because the factors of production are likely to be less well marketed there. A key challenge to entrepreneurship will therefore be to mobilize the supply of those factors to ensure continuous linkages. Finally, risk and uncertainty bearing are also likely to be greater in less developed regions, because of factor market gaps and the lower availability of information, thus the need for greater vertical integration is reinforced.

The study of vertically integrated monopolies and oligopolies in less developed nations, also applicable in many cases to less developed regions, can provide significant insights on the operation of the intermarket linkage role in such firms.[46] Their expansion is often achieved, for example, without separating ownership from control, as finance capital is mobilized through family or personal ties, or through horizontal integration with financial institutions. A second feature is that the decline of family participation in such enterprises is less likely to occur in less developed areas than in advanced regions with well-established financial markets. From an evolutionary standpoint, the inverse of this phenomenon, which is more common in advanced regions and nations, was stressed by Schumpeter (1950) as a precondition facilitating the eventual socialization of production and the trend toward state ownership of productive capacity. A third aspect is that government-owned monopolies, operating in place of private entrepreneurs, do not usually guarantee innovative entrepreneurship, greater efficiency, or the attainment of social goals in connection with the intermarket linkage role. In fact, their performance has often been found to be less than desirable in promoting long-term socioeconomic goals and objectives, insofar as any factor upgrading is concerned.[47]

Horizontal integration, a second important outcome of intermarket linkage, is achieved primarily through mergers and acquisitions, rather than through the creation of new enterprises. Linkages to horizontally integrated firms tend to be financially oriented. They are nonmonopolistic in character but can nevertheless influence enterprises substantially, by providing finance capital at crucial times to the parent enterprise. In this sense, Stigler's (1968, pp. 303–304) definition of this form of restructuring as "non-monopolistic concentrations of wealth" has further reaching implications than have so far been supposed.

The development of a major analytical technique, input-output analysis, and its application to spatial economic analysis since the 1950s and 1960s, would make it feasible to trace both the spatial input linkages of any given region's economy systematically, and their restructuring over time. This was made possible by Leontief's (1936, 1941) publication of the first input-output matrix of the U.S. economy, followed by Isard's (1951, 1953) seminal conceptualization and application to the study of regional and local economic structure.[48] In more than one way, the input-output technique would allow the aggregate measurement of entrepreneurial intermarket linkages to be made. Unfortunately, its use for the study of long-term spatial economic change remains quite limited at this point, because of the longitudinal data requirements.

Two very significant conceptual developments related to linkage research during the 1960s and 1970s can also be related to this entrepreneurial role. One of these was the growth pole concept, developed after Perroux's (1955) seminal contribution, where intermarket linkages played a significant role in promoting expansion of localized activities and industrial complexes.[49] The second was the enormous interest in conceptualizing linkage structures, developed primarily in the geographical literature, which has supported innumerable case studies of organizations and their spatial linkages. A typology of topics covered in these studies would be too long to discuss here; however, a vast number of the conceptualizations and case studies can be directly related to this entrepreneurial role. A large number of the empirical studies in this area were based on survey research and focused on such interests as information flows, contact networks, industrial plant sizes, ownership characteristics, and organizational structure.[50]

Productive Coordination and Organizational Capability

Productive coordination plays an important role in spatial economic change. As opposed to resource allocation, which is primarily static, coordinative activities are inherently dynamic, allowing managerial entrepreneurs the possibility of becoming innovators and agents of change.

Middle and line managerial activities in organizations are characteristic of this role. These include, for example, "routine" tasks, such as combining available processes and techniques in proportions that can satisfy production requirements, avoiding the wasteful use of inputs, and ensuring that schedules and contracts are met. Innovative activities that are also characteristic of this role are, for example, the adaptation of inventions and new techniques in the production process, finding new ways to organize production in order to raise productivity without changing technology, conceiving new measures to raise the motivational state of personnel, and transacting with labor to develop new working arrangements.[51]

One of the most frustrating aspects in searching for this role in both the economic and spatial literature is the widespread neglect it has endured.[52] As such, there is no actual theory of the firm in either the orthodox economic or the spatial literature; instead, a theory of production is usually presented as a theory of the firm.[53] In such approaches, firms are typically represented as production functions, relating a firm's inputs to its outputs, and assuming the organization to be a "black box" that automatically transforms factors of production into products in optimal ways. Issues related to the internal workings and processes of the firm are thus ignored, and attention is deflected toward factor and product prices, or the quantity of outputs.

The systematic neglect of these "micro" concerns on the firm's operation is partly a result of the emphasis placed on "macro" issues in the orthodox economic literature over the past five decades. Organizations have therefore tended to be dealt with mostly in connection with "macro" concerns, usually in a very simplistic and stylized manner. Nelson and Winter (1982a, p. 51) have noted, for example, that "the theoretical firm is not merely a 'black box'—it is a black box whose input and output channels may be modified by assumption, at the convenience of the investigator."

In the Classical economic literature, references to this entrepreneurial role are very sparse. In the early nineteenth century, Jean Baptiste Say's (1803) distinction between strategic risk bearing (related to capital investment) and managerial decision making opened the possibilities to eventual recognition of this role in the literature. Say's view of the entrepreneurial function as being basically the combination of the factors of production would later be expanded by John Stuart Mill (1848), who also included the provision of continuous management and risk bearing in this role. Then, in the late nineteenth century, Alfred Marshall (1961) defined managerial entrepreneurship as the fourth factor of production, along with land, labor, and capital. Marshall's definition was much too narrow, however, as it considered coordinative entrepreneurship to be little more than a specific form of skilled labor.

Schumpeter's (1934) emphasis on innovation would later expand the scholarly perception of this entrepreneurial role, including the design and implementation of "new organizational forms" in his broad view of entrepreneurship. Innovation could then apply as much to the activities of this entrepreneurial role as it could to, say, the creation of new markets, sources of inputs, or the introduction of new technologies.

The introduction of mass production techniques in manufacturing after the turn of the century would further reveal the importance of this entrepreneurial role, laying the foundations for the eventual development of the field of managerial science.[54] Unfortunately, a substantial lag would occur between the implementation of these innovations and the emergence of significant scholarly interest in this role. Thus, management science did not arise as a major field of research and academic pursuit until after World War II.

One of the few early twentieth-century economists to recognize the importance of management in the organization was Austin Robinson (1934), who focused on the relationship between organizational structure and coordination. His research showed that a greater division of labor within the firm eventually increases the problems of coordination, integration, and control. Thus, greater hierarchical differentiation would be traded off with less interrelation between levels, lower knowledge and information handling possibilities, and greater coordination costs at every level.[55] Robinson's work would later inspire Frederick Harbison (1956) to provide a stronger linkage between entrepreneurship, the organization, and the process of economic development. His work applied aspects of communications theory to study the coordinative role in organizational structures, concluding that managerial capability was the most scarce resource in less developed economies.

Substantial interest in management as a field of study and in business history during the 1950s and 1960s then led to significant contributions whose scope can be directly related to this entrepreneurial role. Alfred Chandler's (1962, 1977) seminal work on the historical evolution of corporate hierarchies and structure is one of the most significant examples of this interest.[56] In an early survey of corporate history, Chandler and Redlich (1961) identified three levels of managerial coordination: operational or line management, "locum tenential" or middle management, and top-level management. Organizational objectives associated with the first two types were characterized as being primarily tactical, rather than strategic, including such tasks as the handling of day-to-day operations and the coordination of productive activities. The actual and potential innovative character of these apparently "routine" activities was one of the most important observations of this work, as it provided a direct link between this entrepreneurial role and the Schumpeterian perspectives on innovation.

Greater questioning of the Neoclassical view of the organization in the economic literature of the 1960s and 1970s would then lead Leibenstein (1976, 1979b, 1987) to focus on the coordinative entrepreneurial role as the central component of his "X-Efficiency" paradigm. "Input-completing" activities, such as the ability to obtain and use factors of production that are not well marketed, would be those most closely associated with this role. Input-completing entrepreneurs would be essential to the functioning of any enterprise, labor contracts being always incomplete, since performance specifications can never be perfectly detailed. It was also recognized that not all factors of production, such as leadership and motivational ability, are marketed, and the production function, contrary to Neoclassical assumptions, cannot be completely specified or known. To the extent that there are gaps in factor markets, the coordinative role would then have to make up any deficiencies. In the exercise of this role, enterprises therefore become valuable storehouses of detailed experience and knowledge on its workings, and on that of the factor markets with which it would be most closely linked.

Substantial evidence has been amassed over the past three decades, showing the importance of this role for productivity change. Most contributions have focused on the complexities of management-labor relations and the motivational structures and incentives that condition the workplace. At the core of most of these works is the assumption that a considerable amount of latitude exists to adjust labor's, as well as management's, performance and attitudes, depending on the methods and incentives that are used.[57] Such latitude then leaves considerable room for innovative experimentation in this entrepreneurial role, an aspect that has been continuously verified through case study results in both advanced and less developed economies.[58]

In the spatial literature, the significant interest of industrial geographers in organizational questions can be related to the exercise of this entrepreneurial role. Although important empirical insights have been provided in this area, most research has unfortunately relied on limited aspects of organizational theory. To a great extent, this narrow focus may have prevented broader and more critical views of the relationship between organizational structure and entrepreneurial coordination as they affect long-term spatial economic change.

Since the 1970s, however, the development of contingency theory in organizational analysis has synthesized much previous work and provided a broader and more scientific framework to organizational research. This has expanded the possibility of relating the exercise of the coordinative role and its organizational context to questions of spatial economic change. Unfortunately, most temporal spatial applications and empirical analyses based on contingency theory have focused on short-term change phenomena. Contingency theory may therefore remain limited in its applicability to the analysis of long-term spatial economic change in the future, because of its data requirements and the need to focus on a limited number of firms. Efforts in this area are nevertheless quite commendable, for the innovative perspectives that they have introduced by relating internal organizational questions to the structure of the space economy.[59]

A crucial question on the relationship between the coordinative role and spatial economic change that remains unanswered is how the supply characteristics of this role affect changes in firm location. It is obvious that the previously assumed and verified latitude in adjusting techniques and the motivational state of labor in production also has implications for skills substitution for both labor and management. Skills substitution can result in locational shifts in production, if significant cost reduction can be achieved through skill reductions by changing location. At the same time, the use of less skilled labor often requires less skilled managerial coordination, and thereby helps further cost reduction.[60] The possibilities for such tradeoffs and the consequent locational shifts toward less developed areas have obviously been made easier by recent advances in transportation and communications technology, and the increasing globalization of capital markets.

Strategic Planning and Corporate Entrepreneurship

Strategic planning is, by and large, a product of the rise of the modern, diversified twentieth-century corporation. It has gained greatest recognition in the second half of this century, through the rise of the activist corporation, symbolized by its expansion in interregional and international markets and, its influence on government at various levels, on financial markets, and on public values and perceptions.[61]

The strategic planning role focuses on top management's activities, reflecting ultimate authority and control over the organization. In contrast to the intermarket linkage role, it focuses primarily on product linkages, on marketing strategies, and on resolving regulatory pressures related to demand issues. Medium- and long-term planning related to product market strategies, and the setting of internal overall policy within the organization are also major components of its function.[62]

This is clearly a role that is usually carried out not by one but by several individuals within the organization. Delegation of authority is therefore important, as with the coordinative and intermarket linkage roles. To what extent such delegation occurs depends on the functional differentiation and spatial dispersion of units serving different markets, the overall enterprise size and scale of production, the availability of strategic planning skills, the extent to which they are marketed, and the degree of internal organizational entropy. More often than not, increases in the first, second, and third factors will very likely lead to greater delegation of authority. Greater organizational entropy, on the other hand, whether it results from shortcomings in the coordinative role or inadequacies in the corporate structure, may lead to greater centralization of authority.

The treatment of this role in the historical economic literature can, as with coordinative entrepreneurship, be traced to Say's (1803) early nineteenth-century contribution, where strategic decision making was defined as a component of managerial entrepreneurship. This definition was quite rudimentary, however; it would later be expanded in Schumpeter's (1934) work with the consideration of its innovative possibilities, the "opening up of new markets" being one of its major outcomes.

Chandler and Redlich (1961) and Chandler (1977) trace the emergence of this role to the evolution of the industrial enterprise from being primarily single function–single product organizations in the eighteenth and nineteenth centuries, to the creation of multifunction–single product enterprises in the nineteenth century and, eventually, to the emergence of the modern multifunction–multiproduct industrial corporation in the twentieth century.[63] This process also had major spatial implications since, as Chandler and Redlich (1961, p. 6) note, "modern structure and administration of industrial enterprise began in the United States with the geographical dispersion of such firms . . . geographical dispersion was the initial step in making modern industrial enterprise, because it made necessary the distinction between headquarters and field. . . . The development of such procedures as well as the planning for expansion, maintenance or contraction of the activities in the field became part and parcel of setting the goals and objectives of the firm."

The spatial dispersion of production would be instrumental in the development of the strategic planning role, as more complex organizational structures became a logical outcome of the trend toward multifunctional enterprises, making it necessary to standardize internal operating policies and procedures. This would later be compounded by the development of multiproduct enterprises serving different markets. Here again, Chandler and Redlich (1961, p. 25) note that "business policy seems to be the natural concomitant of geographically dispersed enterprise. In no other way can widely scattered operating decisions be coordinated and supervised."

The emergence of multiregional enterprises was logically made necessary by the need to increase market areas and shares, by the opening up of new markets, and by the effort to rationalize production in the face of competitive pressures. The general relationship between the opening up of new spatial markets and the growth of multiregional enterprises was noted earlier by Lösch (1954, p. 403), when he assumed that entrepreneurial capability, along with natural resource endowments and population density, determines the market area sizes of firms in any given industry.[64] Innovative capabilities in this entrepreneurial role are particularly important, Lösch (1954, p. 191) noted, as in "pioneer industries, where a rather infrequent combination of characteristics is required . . . the actual, though not the necessary, sales areas of the ablest [entrepreneurs] will be larger than those of the others."

Lösch also assumed a simple spatial division of labor to be typical within multiregional firms, where overall strategic planning and decision making would be primarily done at the central operation, with various degrees of authority being delegated to the agents or managers in the regional branches. Thus, again, an emphasis in the quality of entrepreneurial supply in this role, now extended to consider the various spatial dimensions of the enterprise, would lead him to observe (p. 191) that "as the capabilities of a leading entrepreneur can extend his sales area in general, so the special abilities of his regional sales representative can expand it greatly in a certain direction."

Finally, Lösch extended the relationship between the quality of entrepreneurial supply and the firm's market area size to consider a city's aggregate market area. Thus, he provided a linkage with von Thünen's (1826) previous simple model of the spatial division of labor when he stated (p. 406) that "considerable differences in [market area] size [may be found], which may depend partly in differences in market structure, but probably in part also upon a varying power of individual centers to attract qualified entrepreneurs." Thus, the core-periphery relationship that was central to von Thünen's model of agglomeration and market area size could be directly related to the supply characteristics of the strategic planning role.[65]

If these relationships are further extended, it is obvious that urban agglomerations with significant quanta of innovative entrepreneurs could become major generators of new knowledge that would eventually be diffused to the spatial peripheries.[66] Clearly, then, this model can consider not only urban centers, but also "core" regions and nations in the diffusion of innovations in strategic planning and in the other entrepreneurial roles. Their knowledge production capability would then depend not only on their ability to attract and concentrate innovative entrepreneurs, but also on the provision of essential public goods, such as the institutional mechanisms to protect and reinforce property rights, and on natural resource availability.

A further extension of these contributions can be made by differentiating between market innovation and invention in promoting local and regional market area expansion. Thompson (1965) considered innovative marketing and promotional abilities, which are central to this entrepreneurial role, rather than scientific or technological invention, to be the prime generators of spatial economic progress. Thus, he noted (p. 48) that market "advantage may lie with that local economy which serves the oligopolist who, however much he may bide his time in invention, retains a fine sense of timing in market innovation." Concentrations of entrepreneurs with such abilities were assumed by Thompson to be positively correlated with demographic size, up to the point where agglomeration economies decline.

The qualitative and quantitative supply characteristics of this role and the market area changes they promote have major implications for long-term spatial economic change. Their interaction with the rise, leveling off, and decline of demand conditions for any given product is at the source of most corporate strategic planning and decision making. Thus, the exercise of this role is crucial in the adaptation of the firm to changes in product demand pressures.[67] At the same time, the strategic planning role designs and implements the very process by which the firm's most important decision-making rules are learned and modified in the face of environmental feedback.[68]

The internal policy-making activities of this role include locational decision making as a significant component.[69] The way in which such decisions are reached and the effectiveness of their outcomes are influenced by this role's qualitative supply characteristics, and by the organizational context in which it operates, which is to a great extent also an outcome of its decisions. Thus, for example, the decision to follow "ad hoc" approaches to locational decision making, as opposed to either more centralized or autonomous approaches, is influenced greatly by the characteristics of this entrepreneurial role as it is applied to deal with organizational size and structure.[70]

Invention and Technical Innovation

Inventive entrepreneurship is crucial to the introduction of innovations in all the other entrepreneurial roles. It was historically the most significant factor in the origins of the Industrial Revolution, and has acquired increasing importance in the second half of the twentieth century, through the rapid emergence of technologically intensive industries and services.[71]

Unfortunately, significant interest in this role in much of the social science literature did not develop until recent decades.[72] To a great extent, this neglect is due to the lack of an intellectual grounding for invention in the major socioeconomic paradigms. In the Neoclassical approach, for example, technological invention has been commonly treated as an exogenous variable. At the same time, the Neoclassical assumptions have generally prevented a consideration of inventive behavior and the process of invention, both of which involve substantial uncertainty, experimentation, and risk.[73]

A distinction between invention and innovation is essential to the definition of this entrepreneurial role. Invention is defined here as the production of scientific, technical, and organizational knowledge that can be subsequently applied in any entrepreneurial role. Innovation, on the other hand, involves the application of an invention in any entrepreneurial venture. Innovation, as defined here, does have a broader perspective, however, since it may not necessarily involve the application of any technological or scientific invention as, for example, in the implementation of new organizational forms or the opening up of new markets.

Schumpeter (1934) provided an explicit distinction between invention and innovation, following on Say's earlier differentiation between innovative and routine entrepreneurship. He viewed inventive entrepreneurship as a separate role, where the new knowledge it produced would be acquired and applied by innovative entrepreneurs. His definition saw the inventive process as one involving new combinations of ideas and methods, and distinguished between two types of inventions: those that are applied within an existing or already structured process, and those that change the very process in which they are applied. Economic development was then defined as the carrying out of "new combinations" that would result in the introduction of a new good, or of a new quality of a good, and the introduction of a new method of production.

Schumpeter's simple diffusion mechanism, being the acquisition and application of individual inventions by innovative entrepreneurs, has diversified considerably in recent decades. Many enterprises today have developed their own inventive (R&D) capacity, making exclusive use of the new knowledge they produce.[74] In other cases, ventures have been created for the main purpose of producing inventions that are then sold to other enterprises. The participation of government as an inventor in its own right has been a major development of recent decades, providing inventions as a quasi-public good in areas such as health and national defense.[75] At the same time, the success of individual inventors who obtain property rights to be sold on demand, has become increasingly important for many advanced economies.

Despite the institutionalization of inventive entrepreneurship and various diffusion mechanisms, the inventive process remains one of the most elusive and esoteric of human activities. Also, despite all attempts to make the activities of this role routine, it retains an experimental and exploratory nature that is virtually impossible to plan in any detail. Most innovative activities have therefore had to rely on multiple inventive sources, and on selection processes that can determine the usefulness of any invention. The uncertainty and risk involved are therefore higher than for any other entrepreneurial role.

One of the more commonly agreed upon aspects of the inventive process is that it involves a search strategy based on decision rules as a means to reduce uncertainty and risk.[76] These decision rules are assumed to be affected by a number of other variables, such as the quality and preparation of entrepreneurs involved in this role, the potential material and nonmaterial rewards, including appropriability considerations, the competitive pressures faced by the enterprise, its size, and the resources that are available to it, including previous knowledge and experience. Clearly, factors such as potential rewards, enterprise size, and competition have important spatial implications, since they can be very much affected by market area extent and the enterprise's degree of spatial monopoly.[77]

Other variables that may potentially affect the decision rules applied to the inventive process are the degree of regulation encountered, and the evaluation of difficulties involved in achieving satisfactory outcomes. The latter may include, for example, an estimation of a lower potential rate of adoption, or one extending over a longer period of time, a greater potential for successful imitations or substitutions that can reduce appropriability, a large number of alternatives to search into, and difficulties associated with the design of the search process itself, such as the amount of resources to be committed to it.

The positive results of the inventive search process go well beyond the discovery of previously unknown products and methods, to include the broader implications of knowledge and experience gained in experimentation. The benefits of such knowledge can be quite independent of whether successful outcomes are attained or not. In this sense, for example, learning what would not work can be just as valuable as knowing what would. At the same time, the knowledge of related aspects that can lead to unanticipated discoveries, sometimes more valuable than the original objective, can have a major impact on future searches. These aspects are no doubt influenced by the type of entrepreneurial invention being undertaken and the character of its linkages with pure and applied science.[78]

The diffusion of inventions to any of the other entrepreneurial roles can occur in two ways: acquisition through direct purchase, or imitation. Once adoption occurs, it will serve either to substitute or to introduce a new product or process, with the objective of promoting greater efficiency in production, or a more reliable operation. The adopted invention can be embodied in a product, facilitating imitation, or it can be applied as a process. The latter, usually more complex and involving "new ways of doing things," will be more difficult to imitate, thereby prolonging appropriability and the rewards for invention.

The study of inventive entrepreneurship and of its implications for long-term economic change has unfortunately been much neglected in the spatial literature. While this may partly be a result of the recency of interest in technological innovation in this area, it may also be due to the lack of a major theoretical construct to which this research could be adequately linked. A significant amount of interest has nevertheless emerged in the process of spatial diffusion of innovations, dating from Hägerstrand's (1967) well-known contribution.[79] General interest in spatial diffusion processes has also generated substantial research on its impact on local and regional manufacturing activities.[80]

The creation and diffusion of inventions have significant implications for long-term spatial economic change. Substantial inventive activities in any given region will usually improve the supply quantum and quality of all the other entrepreneurial roles. A region with a significant concentration of inventive entrepreneurs is bound to be a major center for the diffusion of inventions and innovations to other areas. Its ultimate effect on the national and regional economies will therefore influence productivity changes and the distribution of spatial economic power.

A redistribution of economic power in favor of regions with greater inventive capacity may result in a more competitive regional position, nationally and internationally. It is very likely that the most successful cases will have strong export-oriented linkages with the international economy, will have very low levels of trade protection, and may become important financial centers.[81] The location of major research universities and supportive institutions is likely to be an important component of the local knowledge production base, although the causal linkages between these institutions and local industry and services may be subtle and difficult to trace.[82]

SYNTHESIS

This chapter has focused on the entrepreneurial function as the single most important factor affecting long-term spatial economic change. A broad typology of the roles that account for every facet of the entrepreneurial function was grounded in a review of major historical and socioeconomic contributions over the past two hundred years.

The contents of this chapter may be seen as a step toward understanding the main components of long-term spatial economic evolution. Providing a "micro" basis for the study and analysis of the process of long-term spatial macroeconomic change has therefore been its main objective. In this sense, its two most distinctive features have been its historical grounding, and the multidisciplinary perspective that combines insights from numerous contributions in various fields.

A first component reflected on the neglect of broad views of entrepreneurship in the social sciences, giving particular attention to the mainstream economic and spatial economic literature. The potential motivations driving entrepreneurial action were then reviewed, considering first the assumptions and shortcomings of the two major paradigms, the Neoclassical and Marxian, and their emphasis on the profit motive. A discussion of other equally important motives followed, grounded in evidence found in the psychological and behavioral sciences. Finally, a review of numerous works in various fields provided a basis for identifying five major entrepreneurial roles: investment, intermarket linkage, productive coordination, strategic planning, and invention.

These five entrepreneurial roles were discussed in the historical order in which they emerged as major developmental factors since the beginnings of the Industrial Revolution, with the exception of invention, which was assumed to have been significant throughout, but relatively more so during recent decades. The innovative potential of every role was emphasized, providing broad Schumpeterian perspectives on their character and application. Each role was then related to numerous relevant contributions found in the spatial economic literature. Unfortunately, a substantial lag was found between the time when some roles acquired major functional importance in the development process, and the time when significant scholarly interest emerged in the literature.

An overview of the analysis provided in this chapter raises numerous questions about the contribution of these roles to long-term spatial economic change, and the supply mechanisms influencing their application. One of these is the importance of opportunity costs in determining the levels of entry in any given entrepreneurial role, and their qualitative characteristics. A second consideration, also related to the effect of opportunity costs, is the supply mix or composition of the various roles found in any given region, and the contribution of different combinations toward enhancing regional comparative advantages. In many ways, it is conceivable that a given combination of roles, and its qualitative characteristics, can in itself become a significant regional comparative advantage.[83]

A third set of questions arising out of this analysis may focus on the composition of the various entrepreneurial roles needed to achieve national and regional macroeconomic objectives. Clearly, not all roles will be equally important or necessary in attaining most objectives. Tradeoffs can therefore be expected between the effects of the various entrepreneurial roles, depending on the objective. Inventiveness and investment can, for example, be crucial if long-term international or interregional competitiveness is the most important goal. On the other hand, strategic planning and intermarket linkage are likely to be most important for short- and medium-term growth. The extent to which interregional and international flows can offset regional imbalances in any given role can therefore become a major force shaping comparative advantages in entrepreneurial supply.

Fourth, the innovative potential of each role and its effect on long-term rewards to entrepreneurship should also be of major concern. It can always be expected that innovative activities will become routinized as the learning process advances and the associated uncertainty and risk are reduced. Rapid routinization can also reduce returns to entrepreneurship, however, by making imitation more feasible, eventually affecting supply characteristics. The extent to which this phenomenon affects long-term regional competitiveness is unclear and deserves careful analysis and research.

The degree of market control exercised by an organization in any given industry can also influence long-term innovation and the qualitative character of entrepreneurial supply. If a Schumpeterian tradeoff occurs, in which greater market control provides opportunities for continuous innovation, and if the resulting long-run social benefits are greater than those obtained through competitive pricing, spatial supply characteristics may shift in favor of inventiveness and intermarket linkage as new industries emerge and develop. In a Schumpeterian tradeoff condition, spatial monopolies and oligopolies would therefore have a crucial role in promoting long-term regional competitiveness in interregional and international markets.[84]

Since organizations are the single most important vehicle of entrepreneurial action, the internal context in which the various roles are developed and exercised has major implications for spatial economic change. Large corporate organizations today usually integrate all the entrepreneurial roles discussed in this chapter in the various units of their operation.[85] The way these roles are structured and allocated within the organization therefore creates a definite division of labor that influences how the enterprise responds to internal and external pressures. This internal division of labor also emphasizes the importance of organizational, over purely technical, innovation in responding to those pressures.

The structuring of the various entrepreneurial roles within the organization and each role's different spatial and temporal horizon also affect the way exogenous and endogenous pressures are responded to. The spatial impact of any given role can be limited primarily to the local, regional, interregional, or international spheres, or any combination thereof. Thus, for example, the spatial operational context of the coordinative role, crucial as it is in maintaining productive continuity, is mostly limited to the locality of a plant or its immediate region. The spatial context of the strategic planning, investment, or intermarket linkage roles can, on the other hand, be far reaching, as their operations and transactions may involve interregional and international markets.

Similarly, every entrepreneurial role can be counted upon to have different temporal operational contexts for the effects of its decisions. Thus, for example, the temporal context of the coordinative role is primarily restricted to the short term, as any changes in productive organization are usually felt quickly, affecting productivity, labor-management relations, and the immediate continuity of productive operations. The temporal context of the strategic planning or inventive roles is, on the other hand, longer term in nature, as considerable lags usually develop between the time when inventions are completed or decisions on product market changes are made, and the time when their full impact is felt.

Extending this perspective further, it is also apparent that some entrepreneurial roles are more affected by the exogenous rather than by the endogenous pressures felt by the organization. In this sense, endogenous pressures related to, for example, the organizational structure, its size, and its prevailing level of entropy, will affect coordinative entrepreneurship relatively more than any of the other roles. Exogenous pressures will more likely impact the strategic planning, intermarket linkage, and investment roles, as market or regulatory changes challenge the organization's capability to modify its practices, outputs, and processes. The discussion of this section has been aimed at pinpointing important themes that can integrate the definition and scope of the entrepreneurial function and its roles, based on the analysis of this chapter. Clearly, at a micro level, organizations are a major vehicle through which all of these roles affect spatial economic processes and the very nature of long-term spatial macroeconomic change. The challenge now is to provide a general conceptual framework that can consider the innovative character of these entrepreneurial roles, their historical significance, and their organizational contexts in the process of long-term regional change.

A Long-Term View of Regional Change

Broad perspectives on long-term economic change have been sub-stantially neglected in both the social science and the spatial economic literature. The reasons for this neglect are similar, in many ways, to those found for the lack of comprehensive treatments of the entrepreneurial function. To a great extent, however, the lack of broad perspectives on long-term economic change is also a product of the neglect of the entrepreneurial function.[1]

Conceptualizing long-term economic phenomena is considerably more difficult than focusing on short-term change, primarily because of the complexity of the forces affecting socioeconomic structures over long periods. The difficulty of conceptualizing the interactions be-tween such forces, a daunting obstacle in itself, is further compounded by the usual lack of sufficiently detailed long-term data. Most often, empirical analyses of long-term phenomena have relied on highly aggregated data that can provide only very limited insights on the processes they evaluate.

Another difficulty in conceptualizing long-term change is the com-mon perception that long-term transformations are beyond human or societal control. This has been partly a byproduct of the uncertain and relatively slow nature of much long-term change, where socioeconomic outcomes, and their spatial implications, are difficult to foresee and measure. Although this may seem difficult to overcome, there are nevertheless ways in which long-term macrostructural phenomena can be conceptualized and explained within reasonably accurate parameters.

A broad conceptualization of long-term regional economic change must rely substantially on the understanding of historical economic processes. Without a significant historical perspective, this task would indeed become little more than a hollow tracing of macroeconomic variables. Such an approach would not only have limited relevance for the explanation of the broad spatial and temporal aspects of long-term economic change, but also might actually hinder our under-standing of the processes it attempts to analyze.

A conceptualization of long-term regional economic change would also be very limited without the incorporation of knowledge from various academic disciplines. This objective must therefore involve a multidisciplinary effort, where the relevant theories and paradigms are integrated in a simplified conceptual framework that can also provide substantial insights on the deeper structures of long-term change. In this sense, a conceptualization of long-term phenomena also involves a substantial synthesis of the various socioeconomic processes that influence major structural changes.

A consideration of the entrepreneurial function and its roles is crucial for the conceptualization of long-term spatial economic change. The continuity of long-term change can be adequately addressed only when the innovative aspects of the various entrepreneurial roles are introduced. Innovative entrepreneurship then essentially becomes the most significant factor that can bridge over, and explain, the apparently discontinuous character of much short- and medium-term phenomena. As we shall see below, the consideration of entrepreneurial innovation also allows many current and past short-term phenomena to be identified as byproducts of long-term processes.

Innovative entrepreneurship greatly determines the outcomes of most secular and cyclical long-term processes. At the same time, it is also the most significant factor linking secular and cyclical phenomena in long-term macroeconomic change. Indeed, the linkage between these two types of phenomena, which has so puzzled scholars over the years, and that between short- and long-term processes, cannot be adequately explained unless changes in the innovative character of the various entrepreneurial roles are also considered.

This chapter will conceptualize the process of secular regional economic change by relating the entrepreneurial function, in all its innovative roles, to long-term sectoral evolution.[2] Syntheses of major historical developments that are related to the exercise of the five entrepreneurial roles, defined in the previous chapter, will be an important component of this effort. The conceptualization of secular long-term change provided in this chapter will also rely heavily on knowledge contributed by various disciplines, especially the historical, economic, geographic, and the managerial fields.

The most significant regional impacts of sectoral economic change will be related to the innovative contributions of the five major entrepreneurial roles, by considering the vehicles and incentive structures that influence entrepreneurial action in each sector. As the most important vehicles of entrepreneurship, the role of corporate organizations will be of special importance in this conceptual framework, and the historical development of corporate functions will therefore receive significant attention. Institutional incentive structures will also be related to secular, long-term sectoral change by considering their effects on interregional differences in entrepreneurial innovation, and on long-term changes in the levels of development.

PERSPECTIVES ON LONG-TERM CHANGE: AN HISTORICAL OVERVIEW

Few subjects are as mystifying to social scientists as the process of long-term change. The sheer magnitude of the temporal dimension involved and the structural impacts of such changes are an enormous challenge fraught with uncertainty. The many possibilities involved can tax anyone's ability to synthesize and simplify what are in fact very complex processes. As will be seen in this and in subsequent chapters, the formidable obstacles to an adequate conceptualization of long-term change are both conceptual and empirical.

The most feasible and convenient way to conceptualize long-term evolution is to visualize it as a sequence of phenomena, usually traceable to human behavioral changes and adjustments at the "micro" level, that are the most significant determinants of socioeconomic change. Such causal sequences of events have been most frequently conceptualized, either explicitly or implicitly, as stages frameworks, with varying degrees of definition and detail. These frameworks have indeed been a versatile tool with which to consider the interrelationships among the many variables affecting the most significant processes and outcomes of each phase, as well as the transitional obstacles to be overcome in advancing from one stage to another. As will be discussed in a subsequent section, stages frameworks are not without significant problems, however. Perhaps one of the most significant examples of these is that such frameworks can often be represented as "one-track" sequences of change without adequate consideration of the regressions and almost indefinite periods of stagnation that occur in any developmental process.

Despite such problems, stages frameworks have generally been most suitable for conceptualizations of historical change whenever a specific typology or direction of change is addressed. A major challenge in such efforts has usually been the delimitation and definition of the phases or stages, partly because identification of the most significant processes and variables must often rely on substantial syntheses. The amount of simplification required has meant that a less than skillful handling of this aspect has often doomed such efforts to be little more than an inventory of macroeconomic variables.

The adequate consideration of the interrelationships between the major causal variables has also been a challenging and decisive aspect in the successful use of stages frameworks. This has been essential in introducing the internal consistency that is so important in providing a meaningful perspective of the whole. A skillful handling of this aspect has in many cases served as a starting point for the development of more elaborate conceptual efforts, empirical analyses, or mathematical modeling. As will become obvious in the following review, the selective handling of the interrelations among the major variables and phenomena can support the application of stages frameworks in ways that will expand their original scope, and contribute to our understanding of the processes and changes involved.

Spatial Stages and Macroeconomic Change

Stage conceptualizations of spatial economic change have, perhaps much to the surprise of some, a long history. Over two hundred years ago, James Steuart (1767), an early British economist, introduced long-term spatial economic change as an essential component of his general theory of economics.[3] His seminal, systematic, and general treatment of the causes of spatial population concentration, location of economic activities, and urban and regional growth, provided a three-stage conceptualization of the process of long-term spatial economic change.

Steuart's first developmental stage can be characterized as a one-sector economy, where primitive agricultural subsistence determines spatial population distribution.[4] Regional population then becomes a function of agricultural productivity, and larger populations are found in areas with relatively greater soil productivity. At the same time, agricultural productivity is assumed to determine the extent to which urbanization and general demographic growth can occur in the following stage.

A more advanced agricultural sector creates a need for some support activities in a second stage. In regard to labor, these are made possible by both demographic growth and increased agricultural productivity, which require relatively fewer workers per volume of output. Thus, commercial and service activities supporting agriculture become important, forming the nucleus of mercantile settlements. In Steuart's framework, it is through the development of these activities that population initially agglomerates in towns and villages, eventually resulting in a significant level of urbanization.

The stimulation of human wants, particularly those of the urbanizing populations, eventually creates a need for manufactures in the third stage of Steuart's evolutionary model. Manufacturing therefore becomes the most important and newest economic sector, employing increasing numbers in the growing settlements. In the new functional division of the regional economy, Steuart assumed commerce and services to be the most urban-oriented activities, while manufacturing would be relatively less so, because of its natural resource requirements (fuel, power, raw materials) and the need for an adequate transport infrastructure. In this third stage, manufacturing nevertheless becomes the prime determinant of regional urbanization, as many industries locate in, or close to, their urban markets because of the availability of labor, lower transport costs (for assembly or weight-losing processes), and better transport facilities.

Perhaps the most significant aspect of Steuart's contribution lies in the rudimentary sectoral perspective that it provided on the process of spatial economic change. As we shall see later in this section, this framework has influenced most contributions on the processes of spatial economic change, right up to our time, although its origins and significance have not always been adequately acknowledged.

Two additional aspects of Steuart's work also deserve to be mentioned, because of their influence on subsequent contributions. One is his assumption that the most significant spatial economic changes and population redistribution are brought about by sectoral changes driven, in turn, by increasing productivity and by changing human wants and needs. Thus, implicit in this framework is the notion that sectoral macroeconomic change, anchored in microbehavioral tendencies, drives long-term regional economic development. The microbehavioral aspect determines economic change in the first stage through the expansion of basic human wants related to food production and shelter and, subsequently, through the development of more superfluous human wants and needs, as in the case of manufacturing and, to a lesser extent, commerce and services.

Almost one decade after Steuart's contribution, Adam Smith's (1776) *Wealth of Nations* ranks as the second major historical contribution focusing on regional long-term change. His regional stages framework, similar in many ways to Steuart's, focuses on trade as the most important determinant of long-term spatial economic change and population distribution.[5] Smith differentiated between intraregional and interregional trade, assuming the former always to be greater and more significant for long-term change than the latter. Additionally, he believed that most intraregional trade would occur between cities and their tributary areas.[6]

In Smith's first stage, as in Steuart's, subsistence agriculture and extraction are the single most important characteristic driving a regional economy. In this stage, whatever limited trade there is is exclusively intraregional. Gradually, this gives way to a second stage, in which generation of an agricultural surplus promotes a greater economic division of labor through the rise of some services and rudimentary manufactures. These new activities are assumed to be exclusively concentrated in towns that are initially agricultural market settlements, where population agglomerates. In this stage, trade remains primarily intraregional, although much of it gradually becomes interurban (but still intraregional), between the agricultural market settlements and their adjacent rural territories.

In Smith's third developmental stage, the promotion of inter-regional trade then becomes a major feature, based primarily on manufactured exports. At this point, manufacturing activities become the most dynamic components of the regional economy, developing as the prime source of extraregional export income, and concentrating additional population and resources in the urban settlements where they locate. Thus, the long-term progression from intraregional-rural to intraregional-interurban, to interregional trade of this rudimentary export base model is completed, with regional and urban population size becoming a function of the volume of trade.[7]

An additional aspect of Smith's conceptualization was the relation-ship he established between institutional structures and the long-term development process, assuming those to be the single most important obstacle to the development of trade. Institutional restrictions thus came to the fore as the prime cause of regional backwardness, lags in the level of regional urbanization, and the lack of regional and urban population growth through in-migration. This argument for greater economic *laissez-faire* would later be elaborated upon and expanded, to become one of the central theoretical and policy concerns of many mainstream economists and social scientists, right up to our time.

Steuart's and Smith's contributions were later significantly comple-mented by von Thünen's (1826) conceptualization of the spatial division of labor within the agricultural sector, and its relationship to long-term regional urbanization and economic change. Although not an explicit stages framework per se, von Thünen's contribution would nevertheless provide significant insights on the characteristics and variables affecting demand-driven spatial economic evolution.

Instead of following the process of change from a primitive agricul-tural stage, von Thünen assumed a given level of development cor-responding approximately to Steuart's and Smith's third stage, and a hypothetical isolated settlement where manufacturing and services would be concentrated. Agricultural activities were then assumed to be distributed around the settlement in concentric rings of equal soil characteristics and fertility, with the more perishable and higher transport cost crops being located closest to the settlement. Converse-ly, the more durable and lower transport cost crops would be located progressively farther away on the concentric rings' gradient, depend-ing on the settlement's aggregate demand for each crop.[8]

Although providing an explicit evolutionary framework was not one of von Thünen's objectives in this contribution, the implications of sectoral demand changes for the long-term regional rural division of labor are enormous.[9] With the growth of manufacturing and services, and the consequent expansion of urban demand for agricultural goods in subsequent stages, the restructuring of the concentric zone framework would become an inevitable component of the process of regional change, trading off lower value agricultural resources (land area, soils, skills) for higher value urban activities in services, commerce and manufacturing. As urbanization advanced, such spatial-sectoral restructuring would require additional agricultural resources to be invested farther away from urban places, driven by additional urban demand and the ever present need to increase productivity, through the application of better and more efficient techniques.

At the same time, it is obvious that von Thünen's primarily intraregional trade focus between town and country, following Smith's model, would eventually shift in favor of a relatively greater emphasis on interregional trade, as the agricultural sector responded to demand from regions with fewer comparative advantages in that sector, by generating increasing surpluses. In a hypothetical sense, this could be expected to follow the manufacturing sector's (and later, services') lead in establishing interregional exchange flows.

Another major contribution of the early nineteenth century is that of the English statistician and economist, Simon Gray (1819), whose work on income and population change and the stages framework on which he based his analysis remain one of the pioneering efforts of nineteenth century social science. Disagreeing with Malthus' apocalyptic vision of the future, Gray argued that population growth would eventually result in a greater increase in per capita income.[10] To support his assumptions, he provided convincing empirical evidence on the relationship between British population growth and income change.[11]

Gray's stages framework was primarily concerned with illustrating the spatial population distribution of a settlement and its surrounding region from hamlet to village to town, and eventually to city and metropolitan size.[12] He assumed, as noted in the preceding discussion, not only that increasing population size would result in greater per capita income, but also that such growth would lead to an increasing division of labor in the urban and regional economy, and to better and lower priced goods. Implicit in Gray's hypothesis was the idea that increasing agglomeration economies, coupled with expanded regional demand for manufactured goods and services, and with greater competition among urban firms, would eventually lead to greater economic efficiency and a higher standard of living for the population. As many spatial scholars will recognize, this line of thought can be considered the embryo of what would become known, almost a century and a half later, as regional growth theory.

The spatial diffusion of urban goods and of new techniques, Gray assumed, would occur from the largest metropolitan areas to the hinterland of their immediate regions, and eventually farther afield to other areas and regions, as metropolitan size expanded and its entrepreneurs explored other markets. Unfortunately, this striking yet simple conceptualization of the spatial innovation diffusion process would be neglected in almost every subsequent major contribution, up to and through the middle of our century. To many, it should be surprising not only that recent works dealing with spatial diffusion provide perspectives similar to Gray's, but that our knowledge of such processes has actually advanced relatively little beyond his conceptualization.

Carrying Gray's assumptions a step further, we can assume that a greater quantum and quality of entrepreneurial supply would be a function of increasing urban size. From a broader evolutionary perspective, however, we cannot ignore that entrepreneurial action was responsible for such urban agglomerations in the first place, as their activities made the rise of commerce and services, and later manufacturing, possible in the earlier transition from primitive agriculture. The original cause and this subsequent symbiotic relationship between urban size and entrepreneurship are further strengthened, if we fully consider the spatial diffusion effect of large urban size on the regional economy.

After Gray's and von Thünen's contributions, and the accumulation of insights, analyses and conceptualizations from these and other scholars, it was obvious that a great synthesis of much of the accumulated spatial knowledge was needed by the end of the nineteenth century.[13] Adna Ferrin Weber's (1899) contribution filled this need extremely well, providing a synthesis of much of the spatial economic knowledge accumulated up to that time, in the form of both theory and empirical analysis. Stimulated by Darwin's work on biological evolution, like so many other social scientists of the time, Weber would devote significant attention to the process of long-term spatial change, by providing a biological analogy as a major component of his conceptual discussions.[14]

Weber assumed two complementary evolutionary processes to affect long-term urban and regional change: differentiation, distinguished by progressively increasing spatial heterogeneity; and integration, defined as the increasing interdependence of heterogeneous elements.[15] Comparing the process of spatial economic development with the evolution of individual cells into tissue and, eventually, into organisms, Weber provides a stages framework that, similar to those of earlier scholars, begins with a vision of the primitive economy, characterized by subsistence agricultural and extractive activities and a rudimentary division of labor.

This primitive division of labor eventually produces increases in per capita product, as new techniques or materials are found or substitution occurs, generating surpluses that in turn result in greater sectoral and spatial differentiation. Weber then assumed the surplus generated by agricultural and extractive activities to be channeled toward urban markets, along with the labor released by more productive techniques, supporting commerce and services already concentrated there, and providing additional urban manpower. In this scheme, trade therefore becomes the original attraction factor for rural-urban migration. At the same time, manufacturing activities become increasingly differentiated and develop from the household to the handicraft and cottage stages, and eventually to the factory system, concentrating and employing workers from services and agriculture. Following and synthesizing Smith's earlier model, trading flows are then assumed to expand from their intraregional frontiers to interregional and eventually international markets.

In his biological differentiation analogy, Adna Weber assumed the enlargement of markets at all levels, especially for manufacturing, supported by increasing extraregional demand, to result in an expanding division of labor for the regional economy. This would become obvious, for example, in the ever increasing levels of detail and additional breakdowns of categories found in the industrial product classifications.[16] At the same time, Weber significantly considered the broader role of noneconomic factors in long-term evolution, such as the psychological, sociological, and political motives that tend to preserve and promote a city's or region's position in the national and international division of labor, in the face of greater economic disadvantages and reduced competitiveness.

After Adna Weber, it would be up to the early twentieth-century German school of location theorists to add to the stages conceptualizations elaborated upon over the previous century. With the enormous popularity enjoyed by spatial economic topics, even in the mainstream economics literature of the time, it would have been unusual indeed for long-term spatial evolution to be neglected, even as the static analysis approach began to gain increasing acceptance in the spatial literature. It should therefore not be surprising that Alfred Weber, the scholar most often associated with the early development of static locational analysis, provided a significant extension of the stages frameworks developed by earlier spatial scholars.

Presaging Christaller's (1966) work on central place theory, Alfred Weber (1929, p. 125) viewed long-term regional evolution as the development of sectoral "strata" with a definite spatial dimension. The first such stratum would be agricultural, supplying the basic necessities, with a widely dispersed regional population required for cultivation. Weber assumed this simple division of labor to be the essential geographical foundation of all subsequent sectoral strata. A second stratum comprising "primary industrial activites" would then be developed, determined by the raw materials provided by extractive and agricultural production, and the consumption levels generated at the places where industries agglomerate. In such places, a range of support activities, such as professional services, transportation, commerce, and government, would also develop.

The third stratum, composed of "secondary industrial activities" would be primarily determined by the growth and differentiation of the previous one. This would comprise industries that process, refine, or assemble the products of the primary industrial stratum, and would be supported in turn by more diversified service and commercial activities, adding increasing importance to the cities where they concentrate.

Weber thus conceived the process of spatial evolution as a three-stage, hierarchical and interdependent system whose development would be determined, first, by primitive agriculture, and subsequently by a greater differentiation and spatial division of labor in manufacturing. Being more abstract than previous conceptualizations, Weber's scheme broke with the biological analogies elaborated over previous decades. It was also based on this general evolutionary framework that Weber, incongruously enough, designed his static theory of industrial location.

It was precisely the shift of interest toward static analysis, motivated in great part by the Neoclassical movement, that is the single most important cause of the neglect of evolutionary frameworks in the spatial literature, over the five decades following Alfred Weber's contribution. In this respect, it is curious nevertheless that Lösch's and Hoover's acknowledgment of the role of the entrepreneur, noted in the previous chapter, would not lead them to explore the obvious linkage with processes of long-term change, inasmuch as Schumpeter's work had already revealed the potentialities of that approach decades earlier, albeit nonspatially.[17]

By the 1950s, however, some stirrings in mainstream economics would draw significant interest back to the evolutionary concern with long-term change. Much of this interest was partly due to the realization of the inadequacies of static, Neoclassical analysis to deal with long-term phenomena. On another level, the rise of development economics at the time, and greater interest in economic history, made it necessary, indeed essential, to look at the long-term implications of the process of development from a dynamic perspective. To a great extent, the significant empirical analyses of Fisher (1933, 1939) and Clark (1940) provided much intellectual support to renewed efforts in developing long-term stages frameworks.[18] As we shall see, this shift of interest would have significant impact on the spatial literature, inasmuch as many of the long-term conceptualizations there developed would follow, and be derived from, the economics literature.[19]

In contrast with the unified treatments of regional and urban stages frameworks of the eighteenth, nineteenth, and early twentieth centuries, the spatial stages literature of the 1950s and beyond can be clearly divided into two separate groups. These are, first, those dealing primarily with long-term intraurban change, such as the economic base and land use stages theories, and those with a broader regional focus. The latter would also include the consideration of urban aspects, including those dealing with the urban-regional interface, such as the growth pole and regional growth theories. In some ways, the broader region-focused stages frameworks also were more directly influenced by the nonspatial stages theories found in the economic development and economic history literature of the 1950s and 1960s.

The renewed interest in stages frameworks of the 1950s and 1960s occurred primarily through the extension of the urban economic base concept to consider long-term change. In many ways, the basic thrust of these efforts can be traced back to Adam Smith's rudimentary spatial export base model, and its linkage with von Thünen's concentric ring theory through the urban form and economic base concepts developed by Haig (1926), Nussbaum (1933), and Hoyt (1941).[20]

Wilbur Thompson's (1965, pp. 15–16) general stages framework of long-term metropolitan change was perhaps the most representative example of the intraurban interest in export base theory of the 1950s and 1960s. His first stage, "export specialization," was determined by the presence of a single industry or firm monopolizing urban export activity. From a basic activity standpoint, a settlement's economy would therefore be little more than that of a highly specialized "company town." It is implicit here that Thompson's framework took the development of urban industry for granted; historically, it therefore starts where most of the eighteenth- and nineteenth-century stages frameworks left off.

Thompson's second stage, "export complex," involved greater relative diversification, and the gradual "filling in" of forward and backward linkages with locally made products. This would eventually give way to a third, "economic maturation" stage, during which greater import substitution in manufacturing would occur, along with an expansion in the range and quality of local services. In the fourth, "regional metropolis" stage, a regional projection of the urban economy would occur, serving other cities' economies and population with hierarchically higher functions, activities, and goods. In this stage, the export of some services becomes a significant contributor to metropolitan export income.

Finally, Thompson assumed a more esoteric fifth stage of "technical-professional virtuosity" to develop, either subsequently or in conjunction with the third or fourth stages above, by developing a basic industry or service activity where the metropolis attains national or international prominence. Examples of this condition would be New York City's with respect to international finance, Los Angeles' with respect to film making, or Detroit's automobile industry. It is obvious here, as in the previous stages, that one of Thompson's uppermost concerns in developing his stages framework was the specialization and diversification of the urban economy. Indeed, the exclusively urban-metropolitan focus and the initial assumption of an already existing manufacturing base were the most significant traits setting his framework apart from those of the early twentieth-, nineteenth-, and eighteenth-century theorists.

The broadening of the intraurban stages focus to consider demographic, as well as more detailed sectoral, aspects of long-term change was perhaps the most significant characteristic of this interest during the 1970s and 1980s. To some extent, the rising attraction of the product cycle and issues of manufacturing change in the spatial literature, to be discussed in a subsequent section, influenced this shift.[21] Among the most significant contributions of this period is Norton's (1979) analysis of growth patterns and life cycles of concentric ring urban zones, which obviously develops von Thünen's and the urban sector theorists' earlier contributions.[22]

Norton's empirical analysis showed how various urban zones followed different life cycle trajectories, while at the same time revealing the relative permanence of mature metropolitan size over the long-term, once a certain population threshold is reached. Thus, unlike the typical bell-shaped life cycle functions, urban demographic concentration resembles a logistic functional distribution over the long-term, where absolute decline seldom occurs for periods longer than the short term. If this conclusion is taken a step further, and a broader regional scale is considered, it becomes obvious that the regional dispersion of urban population occurs at the expense of further metropolitan growth, rather than metropolitan decline, at least over the long term. Thus, a relatively greater proportion of new population growth can be assumed to occur outside the metropolitan boundaries, over and above the population replacement needs of the metropolis.

The broader regional focus of the stages frameworks of the 1950s and 1960s, noted earlier, was greatly influenced by both regional export base theory and the development stages concepts, found in the economic development literature, that attracted much interest during that time.[23] Thomas' (1964) significant integration of these approaches provides a representative example and critique of the regional stages focus, assuming four phases that trace the process of regional development, starting with the movement from subsistence to specialized commercial agriculture. A second stage then focuses on the rise of manufacturing, based on indigenously available raw materials, and producing primarily for intraregional consumption. This is followed by a third, where manufacturing production also serves interregional and international demand. As per capita incomes rise, services and commerce begin to export as well, primarily to interregional markets, in the fourth and final stage.

An important difference, perhaps developed with the benefit of better hindsight, between the framework outlined by Thomas and those of the eighteenth-, nineteenth-, and early twentieth-century theorists, was the increasing importance gained by the tertiary sector over the fourth stage of development. Interesting, in this respect, was the changing character of these activities within the export base concept, as services become more "basic" over time.[24] Another significant aspect is the role that increasing per capita incomes would play in the rise of every sector, and especially services, during the fourth stage. As we shall see later on, this assumption would become one of the cornerstones of regional growth theory.

The development of growth pole theory during the late 1960s and early 1970s, based on Perroux's (1955) important early, though quite general, conceptualization, helped scholars applying stages frameworks to consider the role of urbanization in long-term change. This concept focused on the early rapid growth phases of a region's primate cities, with the manufacturing sector as the source of local dynamism. Although it never encompassed a full fledged birth-to-maturity analogy, growth pole theory nevertheless provided significant insights on the dynamics of the urban-regional interface, and how the sustained growth of a few selected centers and their industries could restructure a regional economy.

As with most earlier stages theories, the growth pole concept's temporal dimension can be easily related to the nineteenth century contributions discussed earlier. In Steuart's and Smith's frameworks, for example, the growth pole stage would occur whenever a mercantile center begins to develop as a major industrial agglomeration, or when a settlement's export trade flows begin to serve interregional markets, through the rapid growth of the local economy. In the growth pole concept, however, the manufacturing sector would become the catalyst of all subsequent growth and development in services and commerce. This causal relationship, although implicit in many earlier stages frameworks, would be most explicitly articulated in this concept.[25]

Much related to the growth pole concept, regional growth theory expanded that concept's temporal dimension, by considering the long-term regional impacts of population concentration and dispersion, and their relationship to economic growth.[26] The possibility of an urban population concentration "turnaround" therefore became an explicit aspect of the regional dynamic, that could potentially be linked to long-term sectoral shifts and restructurings. Richardson's (1973) seminal contribution on regional growth theory considered three phases: one of "initial concentration," related to the beginnings of the process of industrialization, when population and economic activities agglomerate rapidly, as per the growth pole dynamic. This is followed by a second phase that von Böventer (1975, p. 14) aptly describes as "concentrated decentralization," where the regional economic growth leadership passes to, or is shared with, other economic sectors, such as services and commerce.

The third phase in Richardson's framework is characterized by regional deconcentration or, to a great extent, "decentralized concentrations" (von Böventer, 1975, p. 14), with significant population and economic activities decentralizing from major metropolitan areas, driven by reduced or insignificant real wage differentials between metropolitan and nonmetropolitan urban areas, improved transportation and communications infrastructure, and rising income levels. This third phase, which, in many ways, presaged the U.S. metropolitan turnaround phenomenon of the 1970s, is the most significant addition to the previous regional stages frameworks.[27] In previous conceptualizations, it may be recalled, a leveling off of metropolitan population growth, at most, but never a concentration turnaround, was assumed to occur. At the same time, the historical progression from agricultural subsistence to the start of industrialization, outlined in Steuart's and Smith's contributions two centuries earlier, was now being taken for granted. This was, to a great extent, justified by the experiences of many developing nations, where industrialization became an inevitable and almost automatic outcome of the process of economic development.[28]

Although the field's interest in regional growth theory has subsided in recent years, its concern over processes of economic change has increased significantly. In many respects, the issues and phenomena that motivated the original interest in growth theory are now motivating increased scholarship on broader aspects of economic change. Thus, the original concern with the impacts of growth has now been expanded to consider decline as well as stagnation, at the sectoral, spatial, and demographic levels.[29]

The revival of interest in macroeconomic stages conceptualizations of recent years has been greatly concerned with questions of sectoral economic restructuring. Thus, changes in manufacturing and services, and their broader economic and societal implications over the long-term, have been at the center of this interest. On another level, recent interest in stages conceptualizations has also been more concerned with nonspatial aspects of economic change, such as the role of organizations and government, and issues of international competitiveness.[30]

A Constructive Critique of Stages Conceptualizations

Perhaps the most certain conclusion that can be derived from the previous section is that stages frameworks are undoubtedly a very significant and useful conceptual tool. It is indeed hard to find any other vehicle, conceptual or methodological, that has survived over two hundred years of scholarly theorizing. Just as surprising is the increasing amount of interest that this approach has generated in recent years, and the frequency with which it is being applied.

The versatility of the stages approach for synthesizing complex interrelationships and phenomena is perhaps its most important advantage. Although much of this depends on the skills employed in the development of the underlying conceptual relationships, there are obvious inherent benefits in its application to the study of temporal phenomena, as discussed earlier. Perhaps the ultimate proof of this approach's utility is the fact that even its detractors eventually find themselves implicitly applying it in their work.

The drawbacks of using stages frameworks arise primarily from the ways in which they are applied. Important keys to the majority of the shortcomings are, first, the contexts to which the frameworks are applied, related to, for example, the type of phenomena, the temporal span involved, and the complexity of the interrelationships considered. A second aspect is the skill with which they are applied, related primarily to the development of the conceptual underpinnings. This aspect is of crucial importance, over and above any issues related to the level of detail involved in, for example, the number of stages, the number of variables, or the characteristics of the phenomena being explored. In this respect, therefore, the solid conceptual grounding of the relationships being considered in the framework is of the greatest importance.

Perhaps the most significant shortcoming found in the application of stages frameworks to the study of long-term change is the neglect of the micro level, especially the microbehavioral underpinnings of the phenomena being analyzed. This is particularly obvious with respect to the entrepreneurial function as the major vehicle of economic change.[31] Thus, entrepreneurship, as a deeper determinant of the causes usually assumed to promote advance from one stage to another, such as rising per capita income, productivity, or demographic concentration, is ignored. Similarly, behavioral factors affecting demand, such as changes in the population's perceived wants or needs, are ignored. The result is that all too often the process of change either appears to be automatic, or seems to be driven by factors that are not the root causes of the changes being examined.

A second important shortcoming is the lack of sufficient concern with sectoral structure and its interrelationships, especially in terms of how the leading sectors relate to all the other macroeconomic components. Thus, for example, the importance of agriculture to manufacturing is often ignored during the stages of industrialization, disregarding the fact that agricultural productivity has been crucial to the development of industry in most of the successful development trajectories. Similarly, the significance of manufacturing to the development and dynamism of the services sector in "post-industrial" stages is often disregarded. This failure leads to misunderstandings about the importance of nonleading sectors for the development and maintenance of the most dynamic economic sector. Thus, for example, in terms of the significance of the intersectoral relationships involved, it makes about as much sense conceptually to define a "post-industrial" stage as it does to conceive of a "post-agricultural" era, despite the fact that the decline of employment in agriculture has been many times more severe and sustained than that in manufacturing during both the industrialization and the so-called "post-industrial" stages.

The third most important shortcoming on the application of stages frameworks has been an insufficient concern with process over outcomes. This has often led to either a high degree of historical determinism, or a lack of sufficient historical perspective. To some extent, this problem can be expected of any framework that attempts to abstract something as complex as long-term change. Moreover, it is often worsened by the common practice of abstracting stages characteristics on the basis of the most successful cases or trajectories, without considering major structural differences between contexts.

When combined with the neglect of sectoral interrelations and their changes, discussed before, this problem often results in a lack, or an inadequate consideration, of possible alternative trajectories. Similarly, medium- or long-term regressions and periods of stagnation are factored out of consideration. At the same time, a mechanistic and poorly documented treatment of the stages' scale and level of detail can prevent an adequate consideration of the transitions between stages, and of the factors that can lead to unexpected outcomes.

In the following sections, a hypothetical construct and a stages framework of long-term regional economic change will be explored. While it may not be possible to avoid all of the drawbacks discussed here, an effort will be made to address and locate the most important macro and micro underpinnings of long-term economic change, in a way that can remedy most of the obstacles and difficulties encountered in previous attempts.

AN EVOLUTIONARY FRAMEWORK OF LONG-TERM CHANGE

Relating long-term regional change to the development of the entrepreneurial function requires significant insights on the forces of supply and demand that affect entrepreneurship. The identification of demand-side factors requires an understanding of individual behavior that is much broader than that postulated by either the Neoclassical or the Marxian self-interest assumptions. Similarly, on the supply side, broader insights than those provided solely by profit-seeking motives and assumptions are needed for a fuller understanding of the effects of entrepreneurial action.

Of crucial importance to the treatment of long-term phenomena is understanding how changes in individual behavior are reflected in the long-term demand shifts that determine entrepreneurial action. The lack of sufficient research and evidence on both entrepreneurial and consumers' behavior, apart from that of the Neoclassical perspective, unfortunately makes it difficult to provide answers to these questions. At the same time, it is quite obvious that the oversimplifications of reality provided by the major paradigms are inadequate in providing all the insights needed on these questions.

This deficiency presents a serious dilemma to any theoretical effort trying to account for the underpinnings of supply and demand that determine entrepreneurial action. Still, a selective study of past conceptual developments in demand theory can provide some clues on the major forces affecting entrepreneurship, without adopting any of the limitations imposed by the orthodox paradigm. Similarly, at a macro level, past research on supply-side factors can also provide some indications on the results of entrepreneurial adjustment to demand changes. This is not to say that the hypothetical construct elaborated in the following section will be complete. It will, however, provide some basic indications on the general microeconomic forces that help shape the entrepreneurial roles identified in the previous chapter. At the same time, it will also lay the groundwork for the elaboration of the historical stages framework to be presented in a subsequent section.

Wants, Entrepreneurship, and the Economic Process

Human wants are the single most important force driving market demand. This is perhaps one of the least questioned precepts in the Classical and Neoclassical economic literature. Yet, the question of how those wants change over the long-term has been substantially neglected. This neglect, coupled with an even greater one regarding the process through which entrepreneurs adjust to those changes, and their broader sectoral implications, is a serious obstacle to a better understanding of the major forces driving long-term change.

Human economic wants, and their changes, are primarily motivated by both physiological and psychological needs. Of these, the physiological wants can be considered basic, such as the need for food and shelter, while psychological needs are usually more superfluous, and need not be solely material. Throughout the evolution of mankind, the first economic endeavors were directed at the satisfaction of basic, or physiological, needs. As progress unfolded and these became satisfied, wants became more complex and superfluous, driven more by psychological motives than by physiological subsistence.[32]

At an aggregate level, in the stages frameworks discussed in the previous section, long-term changes in these wants were reflected, first, in the transition from subsistence cultivation and extraction toward market agriculture, and eventually in the development of communication and distribution networks, based on commercial activities. The eventual production of what, at the time, must have seemed to many as less essential or even superfluous goods, eventually led to industrialization. Differences in perceptions between what is basic and what is superfluous could not be more evident today, in the contrasts in levels of development between advanced and less developed nations, where services and goods that are increasingly considered essential in the former are perceived as unnecessary or frivolous in the latter.

The essence of this dynamic is, to some extent, summarized by Engel's law, as the tendency for the proportion of total income spent on essentials, such as food, clothing, and shelter, to decline as personal or family income increases.[33] Thus, it is well known that income elasticity of demand, driven by long-term income and price effects and aided by entrepreneurial invention and innovation, has favored what were initially thought to be less essential goods and services. This phenomenon has enormous long-term sectoral implications, as demand shifts favor new activities and sectors, and entrepreneurs adjust to meet those challenges. It is thus that the forces driving restructurings, for both the old and "new frontier" sectors leading demand growth, occur, along with the spatial changes and adjustments required to meet either output growth or the new competitive challenges.

For the "new frontier" sector, meeting new demand through rapid output growth requires the attraction of greater entrepreneurial talent to the new productive opportunities. The speed with which such opportunities are tapped depends on the quantum and quality of entrepreneurial supply, in some roles more than others. Generally, however, a lower degree of competition, due to the new products' early life cycle condition, and better possibilities for larger market share—along with some behavioral and social considerations such as greater status, community leadership, and opportunities for patronage—are likely to attract better entrepreneurial talent to a sector favored by increasing demand elasticities.

Some entrepreneurial roles will obviously be better suited to support a new frontier sector, and will become crucial to the principal objective of promoting rapid output growth and greater market share. Strategic planning is one such entrepreneurial role, determining opportunities and strategies for market expansion through the introduction of new products or services. The spatial implications of this role are quite obvious for a new frontier sector, inasmuch as such market expansion will have regional, interregional, or international impacts. This role would also be crucial for internal enterprise policy-making and planning designed to meet the new challenges through, for example, the budgeting function, or for making major changes in the organizational and productive structure. Similarly, the capital investment role is of great importance when it comes to such decisions as investing the enterprise's own resources, or attracting new finance for expansion.

Also important to a new frontier sector is the intermarket linkage role, especially as extensive new input linkages are established and require maintenance and rapid expansion. In very new activities, this may be related to opening up new sources of inputs, or finding better substitutes for existing ones. Its spatial dimension may very likely reach across regional and national boundaries. In a less direct and often temporally disconnected way, invention is also a major contributor to the rise of a new sector, as new technologies or organizational arrangements make it possible for new products and services to be provided at lower costs, thereby increasing the enterprise's market opportunities.

A very different situation is faced, on the other hand, by sectors and activities shifting out of a growth leadership position. For the goods and services of these sectors, aggregate income elasticities of demand are less favorable than for a new frontier sector. Sectors thus supplanted are most likely to undergo some restructuring, as some of their products face greater competition and market saturation, maturity or decline in their product cycles, changing input and product price structures, and fewer possibilities of applying radically new inventions in their routine activities.

The sectors thus affected will undergo substantial rationalization of their productive activities over the long-term. The most common and important objective of such restructurings will be to increase long-term productivity, as a means of dealing with the uncertainties of input and product market change. Increasing productivity in those sectors therefore becomes the most serious entrepreneurial challenge, where the innovative capabilities of some roles will be more important than others.

Among the entrepreneurial roles that are crucial to productivity change, productive coordination is undoubtedly the most important, for it is in changing the daily, routine activities related to labor's tasks, management-labor relations, and the organization of production, that productivity battles are often won or lost. It is in dealing with such fine, yet subtle, points as the motivational aspects of the workplace, addressing potential or actual conflicts among individuals or between labor and management, and introducing new forms of work organization, that this entrepreneurial role can be most effective. Its importance becomes all the more crucial whenever the enterprise's only possible means of long-term survival occurs through internal cost reduction and reorganization, and its failure to provide acceptable outcomes may result in locational changes of productive operations.

Intermarket linkage may also become significant in the effort to increase productivity, whenever input substitution becomes feasible or necessary as part of cost reduction objectives. Major positive impacts on productivity may therefore be achieved through this role by finding either less costly sources of existing inputs, or more efficient alternatives. In such efforts, the strategic planning role may also become important, especially if the restructuring effort includes the possibility of locational change to lower input cost sites, be they raw material, labor, or transport. Such locational moves indeed often provide a respite from the all-out effort to increase productivity, by employing more cost-effective labor and raw material inputs at the new sites.

In many ways, the effort to increase productivity in sectors with less favorable income elastic demand is limited only by entrepreneurial ingenuity and the willingness to undertake the risks involved.[34] Inasmuch as institutional structures hamper entrepreneurial effectiveness, they preempt the possibilities for raising productivity and enhancing the competitiveness of the less favored sectors. The regional implications of the failure to raise productivity in the face of external competitive pressures are too serious and tragic to be ignored. Plant closings, employment loss, declining export income, so well known in many advanced regions and nations, are some of the unfortunate outcomes of productivity lags in the less favored activities and sectors.

One of the most important spatial impacts of the restructurings occurring in both the new frontier and less favored sectors is employment change and reallocation. Thus, labor released through productivity increases in less favored activities can be expected to be absorbed by the new frontier sector. Reallocation is both spatial and sectoral, however, since major differences in spatial distribution and orientation can be expected for both the new frontier and the less favored sectors.

Thus, from a historical perspective, efforts to raise agricultural productivity, as this sector became less favored in its income elasticity position, resulted in a massive reallocation of actual and potential agricultral manpower toward the more income-elastic manufacturing activities. The spatial corollary of this shift was a substantial flow of rural-urban migration, and a relatively rapid agglomeration of population in industrial cities. Later, as the services sector attained the most favored income elastic position, labor reallocation has occurred from manufacturing toward this sector. Since service activities are primarily traditional central place functions, a greater spatial dispersion of population toward medium size and other urban places could be expected.[35]

Interregional flows are another aspect of the employment reallocation process, inasmuch as regions with greater comparative advantages for a new frontier sector can become major destinations for out-migrants from other regions, where less favored sectors predominate. The essential entrepreneurial roles, if available in sufficient quantum and quality, then become a comparative advantage in their own right in the favored regions, creating employment opportunities and attracting additional in-migration. At the same time, the intersectoral impacts of the new frontier sector can compound the process, as linked or accessory activities experience expansion. In this respect, it is obvious that not all activities or subsectors of a less favored sector will stagnate or experience decline. Those subsectors that are most closely linked with new frontier activities will grow as well, increasing their sector's share of total employment.

An obvious corollary of the previous discussions is that regional productivity is only an adjustment mechanism for coping with long-term uncertainty, if not adversity. In a relative sense, regions that attain competitive productivity levels in the less favored sectors will not be the most successful performers in the national division of labor.[36] It is, rather, the regions that are able to grow rapidly, through the comparative advantages they offer new frontier activities, or those that are closely linked with them, that will be most successful in attracting additional resources and population.

Placing these sectoral restructurings and reallocations in an historical context, along with their spatial impacts and relationship to the development of the various entrepreneurial roles, is a most challenging aspect. This will be the major objective of the following sections. For this purpose, a general stages framework that can account for both the sectoral shifts and intersectoral impacts will be elaborated.

Entrepreneurship and Sectoral Restructuring: Historical Stages

The relationship between the historical development of the entrepreneurial roles, and the sectoral restructurings determined by changing wants and needs, is crucial for an understanding of the process of regional economic change. Thus, the development of entrepreneurship and enterprise forms, changes in sectoral leadership in output growth, employment, productivity, and the consequent spatial changes that reflect regional growth or decline, and inter-regional flows of population and goods will be treated here as central aspects of the process of long-term change.

The conceptualization of historical stages presented in this section is primarily designed to consider the rise and development of the five major entrepreneurial roles. This scope therefore sets this framework apart from other stages conceptualizations, including the selection of the specific historical periods involved.[37] In addition, two other distinguishing aspects are crucial in tracing the historical differentiation of entrepreneurship over the various stages. One is the intimate relationship that exists between the entrepreneurial function and the development of industrialization. It is, in fact, through this relationship that most innovative entrepreneurial applications have occurred. A second aspect is the close connection found between the entrepreneurial function and the development of the firm's organization, ranging from the household workshop typical of late eighteenth-century America, to the rise of conglomerate firms in the 1960s and 1970s.

The historical periods selected for this stages framework, as shown in Table 3-1, are specific to the U.S. experience. This focus is important for two reasons. First, temporal specificity is essential to a consideration of historical development. The alternative, which would be to provide a more general framework, would be much too vague for the purposes of this study. Second, outlining specific periods will be essential to the empirical analyses of the subsequent chapters. All too often, a sequence of stages is presented as a model through which regions and nations should pass if they are to attain a certain level of development. Although similarities do exist among the evolutionary experiences of some national and regional economies, it will not be an objective of this effort to provide such a model.

The historical approach adopted in this study has governed the selection of the various periods to be considered. This has therefore avoided a mechanistic selection of the temporal parameters based solely on, and following, macroeconomic cycles and fluctuations. As such, the contents of this chapter are an effort to provide a plausible explanation of the underlying causes of long-term macroeconomic change, rather than to measure cyclical fluctuations, which were the primary objectives of Kondratieff's (1935) and Kuznets' (1930) classical works.

The exact beginnings and endings of each historical stage have been treated as approximates, primarily because it is difficult to find any consensus among historians on exact dates and time periods, and because of the gradualness of change involved. Unlike other events, political, demographic, or social, the Industrial Revolution had no exact beginning and end. There is conceptual disagreement among historians as to whether it was a revolution at all, as opposed to an evolution, or whether it has even ended.

The Industrial Revolution

The beginnings of the Industrial Revolution mark the first stage of industrialization, starting in the United States during the latter part of the eighteenth century. The most important changes typical of this era were, first, the substitution of power-driven machinery for physical labor, resulting in the establishment of specialized workshops in such industries as textiles and iron processsing. A second major feature was the discovery and substitution of new mineral fuels and raw

Table 3–1 Entrepreneurship and Macroeconomic Change: Historical Stages and Regional Impacts.

	Industrial Revolution (U.S. 1780s–1840s)	Capital Goods Industrialization (1840s–1890s)	Mass Production Industrialization (1890s–1950s)	Services-Oriented Industrial Change (1950s– –)
Entrepreneurial Roles	capital investment (invention)	intermarket linkage (invention)	productive coordination (invention)	strategic planning (invention)
Enterprise Form	single function/ single product	multifunction/ single product (factory system)	multifunction/ multiproduct (process integration)	multifunction/ multiproduct (conglomerate)
Sectoral Leadership				
Productivity	agriculture	agriculture	1. agriculture 2. manufacturing	1. agriculture 2. manufacturing
Output	transitional: agricultural to manufacturing	manufacturing	transitional: manufacturing to services	services
Employment	transitional: agricultural to manufacturing	manufacturing	transitional: manufacturing to services	services
Regional Impacts				
Heartland				
Economic	1. employment/output (manufacturing) 2. productivity (agriculture)	1. employment/output (manufacturing) 2. productivity (agriculture)	productivity (agriculture, manufacturing)	productivity (agriculture, manufacturing)
Demographic	urban concentration* (mercantile functions)	urban concentration (rural-urban migration/ interregional migration)	metropolitan concentration (rural-urban migration/ interregional in-migration)	metropolitan deconcentration
Hinterland				
Economic	employment/output (agriculture)	employment/output (agriculture)	1. employment/output (services, manufacturing) 2. productivity (agriculture)	1. employment/output (services) 2. productivity (manufacturing, agriculture)
Demographic	rural dispersion	rural dispersion/ urban concentration* (interregional migration/rural-urban migration)	urban concentration* (rural-urban migration)	metropolitan/ urban concentration* (interregional migration)

*population growth leadership for historical stage.

materials, such as coal, for agriculturally produced resources, such as wood and charcoal. As a result, the linkages between the primary, extractive sector and manufacturing were substantially deepened. Thus, steam engines, perhaps the main symbol of this era, were built of iron and made to run on coal, two of the newly used minerals. Cotton textiles, steam engine manufacturing, and the development of a wide variety of iron-based manufactures for agricultural, household, and power generation became the most dynamic industries of this period.[38]

The marshaling and channeling of capital investment for industrial enterprise became the most important entrepreneurial activities of this first stage, along with the decisive technological inventions, such as the steam engine and the new iron manufacturing techniques.[39] In the absence of established financial markets for industrial investment, the importance of the capital investment role becomes all the more obvious, as securing and generating the necessary venture capital were far from trivial undertakings. Capital resources thus had to be obtained from the industrial entrepreneur's personal resources, from the surpluses and working capital generated by small-scale industry, or from other entrepreneurs in commerce and agriculture.

Even after the growth and consolidation of industrial workshops had attained significant scale economies, the organization of enterprise was nevertheless quite rudimentary. Enterprises incorporating the most advanced productive and organizational techniques of their day were primarily single function, single product organizations. The single function involved was relatively small scale, narrowly defined production, with all other accessory activities (distribution, marketing, service) being undertaken by independent entrepreneurs. At the same time, the degree of specialization required of productive activities, given the organizational and technological resources available, pretty much determined that single product manufacturing, with relatively little product differentiation, would become the norm for the larger workshops of this period.

This first stage also witnessed a remarkable shift of the output growth leadership from agriculture to manufacturing, based on the greater, and growing, difference in income elasticities of demand between the latter and the former. This shift, according to the assumptions of this framework, inevitably generated a long-term effort to increase productivity in agriculture. The long-term implications of this development were a substantial deepening of the linkages between agriculture and manufacturing, as more manufactured goods began to be used in cropping and extractive activities, such as iron implements for tilling and harvesting, steam engines for mining, and cotton manufactures for clothing and household uses.

Few other sectoral restructurings have had as predictable regional impacts as those of the Industrial Revolution in its first decades. In the region undergoing the most rapid industrialization, the future industrial heartland (in the United States, the Northeast and, later, the Midwest also), the gradual concentration of population in cities where industrial workshops agglomerated became a certain outcome. Population was also attracted to these regions, mainly from abroad, by urban mercantile activities supporting both agriculture and manufacturing.

Several cities would eventually emerge as major industrial centers in the heartland region, such as Boston, Philadelphia, and New York. Still, the small scale of most industrial workshops was a poor indicator of the subsequent changes to come. Chandler (1977, pp. 51–52) provides an excellent description of urban industry in America at the end of the nineteenth century, noting that "in the seaboard cities and the small towns of the interior, manufacturers were largely artisans who lived above or near their shops. They worked at a specialized trade such as the making or processing of cloth (spinners, weavers, tailors, and makers of stockings, gloves, hats, and sails), leather (tanners, shoemakers, and harnessmakers), wood (makers of furniture, carts, wagons, carriages, paneling, and clocks), metals (smiths of gold, silver, copper, tin, blacksmiths and whitesmiths, gunmakers and ironmongers), or clay and glass."[40]

The enlargement of workshops during this first stage was primarily carried out by expanding the workforce rather than through the "putting out" system, or the substitution of machinery for labor.[41] This pattern is consistent with the assumptions of the previous section, where a sector assuming the growth leadership through greater income elasticity of demand would not be expected to attempt to increase productivity in significant ways. Rather, its main way of meeting rapid output growth would be through simple expansion.

If agriculture saw its growth leadership eroded, and lost, to manufacturing in the industrial heartland region, its output and employment growth (including that of agricultural commerce) in the hinterland regions of the United States would remain unrivaled throughout this period. Thus, the pressure to increase productivity would be felt initially in heartland agriculture. The great dynamism of the agricultural frontier regions, so peculiar to the American context, would continue until the end of the nineteenth century, through major increases in cropland area and livestock. This ensured the prolonged rural dispersion of population for almost a century, preventing the formation of large urban agglomerations, except in some states closest to the heartland.

Capital Goods Industrialization

The second historical stage, Capital Goods Industrialization, witnessed a vast transformation and expansion of productive and distributive capacity, consolidating the manufacturing sector's leadership in output and employment growth in the heartland region (see Table 3-1). By the 1840s, less expensive coal and iron had allowed large scale factories to be set up in various metal manufacturing industries, bringing fundamental changes to these and other activities. The sectoral and spatial impacts of heavy, capital goods industrialization were enormous, especially in railroad construction and shipbuilding, bringing about an unprecedented revolution in transportation.

At the same time, the expansion of distributional possibilities supported the growth of the factory system, making it feasible to transport resource inputs from farther away, and more reliably. The expansion of workshops and factories, along with a greater diversity of inputs, resulting from the discovery of new sources, required many entrepreneurs to delegate managerial authority to subordinates, in order to supervise and coordinate the flow of raw material and intermediate inputs. This need was in contrast to that for the marketing of products, which was usually handled by independent firms and entrepreneurs in the commercial sector.

The rise and development of the intermarket linkage role were therefore most appropriate and timely to this historical stage. Its importance was made all the more obvious when the lack of sufficient raw material inputs, such as coal, became a major obstacle to industrial expansion during the 1830s and 1840s. With the exception of textile mills and armories, obstacles to increasing the flow of inputs to factories, such as the lack of sufficient transport, coordination, and organizational arrangements, were preventing both the integration of production processes and a greater division of labor in American manufacturing. Demand for almost every variety of manufactured good was in fact so high throughout much of this period, that many British and European industries were shipping a significant amount of their output to the United States.[42]

The intermarket linkage role was also important in extending backward linkages from capital goods industries to primary resource-producing activities. Thus, steam engines built of iron used coal for fuel and had a major effect on coal mining, where they helped increase output dramatically. Later, steam engines became the primary source of power for iron mining as well as railroad transportation and shipping, providing more access to greater and more diversified raw material sources. The new raw materials, particularly coal and iron, became inputs to virtually every manufacturing activity, either as raw inputs or as intermediate goods. Thus, iron-made machines were used in textile mills; other iron-made machines and parts became crucial to railway locomotive manufacturing, to shipbuilding, and to bridge and architectural constructions. It is therefore not surprising that iron and its derivatives soon became symbols of the new industrial age. As a result, industrial output increased at rates far above those of demographic growth.[43]

The most important organizational advance of this stage was the development of multifunctional industrial enterprises. These were characterized by the integration of all productive operations required to manufacture a product within a single plant. Among the first industries to move toward the multifunctional form were the textile mills and, later, armories. These and other industries' experience with multifunctional integration would later be instrumental to the development of mass production. At the same time, this trend made it even more crucial for input flows to be competently managed and coordinated, especially with respect to their quality, quantity, reliability of supply, and substitution.

Generally, the greater the distance between input source and factory, and the larger its proportion of total input value, the more important input management and coordination became. Thus, an increasing preoccupation with the monitoring of input sources and flows led to the establishment of input accounting and purchasing functions in many factories, during the 1850s and 1860s. In an increasing number of cases, the purchasing function of the larger factories became a separate unit of the enterprise, with complete supervision over issues concerning input supply logistics and management.[44]

The regional impacts of this stage involve substantial contrasts between the U.S. heartland and hinterland regions. In the heartland, the rapid growth of manufacturing employment and output, supported by the development of the railroads and shipping, facilitated access to newer input sources in both the heartland and the hinterland, and helped expand markets for manufactured goods to frontier areas. Despite vast improvements in transport and communications, capital goods industries nevertheless remained greatly concentrated in the heartland region throughout this stage. Agriculture remained the most important and dynamic sector in most of the hinterland states and territories, with rising output and employment, as the agricultural land area was increased through frontier expansion.[45]

The pace of urbanization accelerated in the industrial heartland's major cities as factories expanded, attracting other industries and much commercial activity. The integration of production in multifunctional operations housed in single plants had significant spatial impacts in this respect, as it created much demand for support services, including marketing, business, and financial activities. In contrast, rural population dispersion remained a major characteristic of the hinterland region throughout much of this period, because of frontier expansion, especially after the 1850s. Areas and states closer to the heartland region, such as those in the Midwest (which only became part of the heartland after the 1890s), the South and Southwest, experienced the growth of mercantile towns and cities for agricultural and manufactured goods. These growing hinterland urban settlements would usually be found along major transport routes, such as navigable rivers, railway routes, and ports.

The Age of Mass Production

It is not difficult to foresee that the long-term increase in income elasticity of demand for manufactured products, aided by the development of multiregional markets and greater urbanization in both the heartland and hinterland, would eventually generate enormous possibilities for consumer durable goods. Market size would be an important determinant of this expansion, particularly in a nation as large as the United States, where population more than tripled from the mid-eighteenth century through the 1920s.

Many important inventions in the latter part of the nineteenth century, such as the development of the diesel engine, electric lamps, and the automobile, along with the establishment of a large domestic capital goods subsector and the standardization of many intermediate goods and processes, brought unprecedented opportunities for industrial production. During this stage, many new manufactured goods hardly dreamed of a few decades before, would become part of daily household routines. Refrigerators, radios, electrical appliances of various types, the automobile, would virtually come to be taken for granted in twentieth-century America.

This quantum increase in final demand goods, coupled with the gradual but substantial import substitution of previous decades, also generated much domestic demand for intermediate manufactures. Thus, the development of fuels technology and processing, steel, metals, and machinery manufacturing made enormous strides in the early decades of this stage. At the same time, the increased demand for intermediate and producers' goods generated greater linkage between resource processing industries and consumer durables manufacturers. As a result, major interregional linkages in the United States between the heartland, where most consumer durable goods manufacturing concentrated, and the hinterland, where many new resource processing industries were being established, began to develop. Gradually, for example, oil production in the Southwest would find it economical to establish processing industries there, thus changing the structure of the region's linkages with downwardly linked industries in the Northeast and Midwest.

The revolution in productive organization and technology that accompanied these changes created a new industrial structure where productive coordination became crucial to the operation of any major industrial firm (see Table 3-1). In an increasing number of industries, the multifunctional structure of production, the rapid growth of plant sizes, and the simultaneous production of various products increasingly separated ownership from management. At the same time, a greater participation of capital markets in the financing of industry required more specialized, professional expertise in the management of production.[46] Mass production, or the standardization of productive activities as repetitive tasks, would be the most significant achievement of the coordinative entrepreneurial role. It would be adopted by virtually every industry producing consumer goods, and by many producer goods manufacturers, after the 1910s. It would also be the single most important source of demand for managerial expertise in the subsequent decades.[47]

It is also clear that the inventive role was quite important to this stage, through the development of various major scientific and technological inventions in the late nineteenth century. The establishment of the U.S. patent system, and the safeguarding of inventors' property rights, contributed much to this inventive surge, as the number of patents granted increased from an annual average of about 12,000 in the 1860s to 25,000 in the 1880s, and to about 40,000 by the middle of the 1910s. Unfortunately, a great deal of imbalance existed in the regional distribution of inventions, as the industrial heartland region concentrated the vast majority of patent holders and inventors from the eighteenth century through the first half of the twentieth.

Toward the end of the nineteenth century, some firms had begun to establish research laboratories, engaging in organized, systematic invention, in what would be the early beginnings of the modern corporate research and development function. It also became clear that an important correlation existed between the number of capital goods inventions in an industry, and the purchase of capital goods inputs by that industry.[48] Thus, consistent with the assumptions of the previous section, inventive entrepreneurs channeled their ideas toward industries and activities that either were already experiencing, or were perceived close to experiencing, substantial demand growth.

Structural changes in productive activities through the creation and expansion of multifunctional, multiproduct organizations, and the introduction of mass production, led to the start of substantial vertical integration in the larger industries. The previous marketing arrangements with independent wholesalers that served most final demand goods industries, were proving inadequate in moving the vastly increased amount and diversity of goods in many industries. Thus, since the late eighteenth century, a process of vertical integration had started for some industries, especially those manufacturing low priced consumer nondurables, such as cigarettes, flour, cereals, and canned goods. This was later expanded to consumer durables industries, such as sewing machine, agricultural implements and machinery, and electrical equipment manufacturing, as independent wholesalers were unable to provide all of the essential marketing functions, such as service, repair, and installation.

Thus, by the first and second decades of the twentieth century, many industrial firms were integrating vertically toward their markets, especially in the U.S. industrial heartland region, effectively taking up the functions formerly performed by independent wholesalers. At the same time, the development of the intermarket linkage function in previous decades, as discussed earlier, also led to a backward vertical integration toward input sources in the heartland and hinterland regions, as a way of ensuring a steady flow of supplies.[49]

From a macroeconomic standpoint, the emergence of the Mass Production stage implied a continued and pronounced shift of the national, and the heartland region's, economic base away from agriculture. Even with the growth of agriculture through frontier expansion, this sector's share of national economic growth actually declined throughout the nineteenth century. By the start of this stage, agricultural employment had declined to less than 50 percent of the nation's labor force, with a lower, and rapidly declining, proportion in the industrial heartland region. The obvious outcome of this shift was a long-term effort to increase productivity, thereby releasing manpower and inducing its reallocation toward urban manufacturing in the heartland, and toward services in both heartland and hinterland.

In the latter part of this stage, a shift of the sectoral growth leadership from manufacturing toward services could be expected, according to the assumptions of this framework, as greater relative demand for this latter sector's goods occurred. This would force a need to increase productivity in manufacturing that would initially be felt in those industries with relatively lower income elasticity, eventually expanding to many others in subsequent decades. In the early decades of this stage, manufacturing remained strong, however, consolidating the long-term dynamism attained through the earlier domestic establishment of a capital goods base.

Regionally, an emerging manufacturing belt located along the Detroit-Chicago corridor would begin to rival that of the Northeastern Atlantic seaboard, running from Boston to the Philadelphia area. In the hinterland, natural resources-related manufacturing began to expand rapidly during this stage, being linked with heartland industries. On the other hand, some concern with hinterland agricultural productivity began to develop, as this sector's share of total hinterland economic product began to decline.[50]

The metropolitanization of the industrial heartland occurring during this period brought unprecedented problems in transportation and communication that began to affect urban manufacturing and services greatly. These required better metropolitan self-organization through land use and transportation planning, as a means of rapid growth management. In the hinterland, increasing urban population concentration in the previous major mercantile centers, such as New Orleans, St. Louis, and Minneapolis, and in newer settlements with physiographic advantages, such as ports, as in the case of San Francisco, San Diego, Houston-Galveston, Tampa, and Jacksonville, became a major development.

Services-Oriented Change

The unprecedented interrelations that have developed between the manufacturing and the services sectors during the post–World War II era are the most significant general characteristic of the fourth historical stage (see Table 3-1). The major outcomes of the restructurings that these relationships involved are, first, the search for, and expansion of, foreign markets as a way to counteract the lower domestic income elasticity of demand for many manufactured goods and the loss of the growth leadership to services. The second outcome was the great momentum toward horizontal integration that developed during the 1960s, linking many manufacturing firms with services enterprises through the formation of conglomerates.

These changes had the greatest impact on the internal organization and formulation of long-term enterprise strategy and resource allocation. The uncertainty and complexities of long-term planning, along with the management of horizontally integrated firms that were not similar or even related to the parent company, required considerably more foresight and expertise than had ever been needed by any business organization. Thus, the emergence and institutionalization of strategic planning, the most important entrepreneurial role of this stage, became crucial to the development of many organizations.[51]

In many cases, the knowledge and implementation of top level corporate planning and strategy making have diffused well beyond the realm of the large, departmentalized enterprises to smaller firms. In the process, enterprise strategic planning has become institutionalized as a major component of the field of management science. A good many of the procedures incorporated in the exercise of this entrepreneurial role had their beginnings decades earlier, in the industrial enterprises expanded or created by vertical integration, through mergers or acquisitions, rather than through simple, internally generated expansion. Thus, the knowledge and experience acquired in such restructurings would later be essential to the establishment of large-scale conglomerates.

The development of strategic planning has further advanced the separation between ownership and management, as owners of the widely dispersed stock usually have little or no opportunity to participate in top level decision processes. Thus, strategic planners in most large organizations today have virtually complete control over all decision making related to resource allocation, marketing, and budgeting. The enormous attention devoted to strategy in most major enterprises has prompted Chandler (1977, p. 479) to note that "the divisionalized firms further refined their strategy of diversification by exploiting what became known as the product cycle. Strategies became designed to obtain the maximum return from a new product as it moved through the cycle from its initial commercialization to full maturity. An effectively diversified enterprise attempted to have a number of product lines, each at a different stage of the product cycle."

The increasing focus on strategy also emphasized the importance of the inventive entrepreneurial role, as organized research and development became a major component of long-term planning. Now, the planning of inventions and innovations, anticipating obsolescence in products and processes, became entrenched in corporate strategy. The underlying premise was that replacement or differentiation of products and production processes could be planned for, to a great extent, thereby reducing the uncertainty involved in dealing with future events. Thus, what had in previous times been primarily an uncertain, unpredictable and individual venture, became institutionalized as an almost routine component of daily corporate practice.[52]

The development of the large multifunctional, multiproduct organization not only required the further differentiation and routinization of the entrepreneurial function, through the implementation of strategic planning; it also elaborated new interorganizational arrangements through the capabilities of this entrepreneurial role. Thus, the conglomerate became a distinctive form of enterprise development during this stage. This trend can be interpreted as an effort by manufacturing enterprises to develop financial and ownership linkages with firms in the sector (services) that was being favored by greater income elasticity of demand, and which was decisively taking the growth leadership in the American economy.

This trend toward the conglomerate allowed many industrial firms greater access to financing, and better returns than they would have otherwise enjoyed, had they limited themselves to manufacturing. At the same time, the formation of conglomerates helped reduce the uncertainty generated by less promising horizons in manufacturing, as far as future output growth was concerned. Increasing foreign competition and the pressures to increase productivity were powerful inducements. There should also be little doubt that, interregionally, the development of conglomerates extended the corporate power of the U.S. heartland to many of the acquired firms in the hinterland, where services had the greatest growth prospects. The interregional reach of many conglomerates was also greatly enhanced by the establishment of branch plants and regional sales and service networks in the hinterland, particularly in the Sunbelt states.

In no other sector but agriculture has there been a greater need to increase productivity during this stage. Aided by government support, the agricultural sector was nevertheless most pressed to increase productivity, as the relative income elasticity of its goods trailed well behind that of manufacturing and services. This effort has undoubtedly strengthened the linkages between manufacturing and agriculture, especially in the major agricultural states, as an increasing amount of manufactured goods, such as tractors, harvesters, fertilizers, and even computers, have been used in production. Major restructurings have also continued to occur in this sector as, for example, family farming in the traditional agricultural areas has been disappearing, while corporate agriculture and agribusiness interests produce an increasing proportion of output.[53]

Perhaps the most important heartland-hinterland contrast of this stage is that found between the Sunbelt states and the industrial heartland region, which includes the Northeastern and Midwestern states. In the Sunbelt, the rapid growth of urban services and some manufacturing industries has prolonged the process of urbanization and metropolitanization, while in the heartland significant deconcentration from metropolitan places toward adjacent areas and medium-sized cities has occurred. At the same time, a significant amount of interregional migration from the heartland to the Sunbelt states has been taking place, reflecting a sectoral reallocation of labor from manufacturing and services in the heartland, toward services in the Sunbelt.

A most pressing concern for the heartland manufacturing sector has been that of increasing productivity, in order to meet both hinterland and foreign lower cost competition. An ongoing restructuring in the heartland's manufacturing sector has seen the decline of capital goods industries, such as steel, while in some areas increasing concentrations of high technology electronics, computers, aerospace, and biotechnology manufacturing have developed. The fact that the latter industries had earlier established themselves strongly in some areas of the Sunbelt, such as California and Texas, raises the possibility of a new competitive rivalry between the Sunbelt and the heartland. For many of these industries, however, the inversion of regional roles would properly place the Sunbelt as the heartland, while the regions of the Northeast and Midwest would find themselves in the hinterland's former role.

INTERSECTORAL CHANGE AND THE ROLE OF MANUFACTURING

The relationship among industrial change, entrepreneurship, and long-term regional macroeconomic development has been an important feature of the stages framework presented in this chapter. So far, however, the spatial and intersectoral relationships that exist between manufacturing and the other economic sectors have not been adequately addressed. Growth and changes occurring in agriculture and services have been assumed to occur somehow hand in hand with the differentiation and deepening of industrial structure, without consideration of how changes in manufacturing affect those sectors.

It has been an implicit assumption in the discussions provided in this chapter that sectoral transformations, driven by the development of entrepreneurship, are at the core of long-term spatial change. The sectoral approach has been assumed to be vastly more significant than the more orthodox factor costs perspective, followed in other analyses of spatial change. A major issue in this respect is that the factor costs approach is best applied to the analysis of short- or, at most, medium-term changes. Second, that approach, and its virtually exclusive concern with labor and capital costs, basically neglects the most important agent of economic change: entrepreneurship, in all its roles and activities. A third issue is that factor costs analysis has traditionally adopted the Neoclassical assumptions that preempt a discussion of entrepreneurship and organizations, assuming entrepreneurial action to be an automatic, if not downright trivial, endeavor.[54]

Innovation Diffusion

The importance of manufacturing in the historical development process transcends any changes in its growth leadership position. Even during times of industrial stagnation, this sector has been crucial to the development of agriculture and services. Its importance therefore reaches far beyond what any of the traditional indicators, such as employment, contribution to national income, or export performance, can reveal.[55]

Because most scientific and organizational inventions have historically been first applied in, or developed for, manufacturing production, innovation diffusion is the manufacturing sector's most significant contribution to intersectoral dynamism and long-term spatial development. The close relationship that exists between inventive entrepreneurship and manufacturing has therefore made this sector the source of most innovation diffusion to all other economic activities.[56]

The implications of this linkage are enormous for regional competitiveness in international and interregional trade, since innovative leadership in manufacturing has greatly affected the long-term fortunes of the agricultural and services sectors. Similarly, the importance of innovation in manufacturing for maintaining and increasing living standards cannot be ignored, as its knowledge and qualitative spinoffs reach far beyond what can be quantitatively traced by any analytical technique.

Two major types of innovations are commonly diffused through the manufacturing sector: organizational and technological innovations. Organizational innovations have suffered great neglect in the social science literature, whereas technological innovation diffusion has received overwhelming attention over the years.[57] Organizational innovation diffusion is as important as technological diffusion, although more difficult to trace, since its ownership rights are virtually impossible to appropriate. Innovations in such areas as organizational structuring, labor-management relations, and the organization of quality control procedures have traditionally been applied and developed in manufacturing operations, before they were diffused to commercial and service activities.

Many technological innovations diffused from manufacturing to the other sectors have been embodied in specific products. In many cases, the adoption of these products has required significant organizational and behavioral changes in the enterprises that adopt them. In many commercial activities, for example, the introduction of computers for inventory control led to substantial organizational restructuring, and not a few changes in labor relations and the productivity of many enterprises. Similarly, the introduction of sophisticated electronics in medical technology has revolutionized the diagnostic processes of the medical profession in many areas. In agriculture, sophisticated harvesting combines and biotechnology products have changed the way many crops are planted and harvested, and have contributed to dramatic increases in productivity.

Multiplier impacts on agricultural and service activities, an aspect that is not usually related to innovation diffusion, are also affected by the adoption of organizational and technological innovations in manufacturing. New industries and manufacturing processes require services such as transportation, business support activities, and marketing that would not occur without their introduction. These services are usually local in character and can become an important component of urban and regional economies. Labor income generated in manufacturing, in both older and newer industries, is generally higher than that generated by most activities in the other economic sectors. Clearly, then, a decline of innovation in manufacturing has serious implications for the long-term dynamism and well-being of the other economic sectors, nationally and regionally. The importance of manufacturing for the regional and national economies therefore reaches far beyond this sector's overall growth leadership and relative size.

Intersectoral and Interindustry Dynamics

Innovation diffusion from manufacturing can best be understood through the changes that occur in the input and product linkages between sectors. Similarly, shifts in emphasis between consumer and producer goods manufacturing, and between durable and nondurable goods production, and their impact on other sectors, can reveal major changes in the population's wants and preferences.

Table 3-2 outlines these relationships and their potential regional impacts for each historical stage. What limited documentation we have on the period of the Industrial Revolution in America indicates that input linkages from agriculture and services were significant, even during the initial decades of this stage. Finance capital from mercantile activities was probably the most significant input from the tertiary sector to manufacturing. From agriculture, raw materials, such as cotton for the textile workshops, and wood and charcoal for iron manufacturing, were essential to the development of industrialization.[58]

At the same time, manufacturing's contribution to agriculture, in the form of better implements and tools for farming and mining, was

Table 3–2 Intersectoral Change and Manufacturing: Historical Stages and Regional Impacts.

	Industrial Revolution (U.S. 1780s–1840s)	Capital Goods Industrialization (1840s–1890s)	Mass Production Industrialization (1890s–1950s)	Services-Oriented Industrial Change (1950s– —)
Entrepreneurial Roles	capital investment (invention)	intermarket linkage (invention)	productive coordination (invention)	strategic planning (invention)
Enterprise Form	single function/ single product	multifunction/ single product (factory system)	multifunction/ multiproduct (process integration)	multifunction/ multiproduct (conglomerate)

Intersectoral Linkage

Agricultural & Extractive outputs⁺	farm products (e.g. fibers)	mined raw materials (e.g. ore)	mined raw materials (e.g. fossil fuels)	farm products and mined raw materials (e.g. primary food products, minerals)
inputs⁺⁺	durable goods (e.g. farm tools)	durable goods (e.g. mining eqpt.)	nondurable goods (e.g. chemicals, fertilizers) durable goods (e.g. farm eqpt.)	nondurable goods (e.g. biotech products, chemicals) durable goods (e.g. farm eqpt., computers)
Services outputs⁺	finance	energy	marketing	information (market. technical)
inputs⁺⁺	durable goods (e.g. apparel)	durable goods (e.g. railroads, ships) nondurable goods (e.g. processed fuels)	durable goods (e.g. autos) nondurable goods (e.g. chemicals)	durable goods (e.g. computers, medical) nondurable goods (e.g. medical and business supplies)
Interindustry Emphasis	consumer goods (durables)	producer goods (durables, nondurables)	consumer goods (durables, nondurables) producer goods (nondurables, durables)	consumer goods (nondurables, durables)

Regional Impacts

Intersectoral	manufacturing (heartland*) agricultural (heartland/hinterland)	manufacturing (heartland*)	services (heartland/hinterland*) manufacturing (heartland)	services (hinterland*)
Interindustry input/product markets	local/regional (heartland)	interregional (heartland-hinterland)	national/interregional (hinterland-heartland)	international/national (toward hinterland)
locational dynamics	relative dispersion (heartland rural/urban*)	concentration (heartland urban*)	dispersion (hinterland urban*) production complexes (heartland metropolitan)	dispersion (hinterland urban/ metropolitan*) dispersion (heartland metropolitan)

⁺to manufacturin   ⁺⁺from manufacturing   *growth leadership for historical stage important to the development of this sector. Manufacturing's greatest impact was on the tertiary sector, however, as marketing arrangements spawned new commercial ventures, linked to the emerging textile industries. Gradually, iron manufactures would find wider applications, and both retail and wholesale commerce would become increasingly linked to this important industry.

The regional impacts of the intersectoral linkages developing during this stage were confined to the industrializing Northeast, in such states as Massachusetts, New York, and Pennsylvania. Distance and transport difficulties were obviously a major obstacle to the diffusion of innovations from manufacturing, as well as to the development of raw material input linkages and product distribution. At the same time, the expansion of hinterland agriculture in the Midwest and South was opening up new possibilities for industrialization in the Northeast, by diversifying and enlarging the potential supply of raw material inputs. This would help innovation diffusion by making it possible for many industries to grow larger, applying new methods and techniques as they expanded.[59]

The next stage, Capital Goods Industrialization, witnessed both the rise of the new, heavy industries, and the diversification of producers' durable and nondurable goods manufactures. One of its greatest impacts would be on trade and infrastructural construction, as railroads, bridges, shipping facilities, canals, and roads were built to accommodate the supply needs of a rapidly growing manufacturing sector and the commercial opportunities of an expanding frontier. The growth of manufacturing created enormous demand for mined raw materials, such as iron ore, developing significant new backward linkages to these activities as well, in the form of new or improved mining tools and equipment.[60]

The emergence of the intermarket linkage role was, as we have seen before, a major factor in this stage, as its innovative capabilities were instrumental in resolving the logistical complexities involved in developing and maintaining input flows and linkages. Although little documentation exists on this aspect, it is quite logical to expect that the innovative capacities of this role were not confined to manufacturing, although they were originally introduced and developed in this sector. Clearly, the expertise gained in purchasing, and in the technical coordination and administration of industrial input sourcing, was also very applicable to commercial and service enterprises.[61]

Such enterprises, especially the larger and more diversified ones, would also have substantial supply obstacles to overcome, as they managed to maintain and expand marketing arrangements with manufacturers. Managing the reliability of the industrial supply linkages that replenished their inventories, and finding adequate substitutes, required much the same intermarket linkage and coordination skills as in manufacturing. Similarly, in transportation, the skills and techniques of intermarket linkage were valuable in the operation and rapid expansion of the railroads.[62]

The regional impacts of the intermarket linkage role and its innovative intersectoral diffusion during this stage were substantial. Although industry remained largely concentrated in the industrial heartland states of the Northeast, where it continued to be the most dynamic sector, substantial intersectoral-interregional input linkages began to develop between the industrial heartland and hinterland, primarily in the Midwest and South. Second, the development of new raw material sources and sites inevitably promoted the creation of raw material processing industries in the hinterland, especially in the Midwest, as the transport cost advantages gained through initial on-site processing became quite substantial, the larger the raw material source. This step further strengthened the innovative interregional and intersectoral diffusion posibilities of the intermarket linkage role, as more interrelationships developed between heartland and hinterland industries. At the same time, it led to some spatial filtering of industry toward the hinterland, as some enterprises integrated vertically and created subsidiaries and branch operations there.

During the third historical stage, Mass Production Industrialization, the rapid growth of durable consumer goods' industries substantially transformed many agricultural and service activities (see Table 3-2). In agriculture, the introduction of tractors and harvesting machinery, along with agricultural chemicals and fertilizers, promoted rapid increases in productivity.[63] In services, this stage brought dramatic increases in retail commerce for both durable and nondurable goods, along with substantial increases in some marketing activities, such as advertising. Innovations diffused through the intersectoral linkages that developed among manufacturing and services and agriculture would reach and transform even the most trivial household routines.

The emergence of productive coordination as a major entrepreneurial role, linked to the rise of large-scale manufacturing, had important innovative impacts both within and outside manufacturing. It would indeed be too short-sighted to think that the coordinative techniques developed in production, such as the measurement and coordination of work tasks, labor-management relations, and innovations in organizational structuring, would not have substantial impacts on the other economic sectors. Innovative techniques developed in industrial productive coordination were quite applicable to the management of large retail and service organizations, especially in the areas of labor-management relations and organizational structuring.[64] Some of the same techniques would also be applicable to agriculture as, for example, plans for more efficient mechanized plowing and harvesting drew important lessons from principles developed in industrial engineering.[65]

The importance of consumer durable and nondurable goods industries, along with their related service activities, promoted a more dispersed spatial distribution of industries, as market-oriented plants were established to satisfy local and regional demand. In many cases, this occurred through the creation of new firms, but, in others, establishment of subsidiaries and branch plants of Northeastern firms was an important diffusion vehicle. In both cases, the diffusion of coordinative techniques in production was essential to a more spatially dispersed distribution of industries. It was precisely this process that brought about the transformation of the Midwest as a major industrial producer, making it a part of what is now the modern American industrial heartland.

Population growth in the urbanizing hinterland states, coupled with the diffusion of coordinative techniques and the organizational forms to which it was linked, provided substantial opportunities for the growth of large service and commercial enterprises, many of which were headquartered in heartland metropolises.[66] This helped make the tertiary sector the most dynamic component of the national economy throughout this stage. In the older industrial heartland cities, where productive coordination techniques had been pioneered, the growth of linked, large-scale industries helped form metropolitan industrial complexes, especially as some of these cities became highly specialized in one or more manufacturing activites.

Never before had consumer durable and nondurable goods manufacturing affected intersectoral linkages as they have during our own, Services-Oriented Industrial stage. The rise of innovation-diffusing "high technology" industries, linked with such service fields as health and information processing, has been a major characteristic of this stage. Organizational and technological innovations diffused from manufacturing have revolutionized the daily routines of commercial activities and many professional occupations. In agriculture, the introduction of biotechnology products is inducing yet another productivity surge, as better crops and crop yields are increased and made more reliable, through industrially based genetic selection processes.

To a great extent, innovation diffusion to many personal service activities, such as health, nutrition, and information, reflects a shift in societal preferences toward an emphasis on individual self-development over more basic forms of material consumption. Having made autos, refrigerators, and consumer electronics widely affordable, our society has once again redefined its perceptions of wants and needs, and has shifted its attention toward yet another economic frontier.

The marketing of new "high tech"-based services and products and the organizational and productive restructurings required to satisfy the new demands have added to the importance of the strategic planning role. Many innovations developed in connection with this role in manufacturing have been diffused to service and commercial enterprises. Marketing analyses and product planning, and enterprise budgeting and policy making, originally developed in manufacturing, have been adopted in many service enterprises. The formation of intersectoral conglomerates has no doubt enormously helped innovation diffusion in this role, by reducing barriers to communication and unifying managerial procedures for the disparate enterprises.

The regional impacts of intersectoral and interindustry innovation diffusion in the strategic planning role have promoted a greater national dispersion of manufacturing. Regional dispersion and innovation diffusion have both been helped by the stronger linkages that developed between manufacturing and services, where the latter are usually traditional central place functions. Thus, services-oriented industries have followed regional and national population distribution toward the hinterland.

The spatial filtering of services-linked consumer good, assembly-type industries toward the hinterland has been unprecedented during this fourth stage.[67] Mergers and acquisitions through conglomerate strategies, and the establishment of branch plants, have accounted for the bulk of interregional filtering toward the hinterland, while in some cases the growth of indigenous firms in very new industries has been an important factor. At the same time, the spatial perspectives of some services, such as finance, insurance, and transportation, have expanded enormously during this period, reaching interregional and global markets, aided by the development and application of strategic planning to their marketing functions.

The intersectoral diffusion of innovations in the four historical stages has been supported by some very important intra- and interindustry processes occurring within the manufacturing sector. Product cycles play a major role in diffusing embodied technological innovations between sectors, industries and firms. In some cases this may involve a completely new good, while in others the innovation may be embodied in a differentiated product.[68]

The importance of embodied technological innovation diffusion for service activities is all too often neglected in the literature. This process has nevertheless been of paramount historical importance, especially in the third and fourth historical stages. To this day, the development of many service activities has depended on the diffusion of embodied technological innovations, through new or differentiated manufactured goods. It is impossible to think that health services, for example, could have advanced to their present state without the wide range of innovative goods developed by the medical technology industries. Similarly, the so-called information age would never have occurred without the development of advanced electronics and computers.

The intersectoral diffusion of embodied technological innovations from manufacturing is usually most important during the rapid growth product cycle phase, when the market introduction of a new product occurs and its innovative possibilities attract the greatest interest.[69] It is also during this product cycle phase that the strategic planning role is most important, as marketing strategies are charted and the strongest intersectoral linkages are identified and established.[70]

If product cycles are a major vehicle for the diffusion of embodied technological innovations, process cycles are then the major vehicle for the diffusion of organizational innovations. Innovations diffused through process cycles are therefore more complex and difficult to imitate, since they involve new "ways of doing things." If these innovations are closely related to new technologies, the technologically innovative aspect is disembodied, and could be only indirectly inferred from the new organizational forms or processes.[71]

As with product cycles, most intersectoral and interindustry innovation diffusion through process cycles can be expected to occur during the early growth phase, when the new techniques are learned and implemented. In many cases, however, the complexities of a new process may involve substantial trial and error until it is effectively mastered. In some cases, the mastery of any given process may not occur until the late phases, especially if its structure is significantly differentiated over time. During the early process cycle growth phase, both the intermarket linkage and strategic planning roles become essential for innovation diffusion. The former is important because of the need to manage and coordinate input sourcing. Strategic planning becomes essential with respect to internal policy making and any overall organizational restructuring needed to implement the new techniques.

Intersectoral organizational innovation diffusion through process cycles has taken many forms. New approaches to organizational structuring in service enterprises, originally pioneered in manufacturing, have been one major type of innovation diffusion. These have included, for example, the elaboration of hierarchical levels of authority to manage specific functions, and the decentralization of organizational structures through the creation of autonomous divisions. At a more micro level, the organization of individual work tasks in, for example, many large commercial retail and wholesale enterprises, has occurred through process cycle–induced innovation diffusion from manufacturing.

Intersectoral innovation diffusion through process cycles became most significant historically during the third and fourth historical stages. The growing and important linkages that developed between manufacturing and services during the Mass Production stage were a major factor, and this has intensified during the fourth, Services-Oriented Industrial Stage. Earlier on, however, process cycle-induced innovation diffusion also affected upstream and backwardly linked activities, such as mining, as capital goods industrialization got under way, and new techniques and organizational forms were needed to' operate and sustain the new and expanded input sources.

The interindustry impacts of innovation diffusion during the process cycle's growth phase are also very important, inasmuch as any new production process will have significant forward and backward linkages within the manufacturing sector. Rapidly growing demand for manufactured and raw material inputs will occur during this phase, as a productive process becomes routinized and expands rapidly to gain additional market shares. Imitation and adoption also become important, as far as intra- and interindustry diffusion are concerned, as firms in any reasonably competitive industry seek to gain the advantages of increased output or productivity.

It is obvious from this discussion that substantial intersectoral and interindustry spatial linkage structuring will occur during both the product and process cycles' growth phases. Regions with significant concentrations of industrial activities whose products and processes are in the early growth phases, are bound to be more dynamic and competitive, interregionally and internationally. These regions are also most likely to be the locomotives of the national and international economy. There, a greater and qualitatively better supply of virtually every entrepreneurial role will likely be found.[72]

SYNTHESIS

Providing a broad conceptualization of long-term regional change that relates the entrepreneurial function and all its innovative roles to macroeconomic change, has been the most important objective of this chapter. This has required a consideration of human wants as major determinants of entrepreneurial action, the historical emergence of the various entrepreneurial roles, and shifts in the growth leadership of the various economic sectors.

A review and a critique of major spatial stages conceptualizations found over the past two hundred years were first provided. These helped place the stages framework elaborated in this chapter in perspective, by showing how it could add to previous conceptualizations. More important, the conceptual underpinnings of the historical stages were discussed, by considering the role of long-term changes in human wants, and their effects on sectoral growth.

Changes in human wants and needs, based on individual and collective perceptions of what is necessary to improve well-being and survival, were assumed to be a major societal determinant of entrepreneurial action. A long-term perspective must therefore consider how those wants are reassessed as income increases. Long-term changes in wants and needs determine, through innovative entrepreneurial action, the sectoral dynamics. Most favored sectors will grow fastest, while less favored ones will undergo a rationalization of their productive activities, in an effort to increase productivity and face competitive pressures. This dynamic then shapes the long-term changes occurring in the space economy, by determining the reallocation of employment among the various sectors, and the consequent spatial population distribution.

The historical stages framework has conceptualized long-term regional economic change by relating the emergence of each innovative entrepreneurial role to changes in every economic sector's growth leadership. For this purpose, four historical stages, all very much related to the rise and development of industrialization, were identified. Major hypothetical shifts from one stage to another were discussed, based on our limited historical evidence on the process of industrialization. In this framework, major spatial changes are therefore determined through innovative entrepreneurial action and its impact on sectoral change.

The historical importance of the process of industrialization also reveals the significant role of manufacturing in promoting intersectoral innovation diffusion. Most technological and organizational innovations have historically been developed for, or pioneered in, manufacturing before they were adopted in services and agriculture. Indeed, an examination of two industrial dynamics phenomena, the product and process cycles, helps explain how intersectoral innovation diffusion from manufacturing occurs.

This broad perspective provides a general framework for understanding how some regions and nations become sources of economic growth and change over the long-term. It also provides a viable explanation of why those changes occur, and how they shape the spatial distribution of entrepreneurship, employment, and population.

The historical patterns of sectoral growth leadership, and the shifts in the innovative entrepreneurial roles that determine them, have obviously favored some regions more than others. Changes in interregional and international competitiveness and innovation diffusion, the relative spatial concentration of enterprises in some sectors and industries, and the human impacts of long-term adjustment, all of which are a product of these shifts, are today an important component of our daily lives.

Sectoral Perspectives on Long-Term Change

The broader societal impacts of entrepreneurial action are best gauged through an analysis of sectoral performance. The long-term rise, stagnation, or decline of economic activities, the changes occurring in intersectoral and interindustry linkages, and the resulting distributions of urban and rural population are all at the core of the drama of economic change. All of these changes reflect the micro-level decisions, adjustments, and strategies designed to cope with adversity that are very much a part of our daily lives.

The interplay of sectoral growth, employment reallocation, and productivity is of crucial importance for understanding the process of long-term economic change. In these interrelations, the rise of "new frontier" sectors plays a major role, as their growth performance will reflect on the quality and quantity of entrepreneurial supply, along with the institutional incentives and rigidities that affect entrepreneurial action. A new frontier sector will thus be the growth leader in output and employment in any given historical period, with its performance ultimately being determined by the demand levels of new wants and needs.

Any sector supplanted from the growth leadership position can be expected to experience a relatively lower level of demand elasticity. Such sectors will then be forced to achieve greater productivity, in order to remain competitive nationally and internationally. The level of productivity attained will depend, as with a new frontier sector, on the quantum and quality of entrepreneurial supply. In these sectors, employment growth may occur, but it can be expected to be significantly slower than in the new frontier sectors; in other instances, employment may be stagnant or declining.

Progressively, a sectoral hierarchy based on growth performances can be expected to emerge. Shifts in the hierarchy's growth leadership position are assumed to be secular rather than cyclical, as discussed in the conceptual framework of the previous chapter. Here again, the dynamism of the hierarchy will depend on the quantum and quality of entrepreneurial supply. Aggregate entrepreneurial effectiveness will determine how rapid and timely a shift to higher productivity occurs, in sectors shifting out of a growth leadership position. Similarly, the speed with which new opportunities are seized in a new frontier sector will be determined by entrepreneurial effectiveness in expanding markets and opening new sources of inputs. In this perspective, the entrepreneurial function therefore serves as a medium through which new wants and needs are fulfilled.

The spatial impacts of these shifts arise from the reallocation of employment between sectors, and the redistribution of population that they generate. Such shifts can, for example, change the urban and rural population distribution dramatically, or favor certain urban-size classes over others.[1] Thus, for example, as the growth leadership shifted from agriculture to manufacturing, urbanization became a major societal trend, and was equated with a higher level of development. A shift from manufacturing toward services then entails faster population growth in some urban-size classes than in others, since service activities are primarily central place functions.

This chapter will analyze the most significant national trends found in the agricultural, manufacturing, distributive, and services sectors. For this purpose, three of the most important indicators of aggregate entrepreneurial action—growth, employment and productivity—will be evaluated over a ninety-four-year (1889–1983) period, corresponding to the third and fourth historical stages of the conceptual framework. The changing structure of intersectoral linkages, with respect to manufacturing, and changes in the most significant interindustry linkages, will also be evaluated. Finally, the population distribution effects of long-term sectoral restructuring will be analyzed, in order to determine urban-rural shifts and changes within the urban population distribution.

Despite all efforts, this analysis faces significant limitations. One of these was the impossibility, due to limitations on data availability, to evaluate the process of sectoral restructuring over the first and second historical stages of the conceptual framework. Even with the more restrictive, ninety-four-year time span, finding longitudinally compatible and uniform data proved to be a difficult challenge, as the quality and reliability of some sources tended to vary over the years.[2] As it is, however, starting the analysis at the beginning of the third historical stage does provide certain benefits. One of these is that, territorially, the United States was completely settled and, as the frontier was already conquered, regional divisions were crystallizing. At the same time, the economic and demographic distortions introduced by the Civil War had pretty well subsided by this time, thereby allowing for a more representative analysis of national trends.

LONG-TERM SECTORAL CHANGE: NATIONAL TRENDS

Growth Leadership and National Income

Sectoral contribution to national income will be used in this study as the main growth indicator. National income contribution estimates will represent net value added by each economic sector, measured at factor costs.[3] Four economic sectors—agricultural, manufacturing, distribution, and services—will be analyzed, along with two variants, fabricative activities (manufacturing and construction) and non-governmental services.

Figure 4–1 illustrates changes in the sectoral contribution to national income for the period of study.[4] A most striking feature of this analysis is the pronounced decline of the agricultural sector, especially after 1920. To a great extent, this reflects the shifting of aggregate demand patterns away from agricultural goods toward manufacturing and services, as household incomes rose. At the same time, the settlement of the frontier had pretty well exhausted the possibility of increasing agricultural output through lower cost, land-intensive cultivation.[5] Although one might be tempted to call this period "post-agricultural," this would not do full justice to the importance of the agricultural sector in our economy.

The agricultural sector's decline is in contrast with manufacturing's increasing share of national income through the mid-1950s. A significant shift of wants and preferences toward services then occurs, reducing manufacturing's share. Another important reason for this trend is increasing competition after the industrial reconstruction of advanced nations in Western Europe and Japan, which had been devastated by World War II. In most cases, reconstructed industries used more advanced technology, making production more efficient and introducing significant pricing advantages in many markets.

A third major trend revealed in Figure 4–1 is the 1950s shift in the growth leadership toward services.[6] Clearly, the linkage of many "new frontier" service activities to manufacturing was not enough to impede the latter's declining share of national income. Here, as in the previous stage, steadily increasing household incomes produced new preferences that shifted the growth leadership away from many manufactured goods. In contrast, distribution's share of national income declined since the 1930s. To a great extent, this decline was due to the strong linkages found between many commercial activities and manufacturing, and the fact that modernization and increases in transport and utilities, though significant, added only marginally to this sector's share of national income.[7]

The convergence of some sectoral trends is of particular interest, insofar as Figure 4–1 is concerned, for the long-term movements that

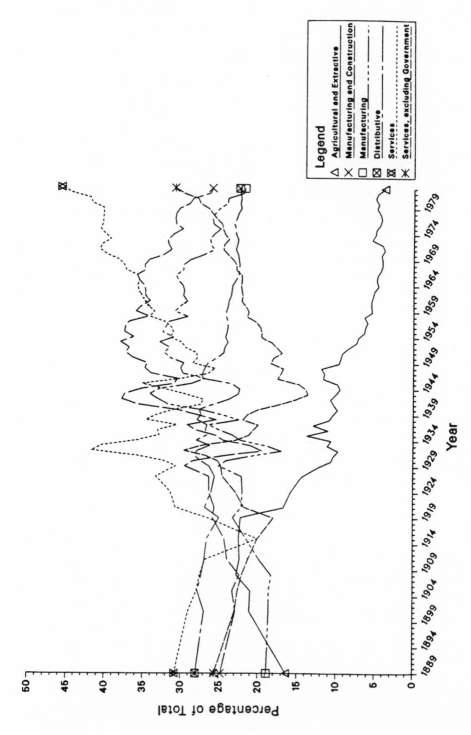

Figure 4-1   Distribution of National Income, by Sector.

Table 4-1 Sectoral Contribution to National Income, 1889–1983.

	Dollars per Employee (x 100)							Dollars per Capita (x 100)						
Year	a	m	m*	d	s	s*	U.S. Total	a	m	m*	d	s	s*	U.S. Total
1889	6.58	17.42	17.42	34.95	61.18+	74.34+	18.53	1.12	1.68	1.30	1.91	2.10	1.75	6.81
1911	18.01	24.66	23.80	35.67	55.29	68.23	27.47	2.32	2.48	2.06	2.79	2.78	2.21	10.35
1919	20.73	24.62	24.14	33.31	46.53	52.06	27.92	2.32	2.69	2.43	2.61	2.76	1.88	10.39
1929	14.93	37.91	37.32	43.50	63.33	81.20	34.76	1.40	3.48	2.96	3.42	4.11	3.20	12.53
1934	12.82	32.10	31.99	41.67	57.33	66.79	30.34	1.11	2.36	2.11	2.63	3.52	2.33	9.70
1941	22.79	52.32	52.20	55.96	64.78	71.55	44.95	1.76	5.92	5.28	4.27	4.99	2.89	17.01
1946	34.17	55.12	54.58	59.80	71.93	72.87	51.73	2.25	6.83	6.13	5.22	6.20	3.29	20.55
1950	36.58	60.76	60.42	56.68	63.10	72.64	51.33	1.95	7.25	6.25	5.12	5.62	3.54	20.03
1960	37.17	72.42	72.70	63.51	75.49	87.06	61.49	1.25	7.80	6.67	5.36	7.73	4.87	22.27
1970	59.08	88.21	86.62	71.70	86.42	95.77	77.26	1.21	9.84	8.23	6.80	11.77	7.15	29.82
1980	86.74	87.18	93.33	70.18	89.58	100.62	84.30	1.72	10.63	8.87	8.23	15.27	10.11	36.55
1983	82.13	84.55	91.57	68.17	91.11	100.96	83.19	1.60	9.64	8.09	8.02	15.72	10.56	35.64

+1901 estimates.

Sectors: a(agricultural and extractive), m (manufacturing and construction), m* (manufacturing), d (distributive: commerce, transportation, utilities), s (services), s* (services, excluding government).

Contribution to National Income and Employment estimates based on five-year moving averages, 1958 constant dollars.

See Appendix for data sources and details.

they reveal. Some convergence between the manufacturing and distributive sectors does appear to set in, though at different rates of change. Again, this may be expected from the strong domestic linkages found between some of the most important distributive activities, such as wholesale and retail commerce, and manufacturing. The trend in services, in contrast, increases dramatically, revealing the growing importance of this sector in the post—World War II economy.

These trends and shifts are clearly reflected in the estimates of Table 4–1, where percentage changes in sectoral contribution to national income have been tabulated.[8] The agricultural sector's rapid increase during 1889–1911 is only elusively replicated during the 1960s. Between 1919-34 and 1946–60, however, agriculture's contribution experienced declining percentages. These shifts furthermore occurred within agriculture's overall declining share of national income.

Manufacturing's second-ranking increase during 1889–1911 was closest to the national average during this period and, in contrast, was next to lowest during 1970–80, with declines occurring during the Depression and recession years of 1929–34 and 1980–83, respectively. Another contrasting performance is that of services, which experiences the lowest-ranking increase during 1889–1911 and the highest-ranking in 1970–80. The distributive sector's performance shows the least contrast, with an increase larger than that for services but lower than that for manufacturing in 1889–1911, and the very opposite situation in 1970–80, when it was closest to the national average.

Standardizing national income for population change, in Figure 4–2, reveals significant contrasts among the various sectors. The increase in per capita product for the services sector is by far the most significant, especially after the 1940s. Indeed, in constant 1958 dollars, as Table 4–2 shows, per capita contribution to national income of this sector increased from 5.62 to 15.72 for 1950–83, and from 3.54 to 10.56, excluding government, over the same period. The difference in these estimates attests to the growing importance of government in the national economy, through the expansion of administrative and regulatory agencies.[9]

In contrast, the per capita contribution of the agricultural sector declined from 1.95 to 1.60 during the same period. Both the manufacturing and distributive sectors increased their per capita contributions significantly since 1934, though not as strongly as did services, reflecting their continued expansion. For manufacturing, this increase occurred despite its declining share of national income, as we saw in the previous analysis. From Figure 4–2 and Table 4–1, the period from the mid-1930s through the end of World War II was particularly important for manufacturing, as its per capita contribution almost tripled, growing faster than that of any other sector. To a great extent, this growth

Table 4-2 Growth Rates by Sector: National Income, Employment, and Population.

Interval	Contribution to National Income							Employment							Population	
	a	m	m*	d	s	s*	U.S. Total	a	m	m*	d	s	s*	U.S. Total	Total	15-64 age Segment
1889–1911	218.8 (9.9)	126.0 (5.7)	143.8 (6.5)	123.7 (5.6)	102.3 (4.7)	93.5 (4.3)	132.8 (6.0)	16.5 (0.8)	59.6 (2.7)	78.4 (3.6)	119.2 (5.4)	41.3+ (4.1)	38.4+ (3.9)	57.0 (2.6)	53.3 (2.4)	63.2 (2.9)
1911–19	10.5 (1.3)	20.0 (2.5)	30.3 (3.8)	3.4 (0.4)	9.9 (1.2)	-5.7 (-0.7)	11.0 (1.4)	-4.0 (-0.5)	20.2 (2.5)	28.5 (3.6)	10.7 (1.3)	30.6 (3.8)	23.5 (2.9)	9.2 (1.2)	10.6 (1.3)	10.0 (1.25)
1919–29	-29.6 (-3.0)	50.4 (5.0)	42.1 (4.2)	52.7 (5.3)	73.0 (7.3)	98.0 (9.8)	40.3 (4.0)	-2.3 (-0.2)	-2.3 (-0.2)	-8.1 (-0.8)	17.0 (1.7)	27.1 (2.7)	26.9 (2.7)	12.7 (1.3)	16.3 (1.6)	19.2 (1.9)
1929–34	-18.1 (-3.6)	-29.7 (-5.9)	-26.0 (-5.2)	-20.1 (-4.0)	-11.0 (-2.2)	-24.6 (-4.9)	-19.7 (-3.9)	-4.6 (-0.9)	-17.0 (-3.4)	-13.7 (-2.7)	-16.6 (-3.3)	-1.7 (-0.3)	-8.3 (-1.7)	-7.9 (-1.6)	2.7 (0.5)	4.6 (0.9)
1934–41	67.1 (9.6)	164.4 (23.5)	163.3 (23.3)	70.9 (10.1)	49.4 (7.1)	31.0 (4.4)	84.7 (12.1)	-6.0 (-0.9)	62.2 (8.9)	61.4 (8.8)	27.2 (3.9)	32.2 (4.6)	22.2 (3.2)	24.6 (3.5)	5.3 (0.8)	8.5 (1.2)
1941–46	34.6 (6.9)	21.3 (4.3)	22.2 (4.4)	28.5 (5.7)	30.5 (6.1)	19.7 (3.9)	27.1 (5.4)	-10.2 (-2.0)	15.2 (3.0)	16.8 (3.4)	20.2 (4.0)	17.6 (3.5)	17.6 (3.5)	10.5 (2.1)	5.2 (1.0)	4.7 (0.9)
1946–50	-6.3 (-1.6)	14.6 (3.7)	10.1 (2.5)	6.0 (1.5)	-2.1 (-0.5)	16.1 (4.0)	5.3 (1.3)	-12.5 (-3.1)	4.0 (1.0)	-0.5 (-0.1)	11.8 (3.0)	11.6 (2.9)	16.4 (4.1)	6.1 (1.5)	8.0 (2.0)	3.2 (0.8)
1950–60	-23.7 (-2.4)	28.1 (2.8)	27.0 (2.7)	24.5 (2.4)	63.6 (6.4)	63.9 (6.4)	32.3 (3.2)	-24.9 (-2.5)	7.5 (0.8)	5.5 (0.6)	11.1 (1.1)	36.8 (3.7)	36.8 (3.7)	10.4 (1.0)	19.0 (1.9)	9.5 (0.9)
1960–70	9.8 (1.0)	42.9 (4.3)	39.7 (4.0)	43.7 (4.4)	72.5 (7.3)	66.1 (6.6)	51.6 (5.2)	-30.9 (-3.1)	17.3 (1.7)	17.3 (1.7)	27.3 (2.7)	50.7 (5.1)	51.0 (5.1)	20.7 (2.1)	13.2 (1.3)	17.6 (1.8)
1970–80	17.9 (5.8)	20.4 (2.0)	20.1 (2.0)	34.8 (3.5)	44.6 (4.5)	57.6 (5.8)	36.6 (3.7)	7.5 (0.8)	21.8 (2.2)	11.5 (1.2)	37.7 (3.8)	39.5 (4.0)	50.0 (5.0)	25.2 (2.5)	11.4 (1.1)	21.7 (2.2)
1980–83	-3.8 (-1.3)	-6.6 (-2.2)	-6.1 (-2.0)	0.4 (0.1)	6.1 (2.0)	7.6 (2.5)	0.5 (0.2)	1.6 (0.5)	-3.7 (-1.2)	-4.2 (-1.4)	3.3 (1.1)	4.3 (1.4)	7.3 (2.4)	1.8 (0.6)	3.0 (1.0)	3.1 (1.0)
1889–1919	252.2 (8.4)	171.1 (5.7)	217.5 (7.2)	131.3 (4.4)	122.3 (4.1)	82.4 (2.7)	158.4 (5.3)	11.8 (0.4)	91.8 (3.1)	129.2 (4.3)	142.7 (4.8)	84.5+ (4.7)	71.5+ (4.0)	71.5 (2.4)	69.5 (2.3)	79.5 (2.7)
1919–29	-29.6 (-3.0)	50.4 (5.0)	42.1 (4.2)	52.7 (5.3)	73.0 (7.3)	98.0 (9.8)	40.3 (4.0)	-2.3 (-0.2)	-2.3 (-0.2)	-8.1 (-0.8)	17.0 (1.7)	27.1 (2.7)	26.9 (2.7)	12.7 (1.3)	16.3 (1.6)	19.2 (1.9)
1934–41	67.1 (9.6)	164.4 (23.5)	163.3 (23.3)	70.9 (10.1)	49.4 (7.1)	31.0 (4.4)	84.7 (12.1)	-6.0 (-0.9)	62.2 (8.9)	61.4 (8.8)	27.2 (3.9)	32.2 (4.6)	22.2 (3.2)	24.6 (3.5)	5.3 (0.8)	8.5 (1.2)
1946–70	-21.6 (-0.9)	109.8 (4.6)	95.3 (4.0)	89.7 (3.7)	176.4 (7.3)	216.0 (9.0)	111.2 (4.6)	-54.6 (-2.3)	31.1 (1.3)	23.1 (1.0)	58.2 (2.4)	130.0 (5.4)	140.5 (5.9)	41.4 (1.7)	45.5 (1.9)	32.9 (1.4)
1970–83	51.8 (4.0)	12.4 (1.0)	12.9 (1.0)	35.3 (2.7)	53.3 (4.1)	69.6 (5.3)	37.3 (2.9)	9.2 (0.7)	17.3 (1.3)	6.8 (0.5)	42.3 (3.2)	45.4 (3.5)	60.9 (4.7)	27.4 (2.1)	14.8 (1.1)	25.4 (1.9)

+1901–1911

Annual averages in parentheses. See Appendix for data sources and details.

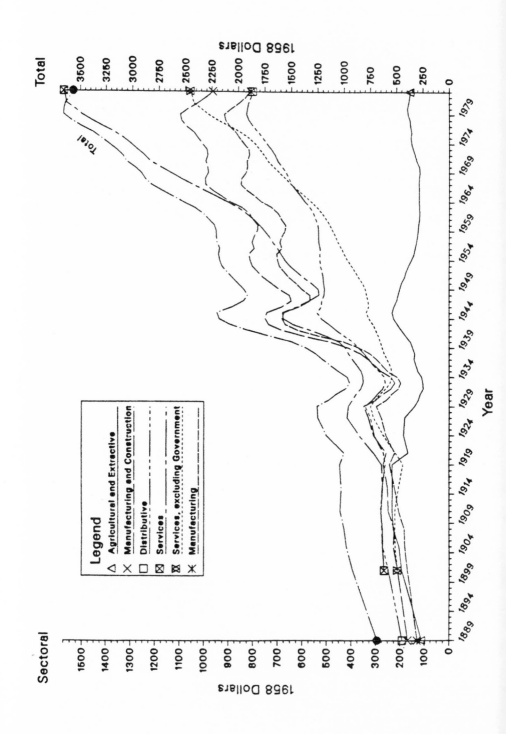

was due to industry's rebound from the Depression and the acceleration of industrial production with the onset of the war.

The increasing divergence of sectoral per capita contributions, readily apparent from Figure 4–2, is a significant development of the postwar era. The relative convergence of manufacturing and distribution therefore stands in contrast with the sharply divergent trends of agriculture and services. Thus, the deepening of demand patterns favoring services over all other sectors was fueled by a twofold increase in national per capita income since 1941.

These divergent trends are also reflected in the changing shares in per capita national income contribution provided in Table 4–3. There, percentage shares can be assumed to approximate cents spent per each dollar of income for the output of each sector. In those estimates, the increasing sectoral divergence promoted by the services sector's unprecedented 44 percent share of national income in 1983, is underscored by the rapid expansion of government throughout the post–World War II period. This becomes obvious when government is

Table 4–3 Percentage Shares by Sector, 1889–1983.

Year	Per Capita Contribution to National Income					
	a	m	m*	d	s	s*
1889	16.4	24.7	19.0	28.0	30.9	25.6
1911	22.4	24.0	19.9	26.9	26.8	21.3
1919	22.3	25.9	23.3	25.1	26.6	18.1
1929	11.2	27.8	23.7	27.3	32.8	25.6
1934	11.4	24.3	21.8	27.2	36.3	24.0
1941	10.3	34.8	31.1	25.1	29.4	17.0
1946	10.9	33.2	29.8	25.4	30.2	16.0
1950	9.7	36.2	31.2	25.6	28.1	17.7
1960	5.6	35.0	30.0	24.1	34.7	21.9
1970	4.1	33.0	27.6	22.8	39.5	24.0
1980	4.7	29.1	24.3	22.5	41.8	27.7
1983	4.5	27.0	22.7	22.5	44.1	29.6

Sectors: a (agricultural and extractive), m (manufacturing and construction),
m* (manufacturing), d (distributive: commerce, transportation, utilities), s (services),
s* (services, excluding government).
See Appendix for data sources and details.

excluded from the services' total, where the latter's share drops to 29.6 percent in 1983. Also evident in Table 4–3 is agriculture's dramatic decline since the turn of the century. A consistent, steady shift away from agricultural goods then becomes obvious, as incomes rose and American society became increasingly urbanized.

Additional insights on these trends can be provided by estimating the percentage changes in per capita sectoral contribution to national income (see Table 4–4). Agriculture, with the largest per capita increase in 1889–1911, mostly declines throughout the post–World War II era, with the exception of the 1970s. The manufacturing sector's increases, which were significantly higher than those for services through the 1910s and the post-Depression years, are then substantially overshadowed by the latter's throughout the postwar years. Undoubtedly, government's participation in services substantially increased the latter's per capita contribution throughout, with the exception of the 1920s, 1970s, and the late 1940s. Major contributors to this trend were rapidly increasing federal, state, and local government employment and payrolls.

Employment Change and Reallocation

Employment reallocation is one of the most significant social impacts of long-term shifts in the sectoral growth leadership. A new frontier sector thus faces the formidable task of absorbing reallocated manpower from any of the less favored sectors and, especially, from the one supplanted from the growth leadership position. The dynamics of this process underlie the drama, successes, and failures of long-term macroeconomic change.

As Figure 4–3 shows, the services sector enjoyed the most rapid increase in post–World War II employment growth. Again, the difference between the total and nongovernmental services trends reflects the rapid growth of the public sector in our economy. The distributive sector accounted for the second fastest employment growth performance, while manufacturing and the fabricative sector showed more modest increases. The deepest contrast occurs in agriculture, however, where a consistent decline in employment occurred since the 1920s. As with sectoral contribution to national income, employment reallocation also reflects greater postwar divergence, in contrast to the prewar performance. Services and agriculture provide the most divergent postwar trends, while some relative convergence occurs between distribution and manufacturing. The latter is no doubt due to the closer linkages that have traditionally existed among transportation, commerce, and industry.

Interval	Per Employee							Per Capita						
	a	m	m*	d	s	s*	U.S. Total	a	m	m*	d	s	s*	U.S. Total
1889-1911	173.7 (7.9)	41.6 (1.9)	36.6 (1.7)	2.1 (0.1)	-9.6+ (-10.0)	-8.2+ (-0.8)	48.3 (2.2)	108.0 (4.9)	47.3 (2.2)	59.0 (2.7)	46.0 (2.1)	32.0 (1.5)	26.3 (1.2)	51.8 (2.4)
1911-19	15.1 (1.9)	-0.2 (-0.02)	1.4 (0.2)	-6.6 (-0.8)	-15.8 (-2.0)	-23.7 (-3.0)	1.6 (0.2)	-0.1 (-0.01)	8.5 (1.1)	17.8 (2.2)	-6.5 (-0.8)	-0.6 (-0.1)	-14.8 (-1.9)	0.4 (0.1)
1919-29	-28.0 (-2.8)	54.0 (5.4)	54.6 (5.5)	30.6 (3.1)	36.1 (3.6)	56.0 (5.6)	24.5 (2.4)	-39.5 (-4.0)	29.3 (2.9)	22.3 (2.2)	31.4 (3.1)	48.8 (4.9)	70.3 (7.0)	20.6 (2.1)
1929-34	-14.1 (-2.8)	-15.3 (-3.1)	-14.3 (-2.9)	-4.2 (-0.8)	-9.5 (-1.9)	-17.7 (-3.5)	-12.7 (-2.5)	-21.1 (-4.2)	-32.3 (-6.5)	-28.7 (-5.7)	-23.1 (-4.6)	-14.2 (-2.8)	-27.4 (-5.5)	-22.6 (-4.5)
1934-41	77.8 (11.1)	63.0 (9.0)	63.2 (9.0)	34.3 (4.9)	13.0 (1.9)	7.1 (1.0)	48.2 (6.9)	58.7 (8.4)	151.0 (21.6)	149.9 (21.4)	62.2 (8.9)	41.9 (6.0)	24.3 (3.5)	75.3 (10.8)
1941-46	49.9 (10.0)	5.4 (0.8)	4.6 (0.9)	6.9 (1.4)	11.0 (2.2)	1.9 (0.4)	15.1 (3.0)	27.9 -(5.6)	15.3 (3.1)	16.1 (3.2)	22.1 (4.4)	24.1 (4.8)	13.8 (2.8)	20.8 (4.2)
1946-50	7.0 (1.8)	10.2 (2.6)	10.7 (2.7)	-5.2 (-1.3)	-12.3 (-3.1)	-0.3 (-0.1)	-0.8 (-0.2)	-13.3 (-3.3)	6.2 (1.6)	2.0 (0.5)	-1.8 (-0.5)	-9.3 (-2.3)	7.5 (1.9)	-2.5 (-0.6)
1950-60	1.6 (0.2)	19.2 (1.9)	20.4 (2.0)	12.1 (1.2)	19.6 (2.0)	19.9 (2.0)	19.8 (2.0)	-35.9 (-3.6)	7.6 (0.8)	6.7 (0.7)	4.6 (0.5)	37.5 (3.8)	37.7 (3.8)	11.2 (1.1)
1960-70	59.0 (5.9)	21.8 (2.2)	19.1 (1.9)	12.9 (1.3)	14.5 (1.4)	10.0 (1.0)	25.6 (2.6)	-3.0 (-0.3)	26.2 (2.6)	23.4 (2.3)	26.9 (2.7)	52.3 (5.2)	46.7 (4.7)	33.9 (3.4)
1970-80	46.8 (4.7)	-1.2 (-0.1)	7.7 (0.8)	-2.1 (-0.2)	3.7 (0.4)	5.1 (0.5)	9.1 (0.9)	41.7 (4.2)	8.0 (0.8)	7.8 (0.8)	21.0 (2.1)	29.7 (3.0)	41.4 (4.1)	22.6 (2.3)
1980-83	-5.3 (-1.8)	-3.0 (-1.0)	-1.9 (-0.6)	-2.9 (-1.0)	1.7 (0.6)	0.3 (0.1)	-1.3 (-0.4)	-6.7 (-2.2)	-9.4 (-3.1)	-8.8 (-2.9)	-2.6 (-0.9)	2.9 (1.0)	4.5 (1.5)	-2.5 (-0.8)
1889-1919	215.0 (7.2)	41.3 (1.4)	38.6 (1.3)	-4.7 (-0.2)	-23.9+ (-1.3)	-30.0+ (-1.7)	50.7 (1.69)	107.1 (3.6)	60.1 (2.0)	86.9 (2.9)	36.6 (1.2)	31.4 (1.0)	7.4 (0.2)	52.6 (1.8)
1919-29	-28.0 (-2.8)	54.0 (5.4)	54.6 (5.5)	30.6 (3.1)	36.1 (3.6)	56.0 (5.6)	24.5 (2.4)	-39.5 (-4.0)	29.3 (2.9)	22.3 (2.2)	31.4 (3.1)	48.8 (4.9)	70.3 (7.0)	20.6 (2.1)
1934-41	77.8 (11.1)	63.0 (9.0)	63.2 (9.0)	34.3 (4.9)	13.0 (1.9)	7.1 (1.0)	48.2 (6.9)	58.7 (8.4)	151.0 (21.6)	149.9 (21.4)	62.2 (8.9)	41.9 (6.0)	24.3 (3.5)	75.3 (10.8)
1946-70	72.9 (3.0)	60.0 (2.5)	58.7 (2.4)	19.9 (0.8)	20.1 (0.8)	31.4 (1.3)	49.3 (2.1)	-46.2 (-1.9)	44.1 (1.8)	34.3 (1.4)	30.3 (1.3)	89.8 (3.7)	117.3 (4.9)	45.1 (1.9)
1970-83	39.0 (3.0)	-4.1 (-0.3)	5.7 (0.4)	-4.9 (-0.4)	5.4 (0.4)	5.4 (0.4)	7.7 (0.6)	32.2 (2.5)	-2.0 (-0.2)	-1.7 (-0.1)	17.9 (1.4)	33.6 (2.6)	47.7 (3.7)	19.5 (1.5)

+1901-1911   Annual averages in parentheses.   See Appendix for data sources and details.

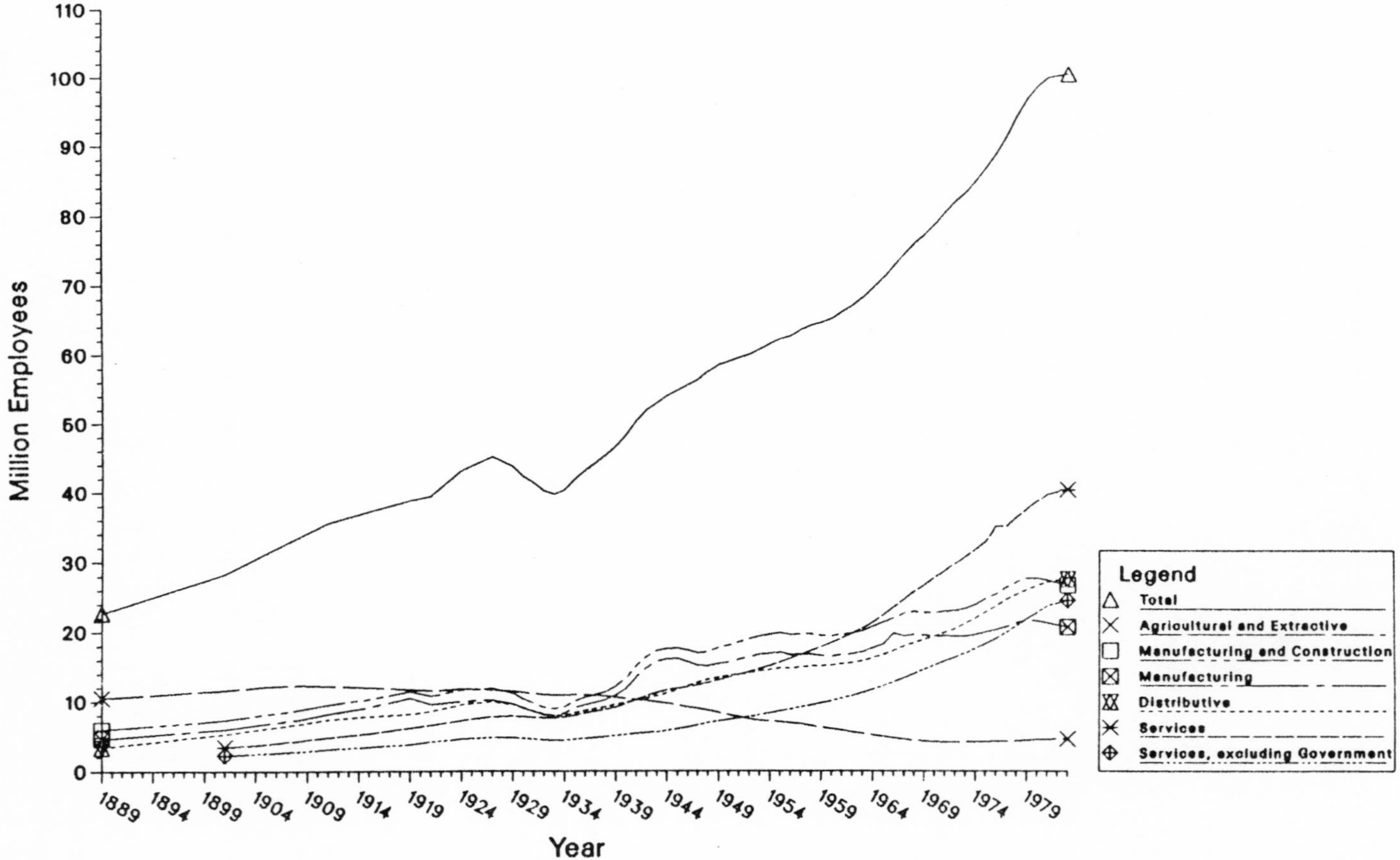

Million Employees

Legend

△	Total
✕	Agricultural and Extractive
☐	Manufacturing and Construction
⊠	Manufacturing
⊠	Distributive
✳	Services
⊕	Services, excluding Government

Year

Figure 4-3. Sectoral Employment

If we standardize for population change, the agricultural sector had the highest employment per hundred total population in 1889 (see Table 4–5). In contrast, employment in the services sector was lowest, with 4.3 per hundred population (2.8 excluding government), in that same year. The end of World War II then marks a turning point for manufacturing and services. Driven by the war effort, manufacturing had achieved the highest sectoral employment per hundred population in 1946. Subsequently, manufacturing employment would remain virtually stagnant, especially since the 1960s.[10] In contrast, employment per hundred population in the services segment doubled over the postwar period, rising to 17.3 per hundred population in 1983 (10.5 excluding government).

Standardizing for working age population provides additional insights on the structure of sectoral employment reallocation (see Table 4–5).[11] The decline of agricultural employment is all the more astounding with this measure, falling from 28.4 in 1889 to 2.9 per hundred working population in 1983. The most important reason for this change is this sector's success with productivity increases, originally stimulated by its loss of the growth leadership and, subsequently, by the application of technological and organizational innovations in production.

Another significant trend is the services sector's rising employment per hundred working age population, from 6.9 in 1901 to 25.4 in 1983 (4.5 and 15.4 excluding government, respectively). While the growth rates of these two trends are relatively close (3.7 versus 3.4, respectively), the growing importance of government in our society again becomes all the more noticeable in the much higher absolute level of total services. In contrast, manufacturing's employment situation is relatively unchanged from the estimates obtained with total population. The national totals for employment change in the working age population then reveal a significant decline from 1889 through the 1930s, due to greater restrictions on the employment of minors and significant changes in the age structure of the population. This is in contrast to significant increases throughout the post–World War II era, as the well-known baby boom and the redefinition of women's roles increased the pool of available manpower.

Figure 4–4 provides a vivid graphic illustration of the process of sectoral employment reallocation through changing percentage shares. Agriculture's astonishing decline is to a great extent offset by that of services, the latter's performance being substantially strengthened by rising government employment. Manufacturing's performance is less dramatic than might be expected, especially through the post–World War II era. Here, the long-term view provides an unquestionably better perspective on this sector's performance.

Table 4–5 Sectoral Employment per Hundred Population, 1889–1983.

Year	Per Total Population							Per 15-64 Age Segment						
	a	m	m*	d	s	s*	U.S. Total	a	m	m*	d	s	s*	U.S. Total
1889	17.0	9.7	7.4	5.5	4.3+	2.8+	36.8	28.4	16.2	12.4	9.1	6.9+	4.5+	61.5
1911	12.9	10.1	8.7	7.8	6.1	3.2	37.7	20.3	15.8	13.6	12.3	9.8	5.1	59.2
1919	11.2	10.9	10.0	7.8	5.9	3.6	37.2	17.7	17.3	15.9	12.4	9.4	5.7	58.7
1929	9.4	9.2	7.9	7.9	6.5	3.9	36.1	14.5	14.1	12.2	12.1	10.0	6.1	55.5
1934	8.6	7.3	6.6	6.3	6.1	3.5	32.0	13.0	11.0	9.9	9.5	9.2	5.2	48.1
1941	7.7	11.3	10.1	7.6	7.7	4.0	37.8	11.3	16.5	14.8	11.2	11.3	5.9	55.2
1946	6.6	12.4	11.2	8.7	8.6	4.5	39.7	9.7	18.2	16.5	12.8	12.6	6.6	58.3
1950	5.3	11.9	10.4	9.0	8.9	4.9	39.0	8.2	18.3	15.9	13.9	13.7	7.5	59.9
1960	3.4	10.8	9.2	8.4	10.2	5.6	36.2	5.6	18.0	15.3	14.1	17.1	9.3	60.4
1970	2.1	11.2	9.5	9.5	13.6	7.5	38.6	3.3	17.9	15.3	15.2	21.9	12.0	62.0
1980	2.0	12.2	9.5	11.7	17.0	10.0	43.4	2.9	17.9	14.0	17.3	25.1	14.8	63.8
1983	2.0	11.4	8.8	11.8	17.3	10.5	42.8	2.9	16.8	13.0	17.3	25.4	15.4	63.0

+1901 estimates.

Sectors: a(agricultural and extractive), m (manufacturing and construction), m* (manufacturing), d (distributive: commerce, transportation, utilities), s (services), s* (services, excluding government).

Employment estimates based on five-year moving averages. See Appendix for data sources and details.

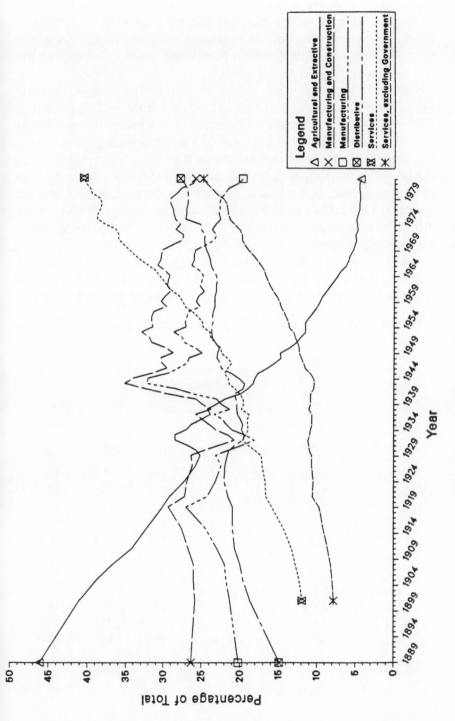

Figure 4-4 Employment Distribution, by Sector.

Legend
△ Agricultural and Extractive
✕ Manufacturing and Construction
☐ Manufacturing
⊠ Distributive
⊠ Services
✳ Services, excluding Government

Year

Percentage of Total

105

Over the postwar years, the decline in manufacturing's employment shares has not been as significant as might be expected. Over the full ninety-four-year period, its employment share has in fact remained virtually constant, with significant fluctuations occurring during the Depression and World War II years.

Standardizing percentage shares for population change, in Table 4–6, shows the agricultural sector's decline from 46.2 to 4.7, from 1889–1983, to be much more pronounced than services' increase, from 11.7 to 30.4 over the same period.[12] The manufacturing sector's performance with this indicator fluctuates throughout, in what is a virtually cyclical pattern, with troughs in 1889, 1934, and 1983, and peaks in 1919 and 1946. Some similarity may also be noticed between the declines of the 1920s and 1930s with those of the 1960s and 1970s. Very different technologies and skills characterize the industries of these two periods, however.

If we review the analysis of this section, it is obvious that the sector suffering the worst employment decline, agriculture, nevertheless remained an important and vital component of our national economy.

Table 4–6 Percentage Shares: Sectoral Employment per Hundred Population, 1889–1983.

	Per Total Population					
Year	a	m	m*	d	s	s*
1889	46.2	26.4	20.9	14.9	11.7+	7.6+
1911	34.2	26.8	23.1	20.7	16.2	8.5
1919	30.1	29.3	26.9	21.0	15.9	9.7
1929	26.0	25.5	21.9	21.9	18.0	10.8
1934	26.9	22.8	20.6	19.7	19.1	10.9
1941	20.4	29.9	26.7	20.1	20.4	10.6
1946	16.6	31.2	28.2	21.9	21.7	11.3
1950	13.6	30.5	26.7	23.1	22.8	12.6
1960	9.4	29.8	25.4	23.2	28.2	15.5
1970	5.4	29.0	24.6	24.6	35.2	19.4
1980	4.6	28.1	21.9	27.0	39.2	23.0
1983	4.7	26.6	20.6	27.6	40.4	24.5

+1901 estimates.

See Appendix for data sources and details.

Qualitatively speaking, American agricultural output in the late twentieth century is both qualitatively and quantitatively superior to that of the late nineteenth century. Yet, the loss of employment in this sector has been astounding over the years.

With the shift in the growth leadership from manufacturing toward services, not a few may wonder whether a fate similar to agriculture's also awaits manufacturing employment. Clearly, recent trends toward greater automation and the application of robotics technology in production have eliminated much potential employment in this sector. If we analyze the percentage changes in Table 4–2, it is clear that manufacturing employment has increased significantly over the postwar period, at annual average rates that vary from 0.6 in the 1950s to 1.7 and 1.2 in the 1960s and 1970s, respectively. Only during the recession years of 1980–83 and the post–World War II demobilization years has employment in this sector actually declined.

Such growth is significant, despite the fact that it has been greatly overshadowed by services' performance, and stands in stark contrast with agriculture's decline throughout most of the pre- and post–World War II eras. This observation is further supported by the abbreviated period estimates found in the bottom of Table 4–2, where the manufacturing sector's increase of 23.1 percent (1.0 annual average) for 1946–70 is far from negligible. The subsequent estimate of 6.8 percent for 1970–83 is more worrisome, but this slower growth rate is exaggerated by the 1980–83 recession. This is obvious from the 1970–80 estimates, at 11.5 percent (1.2 annual average), in the upper portion of the table. Despite these increases, manufacturing employment nevertheless had the second lowest-ranking growth rate throughout the postwar era, after agriculture.

Productivity Trends and Shifts

Productivity change is by far the most important adjustment mechanism for sectors facing a less favorable income elastic situation for their goods and services. Generally, the less favorable the income elasticity of demand experienced by a sector, the greater the need to raise its productivity performance. Productivity differences are relative, however, and even a new frontier sector can be expected to experience significant productivity increases, although these can be expected to be lower than for the less favored sectors. As we saw in the previous section, the most obvious social impact of increasing productivity is a slowdown in employment growth, or an outright decline, for the sectors in question.[13]

Generally, the long-term trends shown in Figure 4–5 and Table 4–4 confirm this study's conceptual assumptions regarding productivity change.[14] Two main periods can be distinguished: pre– and post–World War II. In the prewar period, agriculture experiences the greatest increase of any sector through 1919. Its productivity then declines through the 1920s and the Depression years, partly because of various crises in the nation's main agricultural regions.[15] This decline is then followed by a substantial recovery from the mid-1930s through the end of World War II.

Manufacturing, on the other hand, experiences significant fluctuations, declining during the Depression years, as could be expected, with construction influencing the fabricative sector's overall decline during the 1910s. By and large, however, the manufacturing sector's prewar positive productivity trends overshadowed the downturns. The distributive sector's performance, though less positive than manufacturing's, nevertheless parallels the latter's fluctuations. Services' performance, in contrast, declines through most of the prewar period, with the exception of the 1920s and late 1930s.

In the postwar period, agricultural productivity increases throughout, and especially from 1960–80, when it obtained the largest sectoral increase. The manufacturing sector's productivity performance also increases, up to 1970, when it slows and flattens out. The services sector's productivity trend is generally higher when government is excluded, in Figure 4–5, and its percentage increases are also generally greater, as shown in the abbreviated intervals of Table 4–3. The services sector's estimates are also generally higher than distribution's, partly because of the greater possibilities for application of organizational and technological innovations in the former.

Various explanations can be offered for the long-term productivity changes observed so far. For agriculture, rapid mechanization due to mass production of farm machinery was an important factor during the pre–World War II era. During the postwar era, new fertilizers, improvements in irrigation techniques, biotechnology, and better cropping methods were also important. Manufacturing's pre–World War II productivity increase was greatly due to the widespread introduction of factory mass production techniques, especially in consumer durable and nondurable goods industries. Further advances in the organization of production, automation, and greater scale economies were important during the postwar era. In services, where the greatest contrast is found between pre– and post–World War II performances, with substantial increases in the latter, innovation adoption was facilitated through better information and mergers with industrial enterprises.

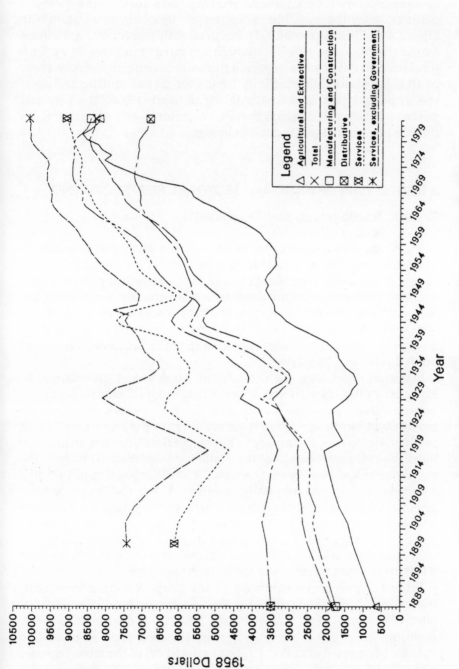

Figure 4–5 Sectoral Contribution to National Income, per Employee.

In general, it may be stated that a tendency toward greater sectoral convergence in productivity trends appears during the postwar decades, with the possible exception of distribution, as shown in Figure 4–5. This is particularly obvious with respect to agriculture, manufacturing, and services, though the rates of increase in agricultural productivity can be expected to continue to be higher than those of all other sectors. Productivity trends for manufacturing and services appear closest to the national trend, during both the pre- and postwar periods, indicating these two sectors' very substantial influence on national productivity change.

A BROAD VIEW OF NATIONAL SECTORAL RESTRUCTURING

Growth, Employment, and Productivity

The shifts to new frontier sectors are secular phenomena specific to a historical period. Sustained long-term trends thus become the most visible indicator of permanent change, in the historical process where wants and entrepreneurship drive sectoral restructurings. Because the socioeconomic impact of the major trends discussed in the previous sections is so important to an evaluation of economic change, employment will become the pivotal variable to which sectoral growth and productivity will be related.

In a simplified way, the most rapid employment growth can be expected in the (new frontier) sector that enjoys the most favorable income elastic position. In the less favored sectors, employment growth will be slower, when it occurs, or may decline altogether, as productivity is raised. Employment change thus becomes an effect of the differential application of the various entrepreneurial roles in the new frontier and less favored sectors.[16] The differential application of entrepreneurship is originally motivated by the opportunities generated by an increase in income elasticity of demand for a sector's goods, where a new frontier sector will enjoy the most favorable position. Changes in the position of any given sector will then be motivated by changing human wants and preferences, and by their effect on any given sector's income elastic position.

Table 4–7 provides a summary of the shifts occurring in sectoral leadership in employment, growth, and productivity. Two sets of intervals are provided, the upper one being more detailed and incorporating virtually all the crucial years for each sectoral trend and indicator (except World War II). The bottom part of the table provides abbreviated intervals, and a more general perspective that excludes both the Depression and World War II years. In both sets, construction

Table 4–7 Growth Rates: Sectoral Magnitude Sequences.

Interval	Contribution to National Income	Per Capita Contribution to National Income	Employment	Contribution to National Income per Employee
1889-1911+	a > m* > d > s*	a > m* > d > s*	d > m* > s* > a	a > m* > d > s*
1911-19	m* > a > d > s*	m* > a > d > s*	m* > s* > d > a	a > m* > d > s*
1919-29	s* > d > m* > a	s* > d > m* > a	s* > d > a > m*	s* > m* > d > a
1929-34	a > s* > m* > d	a > d > s* > m*	a > d > s* > m*	d > a = m* > s*
1934-41	m* > d > a > s*	m* > d > a > s*	m* > d > s* > a	a > m* > d > s*
1946-50	s* > m* > d > a	s* > m* > d > a	s* > d > m* > a	m* > a > s* > d
1950-60	s* > m* > d > a	s* > m* > d > a	s* > d > m* > a	m* > s* > d > a
1960-70	s* > d > m* > a	s* > d > m* > a	s* > d > m* > a	a > m* > d > s*
1970-80	s* > d > m* > a	a = s* > d > m*	s* > d > m* > a	a > m* > s* > d
1980-83	s* > d > a > m*	s* > d > a > m*	s* > d > a > m*	s* > m* > d > a
1889-1919	a > m* > d > s*	a > m* > d > s*	d > m* > s* > a	a > m* > d > s*
1919-29	s* > d > m* > a	s* > d > m* > a	s* > d > a > m*	s* > m* > d > a
1934-41	m* > d > a > s*	m* > d > a > s*	m* > d > s* > a	a > m* > d > s*
1946-70	s* > m* > d > a	s* > m* > d > a	s* > d > m* > a	a > m* > s* > d
1970-83	s* > a > d > m*	s* > a > d > m*	s* > d > a > m*	a > m* = s* > d

+s and s* estimates based on 1901-1911 percentage changes.

and government were excluded from the manufacturing and services sectors, respectively. These components will nevertheless be considered in the evaluations provided in this section.

Two basic hypothetical questions will be evaluated on the basis of information provided in Table 4–7. The first one is that sectors leading employment growth will also be expected to experience fastest growth in their contribution to national income; these are therefore the new frontier sectors. Sectoral growth in response to changing income elastic conditions will therefore reflect the performances of the entrepreneurial roles that most closely deal with exogenous market conditions and processes, such as strategic planning and intermarket linkage. The second hypothetical question assumes that sectors experiencing the greatest slowdown or decline in employment growth should also experience the largest increases in productivity, as measured by their per employee contribution to national income. This situation will therefore reflect the performance of the roles dealing with internal organization, such as productive coordination. In more than one way, therefore, the success of entrepreneurial adjustments to long-term shifts will depend on how well the outcomes of this analysis correspond with the assumptions of the two hypothetical questions.

If we evaluate the changes in employment and sectoral growth leadership, eight out of ten intervals in the upper portion of Table 4–7 confirm the assumptions of the first hypothesis. In the bottom section, four out of five intervals correspond with its assumptions. If we evaluate these changes with national income standardized for population change, seven out of ten intervals in the upper portion, and four out of five in the lower portion, also correspond with the assumptions of the first hypothesis. With construction and government included in the fabricative and services sectors, the results correspond with the hypothetical assumptions in six out of ten intervals. Thus, including these two components in the respective sectoral estimates reduces support for the first hypothesis, but not enough to contradict previous results.

Insofar as employment and productivity change are concerned, correspondence of trends with the second hypothesis occurs in seven out of ten intervals in the top portion of Table 4–7. With the abbreviated intervals of the bottom portion, correspondence occurs in four out of five cases. Including construction and government in the fabricative and services sectors' estimates, correspondence with this hypothesis occurs in six out of ten cases in the more detailed set of intervals, and in four out of five cases in the abbreviated set. As before, the inclusion of government and services in these estimates therefore also reduces support for the second hypothesis.

Evaluating changes in the sectoral growth leadership, and in productivity and employment, according to the assumptions of the third and fourth historical stages, provides additional insights on this analysis (see Chapter 3 and Table 3–1). As far as the third historical stage is concerned, the assumptions on leading sectors are confirmed in four out of six intervals, in both the absolute and standardized national income contribution estimates, in the top portion of Table 4–7. The assumptions on employment growth are supported in five out of six intervals, while correspondence for the productivity assumptions is found in four out of six. In the abbreviated intervals, the assumptions on leading sectors for all three indicators—growth, employment, and productivity—are supported in two out of three intervals.

Over the fourth historical stage, the assumptions on sectoral leadership are confirmed in all four, and in three out of four intervals, for the absolute and standardized national income estimates, respectively. On employment and productivity growth, the sectoral leadership assumptions are supported by all four, and by three out of four intervals, respectively. All of the abbreviated intervals, found at the bottom of Table 4–7, support the assumptions on sectoral leadership for all three indicators of growth, employment, and productivity. In general, therefore, the findings of this section are consistent with the sectoral roles, shifts, and performances assumed for the third and fourth historical stages of the conceptual framework.

An additional and significant observation on the results of this analysis is that manufacturing has seldom been the most important source of either employment or output growth over the full period of this study. This is certainly the case even for the third historical stage, when this sector was relatively more important in the national economy. As far as employment growth is concerned, for example, manufacturing was first-ranking in two out of six intervals in the third stage, and was second-ranking in only one other case. The fact that including government in the services sector's estimates reduced support for the assumptions of this study, should raise some questions about its role in long-term restructurings and adjustments. It is impossible to tell to what extent unnecessary government bureaucracy and regulation have been serious obstacles to sectoral shifts to higher output, productivity, or employment. Nevertheless, it does stand to reason that these activities have in many cases prevented or delayed the sectoral restructurings that were necessary to achieve greater productivity, output, or employment growth. The obstacles have mostly been in the form of ineffective programs that could never hope to achieve the objectives that were set for them, and in regulatory measures with unintended, perverse effects on innovation and entrepreneurial action.

Intersectoral and Interindustry Change

Changes in intersectoral linkages are an important indicator of long-term economic change. Especially important in this respect are the linkages that develop between manufacturing industries and economic activities in all the other sectors. These linkages usually serve as vehicles of innovation diffusion, and the changes that occur in the most important linked industries and activities can provide a good indication of long-term sectoral restructurings.

Data from the national input-output matrixes for 1919, 1939, and 1977 for manufacturing inputs in agriculture reveal some of the very extensive restructurings and adjustments that occurred in the agricultural sector during the third and fourth historical stages.[17] A major characteristic of manufactured inputs in agriculture is the rapid rise of nondurable, technology-intensive goods and a relative decline of durable, less technologically intensive inputs. Table 4–8 provides the top six ranking manufactured inputs to agriculture over the three years in question, based on current dollars.

Among the nondurable manufactured inputs, food products, chemicals, and refined petroleum products increase in rank and proportion to total inputs. Food product inputs comprise primarily livestock feed and grain, and seeds, and remain top-ranked throughout, increasing their relative share of total inputs from 0.05 to

Table 4–8 Rankings of Manufactured Inputs to Agriculture, 1919, 1939, 1977.

Industry	1919	1939	1977
Food Products	1 (0.05)	1 (0.05)	1 (0.15)
Iron, Steel and Electric Products	2 (0.04)	+	+
Chemicals	3 (0.03)	4 (0.03)	2 (0.09)
Lumber and Wood Products	4 (0.02)	10 (0.004)	9 (0.002)
Leather Products	5 (0.01)	15 (0.001)	*
Textiles	6 (0.003)	8 (0.004)	12 (0.002)
Petroleum Refining	13 (0.0001)	2 (0.03)	3 (0.04)
Agricultural Machinery	*	3 (0.03)	4 (0.01)
Motor Vehicles and Equipment	*	5 (0.01)	11 (0.008)
Rubber and Miscellaneous Plastics	*	6 (0.004)	5 (0.01)
Electrical Machinery and Supplies	n.a.	n.a.	6 (0.005)

+unavailable, due to classification restructurings; this category would mostly comprise agricultural implements and tools in 1919.
n.a.: not available.
*no appreciable inputs.
In parentheses: inputs per dollar of total purchases (1977: per dollar of total intermediate inputs).

Data sources:
Leontief (1941) for 1919 and 1939 data.
U.S. Department of Commerce (1984) for 1977 data.

0.15. Chemical inputs, comprising fertilizers, pesticides, and assorted chemicals, increase from third rank in 1919 to second rank in 1977 (declining to fourth in 1939), with input shares increasing from 0.03 in 1919 to 0.09 in 1977. Petroleum products, primarily fuels to run machinery and generate power, experience the most rapid rise, from thirteenth rank in 1919 to second and third in 1939 and 1977, respectively.

Among the durable manufactured inputs, only Rubber and Plastics rise in rank and share, comprising goods that largely replaced leather and textiles, increasing from sixth rank in 1939 to fifth in 1977. The declining durable goods inputs are Lumber and Wood Products, Leather, Textiles, and Motor Vehicles. Lumber and Wood decline from fourth rank in 1919 to ninth in 1977, because of changes in construction techniques and materials, the substitution of fuels for wood as a primary energy source, and a greater variety of synthetic packaging materials. Leather Products are the most rapidly declining of all inputs, slipping from fifth rank in 1919 to fifteenth in 1939, with no appreciable input quantities in 1977. Textiles, sixth ranking in 1919, steadily decline to eighth and twelfth in 1939 and 1977, respectively. Similarly, Motor Vehicles, comprising primarily farm and livestock transport, decline from fifth rank in 1939 to eleventh in 1977.[18]

National input-output data for manufactured inputs to transportation, provided in Table 4–9, reveal the structural changes that have affected this activity from 1919 through 1977.[19] Changes in the types of inputs and linkage structure of this sector reveal a more balanced performance than for agriculture. Here, both durable and nondurable, technology-intensive inputs rise in rank and share, while less technologically intensive inputs (both durable and nondurable) decline. Among the rising nondurable inputs, Petroleum products advance from fourth to first rank between 1919 and 1977, with their shares increasing from 0.01 to 0.16, obviously because of the rising and widespread use of the internal combustion engine during this period, and the expansion of highway transportation services. Among the rising durable inputs, Rubber and Plastics change from fifth to third rank between 1939 and 1977, as plastics came into widespread use by replacing many metallic parts, and rubber products were more widely used in vehicle manufacturing and maintenance.

Coal and Coke Products, a nondurable input, experience the most dramatic decline of all manufactured inputs to transportation, slipping from the second rank in 1919, to third in 1939, and virtually disappearing in 1977. This trend is very much related to the decline of the railroads as the most important form of interstate and interurban transportation, and the widespread use of the petroleum-fueled internal combustion engine in transportation. Durable goods inputs, such

Table 4–9   Rankings of Manufactured Inputs to Transportation and Services, 1919, 1939, 1977.

Industry	Transportation 1919	Transportation 1939	1977	Services, excluding Government 1939	1977
Iron and Steel Products	1 (0.26)	4 (0.02)	7 (0.007)		
Processed Coal and Coke Products	2 (0.07)	3 (0.03)	*		
Lumber and Wood Products	3 (0.02)	*	*		
Petroleum Refining	4 (0.01)	1 (0.05)	1 (0.16)	3 (0.004)	3 (0.02)
Printing and Publishing	5 (0.005)	n.a.	10 (0.005)	1 (0.07)	1 (0.02)
Non-Metallic Minerals Processing	6 (0.002)	10 (0.002)	++		
Transportation Equipment	* (Autos)	2 (0.03)	2 (0.04)	++	2 (0.02)
Rubber and Plastics	*	5 (0.004)	3 (0.02)	6 (0.002)	6 (0.01)
Eletrical Equipment	n.a.	n.a.	6 (0.007)		
Fabricated Metals	n.a.	n.a.	4 (0.009)	n.a.	5 (0.01)
Machinery	n.a.	n.a.	5 (0.007)	4 (0.003)	14 (0.005)
Furniture				2 (0.006)	++
Chemicals				5 (0.002)	8 (0.009)
Pharmaceuticals				n.a.	4 (0.01)

*no appreciable inputs. ++very low ranking; exact rank impossible to determine.
n.a.: not available.
In parentheses: inputs per dollar of total purchases (1977: per dollar of total intermediate inputs).

Data sources: Leontief (1941) for 1919 and 1939 data. U.S. Department of Commerce (1984) for 1977 data (restaurants and food services excluded).

as Iron and Steel, and Nonmetallic Minerals products, also experience significant decline. The latter, comprising primarily glass and clay products, in fact, dramatically decline from sixth rank in 1919 to tenth in 1939, and to a very low and unestimable rank in 1977. Iron and Steel's decline is less pronounced, slipping from first in 1919 to seventh in 1977. An important reason for this decline is the substitution of synthetic, lightweight materials for many metal parts in vehicle manufacturing and maintenance, and a shift of commercial activity in vehicle parts and accessories toward vehicle manufacturing industries. In this respect, it is hardly surprising that the Transportation Equipment industries rapidly rise to second rank in 1939 and 1977, from a minimal input position in 1919.

Data on manufactured inputs to nongovernmental services for 1939 and 1977, also in Table 4–9, show a balanced performance between durable and nondurable goods inputs in the top ranks. Nondurable goods inputs, Printing and Publishing, and Petroleum Products, are found in the first and third ranks in both 1939 and 1977. Durable goods inputs, Furniture and Transportation Equipment, are second-ranking; the former in 1939 and the latter in 1977. The shift in consumer wants and preferences between 1939 and 1977 could not be more obvious, however, as Machinery inputs (durable goods), fourth-ranking in 1939, decline to the fourteenth rank in 1977, and are replaced in the fourth rank by Pharmaceuticals (nondurable inputs) in 1977. Thus, the health concerns of the population surface as an important driving force of sectoral restructuring and entrepreneurial action during this period.

Changes in interindustry inputs, in Table 4–10, show technology-intensive producer durables and nondurables, and consumer nondurables, to be rising between 1919 and 1977. Among the latter, Food Products increased from the second to the first-ranking position between 1919 and 1939, remaining as the top ranked input in 1977. This trend is closely related to population growth and lifestyle shifts favor-

Table 4–10 Rankings of Interindustry Inputs, 1919, 1939, 1977.

Industry	1919	1939	1977
Iron and Steel Products	1	3	4
Food Products	2	1	1
Textiles	3	7	8
Apparel	4	4	6
Chemicals	5	6	5
Motor Vehicles	6	5	3
Petroleum Refining	9	2	2

Data sources:
Leontief (1941) for 1919, 1939 ("Net Total Outlays").
U.S. Department of Commerce (1984) for 1977 ("Total Intermediate Inputs").

ing higher quality food products. However, these linkages mostly occur between related activities within the Food Products industry. A nondurable input, Petroleum Refining, increases from ninth to second place between 1919 and 1939, remaining in that rank in 1977. Another technology-intensive producer nondurable input, Chemicals, sustains its rank over that period, mostly because of its wide variety of applications, and substantial usage in food production and health-related goods. Motor Vehicles, a producer durable, increases from sixth to third rank between 1919 and 1977. These linkages occur mostly between related activites in the Transportation Equipment category.

The declining interindustry linkages primarily involve durable goods inputs. Thus, Iron and Steel Products slide from the first to the fourth rank between 1919 and 1977, partly a result of the domestic decline of steel, and the substitution of more lightweight materials for metal parts in many manufactured goods. Another declining rank industry is Textiles, which took a third rank in 1919 and the eighth in 1977. Similarly, Apparel descends from fourth to sixth place between 1919 and 1977. To a significant extent, the rise of more technology-intensive consumer durables and nondurables helped reduce the ranking of these two industries. The majority of their input linkages nevertheless occur between related activities within and between these two industries.

Population Redistribution

Population redistribution is one of the most important socioeconomic impacts of the process of sectoral restructuring. It affects virtually all social classes and groups, and has substantial long-term implications for the nation's social fabric and the distribution of wealth. Population redistribution follows from shifts in the sectoral growth leadership, from which employment reallocation occurs, as assumed earlier, and as has so far been demonstrated by the analyses of this chapter.[20]

If we assume population to follow employment opportunities, redistribution will tend to adjust to the spatial orientation of the new frontier sectors. Thus, a change in the growth leadership from agriculture to manufacturing involves a long-term shift from rural to urban population concentration. The urbanization of American society in this century is the most obvious outcome of this shift. Afterward, a change in the growth leadership from manufacturing to services has promoted the redistribution of population from the largest metropolitan areas to medium-sized and smaller centers in the national urban system.

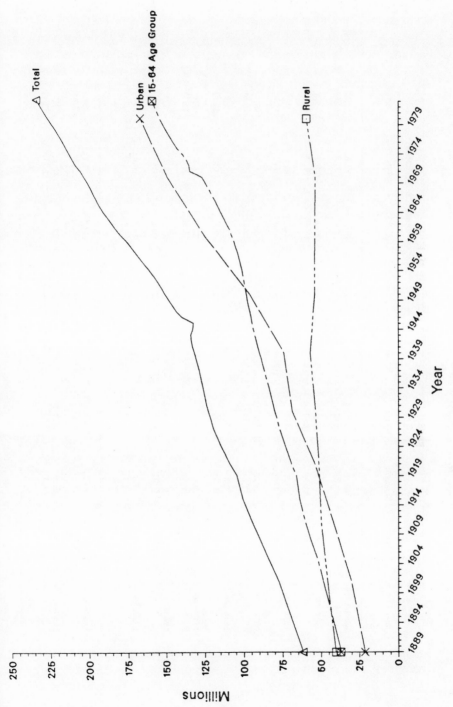

Figure 4-6 Population.

Table 4-11 Growth Rates, Population.

Interval	U.S. Total	15-64 Age Segment	Urban	Rural	Urban Size Classes (x1000)			
					50-100	100-500	500-1000	1000+
1890–1910	53.3 (2.7)	63.2 (3.2)	97.1 (4.9)	23.8 (1.2)	106.1 (5.3)	68.1 (3.4)	273.6 (13.7)	132.1 (6.6)
1910–20	15.4 (1.5)	15.3 (1.5)	29.0 (2.9)	3.2 (0.3)	26.1 (2.6)	25.8 (2.6)	106.7 (10.7)	19.3 (1.9)
1920–30	12.7 (1.3)	15.6 (1.6)	27.3 (2.7)	4.4 (0.4)	23.2 (2.3)	40.1 (4.0)	-7.4 (-0.7)	48.5 (4.9)
1930–40	7.2 (0.7)	12.2 (1.2)	7.9 (0.8)	6.3 (0.6)	13.1 (1.3)	0.8 (0.1)	12.0 (1.2)	5.6 (0.6)
1940–50	14.6 (1.5)	9.3 (0.9)	29.6 (3.0)	-5.3 (-0.5)	21.6 (2.2)	13.4 (1.3)	42.3 (4.2)	9.4 (0.9)
1950–60	19.0 (1.9)	9.5 (0.9)	29.9 (3.0)	-0.3 (-0.03)	54.9 (5.5)	24.8 (2.5)	20.9 (2.1)	0.5 (0.1)
1960–70	13.2 (1.3)	17.6 (1.8)	19.2 (1.9)	-0.3 (-0.03)	20.9 (2.1)	11.8 (1.2)	16.7 (1.7)	7.3 (0.7)
1970–80	11.4 (1.1)	21.7 (2.2)	11.9 (1.2)	10.4 (1.0)	18.3 (1.8)	18.0 (1.8)	-16.4 (-1.6)	-7.6 (-0.8)
1890–1920	76.8 (2.6)	88.2 (2.9)	154.2 (5.1)	27.7 (0.9)	159.8 (5.3)	111.5 (3.7)	672.2 (22.4)	177.1 (5.90)
1950–70	34.8 (1.7)	28.8 (1.4)	54.8 (2.7)	-0.6 (-0.03)	87.3 (4.4)	39.5 (2.0)	41.1 (2.1)	7.8 (0.4)

Annual averages in parentheses. See Appendix for data sources and details.

Figure 4–6 provides an overview of urban, rural, and total population trends during the third and fourth historical stages of this study. Rural population has been virtually stagnant throughout. This stagnation can be assumed to result from the previous shift in the sectoral growth leadership from agriculture to manufacturing during the second historical stage. In contrast, urban population increases throughout. Thus, the shift from manufacturing to services has affected the aggregate urban population situation little. Since both sectors are primarily urban-based, however, as we shall see later on, changing trends in the urban population distribution will emerge as a result of this shift.

The fact that the urban population trend parallels total population reflects how virtually all of the national population increase throughout this period has occurred through urban population growth.[21] In the early 1950s, urban population intersects and rises well past the working age (15–64 group) population trend. Thus, urban population begins to account for an increasing share of those in the youngest and oldest age group, as well as the vast majority of the working age population. At the same time, the increasing divergence between the total and working age populations throughout the period of study reflects a rising proportion of the total population in the youngest and oldest age group.

We can gain additional insights on these changes from Table 4–11, showing percentage changes for total, working age, and urban and rural population. The contrasts in percentage increases between urban and rural population are obvious throughout, with two exceptions: the 1930s and 1970s. During those two periods, increases in urban and rural population tend to approximate each other. The abbreviated interval estimates, which aggregate both the pre-1920 and post–World War II periods, show the longer term contrasts, when urban population grew over five, and almost three times, as fast as the rural population, respectively. The working age population grew faster than total population during the pre-1920 period, but by a lower margin in the 1950–70 period. The only exceptions here are during the decades of the 1940s and 1950s, which primarily reflect the human toll of World War II.

The enormous impact of sectoral restructuring on national population redistribution is reflected in the changes found in the percentage distribution of urban, rural, and working age population in Table 4–12. The shares of working age population fluctuate somewhat, reaching their highest level in 1940 and 1980, and dropping to their lowest level in 1960. The rural population's share declines from its highest level in 1890, at 65.3 percent, to 26.2 percent in 1980, while that of urban population increases from 34.5 to 73.5 percent between 1890

Table 4-12 Percentage Share, Population.

Year	15-64 Age Segment	Urban	Rural	Urban Size Classes (x1000)			
				50-100	100-500	500-1000	1000+
1890	62.4	34.5	65.3	3.3	8.5	1.3	5.9
1910	63.7	44.3	52.8	4.4	9.3	3.2	9.0
1920	63.6	49.6	47.2	4.8	10.1	5.7	9.3
1930	65.3	56.0	43.7	5.3	12.6	4.7	12.2
1940	68.3	56.4	43.4	5.6	11.8	4.9	12.1
1950	65.1	63.8	35.9	5.9	11.7	6.1	11.5
1960	60.0	69.6	30.0	7.7	12.3	6.2	9.7
1970	62.3	73.3	26.4	8.2	12.1	6.4	9.2
1980	68.0	73.5	26.2	8.7	12.8	4.8	7.6

See Appendix for data sources and details.

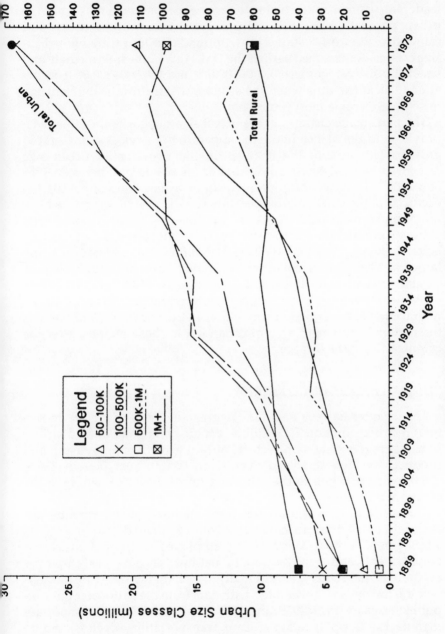

Figure 4-7 Population, by Urban Size.

123

and 1980. This is no doubt a radical and historically unprecedented inversion, even for a period as long as ninety-four years.

The population redistribution impact of the shift in the growth leadership from manufacturing to services becomes obvious when the urban population trend is disaggregated into various urban size categories. Figure 4–7 shows growth trends for four different urban-size classes. As assumed earlier, the "take off" of the intermediate and small city size categories (50,000–100,000 and 100,000–500,000) occurs after 1940, at the time when the structural shift from manufacturing to services became most prominent.

The percentage changes in the urban size categories, in Table 4–11, provide additional insights on the impact of the services sector's rapid growth. The sum of the changes in the two smaller urban size categories is consistently above that of the two largest between 1950 and 1980.[22] Thus, a substantially greater concentration of population occurred in the smaller cities and towns, where services are the most important central place function. In Table 4–12, the share of total national population for the two smaller categories is significantly larger between 1960 and 1980, and also for 1890, and only slightly larger in 1910. For all the other years, the shares are roughly equal. The larger share of the two smaller categories for 1890 and 1910 is best explained by the significant amount of interregional and rural-urban migration that occurred in many places in the West and Southwest, as the national settlement system expanded in those regions, after the colonization of the frontier.

SUMMARY AND CONCLUSIONS

This chapter has evaluated the aggregate effects of long-term sectoral restructurings on the nation's economy and population distribution. Aggregate trends on sectoral output growth, employment, and productivity were analyzed over a ninety-four-year period (1889–1983), corresponding to the third and fourth historical stages of the conceptual framework.

Various indicators and proxies were used to evaluate these trends. Sectoral contribution to national income evaluated output growth, employment annual averages on employed personnel measured employment, and contribution to national income per employee evaluated productitivy. Additionally, the changing structure of intersectoral linkages was evaluated with data from the national input-output matrixes for 1919, 1939, and 1977. Changes in the most important manufactured inputs to agriculture, transportation, services, and interindustry linkages were analyzed and discussed, in order to provide additional insights on the process of sectoral restructuring. This evaluation was followed by an assessment of urban and rural population trends, to determine how the restructuring process has affected population redistribution.

In the vast majority of cases, the evidence on shifts between employment, sectoral growth, and productivity change corresponds with the assumptions of the conceptual framework. Similarly, the analysis of intersectoral and interindustry linkages also provides general support for the assumptions discussed in the previous chapter. An evaluation of population trends related shifts in the sectoral growth leadership, from agriculture to manufacturing, to major changes in the urban-rural population distribution. A second component then demonstrated how a shift in the growth leadership from manufacturing to services, typical of the fourth historical stage, promoted faster growth in some urban size classes, following the services sector's typically less concentrated central place functions.

This chapter has therefore placed national trends in perspective, by evaluating the most important sectoral shifts that influence long-term regional change. If the support provided for the conceptual assumptions is any indication, the historical development of each of the various entrepreneurial roles has been of major importance to the sectoral shifts and restructurings that have been analyzed in the chapter. The degree of timeliness and effectiveness with which such shifts occur reflects the importance of innovative entrepreneurial initiative in the process of long-term economic change.

Regions, Sectors, and Macroeconomic Evolution

The most significant impacts of the national trends analyzed in the previous chapter occur at the regional level. The dynamics of sectoral change affect some regions and local areas more than others, however. Differences in regional performances arise from the uneven spatial distribution of the new frontier sectors, as they historically replace the less favored sectors in the functional economic hierarchy. To a great extent, those differences are a result of the application of the various entrepreneurial roles, as they respond to new opportunities created by changing wants and needs.

One of the most significant regional impacts of sectoral restructuring occurs through employment change. A slowdown in employment growth is indeed the most common initial impact as sectors are supplanted from the growth leadership position. The consequences of this development are too well known in our time, and have potentially serious long-term effects on a region's income distribution, its overall income contribution to the national economy, the level of unemployment, and the potential for substantial outmigration. Additionally, the introduction of greater uncertainty and competition for the regionally headquartered companies producing in the supplanted sectors also reduces their market influence. Over the long-term, their ability to control their destinies, and their impact on the local and regional economies where they operate, will also be reduced.

Employment slowdowns or declines most often come about through efforts aimed at increasing productivity. Indeed, raising productivity is the single most important adjustment mechanism with which regions and communities can deal with the adversities introduced by the decline of less favored sectors. Increasing productivity is also crucially important in maintaining regional competitiveness in the face of greater international and interregional competition. Such efforts are also essential in sustaining a region's position in the national distribution of income, and its overall living standards.

Increasing employment is, on the other hand, one of the most important regional impacts of a new frontier sector. This will most often result in rising levels of individual and household income, and in substantial in-migration. Such in-migration will tend to increase regional income further, even if the new in-migrants are not substantially employed in the new frontier sector. Rapid regional growth in a new frontier sector will also mean that regionally headquartered companies producing in that sector will very likely command increasing influence in the national economy. The effects of this development, although subtle, can be substantial over the long-term. Related activities are bound to grow significantly, increasing both employment and income, along with the region's corporate decision-making power in national and international markets.

The long-term shifts in the sectoral growth leadership generate a regional hierarchy, where the regions most specialized in the new frontier sector become the most important sources of national economic growth. These regions will also, in time, become the most important sources of organizational and technological innovation diffusion, nationally and internationally. Major secular changes in the regional hierarchy, and the innovative diffusion possibilities of the most dynamic regions, can therefore be expected to follow long-term sectoral shifts in the growth leadership.

The spatial impacts of these shifts are most noticeable through changes in the interregional distribution of population. Thus, the leading regions of the hierarchy can be expected to receive substantial in-migration, while spatial population redistribution follows more closely the spatial preferences of the new frontier sector. The major historical changes produced by these shifts have, for example, included the rural-urban population redistribution so typical of urbanizing societies, and substantial redistributions within the national urban hierarchy.

The main objective of this chapter will be to provide insights on these changes, by focusing on the regional trends produced by each of the various economic sectors over the ninety-four-year period of this study. The interplay of regional employment changes with sectoral growth and productivity, and their impact on regional population redistribution, will be a major concern, extending the conceptual perspective of the previous chapters. Longitudinal data on seven U.S. macroregions (Northeast, East North Central, West North Central, Southeast, West South Central, Mountain and Pacific), along with a Heartland (Northeast, East North Central) and Hinterland (all other regions) division will be analyzed.[1]

The limitations of this study arise primarily from the nature and quality of the available regional data. Regional data are less available than national data, especially for the earlier years. In addition, the number and types of variables reported were found to be much more limited and, in some cases, varied from one census year to another. Changes in the classification of the various activities within some of the sectors, and the level of spatial disaggregation, were another significant difficulty. Thus, for example, employment was the only data item available for the services sector over the full period of this study. Similarly, different measures of value had to be used for the various sectors.[2]

A REGIONAL PERSPECTIVE ON LONG-TERM SECTORAL CHANGE

Farm Production and Regional Change

Agriculture has been the most dramatically affected sector over the full ninety-four-year period of this study. The evaluation of national trends in the previous chapter saw enormous decline in agricultural employment, along with major increases in productivity. At the same time, agriculture had the slowest growth in its contribution to national income, becoming the least favored sector in the American economy over most of the period of this study, and especially over the postwar decades.

The regional analysis of this sector should therefore provide a better perspective on the national trends discussed in the previous chapter, by pinpointing the spatial sources of change. In this analysis, Value of Farm Products, being equivalent to the gross value of farm output, will be used as a measure of sectoral growth. Because of data availability constraints, only farming will be considered. Thus, extractive activities such as mining, forestry, and fisheries will be excluded from the regional analysis.[3]

Figure 5–1 provides important insights on the various regional trends with the standardized output (Value of Farm Products per Capita) variable. The West North Central region, the most specialized farming region, corresponding to the Plains states, has the highest value of farm output throughout, and is also the most dynamic farm region through the postwar period and up to the mid-1970s. This region's performance shows the enormous impact of specialization and the application of technological and organizational inventions designed to ensure crop reliability, higher yields, and better quality products.

Most of the other regional performances show fluctuations, though with mostly level performances over the long-term, and especially the postwar era. One exception is the West South Central region, showing

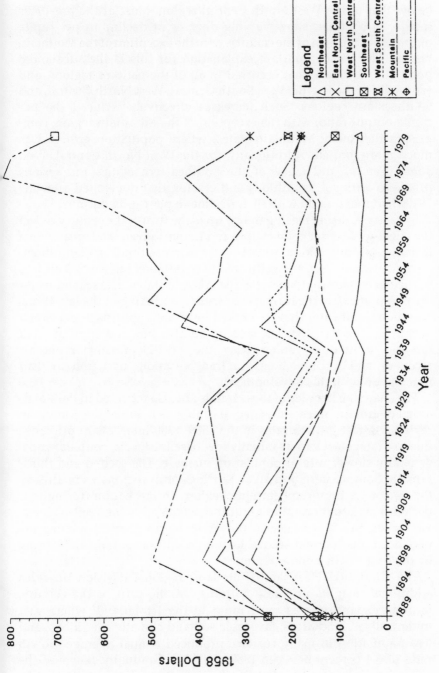

Figure 5–1 Farm Production: Regional Value of Products, per Capita.

a significant increase over the postwar period, though substantially below that of the West North Central region. Most of the pre-1940s trends, in contrast, show varying degrees of decline in per capita output after the turn of the century, with the exception of the Mountain region. The most important explanation for this is the substantial population increase that occurred in all of the nation's regions, and especially in the Pacific, West South Central, West North Central, and Southeastern regions. Such increases effectively reduced the per capita output ratio, with the exception of the Mountain region, comprising the Rocky Mountain states, where population growth was much more limited. Additionally, for the West North Central, West South Central and some of the Southeastern states, the serious problems with soil conditions and erosion that developed after the 1910s had much to do with their decline in per capita output.

In contrast, the increasing trends up to the turn of the century reflect the effects of frontier colonization and underutilized land areas, when farming output could be substantially increased through land-intensive cultivation, keeping well ahead of population increases. This was particularly relevant to many of the Western states. The second major turning point after the turn of the century, occurring in the late 1930s, was then significant, since it marked important upturns in per capita output for every region. The more rapid diffusion and application of farming techniques, along with the post-Depression economic recovery and improvements in transportation, undoubtedly had much to do with this development.

The changing profiles of these trends are also reflected in the standardized growth rates estimated in Table 5-1. First, the Mountain region's fastest growth rates in the 1889–1900 interval are primarily due to a later start and its initially low baseline levels, coupled with a generally slower rate of population increase. The second and third-ranking Southeastern and West North Central regions were already the two most important farming regions in the nation during that period. This situation was significantly changed in the 1969–82 interval, when the Northeastern and West North Central regions experienced the first and second fastest growth rates, followed closely by the East North Central region.

The simplified Heartland-Hinterland regional division provides additional insights on these patterns. At the turn of the century, farming expansion was most rapid in the Hinterland, where vast underutilized land areas, favorable soil and climatic conditions, and less population in many regions, produced annual average growth rates of 6.4 percent between 1889 and 1900. Gradually, however, the Hinterland's position eroded significantly, through the limitations on land-intensive cultivation imposed by the settlement of the Western

Table 5-1 Agriculture: Growth Rates, Value of Farm Products by Region.

Interval	Per Employee									Per Capita								
	North-east	East North Central	West North Central	South-east	West South Central	Mountain	Pacific	Heart-land	Hinter-land	North-east	East North Central	West North Central	South-east	West South Central	Mountain	Pacific	Heart-land	Hinter-land
1889–1900	73.6 (6.7)	97.6 (8.9)	102.0 (9.3)	44.8 (4.1)	64.5 (5.9)	167.6 (15.2)	50.5 (4.6)	87.1 (7.9)	70.6 (6.4)	37.8 (3.4)	72.7 (6.6)	97.4 (8.8)	144.2 (13.1)	67.7 (6.2)	177.1 (16.1)	56.3 (5.1)	56.6 (5.1)	70.0 (6.4)
1900–30	—	—	—	—	—	—	—	—	—	−59.1 (−2.0)	−54.9 (−1.8)	−22.3 (−0.7)	−64.0 (−2.1)	−9.0 (−0.3)	16.4 (0.5)	−42.0 (−1.4)	−56.8 (−1.9)	−26.1 (−0.9)
1930–40	—	—	—	—	—	—	—	—	—	−20.5 (−2.0)	−13.6 (−1.4)	−29.3 (−2.9)	−31.0 (−3.1)	−33.9 (−3.4)	−34.6 (−3.5)	−31.3 (−3.1)	−16.0 (−1.6)	−32.1 (−3.2)
1900–40	−34.8 (−0.9)	−26.9 (−0.7)	−32.2 (−0.8)	−32.0 (−0.8)	6.9 (0.2)	−23.1 (−0.6)	−22.6 (−0.6)	−30.2 (−0.8)	−20.4 (−0.5)	—	—	—	—	—	—	—	—	—
1940–45	62.8 (12.6)	81.6 (16.3)	92.6 (18.5)	109.1 (21.8)	100.0 (20.0)	85.6 (17.1)	108.8 (21.8)	74.9 (15.0)	105.6 (21.1)	57.9 (11.6)	69.2 (13.8)	97.8 (19.6)	82.6 (16.5)	67.4 (13.5)	76.4 (15.3)	70.6 (14.1)	66.1 (13.2)	80.5 (16.1)
1945–50	7.2 (1.4)	7.1 (1.4)	5.8 (1.2)	−1.4 (−0.3)	33.0 (6.6)	23.9 (4.8)	−4.4 (−0.9)	7.5 (1.5)	8.6 (1.7)	−16.0 (−3.2)	−12.0 (−2.4)	−6.64 (−1.3)	−18.7 (−3.7)	6.1 (1.2)	−7.9 (−1.6)	−22.2 (−4.4)	−13.1 (−2.6)	−10.5 (−2.1)
1950–59	22.9 (2.5)	11.7 (2.3)	33.6 (4.0)	69.8 (7.8)	23.1 (2.6)	36.8 (4.1)	31.3 (3.5)	15.4 (1.7)	45.9 (5.1)	−16.3 (−1.8)	−14.1 (−1.6)	0.1 (0.01)	2.8 (0.3)	−11.8 (−1.3)	−13.4 (−1.5)	−9.7 (−1.1)	−13.6 (−1.5)	−5.6 (−0.6)
1959–69	82.6 (8.3)	89.3 (8.9)	85.6 (8.6)	103.0 (10.3)	95.5 (9.6)	76.9 (7.7)	56.0 (5.6)	87.6 (8.8)	91.2 (9.1)	−11.0 (−1.1)	3.5 (0.4)	19.6 (2.0)	0.5 (0.05)	8.0 (0.8)	5.6 (0.6)	−13.5 (−1.4)	−0.6 (−0.1)	4.2 (0.4)
1969–78	60.3 (6.7)	46.5 (5.2)	60.7 (6.7)	36.9 (4.1)	75.8 (8.4)	35.5 (3.9)	40.5 (4.5)	50.2 (5.6)	50.5 (5.6)	36.7 (4.1)	29.4 (3.3)	31.2 (3.5)	10.3 (1.1)	21.6 (2.4)	−5.1 (−0.6)	21.0 (2.3)	32.4 (3.6)	16.9 (1.9)
1978–82	−2.0 (−0.5)	3.8 (1.0)	9.2 (2.3)	−25.4 (−6.4)	2.9 (0.7)	−4.8 (−1.2)	−1.7 (−0.4)	2.1 (0.5)	−5.1 (−1.3)	−7.3 (−1.8)	−7.2 (−1.8)	−11.5 (−2.9)	−30.6 (−7.6)	−28.1 (−7.0)	−18.0 (−4.5)	−9.8 (−2.4)	−7.3 (−1.8)	−19.7 (−4.9)
1889–1900	73.6 (6.7)	97.6 (8.9)	102.0 (9.3)	44.8 (4.1)	64.5 (5.9)	167.6 (15.2)	50.5 (4.6)	87.1 (7.9)	70.6 (6.4)	37.8 (3.4)	72.7 (6.6)	97.4 (8.8)	144.2 (13.1)	67.7 (6.2)	177.1 (16.1)	56.3 (5.1)	56.6 (5.1)	70.0 (6.4)
1900–30 +	−34.8 (−0.9)	−26.9 (−0.7)	−32.2 (−0.8)	−32.0 (−0.8)	6.9 (0.2)	−23.1 (−0.6)	−22.6 (−0.6)	−30.2 (−0.8)	−20.4 (−0.5)	−59.1 (−2.0)	−54.9 (−1.8)	−22.3 (−0.7)	−64.0 (−2.1)	−9.0 (−0.3)	16.4 (0.5)	−42.0 (−1.4)	−56.8 (−1.9)	−26.1 (−0.9)
1930–40	—	—	—	—	—	—	—	—	—	−20.5 (−2.0)	−13.6 (−1.4)	−29.3 (−2.9)	−31.0 (−3.1)	−33.9 (−3.4)	−34.6 (−3.5)	−31.3 (−3.1)	−16.0 (−1.6)	−32.1 (−3.2)
1945–69	140.6 (5.8)	126.5 (5.3)	166.4 (7.2)	239.8 (10.0)	220.2 (9.2)	200.0 (8.3)	95.8 (4.0)	132.8 (5.5)	202.7 (8.4)	−37.5 (−1.6)	−21.8 (−0.9)	11.9 (0.5)	−16.0 (−0.7)	1.1 (0.04)	−15.7 (−0.6)	−39.2 (−1.6)	−25.4 (−1.0)	−11.9 (−0.5)
1969–82	57.0 (4.4)	52.2 (4.0)	75.5 (5.8)	2.1 (0.2)	80.9 (6.2)	28.9 (2.2)	38.1 (2.9)	53.4 (4.1)	42.8 (3.3)	26.8 (2.1)	20.1 (1.5)	16.1 (1.2)	−23.5 (−1.8)	−12.6 (−1.0)	−22.2 (−1.7)	9.2 (0.7)	22.8 (1.8)	−6.1 (−0.5)

+ 1900–40 for Value of Farm Products per Employee estimates.

Annual average in parentheses. See Appendix for data sources and details.

regions, the soil problems that developed in many Southwestern and Plains states, and the rapid population growth that occurred in virtually all Hinterland regions, with the exception of the Plains states.

Additional insights on these trends are provided by the estimates of regional shares in total value of farming output found in Table 5–2. The West North Central region's importance over the period of this study is obvious, as it not only retains the largest share of output, but actually increases it over the years. Perhaps more surprisingly, a Heartland region, the East North Central, retains the second largest share through most of the period of this study, but with significant decline. Contrasting trends are reflected in the Northeastern region's rapidly declining share through the 1960s, and the rise of the Pacific region's, occurring primarily through the development of California farming. These changes, and the relatively stationary ranking of the other regions' shares, provide the Hinterland with the largest, and increasing, share of farming output through much of the period of this study.

Recalling the agricultural sector's dramatic national employment decline, the analysis of regional trends on this variable should provide major insights on the changing spatial distribution of farm employment. These trends are illustrated in Figure 5–2, where the decline of Southeastern farm employment becomes most obvious from 1940 through 1970. Given this region's largest employment level in 1940, it is therefore obvious that it accounted for a large proportion of the national decline in agricultural employment. This is undoubtedly a major factor in the Southeast's very significant rural-urban migratory

Table 5–2 Agriculture: Value of Farm Products, Percentage Shares by Region, 1889–1982.

Year	North-east	East North Central	West North Central	South-east	West South Central	Moun-tain	Pacific	Heart-land	Hinter-land
1889	18.2	22.8	23.0	23.1	6.6	1.4	4.8	41.0	59.0
1900	15.4	23.7	26.6	19.4	7.8	2.8	4.4	39.0	61.0
1930	10.2	16.7	26.3	17.2	13.1	7.0	9.5	26.9	73.1
1940	10.8	19.5	24.2	16.9	11.9	6.7	10.0	30.3	69.7
1945	9.2	18.2	25.2	17.4	11.2	6.6	12.3	27.4	72.6
1950	8.7	18.3	25.8	15.9	13.0	7.4	10.9	27.0	72.9
1959	7.6	17.2	25.7	17.2	12.1	7.8	12.5	24.7	75.3
1969	6.2	16.6	27.7	16.8	12.6	8.5	11.5	22.9	77.1
1978	6.3	16.5	28.1	15.9	13.4	7.8	11.9	22.8	77.2
1982	6.7	17.5	28.9	13.3	12.3	8.2	13.2	24.2	75.8

See Appendix for data sources and details.

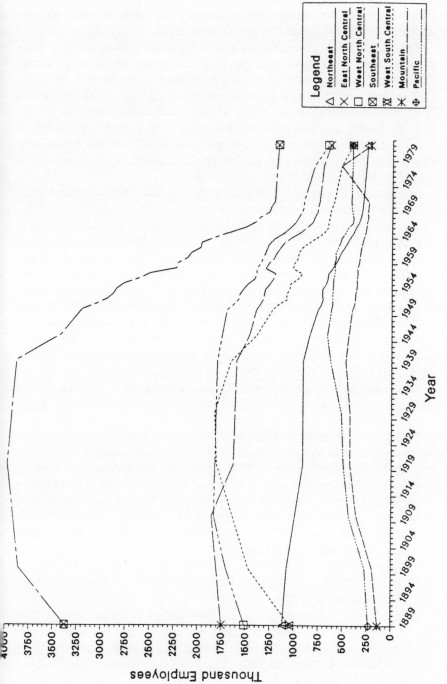

Figure 5-2 Farm Production: Regional Employment.

flow of the postwar era, when Northeastern and Midwestern metropolitan areas, along with the larger Southeastern cities, became major destinations for that region's farm labor.

The West South Central region's farming employment decline is the second most significant since the 1930s, after the Southeast's. There, the most significant factors were a combination of the effects of the Depression and the declining soil conditions that devastated much of Southwestern agriculture. These forced much farm labor out of the region toward the Western states, in search of better opportunities. The West North Central region's employment decline since 1940 is also important. This became a major source of rural-urban migration to the major midwestern cities and to the West.

In the trends shown in Figure 5–2, the late 1930s undoubtedly marked a major long-term turning point on regional farming employment. This can also be considered the beginning of a significant secular shift, promoted by the restructuring of the sectoral hierarchy favoring services over manufacturing. This change permanently relegated the agricultural sector to the least favored position in the hierarchy, and promoted the substantial increases in productivity that were the most important factor in the decline of farming employment.[4] From the turn of the century to the 1940s, farming employment therefore peaked in the most important agricultural regions, such as the Southeastern, West North Central, West South Central, and, to some extent, in the East North Central region.

An examination of the growth rates underlying these trends provides some additional insights on the structure of the changes occurring in the regional economies (see Table 5–3). The West South Central and Pacific regions had the fastest growing employment of the large agricultural regions before the turn of the century. This growth then turned to decline after 1940, reflecting the trends observed in Figure 5–2. The Pacific nevertheless had the slowest farming employment decline of all the regions, mostly due to the development of California agriculture, where more labor-intensive characteristics prevailed. The changes occurring before and after 1940 are also reflected in the simplified Heartland-Hinterland division, where the latter grew faster through the 1930s. After 1940, shifts in the rate of decline appear throughout, with virtually even performances through the 1970s and early 1980s.

The dramatic changes occurring in regional farming employment are surprisingly less obvious when the employment distribution is evaluated (see Figure 5–3). First, the Southeast's employment decline appears less substantial than might be expected, when its employment share is evaluated. This trend very much results from the fact that farming employment also declined significantly for all the other major

Table 5-3   Agriculture: Farm Employment Growth Rates, by Region.

Interval	North-east	East North Central	West North Central	South-east	West South Central	Moun-tain	Pacific	Heart-land	Hinter-land
1889-1900	-3.7 (-0.3)	3.3 (0.3)	12.8 (1.2)	14.5 (1.3)	41.8 (3.8)	43.0 (3.9)	18.8 (1.7)	0.6 (0.05)	19.3 (1.8)
1900-40	-14.9 (-0.4)	-11.1 (-0.3)	5.8 (0.1)	0.8 (0.02)	12.8 (0.3)	145.6 (3.6)	132.0 (3.3)	-12.5 (-0.3)	12.8 (0.3)
1940-45	-6.9 (-1.4)	-8.3 (-1.7)	-3.3 (-0.7)	-11.9 (-2.4)	-15.9 (-3.2)	-5.9 (-1.2)	5.5 (1.1)	-7.8 (-1.6)	-9.2 (-1.8)
1945-50	-10.2 (-2.0)	-4.8 (-1.0)	-2.2 (-0.4)	-6.4 (-1.3)	-11.9 (-2.4)	-8.3 (-1.7)	-6.0 (-1.2)	-6.8 (-1.4)	-6.5 (-1.3)
1950-59	-23.6 (-2.6)	-9.1 (-1.0)	-20.2 (-2.2)	-30.7 (-3.4)	-18.0 (-2.0)	-16.6 (-1.8)	-5.0 (-0.6)	-14.2 (-1.6)	-23.0 (-2.6)
1959-69	-46.6 (-4.7)	-39.2 (-3.9)	-31.2 (-3.1)	-43.0 (-4.3)	-36.6 (-3.7)	-27.0 (-2.7)	-30.4 (-3.0)	-41.5 (-4.2)	-36.6 (-3.7)
1969-78	-13.8 (-1.5)	-8.0 (-0.9)	-14.0 (-1.6)	-5.9 (-0.6)	-17.6 (-2.0)	-8.0 (-0.9)	0.2 (0.02)	-9.7 (-1.1)	-9.6 (-1.1)
1978-82	-5.2 (-1.3)	-10.5 (-2.6)	-17.7 (-4.4)	-1.6 (-0.4)	-22.4 (-5.6)	-3.0 (-0.8)	-0.7 (-0.2)	-9.1 (-2.3)	-9.1 (-2.3)
1889-1900	-3.7 (-0.3)	3.3 (0.3)	12.8 (1.2)	14.5 (1.3)	41.8 (3.8)	43.0 (3.9)	18.8 (1.7)	0.6 (0.05)	19.3 (1.8)
1900-40	-14.9 (-0.5)	-11.1 (-0.4)	5.8 (0.2)	0.8 (0.03)	12.8 (0.4)	145.6 (4.8)	132.0 (4.4)	-12.5 (-0.4)	12.8 (0.4)
1945-69	-63.3 (-2.6)	-47.4 (-2.0)	-46.4 (-1.9)	-63.0 (-2.6)	-54.2 (-2.2)	-44.2 (-1.8)	-37.8 (-1.6)	-53.3 (-2.2)	-54.3 (-2.3)
1969-82	-18.3 (-1.4)	-17.7 (-1.4)	-29.2 (-2.2)	-7.4 (-0.6)	-36.1 (-2.8)	-10.8 (-0.8)	-0.5 (-0.03)	-17.9 (-1.4)	-17.9 (-1.4)

Annual average in parentheses See Appendix for data sources and details.

agricultural regions. Thus, the Southeast's substantial decline is not fully reflected in the regional employment distribution.

For all the other regions, the trends show varying degrees of decline, with the exception of the Pacific, whose employment shares increased throughout the postwar period. This region's overall share situation nevertheless remains below that of the other major agricultural regions. To a great extent, the post-1960s declining shares for the West North Central and West South Central regions are offset by the Southeastern region's increase over the same period. The latter's performance can be attributed to an expansion of the more labor intensive crops, where mechanization became less practical because of the availability of lower cost farm labor, and the complexities involved in mechanizing the harvesting routines.

It was in raising productivity that the agricultural sector performed best nationally, especially throughout the post–World War II period.

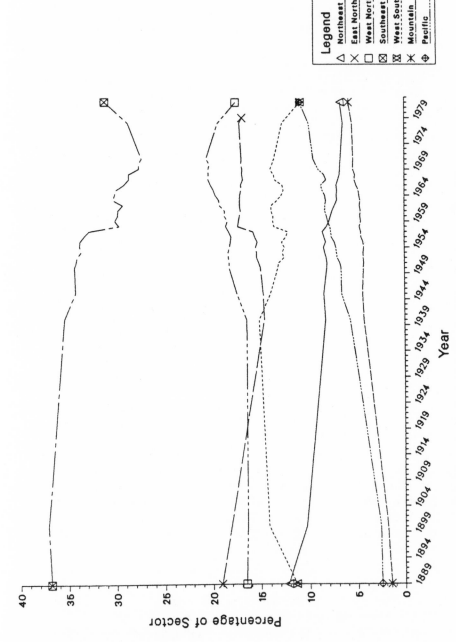

Figure 5-3 Farm Production: Regional Employment Distribution.

It is therefore in the shift toward higher productivity that agricultural entrepreneurship excelled, as this sector became progressively less favored in the sectoral hierarchy. Table 5–1 shows farming productivity, measured as the per employee value of farm products, increasing in all regions after the 1940s and through the late 1970s.

The emphasis on productivity becomes most obvious in the most important agricultural regions. The West North Central region's position, for example, remains among the top two ranks before the turn of the century, through the late 1940s, the 1950s, and 1970s, among the major agricultural regions. The West South Central region, fifth ranking in productivity growth before the turn of the century, becomes top ranked by the 1970s. This is a remarkable achievement over the long-term, considering that this region was one of the hardest hit by the soil erosion problems and the Depression during the 1920s and 1930s. Similarly, the Southeast, often characterized as the most backward agricultural region throughout much of this century, rises from the lowest rank before the turn of the century, to become the top ranking region in productivity growth during the 1950s and 1960s.

A look at the simplified Heartland-Hinterland division also proves to be revealing, insofar as any spatial shifts in productivity growth are concerned. The Heartland had the early productivity growth advantage, as expected, as agriculture was first supplanted from the growth leadership by manufacturing in this region. At the same time, the diffusion of new techniques could be expected to make its impact on the Heartland first. Later, the productivity growth advantage shifts in favor of the Hinterland, as the impact of agriculture's decline in the sectoral hierarchy began to be felt, and the diffusion of new techniques reached the major agricultural regions.

The impact of productivity change was also felt in the increasing regional divergence of per capita farming output throughout the post–World War II era, especially between the West North Central region's performance and those of all the other regions (see Figure 5–1). This divergence was mostly a result of the introduction of new farming techniques and substantial mechanization in that region, and its relatively lower population growth rate. In contrast, the pressures to increase productivity felt in virtually all farming activities, despite crop differences, resulted in substantial regional convergence in farming employment after the 1930s, as becomes obvious from the trends in Figure 5–2.

It was therefore through the raising of regional productivity that the process of sectoral restructuring had its greatest impact on farming. The traditional farming regions experienced substantial productivity growth, due in great measure to the introduction of innovative techniques, many of which were derived from advances made in manufacturing. For farming, it is obvious that the introduction of these advances required the substantial application of productive coordination. More than any other entrepreneurial role, productive coordination can therefore be assumed to account for the majority of the changes introduced to make American farming more productive and competitive.

Manufacturing Change and Regional Diffusion

The manufacturing sector's shift toward a relatively less favored position in the national sectoral hierarchy was a major development of the third historical stage. This involved a significant slowdown in employment growth, and increasing productivity for the least favored manufacturing activities. How these changes affected regional economic performance is a crucial question, inasmuch as manufacturing has historically been the most unevenly distributed activity in the nation's space-economy.

The regional estimates with the standardized value-added variable, in Figure 5–4, show the importance of the Northeastern and East North Central regions' (the industrial Heartland) industrial base.[5] These regions' higher absolute levels throughout the full period of this study, though impressive, are hardly surprising, since manufacturing has been the most spatially stable economic sector over the long-term. An important aspect, in this respect, has been the significant gains made by all the Hinterland regions. The spatial diffusion of manufacturing activities toward the Hinterland, through branch plant creation, along with the rapid growth of new, technologically intensive activities in the Pacific, West South Central, and Southeastern regions, has been a major contributor to this trend.[6] At the same time, a less competitive international situation for many of the traditional Heartland industrial activities has accelerated the spatial diffusion process and has reduced that region's importance.[7]

An important hiatus in all the regional trends was obviously marked by the Depression and World War II years, promoting substantial readjustment, especially in the financial markets. Some of the structural market changes that occurred during this period would no doubt promote greater stability in the postwar period, through better macroeconomic management. Much of the initial postwar growth must nevertheless be attributed to the unique competitive situation of U.S. manufacturing industry, after the destruction of virtually every advanced nation's industrial base during World War II.

Over the pre-1930s era, the predominance of the traditional Heartland regions is quite obvious throughout. Especially noticeable

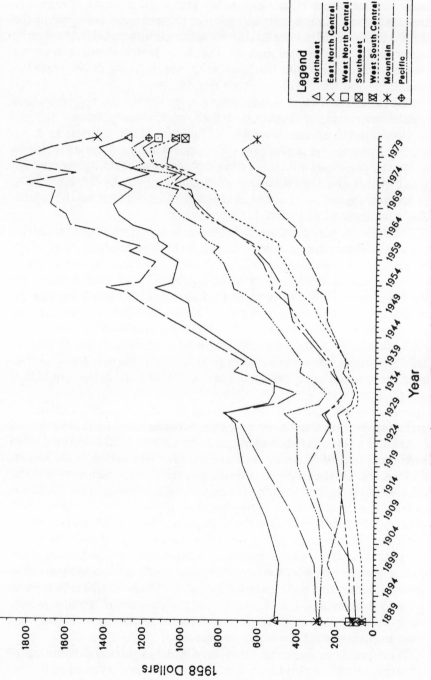

Figure 5-4 Manufacturing: Regional Value Added, per Capita.

Legend
△ Northeast
✕ East North Central
☐ West North Central
⊠ Southeast
⊠ West South Central
✳ Mountain
⊕ Pacific

1958 Dollars

Year

1889 1894 1899 1904 1909 1914 1919 1924 1929 1934 1939 1944 1949 1954 1959 1964 1969 1974 1979

is the rise of the East North Central region, after the introduction of mass production in some industrial activities, such as automobile manufacturing. The industrialization of this region is reflected in the fact that its level of per capita output was virtually equal to the Pacific region's in 1889. Subsequently, the East North Central region's "takeoff" becomes quite obvious, with the growing divergence between this and the Pacific region's trends.

This rapid rise is tempered, however, by the Pacific region's more rapidly increasing population, which undoubtedly biased its per capita output measure downward. The East North Central region's greater comparative advantages were nevertheless a major factor in its initial, pre-1930s industrial development, as shown by the convergence of this and the Northeastern region's trends by the late 1920s. Subsequently, the East North Central region would surpass the Northeast's per capita measure of total output.

The growth rate estimates of Table 5–4 reflect the shift of industrial growth toward the Hinterland's regions. The Southeastern, West South Central, West North Central, and Mountain regions' rapid growth rates are tempered by their low baseline starting figures. By the 1960s and 1970s, the West South Central region had achieved the fastest growth rate, followed by the Mountain, West North Central, and Pacific regions. Thus, the shift of industrial dynamism toward the Hinterland regions became a continuous phenomenon since the 1920s. This is obvious from the estimates provided in Table 5–4, and becomes even more so in the abbreviated intervals of the bottom portion of that table.

Additional insights on the changing regional balance in manufacturing can be found in the percentage share estimates of Table 5–5. The Heartland's regions share of value added consistently declines from 1889 until the 1960s, when it is surpassed by the Hinterland. Nevertheless, the Northeastern and East North Central's shares remain the highest of all regions through the early 1980s, although the Northeast experiences considerable erosion throughout the period of this analysis. Surprisingly, however, the East North Central region's declining share is more stable, partly because of this region's relatively younger industrial base. Significant changes in rank order occur in the Pacific and Southeastern shares, rising to the third and second ranks by 1980, respectively. The fastest growing shares are therefore those of the Southeastern, Pacific, and West South Central regions, where the growth of consumer markets for manufactured goods has been most important over the postwar decades.

Of crucial importance to this study is the regional distribution of manufacturing employment, because of its long-term human and socioeconomic impacts. Figure 5–5 illustrates the most significant

Table 5-4 Manufacturing: Growth Rates, Value Added by Region.

Interval	Per Employee									Per Capita								
	North-east	East North Central	West North Central	South-east	West South Central	Moun-tain	Pacific	Heart-land	Hinter-land	North-east	East North Central	West North Central	South-east	West South Central	Moun-tain	Pacific	Heart-land	Hinter-land
1889–1909 +	-4.1 (-0.2)	-3.4 (-0.2)	0.9 (0.04)	10.6 (0.5)	-5.4 (-0.3)	134.0 (6.7)	-5.7 (-0.3)	-4.0 (-0.2)	8.4 (0.4)	10.0 (0.5)	42.2 (2.1)	26.6 (1.3)	195.7 (9.8)	68.6 (3.4)	62.4 (3.4)	3.6 (0.2)	20.7 (1.0)	49.1 (2.4)
1909–19 +	21.5 (2.2)	23.3 (2.3)	14.9 (1.5)	16.4 (1.6)	11.9 (1.2)	9.1 (0.9)	37.8 (3.8)	22.6 (2.3)	18.7 (1.9)	21.4 (2.1)	38.4 (3.8)	24.9 (2.5)	31.9 (3.2)	28.3 (2.8)	-9.0 (-0.9)	38.2 (3.8)	27.1 (2.7)	25.9 (2.6)
1919–29 +	30.3 (3.0)	39.6 (4.0)	44.3 (4.4)	25.1 (2.5)	13.9 (1.4)	19.6 (2.0)	27.1 (2.7)	34.2 (3.4)	27.7 (2.8)	13.6 (1.4)	36.5 (3.6)	42.6 (4.3)	-25.1 (-2.5)	25.6 (2.6)	21.9 (2.2)	17.7 (1.8)	22.2 (2.2)	34.4 (3.4)
1929–35+	—	—	—	—	—	—	—	—	—	-32.4 (-5.4)	-27.5 (-4.6)	-32.4 (-5.4)	-27.4 (-4.6)	-31.4 (-5.2)	-35.4 (-5.9)	-33.9 (-5.6)	-30.4 (-5.1)	-30.6 (-5.1)
1935–39	—	—	—	—	—	—	—	—	—	—	—	—	—	—	—	—	—	—
1929–39 +	-27.4 (-2.7)	-32.4 (-3.2)	-15.2 (-1.5)	-13.2 (-1.3)	0.8 (0.1)	27.5 (2.8)	—	12.4 (1.2)	42.5 (4.2)	19.6 (4.9)	19.2 (4.8)	23.8 (6.0)	31.6 (7.9)	37.4 (9.4)	21.0 (5.2)	22.8 (5.7)	19.5 (4.9)	29.0 (7.2)
1939–47	83.0 (10.4)	88.1 (11.0)	108.6 (13.6)	102.5 (12.8)	164.9 (20.6)	97.0 (12.1)	—	16.6 (2.1)	32.8 (4.1)	53.0 (6.6)	58.1 (7.3)	72.5 (9.1)	74.4 (9.3)	99.4 (12.4)	64.8 (8.1)	40.7 (5.1)	55.4 (6.9)	71.6 (9.0)
1947–50	8.8 (2.9)	20.5 (6.8)	15.5 (5.2)	12.8 (4.3)	15.1 (5.0)	9.2 (3.1)	12.5 (4.2)	14.1 (4.7)	13.5 (4.5)	1.4 (0.5)	13.6 (4.5)	13.4 (4.5)	4.1 (1.4)	12.6 (4.2)	-0.1 (-0.03)	11.9 (4.0)	7.1 (2.4)	8.3 (2.8)
1950–60	28.2 (2.8)	25.5 (2.6)	30.6 (3.1)	29.2 (2.9)	39.8 (4.0)	27.2 (2.7)	24.2 (2.4)	26.9 (2.7)	30.6 (3.1)	15.1 (1.5)	5.6 (0.6)	39.0 (3.9)	35.7 (3.6)	54.9 (5.5)	49.6 (5.0)	39.8 (4.0)	10.6 (1.1)	41.5 (4.2)
1960–69	26.2 (2.9)	21.9 (2.4)	22.9 (2.5)	23.2 (2.6)	18.9 (2.1)	21.5 (2.4)	25.8 (2.9)	24.5 (2.7)	22.9 (2.5)	22.4 (2.5)	31.8 (3.5)	49.1 (5.4)	49.8 (5.5)	58.0 (6.4)	40.0 (4.4)	27.4 (3.0)	27.0 (3.0)	44.4 (4.9)
1969–80	23.6 (2.1)	17.7 (1.6)	26.7 (2.4)	26.4 (2.4)	34.8 (3.2)	17.4 (1.6)	21.0 (1.9)	20.8 (1.9)	26.6 (2.4)	5.7 (0.5)	0.1 (0.0)	29.6 (2.7)	17.4 (1.6)	46.8 (4.2)	32.0 (2.9)	19.1 (1.7)	3.0 (0.3)	24.1 (2.2)
1980–82	-2.5 (-1.2)	-0.9 (-0.4)	3.7 (1.8)	1.1 (0.6)	-4.3 (-2.2)	-3.2 (-1.6)	1.4 (0.7)	-1.8 (-0.9)	0.8 (0.4)	-10.2 (-5.1)	-14.2 (-7.1)	-6.6 (-3.3)	-7.5 (-3.8)	-11.0 (-5.5)	-10.8 (-5.4)	-7.0 (-3.5)	-12.2 (-6.1)	-8.2 (-4.1)
1889–1919 +	16.6 (0.6)	19.2 (0.6)	15.9 (0.5)	28.8 (1.0)	5.9 (0.2)	155.3 (5.2)	30.0 (1.0)	17.6 (0.6)	28.7 (1.0)	33.5 (1.1)	96.8 (3.2)	58.1 (1.9)	289.9 (9.7)	116.4 (3.9)	47.7 (1.6)	43.2 (1.4)	53.4 (1.8)	87.6 (2.9)
1919–29 +	30.3 (3.0)	39.6 (4.0)	44.3 (4.4)	25.1 (2.5)	13.9 (1.4)	19.6 (2.0)	27.1 (2.7)	34.2 (3.4)	27.7 (2.8)	13.6 (1.4)	36.5 (3.6)	42.6 (4.3)	-25.1 (-2.5)	25.6 (2.6)	21.9 (2.2)	17.7 (1.8)	22.2 (2.2)	34.4 (3.4)
1935–39	—	—	—	—	—	—	—	—	—	—	—	—	—	—	—	—	—	—
1947–69	76.0 (3.4)	84.3 (3.8)	85.4 (3.9)	79.7 (3.6)	91.3 (4.2)	68.6 (3.1)	75.8 (3.4)	80.2 (3.6)	82.2 (3.7)	43.0 (2.0)	58.0 (2.6)	135.1 (6.1)	111.6 (5.1)	175.5 (8.0)	109.2 (5.0)	99.2 (4.5)	50.5 (2.3)	121.4 (5.5)
1969–82	20.6 (1.6)	16.6 (1.3)	31.4 (2.4)	27.8 (2.1)	29.0 (2.2)	13.6 (1.0)	22.7 (1.7)	18.5 (1.4)	27.5 (2.1)	-5.11 (-0.4)	-14.0 (-1.1)	21.1 (1.6)	8.6 (0.7)	30.6 (2.4)	17.7 (1.4)	10.8 (0.8)	-9.5 (-0.7)	14.0 (1.1)

+ 1889, 1909, 1919 per capita estimates based on 1890, 1910, 1920 population, respectively; 1909, 1919, 1929 per employee estimates based on 1910, 1920, 1930 employment.

Annual averages in parentheses. See Appendix for data sources and details.

Table 5–5 Manufacturing: Value Added, Percentage Shares by Region, 1889–1982.

Year	North-east	East North Central	West North Central	South-east	West South Central	Moun-tain	Pacific	Heart-land	Hinter-land
1889	54.8	24.2	6.8	8.4	1.7	0.8	3.3	79.0	21.0
1909	49.0	25.5	6.6	10.4	2.8	1.6	4.1	74.5	25.5
1919	46.6	28.4	5.6	10.1	2.9	1.2	5.1	75.0	25.0
1929	42.1	31.3	5.9	10.6	3.0	1.2	6.0	73.4	26.6
1935	41.1	31.9	5.6	11.4	3.0	1.0	5.9	73.0	27.0
1939	39.6	31.5	5.5	12.4	3.3	1.1	6.4	71.2	28.8
1947	37.1	31.5	5.5	13.2	4.1	1.1	7.4	68.6	31.4
1950	34.4	33.2	5.7	13.3	4.3	1.2	7.8	67.7	32.3
1960	31.6	29.4	6.2	14.8	5.4	1.6	10.8	61.1	38.9
1969	28.3	28.6	6.5	16.8	6.5	1.8	11.4	56.9	43.1
1980	24.2	24.1	7.1	19.0	9.5	2.7	13.3	48.3	51.7
1982	23.8	22.5	7.3	19.7	9.8	2.8	14.0	46.2	53.7

See Appendix for data sources and details.

changes occurring throughout the ninety-four-year period of this analysis. In the decades preceding the 1930s, the Northeastern and East North Central regions remain the largest employers, with increasing levels up to the late 1920s. Among the Hinterland regions, the Southeastern trend is most important, increasing well above the two million mark by 1929, though still far below the East North Central region's level.

In the post-1930s decades, only the Northeastern trend registers decline, while the East North Central region's remains virtually stagnant, with fluctuations, between the mid-1940s and the 1980s. Impressive post–World War II gains occurred in the Southeastern and Pacific regions, with the former approaching the East North Central level by 1980. It is obvious from these trends that industrial employment decline is primarily a regional problem, not a national one.[8] More specifically, it is a Heartland and a Northeastern problem that is particular to that region's industrial structure and degree of national and international competitiveness.

The employment growth rates of Table 5–6 provide additional insights on the various regional trends. The Hinterland's regions are more dynamic throughout, during the 1930s and up to the mid-1940s, when the post-Depression recovery and the war effort shifted the regional balance in favor of the Heartland. The most rapidly growing Hinterland regions are the Western (Pacific and Mountain) and the West South Central. In the latter, industrial employment growth was no doubt helped by the development of the oil industry throughout much of this century. However, these performances are tempered by

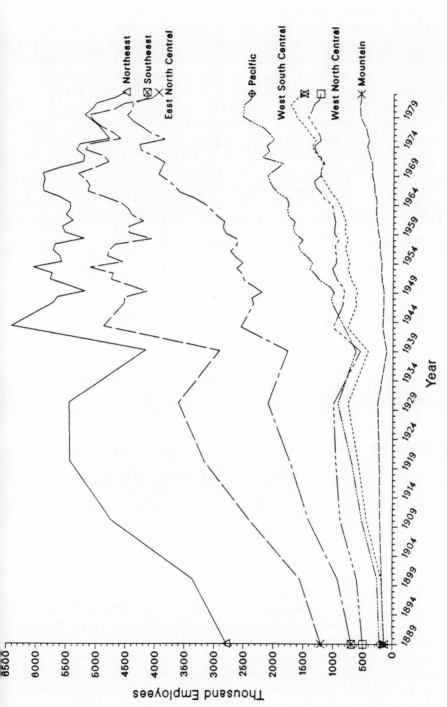

Figure 5-5 Manufacturing: Regional Employment.

Table 5–6 Manufacturing: Employment Growth Rates, by Region.

Interval	North-east	East North Central	West North Central	South-east	West South Central	Moun-tain	Pacific	Heart-land	Hinter-land
1889–1910	70.4 (3.4)	99.5 (4.7)	76.3 (3.6)	102.9 (4.9)	231.6 (11.0)	49.6 (2.4)	143.7 (6.8)	79.2 (3.8)	105.8 (5.0)
1910–20	14.6 (1.5)	32.0 (3.2)	8.7 (1.0)	22.4 (2.2)	33.3 (3.3)	6.1 (0.6)	33.4 (3.3)	20.4 (2.0)	21.0 (2.1)
1920–30	0.1 (0.01)	13.9 (1.4)	4.3 (0.4)	21.5 (2.2)	29.6 (3.0)	12.3 (1.2)	33.3 (3.3)	5.2 (0.5)	20.2 (2.0)
1930–39	−23.5 (−2.6)	−19.1 (−2.1)	−44.6 (−5.0)	−15.6 (−1.7)	−45.0 (−5.0)	−58.4 (−6.5)	−32.4 (−3.6)	−21.7 (−2.4)	−31.1 (−3.4)
1939–47	37.2 (4.6)	55.2 (6.9)	52.5 (6.6)	32.7 (4.1)	47.5 (5.9)	47.2 (5.9)	61.6 (7.7)	44.6 (5.6)	43.3 (5.4)
1947–50	−4.2 (−1.4)	−1.8 (−0.6)	0.7 (0.2)	0.1 (0.03)	2.8 (0.9)	5.8 (1.9)	5.1 (1.7)	−3.1 (−1.0)	1.7 (0.6)
1950–60	1.6 (0.2)	0.3 (0.03)	16.6 (1.7)	22.1 (2.2)	29.1 (2.9)	58.8 (5.9)	57.8 (5.8)	1.0 (0.1)	30.8 (3.1)
1960–69	5.8 (0.6)	19.0 (2.1)	27.6 (3.1)	37.8 (4.2)	49.8 (5.5)	37.4 (4.2)	25.1 (2.8)	11.6 (1.3)	34.5 (3.8)
1969–80	−13.7 (−1.2)	−11.2 (−1.0)	8.5 (0.8)	11.4 (1.0)	35.3 (3.2)	56.7 (5.2)	19.4 (1.8)	−12.5 (−1.1)	18.0 (1.6)
1980–82	−7.6 (−3.8)	−13.5 (−6.8)	−9.1 (−4.6)	−5.8 (−2.9)	−1.0 (−0.5)	−2.3 (−1.2)	−4.7 (−2.4)	−10.5 (−5.2)	−5.0 (−2.5)
1889–1920	95.3 (3.2)	163.4 (5.4)	91.6 (3.0)	148.3 (4.9)	342.1 (11.4)	58.7 (2.0)	225.1 (7.5)	115.8 (3.9)	148.9 (5.0)
1920–30	0.1 (0.01)	13.9 (1.4)	4.3 (0.4)	21.5 (2.2)	29.6 (3.0)	12.3 (1.2)	33.3 (3.3)	5.2 (0.5)	20.2 (2.0)
1935–39	—	—	—	—	—	—	—	—	—
1947–69	3.0 (0.1)	17.1 (0.8)	49.9 (2.3)	68.6 (3.1)	98.7 (4.5)	130.8 (5.9)	107.6 (4.9)	9.2 (0.4)	79.0 (3.6)
1969–82	−20.3 (−1.6)	−23.2 (−1.8)	−1.3 (−0.1)	4.9 (0.4)	34.0 (2.6)	53.0 (4.1)	13.8 (1.1)	−21.7 (−1.7)	12.0 (0.9)

Annual averages in parentheses. See Appendix for data sources and details.

the low initial baseline employment levels found in these regions. In contrast and confirming earlier observations, the East North Central region's relative growth ranking declines from fourth before the turn of the century, to one of the lowest throughout the postwar era. The Northeastern rate declines through many of the intervals, and remains one of the lowest ranking throughout the period of this analysis.[9]

The employment share trends illustrated in Figure 5–6 provide yet another perspective on the regional distribution of this important variable. The Northeastern region's dramatic decline throughout the period of this study is most obvious there, with the exception of the 1930s, whereas the decline of the East North Central region's shares does not set in until after the 1940s. The employment shares of most

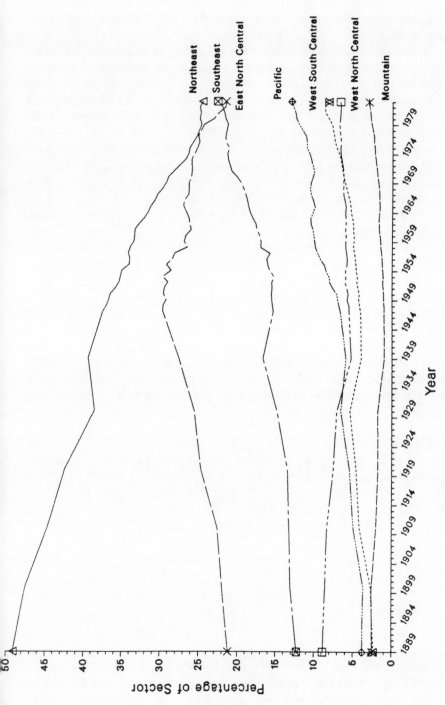

Figure 5–6 Manufacturing: Regional Employment Distribution.

Hinterland regions increase throughout the postwar era, with the exception of the West North Central's, which remains primarily agricultural.

All of the Hinterland regions experiencing increases are part of the so-called "Sunbelt" area, where the fastest growing industrial states can be found. These are California in the Pacific, Colorado in the Mountain, Texas in the West South Central, and Florida in the Southeastern region. The Southeastern region's shares surpassed the East North Central's by the early 1980s. It is historically unprecedented for a Hinterland region, considered industrially backward only a few decades before, to bypass one of the industrial Heartland's largest, not only for the United States but also internationally. This growth reflects not only the Hinterland's dynamism, but also the significant attraction of its comparative advantages for many manufacturing industries.

Again, if declining employment shares can be taken as an indicator of "deindustrialization," it is obvious that this is primarily a regional problem. The Southeastern, Pacific, West South Central, and Mountain regions' rising employment shares have shifted the balance in favor of the Hinterland, where lower production costs and larger consumer markets have created significant comparative advantages. At the same time, these advantages have made Hinterland industry more competitive in national and international markets. Particularly important in this shift are the "high technology" industries that originated and have become established in various Sunbelt states, such as California and Texas.

Additional insights on the Heartland-Hinterland shift can be found in the productivity (Value Added per Employee) estimates of Table 5–4.[10] In the upper portion of this table, the Heartland's productivity is highest in four estimates, versus the Hinterland's six. Both the Northeastern and East North Central's productivity growth rates can be found among the top three ranks in four out of ten intervals. Industry age and structure undoubtedly affected these estimates, as older plants can be expected to reduce productive efficiency substantially. This influence is supported by the fact that the regions with consistently higher productivity, the West North Central and West South Central, have relatively smaller and newer industrial bases, with lower industrial employment shares.

Distribution and the Division of Commerce

The distributive sector's employment performance also reflects the Hinterland regions' growing importance in the national space-economy. Distributive activities more closely follow, and are better correlated with, the spatial distribution of population. Wholesale and retail commerce is one such activity, accounting substantially for the product of this sector. Other activities included are transportation, of both passengers and freight, and utilities generation and distribution.

Subtle shifts can be observed in the trends shown in Figure 5–7, with respect to distributive sector employment in the Hinterland's "Sunbelt" regions. The Southeast, in particular, achieves fastest growth in the post-1950s period, surpassing the Northeast as the nation's most important source of distributive sector employment. An important turning point can be seen to occur for the other Sunbelt regions after the 1950s, as their employment levels increase substantially. Nevertheless, despite the regional population shifts, the Northeast and, to a lesser extent, the East North Central regions generally maintain their overall trends throughout the full period of this analysis, despite some fluctuation and a brief period of stagnation during the 1930s. The growth of the Sunbelt regions does not therefore imply any decline in the Heartland's employment levels.

The longer-term changes underlying the Heartland regions' apparent stability can be observed in the growth rate estimates of Table 5–7. The Hinterland's regions grew faster than the Heartland's throughout the full period of this analysis. Thus, the Western (Pacific, Mountain) and West South Central regions were the growth leaders more frequently than any of the other regions, in both the detailed and the abbreviated intervals.[11] To a great extent, however, their early rapid growth rates were a product of the low baseline employment figures resulting from late settlement and population growth. These regions' growth rates were gradually reduced over time, as population increased and the initially rapid rates of in-migration leveled off.

More revealing still on the distributive sector's changing regional distribution are the employment share trends of Figure 5–8. It is obvious that underneath the Northeastern trend's apparent employment stability in Figure 5–7 lies a substantial decline in its employment share, starting after the turn of the century. The East North Central region's virtually stagnant share and slight decline after the 1950s underlie its apparent long-term stability and post-1950s employment increase. On the other hand the Sunbelt regions' dynamism in this sector is obvious in the Southeastern, Pacific, and West South Central regions' increases.

The regional significance of the distributive sector's most important component, wholesale and retail commerce, is quite substantial, since it serves as an important indicator of general business trends. The growth rate estimates for standardized sales in Table 5–8 reveal greater Hinterland growth throughout the post–World War II era. This

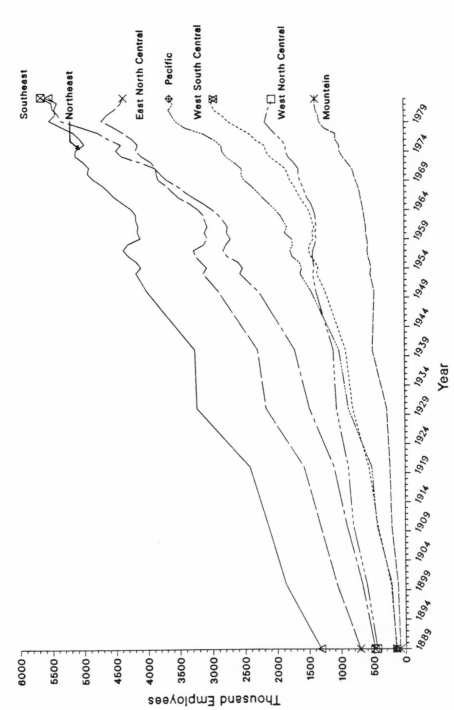

Figure 5-7 Distributive Activities: Regional Employment.

Table 5–7 Distributive Sector: Employment Growth Rates, by Region.

Interval	North-east	East North Central	West North Central	South-east	West South Central	Moun-tain	Pacific	Heart-land	Hinter-land
1889–1910	62.5 (3.0)	86.8 (4.1)	82.0 (3.9)	88.4 (4.2)	201.4 (9.6)	147.0 (7.0)	197.3 (9.4)	71.0 (3.4)	114.8 (5.5)
1910–20	13.0 (1.3)	19.1 (1.9)	9.5 (0.9)	21.4 (2.1)	32.7 (3.3)	12.4 (1.2)	17.6 (1.8)	15.3 (1.5)	18.4 (1.8)
1920–30	33.6 (3.4)	37.6 (3.8)	20.1 (2.0)	34.5 (3.4)	43.3 (4.3)	19.5 (2.0)	69.3 (6.9)	35.2 (3.5)	36.5 (3.6)
1930–40	0.92 (0.1)	6.0 (0.6)	4.5 (0.4)	15.3 (1.5)	13.1 (1.3)	78.7 (7.9)	16.0 (1.6)	2.9 (0.3)	16.4 (1.6)
1940–50	23.0 (2.3)	26.4 (2.6)	21.9 (2.2)	33.0 (3.3)	33.8 (3.4)	−6.5 (−0.6)	42.1 (4.2)	24.4 (2.4)	28.8 (2.9)
1950–60	3.3 (0.3)	7.1 (0.7)	2.2 (0.2)	21.4 (2.1)	16.3 (1.6)	27.6 (2.8)	28.3 (2.8)	4.9 (0.5)	18.5 (1.8)
1960–70	18.6 (1.9)	23.8 (2.4)	18.4 (1.8)	36.7 (3.7)	26.3 (2.6)	30.1 (3.0)	35.9 (3.6)	20.8 (2.1)	31.0 (3.1)
1970–80	10.3 (1.0)	20.2 (2.0)	30.6 (3.1)	42.4 (4.2)	55.6 (5.6)	70.3 (7.0)	42.1 (4.2)	14.6 (1.5)	44.8 (4.5)
1980–83	1.8 (0.6)	−5.6 (−1.9)	−4.0 (−1.3)	4.9 (1.6)	5.2 (1.7)	4.0 (1.3)	1.1 (0.4)	−1.6 (−0.5)	2.7 (0.9)
1889–1920	83.7 (2.7)	122.5 (4.0)	99.3 (3.2)	128.8 (4.2)	300.0 (9.7)	177.6 (5.7)	249.7 (8.0)	97.2 (3.1)	154.4 (5.0)
1920–30	33.6 (3.4)	37.6 (3.8)	20.1 (2.0)	34.5 (3.4)	43.3 (4.3)	19.5 (2.0)	69.3 (6.9)	35.2 (3.5)	36.5 (3.6)
1950–70	22.6 (1.1)	32.6 (1.6)	21.1 (1.0)	65.9 (3.3)	46.9 (2.3)	66.0 (3.3)	74.3 (3.7)	26.8 (1.3)	55.3 (2.8)
1970–83	12.3 (0.9)	13.5 (1.0)	25.4 (2.0)	49.4 (3.8)	63.7 (4.9)	77.2 (5.9)	43.7 (3.4)	12.8 (1.0)	48.8 (3.8)

Annual averages in parentheses. See Appendix for data sources and details.

is not surprising, when the increasing importance of manufacturing and virtually every other type of economic activity in the Western, Southeastern, and West South Central regions is considered. The highest annual average growth rates are nevertheless to be found over the 1930s and 1940s, as a result of the post-Depression recovery and the war effort. When these two periods are excluded, as in the abbreviated intervals of Table 5–8, two Sunbelt regions, the Southeastern and West South Central, achieve the most rapid growth rates from 1948–72 and from 1972–82, respectively. The Pacific and Mountain regions also achieve rapid growth from 1948–72.

Given the Hinterland's higher long-term growth rates, it may surprise some that the Heartland regions (Northeast, East North Central) retain the largest share of total commercial sales throughout the full period of this analysis (see Table 5–9). This is primarily a result

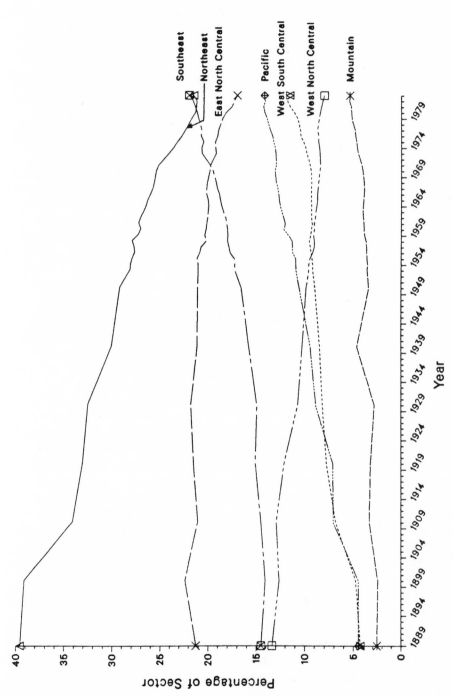

Figure 5-8 Distributive Activities: Regional Employment Distribution.

Table 5–8   Commerce: Sales Growth Rates, by Region.

Interval	North-east	East North Central	West North Central	South-east	Sales per Capita West South Central	Moun-tain	Pacific	Heart-land	Hinter-land
1929–35	-26.5	-25.2	-30.5	-19.5	-33.2	-16.3	-20.7	-25.9	-25.2
	(-4.4)	(-4.2)	(-5.1)	(-3.2)	(-5.5)	(-2.7)	(-3.4)	(-4.3)	(-4.2)
1935–39	25.4	23.5	20.6	26.1	27.1	17.5	17.6	24.5	22.9
	(6.4)	(5.9)	(5.2)	(6.5)	(6.8)	(4.4)	(4.4)	(6.1)	(5.7)
1939–48	46.4	62.7	90.9	74.7	81.8	67.1	32.3	52.1	70.4
	(5.2)	(7.0)	(10.1)	(8.3)	(9.1)	(7.4)	(3.6)	(5.8)	(7.8)
1948–58	-0.6	-2.1	-5.1	13.2	14.6 .	2.5	1.9	-1.4	6.3
	(-0.1)	(-0.2)	(-0.5)	(1.3)	(1.5)	(0.2)	(0.2)	(-0.1)	(0.6)
1958–72	24.5	32.0	31.1	57.3	43.9	33.2	28.0	27.6	40.9
	(1.8)	(2.3)	(2.2)	(4.1)	(3.1)	(2.4)	(2.0)	(2.0)	(2.9)
1972–77	14.0	21.3	24.1	14.1	27.0	15.3	19.7	17.1	19.2
	(2.8)	(4.3)	(4.8)	(2.8)	(5.4)	(3.1)	(3.9)	(3.4)	(3.8)
1977–82	44.8	-12.3	-5.1	-6.5	18.1	-5.5	-4.4	-3.0	-1.1
	(9.0)	(-2.5)	(-1.0)	(-1.3)	(3.6)	(-1.1)	(-0.9)	(-0.6)	(-0.2)
1935–39	25.4	23.5	20.6	26.1	27.1	17.5	17.6	24.5	22.9
	(6.4)	(5.9)	(5.2)	(6.5)	(6.8)	(4.4)	(4.4)	(6.1)	(5.7)
1948–72	23.8	29.2	24.4	78.1	64.9	36.6	30.4	25.7	49.8
	(1.0)	(1.2)	(1.0)	(3.2)	(2.7)	(1.5)	(1.3)	(1.1)	(2.1)
1972–82	19.1	6.4	17.8	6.7	50.0	9.0	14.4	13.5	17.8
	(1.9)	(0.6)	(1.8)	(0.7)	(5.0)	(0.9)	(1.4)	(1.4)	(1.8)

Includes wholesale and retail sales.
Annual averages in parentheses. See Appendix for data sources and details.

of the established trading patterns, particularly in wholesale trade, that are very much related to the traditional industrial concentration of the Heartland regions. The Northeastern region's share, largest throughout, nevertheless declines over the years, from 37.3 percent in 1929 to 24.6 in 1982. A less pronounced decline in share of total sales occurs in the East North Central, and West North Central regions, while significant share increases are found in the Southeastern, West South Central, and Pacific regions. Again, the shift toward the Hinterland's Sunbelt regions becomes quite obvious in this analysis.

Services and Regional Employment Growth

The services sector's dynamism has often been assumed to be synonymous with post–World War II development. Its impressive national performance has affected some regions more than others, however. This influence has much to do with the fact that service activities are traditional central place functions that correlate well

Table 5-9   Commerce: Percentage Shares by Region, 1929–1982.

Year	North-east	East North Central	West North Central	South-east	Wholesale and Retail Sales (1958 Dollars) West South Central	Moun-tain	Pacific	Heart-land	Hinter-land
1929	37.3	21.3	11.8	11.5	7.3	2.3	8.5	58.6	41.4
1935	36.9	20.9	10.9	12.8	6.6	2.6	9.4	57.8	42.2
1939	36.7	21.0	10.2	13.1	6.7	2.6	9.6	57.7	42.2
1948	32.5	21.7	11.0	14.2	7.5	2.8	10.2	54.2	45.8
1958	30.2	20.9	9.6	15.6	8.2	3.2	12.2	51.1	48.9
1972	26.7	19.8	8.7	18.9	9.0	3.7	13.1	46.6	53.4
1977	24.6	19.8	8.9	18.8	10.2	4.0	13.7	44.4	55.6
1982	24.6	16.8	8.3	18.5	13.4	4.3	14.2	41.3	58.7

See Appendix for data sources and details.

with urban population size. For this reason, the spatial distribution of service activities can be expected to follow population redistribution more closely than any other sector.

The employment trends in nongovernmental services support the Northeastern region's predominant role as the most important long-term source of service employment Three important periods can be identified in the trends illustrated in Figure 5–9. These are the pre-1930s, the 1930s and 1940s, and the post-1940s decades. Over the pre-1930s years, the Northeastern and East North Central regions are most important in overall employment and growth, followed by the Southeast. This pattern reflects the substantial concentration of population in the Heartland's regions and its metropolitan areas.

Throughout the 1930s and 1940s a decline in services employment occurs in all regions, due primarily to the Depression's impact on household incomes and spending priorities, since expenditures on many service activities can be more easily cut back in times of austerity. In this period, the war effort undoubtedly also had a substantial impact on services employment, as greater priority had to be given to manufacturing and agriculture in order to meet the nation's emergency needs.

This situation clearly contrasts with the postwar one, where changes in the rank order of regions occur vis-à-vis this period and the pre-1930s. An important indication of the Sunbelt's rising importance is the Southeastern region's increasing trend, which bypasses the East North Central's after the 1960s. The Pacific region's rapidly increasing employment is also important in this analysis, while the West South Central's trend surpasses that of the West North Central region.

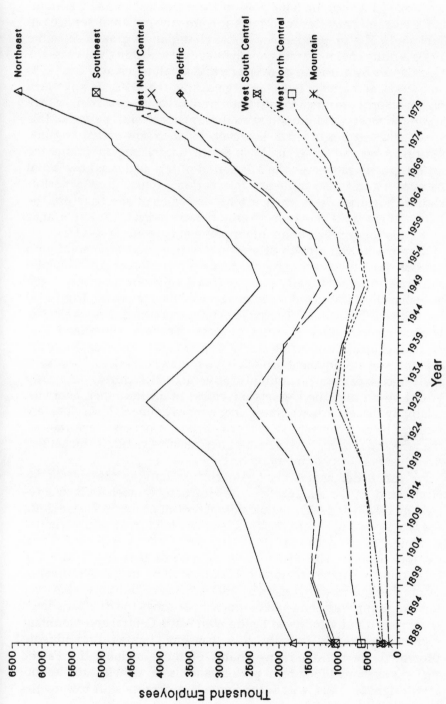

Figure 5-9 Nongovernmental Services: Regional Employment

We can gain additional insights on these regional shifts by examining the employment growth rates for nongovernmental services in Table 5–10 The preponderance of the Hinterland's growth since the 1940s is quite obvious, as its growth rates overwhelmingly surpass the Heartland's by a margin of over one and a half times over the 1950s and 1960s, and almost twice as large during the 1970s. The Western regions contribute much to the Hinterland's overall growth, since they attain the most rapid growth rates throughout the full period of this study. These are tempered, however, by their low initial baseline figures. After the West, the West South Central region attains the fastest growth rates over the full period of this analysis. Low initial baseline figures also influence this region's initial growth performance, however. To a great extent, as we shall see later on, the Hinterland's rapid employment growth rates indicate the importance of population redistribution for employment growth in services.[12]

Comparing the growth rate estimates of nongovernmental with total services, it becomes obvious that the inclusion of governmental activities reduces virtually every regional employment growth rate, as well as the Hinterland's advantage over the Heartland, from 1950 to 1983 (see Table 5–10). The same situation occurs during the 1920s. Higher growth rates in total services for both Hinterland and Heartland do appear during the 1910s and 1930s, however. These are due to faster employment growth in government services, because of the rapid expansion of administrative activities during and after World War I and the Depression years. In all the other intervals, relatively faster growth rates for nongovernmental services are reduced by government's slower growth performances. Nevertheless, the rank order of regional growth rates remains virtually unchanged in the vast majority of intervals.

We can better assess the tendencies underlying the Heartland-Hinterland or, more accurately, the Heartland-Sunbelt shift in services, by estimating each region's employment share. In Figure 5–10, the Northeastern's share declines over the long-term, while slightly declining trends occur for the East North Central and West North Central regions. The distribution of growth patterns within the Hinterland's Sunbelt regions becomes obvious in these estimates, where the Southeastern region's trend remains virtually stagnant over the long-term, with some fluctuations. In contrast, the Pacific region's share rises rapidly, followed by the West South Central and Mountain regions. Although initially low baseline figures undoubtedly promoted the rapidly rising shares of these regions, the Pacific region's sustained long-term performance is nevertheless too important to ignore. Thus, within the Sunbelt, a definite shift toward the West begins to appear.

Table 5–10 Services: Employment Growth Rates, by Region.

Interval	Services									Services, excluding Government								
	North-east	East North Central	West North Central	South-east	West South Central	Moun-tain	Pacific	Heart-land	Hinter-land	North-east	East North Central	West North Central	South-east	West South Central	Moun-tain	Pacific	Heart-land	Hinter-land
1889–1910	—	—	—	—	—	—	—	—	—	46.5 (2.2)	28.6 (1.4)	30.5 (1.4)	24.6 (1.2)	74.1 (3.5)	40.8 (1.9)	81.6 (3.9)	39.6 (1.9)	39.0 (1.8)
1910–20	21.5 (2.2)	29.1 (2.9)	16.4 (1.6)	16.9 (1.7)	32.5 (3.2)	23.7 (2.4)	37.3 (3.7)	24.2 (2.4)	22.4 (2.2)	19.4 (1.9)	27.3 (2.7)	15.9 (1.6)	11.4 (1.1)	24.9 (2.5)	20.0 (2.0)	35.2 (3.5)	22.2 (2.2)	18.3 (1.8)
1920–30	36.2 (3.6)	41.1 (4.1)	25.7 (2.6)	33.7 (3.4)	48.6 (4.9)	24.4 (2.4)	71.0 (7.1)	38.0 (3.8)	39.5 (4.0)	37.7 (3.8)	42.3 (4.2)	26.5 (2.6)	37.7 (3.8)	55.2 (5.5)	29.6 (3.0)	75.1 (7.5)	39.4 (3.9)	43.2 (4.3)
1930–40	-21.3 (-2.1)	-21.6 (-2.2)	-12.6 (-1.3)	5.8 (0.6)	2.2 (0.2)	-4.7 (-0.5)	-3.6 (-0.4)	-21.4 (-2.1)	-1.1 (-0.1)	-25.3 (-2.5)	-25.9 (-2.6)	-17.7 (-1.8)	-2.1 (-0.2)	-2.7 (-0.3)	-12.9 (-1.3)	-11.9 (-1.2)	-25.6 (-2.6)	-8.0 (-0.8)
1940–50	8.2 (0.8)	12.4 (1.2)	3.4 (0.3)	3.4 (0.3)	0.9 (1.0)	43.9 (4.4)	34.2 (3.4)	9.8 (1.0)	11.0 (1.1)	—	—	—	—	—	—	—	—	—
1950–60	32.3 (3.2)	38.6 (3.9)	34.2 (3.4)	51.5 (5.2)	46.0 (4.6)	68.4 (6.8)	56.1 (5.6)	34.6 (3.5)	49.9 (5.0)	34.8 (3.5)	38.5 (3.8)	35.7 (3.6)	65.4 (6.5)	42.8 (4.3)	76.2 (7.6)	56.2 (5.6)	36.1 (3.6)	54.6 (5.5)
1960–70	41.9 (4.2)	51.8 (5.2)	47.1 (4.7)	59.4 (5.9)	60.2 (6.0)	62.8 (6.3)	69.0 (6.9)	45.8 (4.6)	60.2 (6.0)	40.6 (4.1)	51.4 (5.1)	47.8 (4.8)	62.6 (6.3)	71.2 (7.1)	70.5 (7.0)	77.3 (7.7)	44.5 (4.4)	65.7 (6.6)
1970–80	26.7 (2.7)	34.1 (3.4)	38.3 (3.8)	44.6 (4.5)	57.1 (5.7)	68.9 (6.9)	48.7 (4.9)	29.7 (3.0)	48.7 (4.9)	31.4 (3.1)	44.6 (4.5)	52.8 (5.3)	47.4 (4.7)	70.3 (7.0)	94.8 (9.5)	68.4 (6.8)	36.4 (3.6)	61.1 (6.1)
1980–83	5.1 (1.7)	-0.04 (-0.01)	1.4 (0.5)	11.9 (4.0)	9.7 (3.2)	11.4 (3.8)	3.2 (1.1)	2.9 (1.0)	7.9 (2.6)	10.2 (3.4)	4.5 (1.5)	4.2 (1.4)	26.2 (8.7)	14.2 (4.7)	19.6 (6.5)	6.9 (2.3)	7.9 (2.6)	15.2 (5.1)
1889–1920	—	—	—	—	—	—	—	—	—	74.9 (2.4)	63.7 (2.0)	51.2 (1.6)	38.7 (1.2)	117.5 (3.8)	69.0 (2.2)	145.5 (4.7)	70.6 (2.3)	64.6 (2.1)
1920–30 +	65.4 (3.3)	82.1 (4.1)	46.2 (2.3)	56.2 (2.8)	96.8 (4.8)	53.9 (2.7)	134.8 (6.7)	71.1 (3.6)	70.8 (3.5)	37.7 (3.8)	42.3 (4.2)	26.5 (2.6)	37.7 (3.8)	55.2 (5.5)	29.6 (3.0)	75.1 (7.5)	39.4 (3.9)	43.2 (4.3)
1950–70	87.5 (4.4)	110.4 (5.5)	97.4 (4.9)	141.6 (7.1)	134.0 (6.7)	174.2 (8.7)	163.9 (8.2)	96.2 (4.8)	140.2 (7.0)	89.5 (4.5)	109.7 (5.5)	100.5 (5.0)	169.0 (8.4)	144.6 (7.2)	200.5 (10.0)	176.9 (8.8)	96.8 (4.8)	156.2 (7.8)
1970–83	33.2 (2.6)	34.0 (2.6)	40.2 (3.1)	61.8 (4.8)	72.4 (5.6)	88.2 (6.8)	53.5 (4.1)	33.5 (2.6)	60.5 (4.6)	44.7 (3.4)	51.1 (3.9)	59.1 (4.5)	86.1 (6.6)	94.5 (7.3)	133.0 (10.2)	80.0 (6.2)	47.2 (3.6)	85.6 (6.6)

+ 1910–30 for Services.

Annual averages in parentheses. See Appendix for data sources and details.

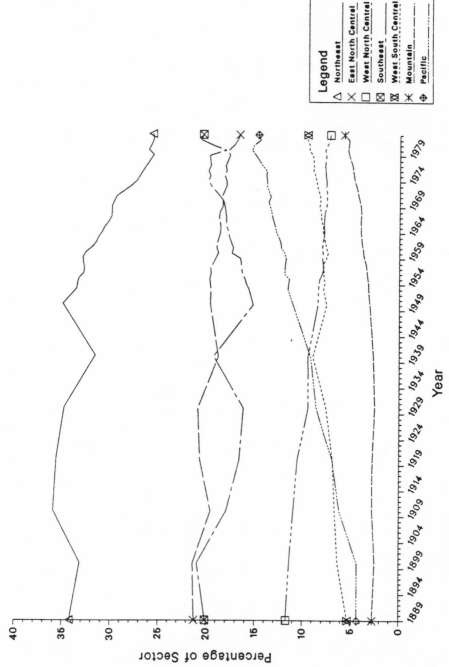

Figure 5-10 Nongovernmental Services: Regional Employment Distribution.

AN OVERVIEW OF REGIONAL POPULATION CHANGE

Population Redistribution and Regional Growth

Changes in the spatial distribution of population are one of the most important effects of sectoral restructuring. Population redistribution is primarily caused by the reallocation of employment from the less favored sectors to new frontier activities. Differences in spatial orientation between the less favored and the new frontier sectors then promote the spatial redistribution of employment and population, toward regions with greater comparative advantages in the new frontier activities.

The shift from manufacturing to services during the post–World War II era introduced a greater degree of spatial economic mobility than had so far been possible. Most service activities, being primarily central place functions, helped redistribute population as they promoted employment growth even in the most isolated regions.[13] In this respect, the question of whether people followed jobs or jobs followed people to the Hinterland's Sunbelt regions would then appear easily settled.

The answer to this question is not quite so simple, however. Given the strong relationship between population and service activities, both propositions are in fact correct. In an era of services-led regional growth, population size itself becomes a significant comparative advantage. Thus, as employment opportunities increased in the Sunbelt regions, because of the spatial distribution of service activities, population growth could be expected to favor the Hinterland. At the same time, the population growth that occurred in these regions helped create new employment opportunities. The broader spatial distribution of service activities also allowed greater possibilities for personal spatial preferences to be exercised. Thus, amenities and seemingly superfluous considerations such as climate and scenery also became significant factors in population redistribution.

The Heartland-Sunbelt population shift of the postwar era becomes obvious in the trends of Figure 5–11. While we can observe little change in the rank order of regional population trends during the pre-1940s decades, the 1940s witness the convergence of the Pacific, West South Central, and West North Central regions. An important factor in this is the urbanization of the Pacific and West South Central regions. After the 1950s, population redistribution toward the Sunbelt becomes obvious as the Southeast passes the Northeast as the nation's most populous region, and the Pacific and West South Central regions continue to increase their population. More significantly, both the Northeastern and East North Central population trends tend to level off after the 1960s.

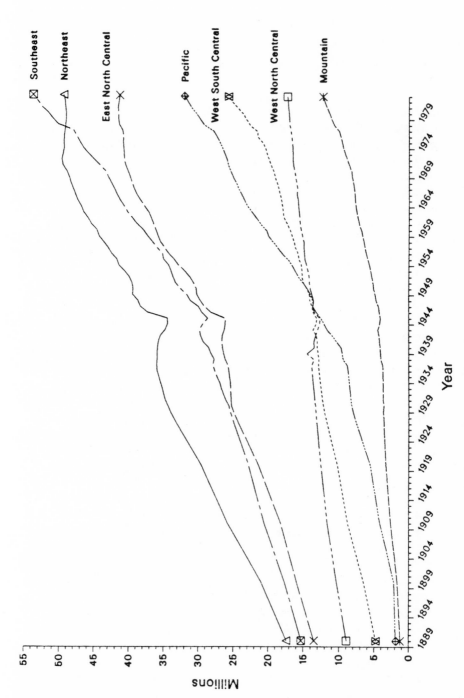

Figure 5-11 Regional Population.

The evidence on the regional distribution of population supports these findings and provides additional insights on the Heartland-Sunbelt shift (see Figure 5–12). Two periods can be easily distinguished: the pre-1950s years, corresponding with the third historical stage of the conceptual framework, and the 1950s and beyond. The decline in the Southeastern and West North Central regions' shares is conspicuous during the prewar decades, undoubtedly as a result of the substantial out-migration that occurred through the restructuring of agriculture. The Northeastern and East North Central regions' stagnant shares during this period are also significant, inasmuch as they are a prelude to the Heartland's decline over the postwar era.

The post-1940s decades then mirror the Heartland-Sunbelt shift so obvious in most of the analyses of this chapter. Significant decline sets in for the Northeastern and East North Central regions' shares, while all of the Sunbelt regions' shares increase. The West North Central remains the only Hinterland region to experience decline. This is very much a product of both the impact of agricultural restructuring on this highly specialized region, and its relatively lower comparative advantages vis-à-vis the Sunbelt regions. Of the most dynamic regions, the Pacific grew fastest, fueled primarily by California's expanding metropolises. The Southeast presents a significant turnaround that contrasts with the prewar years' experiencing an increase that surpasses the Northeast's absolute share.

The postwar era has therefore witnessed one of the most remarkable shifts in America's regional population distribution. As the sectoral growth leadership shifted to the services sector, population redistribution toward the Sunbelt regions became inescapable. In this context, the Pacific became the most dynamic region, while the Southeast experienced a remarkable turnaround from the prewar decades, achieving the largest share of national population by the late 1970s.

Urban Dimensions of Regional Change

Urban population change is the most important component of regional population redistribution. This is especially significant in an economy where first manufacturing, and then services assume the sectoral leadership. Both of these sectors are urban-oriented, though in different ways, as we saw in the previous chapter, and we can expect them to influence the regional distribution of urban population substantially.

We can distinguish two major periods in the regional distribution of urban population (see Figure 5–13). During the decades preceding the 1940s, the Northeast's urban population is by far the largest, rising rapidly up to 1930, followed by the East North Central's. This

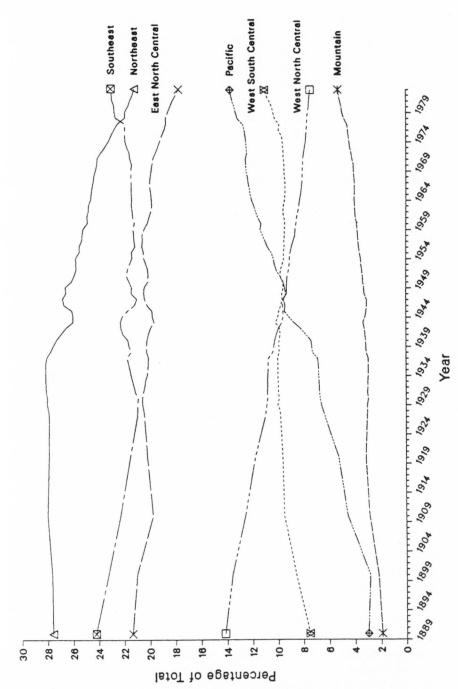

Figure 5-12 Regional Population Distribution.

dominance is very much a product of the urbanization of these two Heartland regions during the nineteenth century. The Heartland's urbanization was greatly influenced by the leading position of manufacturing, and its urban orientation, which promoted the concentration of population in that region's largest urban areas.

During this period, the Pacific region's urban population converges with, and surpasses, the West North Central's. A similar tendency occurs with respect to the West South Central region's, although its urban population will not surpass the West North Central's until the late 1940s. The brief hiatus of the 1930s shows the impact of the Depression on urban population growth. Substantial slowdowns in the Heartland's urban population trends reflect the lack of employment opportunities that discourage further concentration.

After the 1930s, several shifts once again point to the changes favoring the Sunbelt regions. These shifts are less conspicuous than those occurring with the total regional population estimates. The Northeast, for one, retains the lead in total urban population, although its trend levels off after the 1960s. Similarly, the East North Central region's trend stops growing and declines slightly at approximately the same time. More significant is the fact that the Southeast, for many decades considered a primarily rural region, surpasses the East North Central in total urban population by the late 1970s. The Pacific region's rapid urban growth is another significant development of this period, converging toward the East North Central's level, and raising the likely possibility that the Sunbelt regions may occupy two of the top three ranks in total urban population by 1990.

Changes in the urban-rural population balance add more perspective to the Heartland-Hinterland shift observed in the previous analyses. In Table 5-11, we can see that the Hinterland's urban population increases faster than the Heartland's throughout the full period of this analysis. This is hardly surprising, given the Hinterland's later settlement and demographic expansion. By the late nineteenth century, furthermore, much of the Heartland, and particularly the Northeast, was already highly urbanized.

Shifts in the Heartland-Hinterland rural population's growth reflect greater complexity. The Hinterland's rural population grew faster during 1890–1930, primarily because of the Western and West South Central regions' agricultural development. This pattern was pretty well changed after the 1930s by the restructuring of the agricultural sector and the need to increase productivity, which affected the Hinterland much later than the Heartland regions. As we saw in the analyses of the previous chapter, agriculture's least favored status in the sectoral hierarchy was the major force behind this effort. This caused a substantial reduction of agricultural labor demand in the

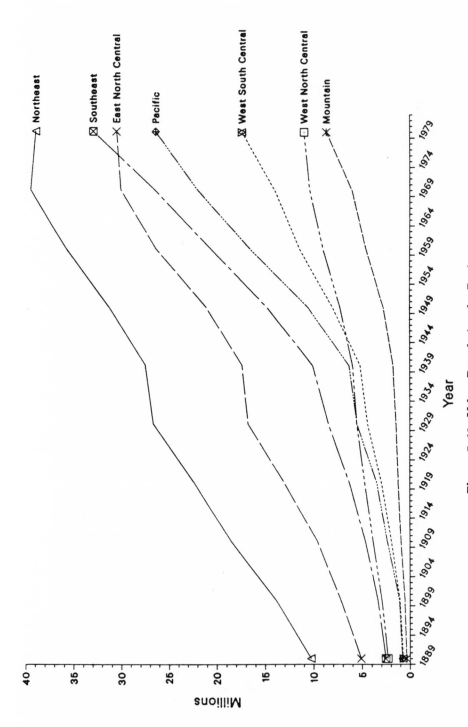

Figure 5-13 Urban Population, by Region.

Table 5-11 Population: Growth Rates by Region.

Interval	Northeast urban	Northeast rural	East North Central urban	East North Central rural	West North Central urban	West North Central rural	Southeast urban	Southeast rural	West South Central urban	West South Central rural	Mountain urban	Mountain rural	Pacific urban	Pacific rural	Heartland urban	Heartland rural	Hinterland urban	Hinterland rural
1890–1910	80.8 (4.0)	2.3 (0.1)	88.2 (4.4)	3.2 (0.2)	67.5 (3.4)	17.3 (0.9)	83.4 (4.2)	25.4 (1.3)	173.3 (8.7)	69.6 (3.5)	165.9 (8.3)	97.0 (4.8)	196.1 (9.8)	67.2 (3.4)	83.3 (4.2)	2.8 (0.1)	105.3 (5.3)	34.4 (1.7)
1910–20	20.7 (2.1)	-0.7 (-0.1)	35.7 (3.6)	-2.4 (-0.2)	22.2 (2.2)	0.6 (0.1)	35.7 (3.6)	3.8 (0.4)	51.7 (5.2)	6.5 (0.6)	29.0 (2.9)	25.3 (2.5)	45.3 (4.5)	16.3 (1.6)	25.8 (2.6)	-1.6 (-0.2)	35.4 (3.5)	5.4 (0.5)
1920–30	19.2 (1.9)	6.4 (0.6)	28.7 (2.9)	0.9 (0.1)	17.6 (1.8)	-1.0 (-0.1)	33.9 (3.4)	3.9 (0.4)	49.1 (4.9)	6.5 (0.6)	19.7 (2.0)	6.1 (0.6)	60.0 (6.0)	26.2 (2.6)	22.7 (2.3)	3.4 (0.3)	36.1 (3.6)	4.8 (0.5)
1930–40	3.2 (0.3)	8.9 (1.0)	3.9 (0.4)	8.0 (0.8)	7.9 (0.8)	-2.8 (-0.3)	19.0 (1.9)	7.6 (0.8)	17.5 (1.8)	1.4 (0.1)	21.5 (2.2)	5.9 (0.6)	14.8 (1.5)	27.0 (2.7)	3.5 (0.4)	8.4 (0.8)	15.5 (1.6)	5.5 (0.6)
1940–50	13.8 (1.4)	-3.6 (-0.4)	21.4 (2.1)	0.3 (0.03)	21.9 (2.2)	-10.2 (-1.0)	47.5 (4.8)	-3.9 (-0.4)	55.3 (5.5)	-17.8 (-1.8)	57.3 (5.7)	-3.7 (-0.4)	70.9 (7.1)	7.3 (0.7)	16.8 (1.7)	-1.5 (-0.2)	49.3 (4.9)	-6.9 (-0.7)
1950–60	14.2 (1.4)	9.0 (0.9)	24.8 (2.5)	6.3 (0.6)	23.8 (2.4)	-6.1 (-0.6)	39.0 (3.9)	-2.5 (-0.2)	42.0 (4.2)	-15.3 (-1.5)	65.1 (6.5)	-1.5 (-0.2)	53.0 (5.3)	2.7 (0.3)	18.5 (1.9)	7.6 (0.8)	42.2 (4.2)	-4.8 (-0.5)
1960–70	10.1 (1.0)	8.5 (0.8)	13.8 (1.4)	3.8 (0.4)	14.8 (1.5)	-6.5 (-0.6)	28.2 (2.8)	-2.2 (-0.2)	22.2 (2.2)	-3.3 (-0.3)	31.6 (3.2)	-1.3 (-0.1)	32.5 (3.2)	-6.2 (-0.6)	11.5 (1.2)	6.0 (0.6)	26.5 (2.6)	-3.5 (-0.4)
1970–80	-1.4 (-0.1)	6.6 (0.7)	1.5 (0.2)	9.7 (1.0)	5.7 (0.6)	4.5 (0.4)	24.4 (2.4)	9.9 (1.0)	24.3 (2.4)	19.3 (1.9)	43.4 (4.3)	20.7 (2.1)	20.1 (2.0)	14.5 (1.4)	-0.1 (-0.01)	8.2 (0.8)	22.2 (2.2)	10.6 (1.1)
1890–1920	118.2 (3.9)	1.6 (0.05)	155.4 (5.2)	0.7 (0.02)	104.7 (3.5)	18.0 (0.6)	148.9 (5.0)	29.9 (1.0)	314.7 (10.5)	80.7 (2.7)	243.1 (8.1)	146.7 (4.9)	330.3 (11.0)	94.6 (3.2)	130.6 (4.4)	1.1 (0.04)	178.0 (5.9)	41.6 (1.4)
1950–70	25.7 (1.3)	18.3 (0.9)	42.0 (2.1)	10.3 (0.5)	42.2 (2.1)	-12.2 (-0.6)	78.2 (3.9)	-4.6 (-0.2)	73.6 (3.7)	-18.0 (-0.9)	117.2 (5.9)	-2.8 (-0.1)	102.7 (5.1)	-3.6 (-0.2)	32.3 (1.6)	14.0 (0.7)	79.9 (4.0)	-8.1 (-0.4)

Annual averages in parentheses. See Appendix for data sources and details.

163

Hinterland's traditional agricultural regions, with the exception of the Pacific. The agricultural troubles of the West South Central and West North Central regions during the 1920s and 1930s, and the Depression years, also had an impact in reducing the Hinterland's rural population growth.

In this context, the reversal of the 1970s, when the Hinterland's rural population once again grew faster than the Heartland's, may seem surprising. This shift was obviously much connected with the metropolitan slowdown of this decade, although most of this period's rural population growth actually occurred within relatively close proximity to the major metropolitan areas. Thus, much of the observed rural growth of this decade may be due to a classification problem, as the delimitation of the metropolitan boundaries failed to keep up with suburbanization and peripheral urban and metropolitan growth.

The shifting regional fortunes in urban population growth are vividly illustrated by the trends in Figure 5–14. Most significant is the trend shown by the Northeast, which attains its maximum share by 1930, and begins a sustained decline throughout most of the subsequent years. The East North Central trend's leveling by the 1960s and its subsequent decline also mirror this pattern, sealing what may well be the Heartland's accelerated long-term decline in total urban population shares. Of all the Hinterland's regions, only the West North Central maintains a level performance throughout, again reflecting this region's high degree of specialization in agriculture and its relatively lower comparative advantages vis-à-vis the Sunbelt regions. In contrast, the Southeastern and Pacific urban population shares take off after the 1930s, followed by the West South Central's. These trends confirm the marked shift of the post–World War II era toward the Sunbelt regions, and the importance of sustained urbanization in regional population redistribution.

SECTORAL RESTRUCTURING AND THE REGIONS

The Less Favored Sectors

The long-term shifts occurring in the sectoral hierarchy, as a sector becomes less favored while another rises to the growth leadership position, are the most important source of regional change. If we recall the analyses of the previous chapter, and those of the preceding sections, it is obvious that the shift from manufacturing to services in the third historical stage and the preponderance of services in the fourth have promoted some of the most remarkable changes ever to occur in America's space-economy.

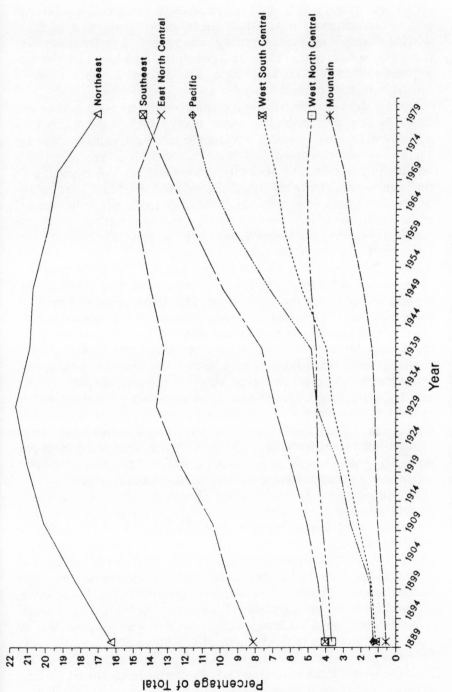

Figure 5-14 Urban Population Distribution, by Region.

In much the same way as the spatial orientation of a new frontier sector determines where employment growth will occur, less favored sectors can influence substantially the long-term patterns of regional decline. Agriculture's restructuring thus promoted major changes in the highly specialized, traditional agricultural regions. Then, the subsequent shift from manufacturing to services was a major source of spatial industrial diffusion away from the Heartland's regions.

Employment growth, a major indicator of sectoral performance, can therefore be expected to slow down or even decline in regions with substantial concentrations of less favored sector activities. Such changes, as has been discussed before, are due to the less favored sector's relatively lower income elasticity of demand, as the population's preferences value more highly other goods and activities. The application of the various entrepreneurial roles then ensures that the sectoral shifts needed to satisfy the new wants occur, while at the same time restructuring the less favored sectors to increase their productive efficiency and competitiveness.

The less favored sectors are not all equally disadvantaged. For example, agriculture has been least favored in the sectoral hierarchy, especially during the postwar period. This status promoted both the most substantial increases in productivity, and the most dramatic employment slowdowns and decline of any economic activity. At the same time, its least favored position produced the lowest sectoral contribution to national income. Manufacturing shifted to less favored status during the third historical stage, in the early decades of this century, as it gradually began to lose the long-term growth leadership to services. Distribution, a less favored sector, performed better than agriculture.[14] This trend was, to a great extent, influenced by its linkages with manufacturing, especially in commerce and transportation.

In many of the spatial stages conceptualizations developed since the eighteenth century, agriculture was always the sector whose initial growth allowed other economic activities to develop and become predominant in the sectoral economic hierarchy.[15] In the evolution of the American economy, farming has been very important, given its crucial role in frontier settlement and hinterland development. The spatial orientation of farming contrasts with that of all the other sectors, primarily because the location of manufacturing, distributive, and service activities is greatly influenced by population agglomeration. The location of farming, in contrast, is influenced more by soil conditions, physiographic characteristics, and accessibility.

The regional summaries in Table 5–12 provide a synthesis of the most important shifts occurring in American farming. The Hinterland shows faster growth rates during the third historical stage (1889–

1950), in both absolute and standardized Value of Farm Products, and in employment, in the majority of the time intervals. For both the absolute and standardized Value of Farm Product variables, higher Hinterland performances occur in four out of five intervals, and in two out of three abbreviated time periods (excluding World War II and late 1940s, bottom portion of Table 5–12). Faster Hinterland employment growth rates also occur in three out of four intervals in the upper portion of Table 5–12, and in both of the abbreviated periods in the bottom portion.

Productivity growth can be expected initially to favor the Heartland during the third stage, primarily because the pressures to increase farming efficiency would be felt first in that region. It was in the Heartland where the shift in the growth leadership from agriculture to manufacturing would first promote employment reallocation from the rural-based farming activities to urban-based industry. At the same time, faster learning and application of innovative techniques and machinery could be expected to occur there earlier, following the usual spatial diffusion patterns from advanced to less developed regions.

The regional summaries in Table 5–12 confirm these assumptions for the first interval (1889–1900). Subsequently, productivity (Value of Farm Products per Employee) increases faster in the Hinterland, as more effective farming techniques were diffused and adopted there. At the same time, the possibilities for substantial additional land-intensive cultivation were pretty well limited by the turn of the century. Thus, after 1900, in all intervals corresponding to the third stage (up to 1950), the Hinterland's productivity rises faster.

The application of better farming techniques could be expected to promote a faster increase of total output (Value of Farm Products) in the Hinterland during the fourth historical stage (post-1940s). The regional summary of Table 5–12 confirms these assumptions in four out of five intervals since 1950. The only exception is the 1978–82 interval, when the Heartland achieves significantly faster growth rates. Less consistency is then found for the standardized output indicator, and for farm employment and productivity For the standardized output summary, the intervals are evenly split between the Heartland and Hinterland. The Heartland is favored from 1969–82, partly a result of this region's slower population growth. Conversely, the Hinterland's rapid population increase tends to reduce the standardized indicator substantially. We can easily observe this change by comparing the standardized and absolute output summaries.

Farm employment change favors the Heartland and Hinterland in one interval each, while in two others both regions grow equally fast. Similarly, the productivity indicator favors the Hinterland in two out

Table 5-12 Agriculture: Growth Rates, Regional Magnitude Sequences.

Interval	Value of Farm Products	Per Employee Value of Farm Products	Per Capita Value of Farm Products	Farm Employment
1889–1900	B > A (M, WSC, WNC)	A > B (M, WNC, ENC)	B > A (M, SE, WNC)	B > A (M, WSC, P)
1900–30	B > A (M, P, WSC)	—	B > A (M, WSC, WNC)	—
1930–40	A > B (ENC, NE, P)	—	A > B (ENC, NE, WNC)	—
1900–40	—	B > A (WSC, P, M)	—	B > A (M, P, WSC)
1940–45	B > A (P, WNC, SE)	B > A (SE, P, WSC)	B > A (WNC, SE, M)	A > B (P, WNC, M)
1945–50	B > A (WSC, M, WNC)	B > A (WSC, M, NE = ENC)	B > A (WSC, WNC, M)	B > A (WNC, ENC, P)
1950–59	B > A (P, SE, M)	B > A (SE, M, WNC)	B > A (SE, WNC, P)	A > B (P, ENC, M)
1959–69	B > A (M, WNC, WSC)	B > A (SE, WSC, ENC)	B > A (WNC, WSC, M)	B > A (M, P, WNC)
1969–78	B > A (WSC, P, WNC = NE)	A = B (WSC, WNC, NE)	A > B (NE, WNC, ENC)	A = B (P, SE, M = ENC)
1978–82	A > B (P, NE = ENC, M)	A > B (WNC, ENC, WSC)	A > B (ENC = NE, P, WNC)	A = B (P, SE, M)
1889–1900	B > A (M, WSC, WNC)	A > B (M, WNC, ENC)	B > A (M, SE, WNC)	B > A (M, WSC, P)
1900–30+	B > A (M, P, WSC)	B > A (WSC, P, M)	B > A (M, WSC, WNC)	B > A (M, P, WSC)
1930–40	A > B (ENC, NE, P)	—	A > B (ENC, NE, WNC)	—
1945–69	B > A (M, WSC, WNC)	B > A (SE, WSC, M)	B > A (WNC, WSC, M)	B > A (P, M, WNC)
1969–82	A > B (P, NE, ENC)	A > B (WSC, WNC, NE)	A > B (NE, ENC, WNC)	A = B (P, SE, M)

+1900–40 for farm employment and value of farm products per employee.

A: Heartland, B: Hinterland. Parentheses: first, second, third ranking regions.
NE: Northeast, ENC: East North Central, WNC: West North Central, SE: Southeast, WSC: West South Central, M: Mountain, P: Pacific.

of four intervals, and the Heartland in one, with both regions being virtually even over the 1969–78 interval. Generally, over the 1970s and early 1980s, the balance with these two indicators shifts in favor of the Heartland. Insofar as productivity is concerned, this shift may be partly due to the wider diffusion of better techniques, through better access to information and technology, which tended to even out the differences between these two regions. This assumption is supported by the fact that the employment decline rate, the most important sign of increasing productivity in farming, is virtually even for both regions from 1969–82.

Manufacturing, a less favored sector since the middle of the third historical stage (the 1920s), can be expected to favor the Hinterland in output and employment growth throughout the third and fourth stages. In regard to productivity, this sector may be expected to favor the Heartland during the third stage, as the impact of a less favored position in the sectoral hierarchy could be expected to be felt there first. The Hinterland's growth leadership in manufacturing can, on the other hand, be explained by the "new lease on life" that lower production costs and greater spatial market shares could bring to some industries. To some extent, the Hinterland's significantly lower level of development during the third and part of the fourth stages could also be expected to favor industrial goods, mainly consumer durables and nondurables.

The industrialization of America's hinterland can then be attributed initially to the establishment of market-oriented industries by local and regional entrepreneurs, and to branch plant creation by national and regional corporations. In some cases, the growth of natural resource industries, such as oil refining in the Southwest, had much impact on regional industrial growth. During the post–World War II era, acquisitions and mergers also influenced industrial growth in the Hinterland's Sunbelt regions, as they promoted additional investment by Heartland and foreign enterprises. After the 1960s, the growth of new "high technology" industries indigenous to this region, such as electronics and computers, became a major force behind industrial expansion.

The regional summaries in Table 5–13 provide a synthesis of the industrial shifts occurring in America's space-economy over the third and fourth historical stages. Over the third stage, growth in the absolute output indicator (Value Added) favors the Hinterland in five out of six intervals, excluding World War II, and in all the abbreviated periods.[16] The standardized output indicator (Value Added per Capita) also favors the Hinterland in four out of six intervals (World War II excluded), and in all three abbreviated periods. Thus, the Hinterland's industrial expansion was sufficiently strong during this

Table 5-13 Manufacturing: Growth Rates, Regional Magnitude Sequences.

Interval	Value Added	Per Employee Value Added	Per Capita Value Added	Employment
1889–1909+	B > A (M, WSC, P)	B > A (M, SE, WNC)	B > A (SE, WSC, M)	B > A (WSC, P, SE)
1909–19+	A > B (P, ENC, WSC)	A > B (P, ENC, NE)	A > B (ENC = P, SE, WSC)	B > A (P = WSC, ENC, SE)
1919–29+	B > A (P, ENC, SE)	A > B (WNC, ENC, NE)	B > A (WNC, ENC, WSC)	B > A (P, WSC, SE)
1929–35	B > A (SE, ENC, WSC)	—	A = B (SE = ENC, WSC, WNC = NE)	—
1935–39	B > A (WSC, P, SE)	—	B > A (WSC, SE, WNC)	—
1929–39+	—	B > A (M, WSC, SE)	—	A > B (SE, ENC, NE)
1939–47	B > A (WSC, P, SE)	B > A (WSC, WNC, SE)	B > A (WSC, SE, WNC)	A > B (P, ENC, WNC)
1947–50	B > A (P = WSC = ENC, WNC, M)	A > B (ENC, WNC, WSC)	B > A (ENC = WNC, WSC, P)	B > A (M, P, WSC)
1950–60	B > A (M, P, WSC)	B > A (WSC, WNC, SE)	B > A (WSC, M, P)	B > A (M, P, WSC)
1960–69	B > A (WSC, SE, M)	A > B (NE, P, SE)	B > A (WSC, SE, WNC)	B > A (WSC, SE, M)
1969–80	B > A (M, WSC, P)	B > A (WSC, WNC, SE)	B > A (WSC, M, WNC)	B > A (M, WSC, P)
1980–82	B > A (P, SE, WSC = M)	B > A (WNC, P, SE)	B > A (WNC, P, SE)	B > A (WSC, M, P)
1889–1919	B > A (WSC, P, M)	B > A (M, P, SE)	B > A (SE, WSC, ENC)	B > A (WSC, P, ENC)
1919–29+	B > A (P, ENC, SE)	A > B (WNC, ENC, NE)	B > A (WNC, ENC, WSC)	B > A (P, WSC, SE)
1935–39	B > A (WSC, P = SE, M)	—	B > A (WSC, SE, WNC)	—
1947–69	B > A (M, WSC, P)	B > A (WSC, WNC, ENC)	B > A (WSC, WNC, SE)	B > A (M, P, WSC)
1969–82	B > A (M, WSC, P)	B > A (WNC, WSC, SE)	B > A (WSC, WNC, M)	B > A (M, WSC, P)

+1889–1910, 1910–20, 1920–30, 1930–39 for employment estimates.

A: Heartland, B: Hinterland. Parentheses: first, second, third ranking regions.
NE: Northeast, ENC: East North Central, WNC: West North Central, SE: Southeast, WSC: West South Central, M: Mountain, P: Pacific.

stage to withstand the impact of population growth on the standardized indicator.

The correspondence between the Hinterland's faster output and employment growth during the third historical stage confirms all the previous assumptions in the relationship between these two indicators.[17] Faster employment growth favors the Hinterland in four out of five intervals, excluding World War II. The productivity indicator (Value Added per Employee) then favors the Heartland, as expected, in three out of five intervals. Thus, the contrast between Heartland and Hinterland industry, promoted by differences in the spatial economic context between these two regions, and the spatial diffusion of manufacturing know-how, is borne out by the productivity indicator.[18]

Over the fourth historical stage, the industrialization of the Hinterland intensifies, because of the rapidly expanding consumer markets. This growth is greatly promoted by the redistribution of population toward the Sunbelt regions, and the importance of services as the growth leader in the sectoral hierarchy Other important factors helping this process are the lower production costs and taxes offered by many Hinterland locations, especially industries.

Both the absolute and standardized output growth indicators favor the Hinterland in all intervals. Similarly, employment growth favors the Hinterland in all periods, thereby confirming once again the relationship assumed for output and employment growth. The productivity indicator shows faster Hinterland growth in three out of four intervals, and in all the abbreviated periods (bottom portion, Table 5–13). The latter can be explained primarily in terms of the Hinterland's changing industrial mix, where newer industries using more advanced technology and organization help turn this indicator in its favor.

Despite its less favored position, the distributive sector's activities are essential for trade in manufactured goods and agriculture, both at the wholesale and retail levels. Transportation and the generation of utilities are very important to all economic sectors, and especially the urban-oriented, such as services and manufacturing. Given the obviously strong relationship between distribution and population size, growth in distributive sector activities—particularly in such market-linked activities as wholesale and retail trade—can be expected to favor the Hinterland.

Over the third historical stage, the regional summaries for distributive employment growth, in Table 5–14, favor the Hinterland in all intervals, as expected. Similarly, the partial coverage for total sales in wholesale and retail trade favors the Hinterland in all time periods (1929–50), while the standardized indicator (Sales per Capita) supports this outcome in two out of three intervals. Over the fourth historical stage, the Hinterland is favored in all intervals in distributive employment, and in the absolute and standardized commercial sales indicators. The temporal evidence on the regional performance of this sector, limited as it may be, therefore overwhelmingly supports the conceptual assumptions.

The New Source of Regional Change

The shift toward services has made this sector the most important source of long-term regional change over the fourth and much of the third historical stages. The rise of services to the growth leadership position became firmly established after World War II. Since then, its expansion has been much associated with Hinterland, and especially Sunbelt, growth and development. As we saw in previous analyses, the expansion of services also promoted an unprecedented redistribution of population away from the nation's Heartland regions.

The regional summaries in Table 5–15 confirm the relationship between services and Hinterland growth. Over the third historical stage (starting in 1910), total services grew fastest in the Hinterland in three out of four intervals. In all cases, the fastest growing regions were part of the Sunbelt (Pacific, Southeast, Mountain). The summaries for nongovernmental services are divided, favoring the Heartland over the first two intervals (1889–1920), and the Hinterland over the following two periods (1920–40).[19] Still, the shift to the Hinterland is clear for both total and nongovernmental services' employment growth. This shift occurs after the 1910s in both indicators, and remains unchanged throughout the full period of analysis, up to 1983. It is revealing that, even when the Heartland was favored in nongovernmental services' employment, from 1889–1920, a Hinterland region (Pacific) grew fastest throughout that period.

Over the fourth historical stage, the Hinterland is favored in all intervals in both total and nongovernmental services employment. In both of these indicators, the regional leadership shifted among several Sunbelt regions (Mountain, Pacific, Southeast). The Mountain region's fastest growth in two intervals (1950s and 1970s) is partly due to its generally lower initial baseline figures, which tend to promote faster growth. Nevertheless, in both of the intervals where this region experienced fastest growth, the second fastest growing regions were also part of the Sunbelt (Pacific, Southeast, West South Central).

To a great extent, the services sector's enormous impact on America's space-economy has occurred because virtually all of its activities are traditional central place functions. Among these, health-

Table 5–14 Distributive Sector: Growth Rates, Regional Magnitude Sequences.

Interval	Wholesale and Retail Commerce Total Sales	Wholesale and Retail Commerce Per Capita Sales	Distributive Sector Total Employment
1889–1910	—	—	B > A (WSC, P, M)
1910–20	—	—	B > A (WSC, SE, ENC)
1920–30	—	—	B > A (P, WSC, ENC)
1930–40	—	—	B > A (M , P, SE)
1929–35	B > A (SE, P, M)	B > A (M, SE, P)	—
1935–39	B > A (P = SE, WSC, M)	A > B (WSC, SE, NE)	—
1940–50+	B > A (WSC, SE, M)	B > A (WNC, WSC, SE)	B > A (P, WSC, SE)
1950–60+	B > A (P, M, WSC, SE)	B > A (WSC, SE, M)	B > A (P, M, SE)
1960–70+	B > A (SE, M, WSC)	B > A (SE, WSC, M)	B > A (SE, P, M)
1970–80+	B > A (WSC, M, P)	B > A (WSC, WNC, ENC)	B > A (M, WSC, SE)
1980–83+	B > A (WSC, M, P)	B > A (NE, WSC, WNC)	B > A (WSC, SE, M)
1889–1920	—	—	B > A (WSC, P, M)
1920–30	—	—	B > A (P, WSC, ENC)
1935–39	B > A (P = SE, WSC, M)	A > B (WSC, SE, NE)	
1950–70+	B > A (M = SE, P, WSC)	B > A (SE, WSC, M)	B > A (P, M, SE)
1970–83+	B > A (WSC, M, P)	B > A (WSC, NE, WNC)	B > A (M, WSC, SE)

+1939–48, 1948–58, 1958–72, 1972–77, 1977–82 for Wholesale and Retail total and per capita sales.

A: Heartland, B: Hinterland. Parentheses: first, second, third ranking regions.
NE: Northeast, ENC: East North Central, WNC: West North Central, SE: Southeast, WSC: West South Central,
M: Mountain, P: Pacific.

Table 5–15 Services: Growth Rates, Regional Magnitude Sequences.

Interval	Services Employment	Services excluding Government Employment
1889-1910	—	A > B (P, WSC, NE)
1910-20	A > B (P, WSC, ENC)	A > B (P, ENC, WSC)
1920-30	B > A (P, WSC, ENC)	B > A (P, WSC, ENC)
1930-40	B > A (SE, WSC, P)	B > A (SE, WSC, P)
1940-50	B > A (M, P, ENC)	—
1950-60	B > A (M, P, SE)	B > A (M, SE, P)
1960-70	B > A (P, M, WSC)	B > A (P, WSC, M)
1970-80	B > A (M, WSC, P)	B > A (M, WSC, P)
1980-83	B > A (SE, M, WSC)	B > A (SE, M, WSC)
1889-1920	—	A > B (P, WSC, NE)
1920-30+	A > B (P, WSC, ENC)	B > A (P, WSC, ENC)
1950-70	B > A (M, P, SE)	B > A (M, P, SE)
1970-83	B > A (M, WSC, SE)	B > A (M, WSC, SE)

+1910-30 for Services total.

A: Heartland, B: Hinterland. Parentheses: first, second, third ranking regions.
NE: Northeast, ENC: East North Central, WNC: West North Central, SE: Southeast,
WSC: West South Central, M: Mountain, P: Pacific.

related activities have experienced enormous growth over the post–World War II decades, along with financial, real estate, insurance, and information-gathering and -processing services. Most of the growth of these activities has occurred in the Sunbelt's metropolitan areas, and especially in its most dynamic megalopolises in Southern and Northern California, Colorado, Texas, and Florida. The continuing expansion of services promises to turn several of the Sunbelt's regions into the nation's most urbanized, surpassing the levels of metropolitan agglomeration found in the Heartland regions.

Population Impacts of Sectoral Restructuring

As one of the most important outcomes of sectoral restructuring, spatial population redistribution has had profound effects on American society. Long-term sectoral changes have affected the regional, rural-urban, and the overall balance of population distribution among different urban sizes. In the analyses of the previous sections, population shifts were found to follow closely major changes in the sectoral growth hierarchy.

The shift of the sectoral leadership from agriculture to urban-based manufacturing never had its full potential impact on rural-urban migration in America. It was very much tempered by the pace of frontier development, which encouraged substantial migration to rural areas in the West and Southwest. Nevertheless, the shift from agriculture to manufacturing promoted the rapid growth of the largest cities in the urban hierarchy. These places were predictably in the nation's most rapidly industrializing regions, the Northeast, and subsequently the Midwest. In this respect, a peculiar aspect of America's development was the fact that, because of frontier growth, the Hinterland (West, Southwest) was also experiencing rapid rural population growth concurrently with this phenomenon.

The subsequent shift in the sectoral leadership from manufacturing to services would then promote an unprecedented redistribution of population within the nation's urban hierarchy. Most service sector activities, being traditional central place functions, would encourage employment and population growth in medium- and small-sized urban places. This trend would promote the redistribution of population away from the nation's most urbanized regions, toward the Hinterland's urban areas, where the vast majority of cities in that segment of the hierarchy would be found.

Initially, during the third historical stage, faster rural population growth could be expected in some regions of the Hinterland, partly as a legacy of late frontier settlement, and of more land- and labor-intensive farming. Thus, the Hinterland would very likely experience faster rural growth over the first decades of this century. This would be substantially diminished as Hinterland agriculture, faced with the need to increase productivity, reduces its manpower needs. At the same time, the urbanization of the Hinterland would attract much rural population to better employment opportunities.

Over the fourth historical stage, as the Hinterland's urbanization progressed, the Heartland might be favored with faster rural growth, because of the Hinterland's rapid rate of rural-urban migration as agriculture became more productive, and better employment opportunities became available in the cities. Also, in the Heartland regions, the shift to services redistributed population from the larger and older metropolitan areas to the adjacent rural peripheries. Advances in urban transportation and communications would make this a viable possibility for many households. This phenomenon would be very much a part of the process of suburbanization that has affected American cities throughout the post–World War II era.

The regional summaries for urban and rural population growth in Table 5–16 provide insights and evidence on these shifts. Urban population grew fastest in the Hinterland's Sunbelt regions over the third and fourth historical stages, in all intervals. Initially, this occurred in part because of late frontier settlement in such regions as the Pacific, Mountain, and West South Central, and their low urban population baseline figures in the early years of the third stage. It is therefore predictable that the Western regions (Pacific, Mountain) should experience fastest growth in almost all the intervals. The West South Central region grows fastest in one interval, and is the second fastest growing region in three other periods. The Southeastern region also shows strong growth, especially from 1910 to 1940 and from 1960 to 1980.

The summaries of rural population growth show the Hinterland's Sunbelt regions growing fastest from 1890 to 1930. Again, late frontier

Table 5–16 Urban and Rural Population: Growth Rates, Regional Magnitude Sequences.

Interval	Urban	Rural
1890–1910	B > A (P, WSC, M)	B > A (M, WSC, P)
1910–20	B > A (WSC, P, SE = ENC)	B > A (M, P, WSC)
1920–30	B > A (P, WSC, SE)	B > A (P, WSC = NE, M)
1930–40	B > A (M, SE, WSC)	A > B (P, NE, ENC)
1940–50	B > A (P, M, WSC)	A > B (P, ENC, NE = M)
1950–60	B > A (M, P, WSC)	A > B (NE, ENC, P)
1960–70	B > A (P, M, SE)	A > B (NE, ENC, M)
1970–80	B > A (M, WSC = SE, P)	B > A (M, WSC, P)
1890–1920	B > A (P, WSC, M)	B > A (M, P, WSC)
1950–70	B > A (M, P, SE)	A > B (NE, ENC, M)

A: Heartland, B: Hinterland. Parentheses: first, second, third ranking regions.
NE: Northeast, ENC: East North Central, WNC: West North Central, SE: Southeast, WSC: West South Central, M: Mountain, P: Pacific.

settlement and the delayed impact of agricultural productivity promoted faster rural population growth in these regions. An interesting shift favoring faster Heartland growth then occurs after 1930, lasting through the 1970s. As was discussed before, rural-urban and interregional out-migration in some of the Hinterland's regions, such as the Southeast, West North Central, and West South Central, was the prime cause of this shift. The reduction in the Hinterland's rural population was also aided by the metropolitan deconcentration that occurred in many Heartland metropolitan areas.

It is revealing, nevertheless, that in two of the four periods during which the Heartland experienced fastest rural population increase (1930–40, 1940–50), a Hinterland region (Pacific) grew most rapidly. The shift over the 1970s, favoring the Hinterland once again, is symbolic of the regional impact of the "metropolitan turnaround." Growth in areas adjacent, or reasonably close, to the major Sunbelt metropolises was the most important force behind the Hinterland's performance during this period.

SUMMARY AND CONCLUSIONS

This chapter has analyzed the long-term regional changes promoted by sectoral restructurings in farming, manufacturing, distribution, and services. Evaluating the interplay and regional impacts of changes in output, employment, and productivity in two less favored sectors, farming and manufacturing, has been an important component of this chapter. Additionally, more limited analyses on total and nongovernmental services, distribution, and commerce, have provided insights on the expansion and comparative regional performances of these sectors.

As with the national analysis of the previous chapter, the conceptual assumptions on the regional impacts of sectoral restructuring are verified in the vast majority of the time intervals that were examined. These analyses also reveal the enormous impact of sectoral restructuring on spatial population redistribution, including urban and rural population growth and decline. The analysis of population over the third and fourth historical stages, in fact, reveals the unprecedented rise and level of urbanization in the nation's Sunbelt regions. For population and the economic sectors, a marked shift favoring these regions also becomes quite obvious.

Increasing productivity becomes the most significant tendency in farming, with substantial impacts on regional agricultural employment and population redistribution. The latter occurs initially through both rural-urban migration in, and interregional out-migration from, various Hinterland regions, such as the Southeastern, Southwestern, and Plains regions. To a great extent, the restructuring of farming has relied much on productive coordination. This has involved the implementation of new farming techniques and organization through, for example, mechanization, the application of advanced chemicals and fertilizers, improvements in harvesting and seeding routines, and advances in overall farm management.

Manufacturing begins to experience major productivity increases as it is supplanted from the growth leadership position in the third historical stage. This trend is, however, more typical of the Heartland regions, where reliance on productive coordination is greatest. Productivity increases are thus achieved through better organization, including the rationalization of tasks, cutbacks on less necessary labor, and automation.

Although the growth of manufacturing initially promoted the concentration of population in the largest Heartland cities, the subsequent spatial diffusion of industries overwhelmingly favors the Hinterland's Sunbelt regions. The comparative advantages of these regions provide lower production costs and taxes, and larger market shares, and have been aided by substantial advances in communications and transportation technology. To a great extent, the spatial diffusion to the Hinterland's Sunbelt therefore provided many older industries with a new "lease on life," where substantial expansion could occur. At the same time, the rise of new "high technology" industries, indigenous to the Sunbelt, has promoted substantial expansion in some states. Thus, industrial stagnation and decline in America have been primarily a regional problem, confined mostly to the Heartland's regions.

As in any growing economic activity, industrial expansion in the Hinterland's Sunbelt regions, through the establishment of new industries, branch plants, or corporate mergers, has relied substantially on strategic planning and investment. These roles and, to some extent, intermarket linkage, are essential in determining market strategies, in marshaling the necessary financial resources, and in developing and coordinating new sources of inputs. The contrasts between the Heartland and Hinterland regions in manufacturing are therefore also reflected in the potential application of the various entrepreneurial roles.

The rise of the services sector to the growth leadership position was a development of the third and fourth historical stages. This has been the most important force underlying the redistribution of population toward the Hinterland's Sunbelt regions. Most service activities, being traditional central place functions, have increased employment opportunities in many medium- and small-sized cities. Because of the territorial distribution of the national urban hierarchy, this growth has benefited the Sunbelt regions most. As in most expanding economic activities, the growth of services in both the Heartland and Hinterland regions has obviously relied substantially on strategic planning and investment. These entrepreneurial roles have promoted the growth leadership of this sector by determining the viability of new opportunities and ventures, acquiring the necessary financial resources, and marketing the new services.

A Retrospective On Regional Evolution

Exploring the relationship between the "micro" determinants of economic change and its broader macroeconomic aspects has provided new perspectives on the process of long-term regional change. Far from being the outcome of coincidental or seemingly random events, regional evolution has been shown to be the product of a deeper structure, where economic sectors, entrepreneurial action, and human wants become major forces in long-term change.

Unique to this approach has been the identification of the major entrepreneurial roles and their historical emergence. To a great extent, the long-term evolution of industry and shifts in the sectoral growth leadership have been historically influenced by the emergence of each role. The conceptual perspective of this study thus established a historical linkage between the regional impacts of sectoral change and the development of the entrepreneurial function.

REINTERPRETING REGIONAL CHANGE

The reinterpretation of long-term regional change has therefore relied, first, on the study of entrepreneurship as a major vehicle and determinant of the dynamics of change. This required a selective analysis of the process of sectoral and regional economic evolution. The emphasis on sectoral restructuring, with a special focus on the development of industry, became a major aspect through which long-term regional change could be evaluated. The historical perspective underlying these linkages then provided a directional sense and an essential background to the analysis, realistically placing it in the broader context of socioeconomic evolution.

The emergence of each of the five entrepreneurial roles in both the classical literature and in economic action served as a first step in providing a more detailed definition of the entrepreneurial function. This helped demonstrate how the historical development of industrialization and the deepening of industrial structure, and their linkages with the other economic sectors, determined the most important functions and scopes of each role. At the same time, the historical emergence of each role and the sectoral structures that they affected were shown to result in distinct spatial impacts. These occurred primarily through the locational preferences of the most dynamic sectors, and the interregional redistribution of employment and population that they promoted.

The identification of four major historical stages of sectoral and spatial macroeconomic change, related to the emergence of each entrepreneurial role, helped provide a conceptual framework to which the various long-term shifts and changes, and their spatial impacts, could be related. In each stage, the development of a new entrepreneurial role promoted the rise of a "new frontier" sector. Rapid increases in sectoral employment and contribution to national income thus became the most important impacts of new leadership in the sectoral macroeconomy. The most significant regional impacts of these changes were shown to occur through the spatial reallocation of employment from the less favored sectors. The spatial redistribution of population, following employment reallocation, thus became an obvious consequence of long-term sectoral restructuring.

In contrast, employment slowdowns or declines in the less favored sectors were shown to result from rising productivity. Thus, productivity increase was identified as the most important aspect of the effort to maintain sectoral income, by the introduction of more efficient organization and technology, as a way of reducing costs. The sectoral restructurings involved were shown to promote relative economic decline in regions that specialized in the less favored activities. Thus, substantial out-migration of employment and population to areas with greater specialization in the new frontier activities was shown to be a major impact of long-term sectoral restructuring.

Tracing the development of modern entrepreneurship to the beginnings of the Industrial Revolution in America helped provide a broad historical perspective on the process of regional change. A first stage, the Industrial Revolution, thus related the development of industry and its linkages with agriculture, commerce, and services, to the emergence of the investment and inventive roles. The concentration of population in industrial towns became a major characteristic of this stage, as employment was reallocated from agricultural activities in the most advanced region. A second stage, Capital Goods Industrialization, then related the emergence of the intermarket linkage role to the development of basic heavy industries. This development promoted both the further concentration of population in metropolitan areas in the industrial heartland, and linkages with the hinterland's natural resource base.

The third historical stage, Mass Production Industrialization, marked the rise of productive coordination as a major entrepreneurial role, and the start of what would become an important shift in the sectoral growth leadership from manufacturing to services. At the same time, the faster growth of industry and services in the Sunbelt regions began to be felt. During the fourth stage, Services-Oriented Industrial Change, the emergence of strategic planning corresponded with the significant dynamism of services in the national and regional economies. This relationship promoted the extensive redistribution of population toward the Sunbelt regions, and greater economic and demographic growth in the nations' medium-sized and smaller cities.

The analyses of trends over the third and fourth historical stages then verified the major conceptual assumptions about the linkages between sectoral restructuring and regional change. Major historical shifts toward manufacturing and services were found to occur in the traditional agricultural regions, with the exception of the Plains states, as agriculture became the least favored economic sector. Thus, the rapid growth of manufacturing, distribution, and especially services toward the Sunbelt regions in virtually all indicators became the most important regional effect of sectoral restructuring. This was followed by substantial population redistribution and growth in the Sunbelt regions, especially in the post–World War II decades. Thus, for example, the Southeast, a primarily rural region only a few decades before, became the nation's second most urbanized region, with the largest share of total population, by the late 1970s.

LONG-TERM CHANGE AND SECTORAL POLICY

Despite the development of policy mechanisms, strategies, and analytical tools, relatively little is known about the spatial impacts of sectoral policies on the phenomena analyzed in this study. Sectoral policy making has all too often been insensitive to the factors and variables driving regional change. Similarly, these policies have all too often lost track of the temporal dimensions of the conditions that they seek to affect.

Most policy making today is unable to distinguish between the long run and the short run, and to limit its actions and functions accordingly. Many sectoral policies are primarily targeted for short-term solutions that are better attuned to the needs of the political process, rather than to the nature of the phenomena that they seek to address. Thus, inherently short-term and "stop-gap" policies have been designed to deal with the long-term problems of, say, farming's declining share of national income, or the need for industrial restructuring to meet international competition.

To a great extent, our ignorance of the dynamics of long-term change has contributed to this problem. Policies designed to meet short-term needs cannot be expected to deal effectively with long-term phenomena. Sectoral policy making that has little understanding of the interface between the "micro" roots of long-term change in its various aspects—entrepreneurial, organizational, and behavioral—and their macroeconomic impacts, cannot be effective in meeting its objectives. Similarly, policies that take little account of their long-term impacts can produce perverse or harmful effects that end up canceling out any beneficial results.

A consideration of the long-term impacts of policy making must deal with its effects on the innovative potential of each entrepreneurial role. These relate to such issues as, for example, the ways in which learning processes in invention and innovation are affected. Unfortunately, the record on the influence of "macro" policies on "micro" events is quite dubious, at best. More often than not, such policies have turned out to be obstacles and constraints, with few beneficial outcomes. Again, the lack of perspective on the "micro" roots of long-term change has been a major obstacle to the development of effective and realistic policy mechanisms on this aspect.

Another question is how sectoral policies influence the composition of the entrepreneurial function in its various roles, in any given region. Clearly, some roles are more important than others in promoting the full growth potential of a new frontier sector. In this respect, for example, a relatively greater supply of, and regional specialization in, invention and strategic planning would be crucial to the development of advanced technology industries. In regions specialized in less favored sectors facing greater interregional and international competition, for example, productive coordination would be crucial in raising productivity to its full potential.

Sectoral policy making has also substancially neglected its spatial impacts. Indeed, few other aspects have been as systematically ignored in policy formulation and implementation. Sectoral policy making must take account of the spatial scopes of the various entrepreneurial roles. Thus, for example, policies that have a substantial impact on both strategic planning and investment must consider these roles' international and interregional scopes of action. Policies that, on the other hand, primarily affect productive coordination must give greater weight to this role's local impact.

A major question, therefore, is how policy mechanisms influence these roles locally and across regions and national boundaries. Are interregional differences actually diminished by policy mechanisms that constrain the spatial perspectives of any one entrepreneurial role? Can greater entrepreneurial effectiveness in any given region result from a lower level of policy interference? Would less restrictive mechanisms be more effective in dealing with the inevitable transition from a sector's growth leadership to a less favored status? Clearly, few definitive answers can be provided to any of these questions. Although the temptation exists to believe that the unimpeded workings of market mechanisms can yield greater positive results than can policy remedies, it would be unrealistic to expect substantially greater restraint in policy making from the political process.

Given the nature of public policy making, perhaps the best that can be hoped for is a more realistic view of long-term change and its deeper structure. In this respect, greater emphasis on policies that create a favorable environment and goodwill toward invention and innovation, and their diffusion, would help the sectoral adjustment process. Policies that understand and facilitate a sector's long-term transition to less favored status, rather than creating obstacles, would be less wasteful of resources. At the same time, such policies would help the productivity effort in those sectors, facilitating the employment reallocation process.

BEYOND THE FOURTH STAGE

Predicting future long-term change is a risky and uncertain task. The identification of the factors on which future changes and trends will hinge should provide a more useful discussion than will soothsaying. Of these, changes in the population's wants and needs are truly the key to long-term regional macroeconomic change. To a great extent, such changes determine the emergence of any new entrepreneurial roles, as well as any shifts in the sectoral growth leadership, productivity, and employment reallocation. The effectiveness with which such changes occur will depend on the quality and quantum of the supply of entrepreneurship, and the institutional structures and obstacles created to deal with those shifts.

Clearly, the tendency for human wants to shift to newer frontiers in a consumer society will determine the structure of demand. Experience should have taught us that the fulfillment of a need, which only a few decades before may have seemed difficult or even impossible to satisfy through existing organizational and technological means, can become commonplace in only a few years' time. As such needs are met through marketplace mechanisms, the human psyche has shown a prodigious tendency to determine and pursue new wants. Thus, what may at one point have seemed superfluous can become a major objective of human economic striving. The broader implications of such behavior for the national and regional macroeconomies are enormous, for they determine the rise of sectors and new activities, and the decline of others in the sectoral hierarchy.

How far future changes can be predicted on the basis of current trends is, of course, an open question. As should have become obvious from the analyses of the previous chapters, incremental change has limits over the long-term. Can services' predominant position in the sectoral hierarchy over the fourth historical stage be expected to continue into a subsequent phase? Can the regional trends based on this sector's dynamism be expected to persist into the long-term future?

The services sector's trends are underscored by shifts in service activities that respond to changes in consumer wants and entrepreneurial action. Over the fourth stage, a greater emphasis on quality over quantity, not only in the demand for services but also in manufacturing and agriculture, has placed increasing stress on entrepreneurial innovation and invention Such innovation has been increasingly directed at the production of goods and activities that promote greater personal development. In this respect, activities that favor more developmentally rewarding tasks have gained growing importance in the continuing restructuring of the services sector.

Thus, for example, an increasing number of technological advances have aimed to replace basic human functions in the exercise of routine service tasks with automated modes. The production of "smarter" manufactured goods with sophisticated self-regulating capabilities has revolutionized many service activities. The current interest in the creation of artificial intelligence is yet one more instance of the far-ranging interest in extending human capabilities beyond advanced automation. In agriculture, the trend toward "designing" better products through the application of biotechnology is driven both by the population's greater emphasis on health and self-development, and by the need to raise productivity in this sector.

Advances in communications technology and infrastructure have contributed to a substantial decentralization of services and manufacturing away from the nation's industrial heartland. The technological limits of this development, coupled with other advances in, for example, computer technology, productive organization, and a wider access to financial services and capital markets, are nowhere in sight. Indeed, the only limits are in the changes in the population's wants, and in the quality of entrepreneurship from which any new activities must draw.

A further decentralization of economic activities will no doubt aid the competitive position of many Sunbelt states nationally and internationally, especially in the provision of exportable services, and in some manufacturing activities. At the same time, a resurgence of the heartland's regions in some activities can be expected, as regional differences in factor costs are reduced. These trends, coupled with additional rapid urbanization in many Sunbelt states, will transform the nation's space-economy in unprecedented ways. The growth of regional megalopolises in the Sunbelt, in such states as California, Texas, and Florida, will very likely rival the heartland's traditional Northeastern and Midwestern metropolitan corridors as major agglomerations of the new service and manufacturing activities.

In coming decades, the pace of regional and sectoral change will very likely accelerate. Rapid change has indeed been one of the most important impacts of innovative entrepreneurship. The rise of some regions and the stagnation or relative decline of others are very much a part of this dynamic. Such changes will no doubt transform our expectations, routines, and the quality of our daily lives.

Data Sources and Definitions for National Sectoral Estimates

The composition of the four major sectors follows the conventional macroeconomic taxonomy. The primary sector comprises all agricultural and extractive activities (farming, forestry, fisheries, and mining). The fabricative sector comprises manufacturing and contract construction. Wholesale and retail trade, transportation, communications, and public utilities are included in the distributive sector category. The services sector, in turn, includes finance, insurance, real estate, professional and health services, local, state, and national government, and government enterprises.

In addition, two variants of the fabricative and services sectors were created, in order that the performance of manufacturing industries and of nongovernmental services, respectively, be assessed. Manufacturing contributes the vast majority of the fabricative sector's output and, as such, deserves careful evaluation. Its trends not only determine the fortunes of this sector, but also affect the regional and national economies in significant ways. The importance of the services' sector in our economy also deserves further disaggregation, in order to gauge differences in the performance of private and governmental activities, and the influence of the latter on this sector's dynamism.

SECTORAL CONTRIBUTION TO NATIONAL INCOME

Broadly defined, the sectoral contribution to national income is a comprehensive account of each sector's total annual production of goods and services. Its measurement is usually based on the annual end products of sectoral activity. Sectoral contribution to national income, as used in this study, is therefore equivalent to the net value added of each sector, measured at factor costs (see Table A–1).

National income is a net measure of gross national product. This variable is not technically equivalent to net national product, however. The latter is usually defined as gross national product minus capital consumption allowances. National income is, in turn, equivalent to

Table A-1 Sectoral Employment and Contribution to National Income

Year	Contribution to National Income							Employment						
	a	m	m*	d	s	s*	Total	a	m	m*	d	s	s*	Total
1889	1.7	2.6	2.0	3.0	3.3	2.7	10.7	10.5	6.0	4.6	3.4	–	–	22.7
1889–1903	3.6	4.0	3.2	4.6	5.0	4.0	17.3	11.6	7.3	6.0	5.3	3.4	2.2	28.3
1903–07	4.6	5.0	4.0	6.0	6.0	4.9	21.7	12.1	8.1	6.8	6.1	3.8	2.5	31.2
1907–10	5.8	5.7	4.6	6.9	7.0	5.6	25.4	12.3	8.7	7.3	6.7	4.3	2.7	33.5
1910–13	6.5	7.0	5.8	7.8	7.8	6.2	29.1	12.0	9.5	8.2	7.4	4.8	3.1	35.7
1913–18	8.7	9.4	8.3	10.3	10.2	7.8	38.6	11.7	10.3	9.1	7.8	5.4	3.4	37.4
1918–20	14.0	16.3	14.6	15.8	16.7	11.4	62.8	11.6	11.4	10.5	8.2	6.2	3.8	39.0
1920–23	10.1	15.5	13.4	16.2	18.6	13.2	60.3	11.8	10.8	9.6	8.6	6.6	4.2	39.6
1923–26	10.9	18.2	15.2	18.0	21.7	15.8	68.9	11.7	11.6	10.0	9.5	7.3	4.6	43.2
1926–29	10.9	19.9	16.8	19.4	25.2	18.6	75.5	11.6	11.9	10.2	10.0	7.8	4.8	45.2
1929	10.6	25.7	21.9	20.7	26.7	21.6	86.8	11.3	12.2	10.7	10.0	8.0	4.9	46.2
1930	8.1	21.5	18.3	22.9	24.4	19.1	75.4	11.1	10.9	9.6	9.5	8.0	4.9	44.2
1931	6.2	14.7	12.5	16.9	21.4	16.0	59.7	10.9	9.4	8.2	8.5	7.9	4.6	41.3
1932	4.2	8.4	7.3	12.0	17.9	12.7	42.8	10.8	7.9	6.9	7.5	7.5	4.6	38.0
1933	4.5	8.5	7.7	10.6	16.3	11.0	40.3	10.9	8.2	7.4	7.4	7.3	4.2	38.0
1934	5.3	12.2	11.1	13.9	17.7	11.4	49.5	11.0	9.4	8.5	8.0	7.7	4.4	40.3
1935	7.9	14.7	13.4	15.3	18.9	12.2	57.2	11.0	10.0	9.1	8.2	8.0	4.5	41.7
1936	7.2	18.3	16.3	17.5	21.6	13.5	65.0	11.0	11.0	9.8	8.8	8.4	4.7	44.0
1937	9.6	21.6	19.5	19.7	22.6	14.8	73.7	10.7	11.9	10.8	9.4	8.7	5.0	46.1
1938	7.4	17.2	15.2	18.9	23.4	14.9	67.4	10.7	10.5	9.4	9.0	8.8	5.0	44.1
1939	7.6	20.4	18.1	20.0	24.1	15.6	72.6	10.6	11.4	10.3	9.4	9.0	5.0	45.7
1940	8.0	25.1	22.5	22.5	25.1	16.3	81.1	10.5	12.3	11.0	9.8	9.4	5.2	47.5
1941	10.8	37.4	33.2	27.0	29.0	18.2	104.2	10.1	15.0	13.2	10.5	10.1	5.5	50.3
1942	14.8	51.9	45.4	32.7	37.3	21.0	137.1	10.2	17.4	15.3	10.6	11.1	5.6	53.8
1943	17.2	63.8	58.3	38.6	50.4	23.4	170.3	10.0	19.2	17.6	10.6	11.7	5.7	54.5
1944	17.5	64.4	60.3	41.0	59.2	25.5	182.6	9.8	18.4	17.3	10.9	11.7	5.6	54.0
1945	18.0	56.5	52.2	42.7	63.9	27.1	181.5	9.4	16.7	15.5	11.2	11.7	5.7	52.8
1946	21.2	55.6	49.1	49.7	54.7	32.0	181.9	9.2	16.4	14.7	12.4	12.0	6.4	55.2
1947	23.1	67.9	59.5	54.3	52.9	34.2	199.0	9.0	17.5	15.5	13.1	12.3	6.8	57.8
1948	26.9	78.2	67.6	60.5	57.6	37.8	224.2	8.6	17.8	15.6	13.5	12.7	7.0	58.3
1949	21.1	75.3	64.8	57.8	62.3	40.3	217.5	8.6	16.6	14.4	13.3	13.0	7.1	57.6
1950	22.8	88.1	76.2	61.6	67.4	43.8	241.1	8.1	17.6	15.2	13.4	13.3	7.3	58.9
1951	25.8	104.1	90.0	68.4	78.0	47.6	278.0	7.7	19.0	16.4	14.0	14.0	7.6	60.0
1952	24.7	107.7	92.5	71.5	86.3	51.6	291.4	7.4	19.3	16.6	14.2	14.4	7.8	60.2
1953	22.6	116.0	100.4	73.3	91.6	56.1	304.7	7.1	20.2	17.5	14.5	14.7	8.0	61.2
1954	21.7	110.2	94.6	73.9	95.9	59.8	303.1	7.0	18.9	16.3	14.3	15.0	8.2	60.1
1955	21.3	124.5	107.9	80.1	103.3	65.2	331.0	7.2	19.7	16.9	14.7	15.5	8.6	62.2
1956	22.1	131.6	113.1	84.6	110.5	69.8	350.8	7.1	20.2	17.2	15.1	16.2	9.0	63.8
1957	22.0	135.6	116.3	88.2	118.1	74.7	366.1	6.8	20.1	15.9	15.1	16.8	9.2	64.1
1958	23.6	126.7	107.7	89.2	126.2	79.3	367.8	6.3	18.7	16.7	14.7	17.2	9.3	63.0
1959	21.5	144.5	124.0	97.0	134.8	85.5	400.0	6.3	19.6	16.3	15.4	17.8	9.7	64.6
1960	22.6	146.6	125.8	99.8	143.2	90.3	414.5	6.2	19.7	16.8	15.2	18.4	10.1	65.8
1961	23.6	146.6	125.1	102.5	151.8	95.2	427.3	5.9	19.1	16.9	15.1	19.0	10.4	65.7
1962	24.2	159.8	137.0	108.4	162.1	101.4	457.7	5.6	19.8	16.9	15.5	19.7	10.8	66.7
1963	24.6	168.0	143.8	113.6	172.4	107.7	481.9	5.3	20.0	17.0	15.7	20.4	11.2	67.8
1964	23.9	182.1	155.6	122.0	186.2	116.2	518.1	5.2	20.3	17.3	16.1	21.3	11.7	69.3

	Contribution to National Income							Employment						
Year	a	m	m*	d	s	s*	Total	a	m	m*	d	s	s*	Total
1965	27.1	201.7	172.6	130.2	201.2	126.0	564.3	5.0	21.2	18.1	16.8	22.2	12.1	71.1
1966	29.0	223.5	191.5	140.9	223.2	138.5	620.6	4.6	22.5	19.2	17.4	23.4	12.7	72.9
1967	27.9	228.4	195.2	148.4	244.2	150.4	653.6	4.5	22.7	19.4	17.9	24.7	13.3	74.4
1968	28.8	249.0	212.7	160.5	268.2	163.5	711.1	4.4	23.1	19.8	18.4	25.9	14.0	75.9
1969	31.6	263.2	222.3	173.5	293.5	179.2	766.0	4.2	23.6	20.2	19.1	27.0	14.8	77.9
1970	33.3	260.3	217.5	182.6	319.7	192.8	800.5	4.1	22.7	19.4	19.4	27.9	15.3	78.6
1971	33.1	272.5	224.7	200.5	353.3	214.3	866.0	4.0	21.9	18.6	19.7	28.6	15.7	79.1
1972	39.3	304.1	251.8	219.0	387.3	234.8	956.8	4.2	22.4	18.9	20.2	29.5	16.2	81.7
1973	58.2	339.9	281.6	244.8	423.9	258.1	1075.7	4.1	24.1	20.1	21.3	30.8	17.1	84.4
1974	57.4	355.3	294.2	267.4	463.0	283.0	1157.5	4.2	24.0	20.0	21.7	32.0	17.7	85.9
1975	61.1	361.0	303.1	295.7	503.4	306.3	1267.4	4.3	24.3	19.3	23.1	32.9	18.2	84.8
1976	60.8	430.6	362.9	325.5	562.5	346.8	1393.8	4.2	25.2	20.0	23.7	33.9	19.0	87.5
1977	67.8	486.1	408.8	359.9	623.7	391.0	1586.0	4.2	26.1	20.6	24.5	34.8	19.7	90.5
1978	79.5	556.8	464.7	410.8	725.3	469.1	1802.0	4.3	27.5	21.5	25.4	36.1	20.7	94.4
1979	95.9	613.2	508.9	451.5	812.7	535.6	2015.8	4.4	28.9	22.5	26.6	38.0	22.1	98.8
1980	99.9	633.7	526.5	487.9	907.2	600.9	2174.0	4.5	28.2	21.9	26.7	39.3	23.1	99.3
1981	119.9	690.4	581.3	539.9	1013.6	676.6	2414.0	4.6	27.9	21.8	27.1	39.9	23.9	100.4
1982	116.1	657.4	549.6	559.2	1106.2	742.1	2486.9	4.6	26.0	20.3	27.3	40.2	24.4	99.5
1983	100.9	692.2	579.9	598.5	1212.3	820.6	2651.9	4.5	26.1	19.9	28.1	41.0	25.1	100.8

National Income estimates in current (billion) dollars. Employment estimates in millions.

Interval estimates based on averages of the years concerned.

Sectors: a (agricultural and extractive), m (manufacturing and construction), m* (manufacturing), d (distributive: commerce, transportation, utilities), s (services), s* (services, excluding government).

net national product plus subsidies, less current surplus of government enterprises, less indirect business tax and nontax liabilities.

A comprehensive and invaluable source of historical statistics is the U.S. Bureau of the Census' (1975) *Historical Statistics of the United States, Colonial Times to 1970* (parts 1 and 2), which includes definitions and discussion of the data compiled, their sources, and reliability. Most of the historical estimates found in this source are based on substantial statistical research by the Census Bureau staff or, in many cases, by distinguished scholars. Various statistical sources, especially for the earlier years, were compared and compiled in the preparation of this source. Other valuable general sources of information for earlier years were Kuznets (1961) and Martin (1939).

The specific sources of data and estimates, for 1889–1970, were U.S. Bureau of the Census (1975, pp. 239–40). The data for 1889–1929 provided in this source were based on the Martin (1939) estimates. All of the post-1970 estimates were obtained from various sources as reported in the U.S. Bureau of the Census' *Statistical Abstract of the United States*. [The general reference for all *Statistical Abstract* sources is the U.S. Bureau of the Census' (1986) bibliographic listing].

Changes in the sectoral contribution to national income were measured in constant 1958 dollars, as reflected in the estimates of Chapters 4 and 5. Ideally, the use of constant dollar prices should only reflect changes in the real volume of goods and services. A major issue, in this respect, is the choice of a year as a weighting base. Adopting an earlier year in the period of study will overestimate each sector's contribution, because of a tendency to consume and produce more of those goods with decreasing prices. Thus, any growth in the contribution to national income will be biased upward in a sector where a significant proportion of goods and services was initially more expensive. For this reason, a relatively late year in the time series (1958) was used as a weighting base in the estimation of constant prices.

Another issue is that the sectoral contribution to national income in constant prices will not reflect fully the qualitative changes in goods and services produced during periods of economic expansion. The use of constant prices will thus understate the growth of the sectoral contribution, since the quality of goods and services will tend to increase over time. This understatement may, however, be counterbalanced by the common tendency of national income estimates to overstate long-term economic growth, because national income estimates typically include, for example, all government expenditures for commodities and services, such as defense, and government services to businesses, which are themselves not end products. The tendency for these expenditures to increase in importance as the economy grows will therefore bias longitudinal estimates of national income upward.

The most important source on price deflators was U.S. Bureau of the Census (1975, p. 224) for 1889–1970 data. For 1971–74 and 1975–83 data, the *Statistical Abstract* of 1975 (p. 416) and 1986 (p. 470), respectively, provided basic information on implicit price deflators. Other useful, general sources of information for various periods were Lewis (1978b), Kendrick (1961), and Strauss and Bean (1940).

Another issue on national income data is the potential difference in reliability between the various sectoral estimates. This is important in sectors where the share of proprietors' and rental income accounts for a significant part of the total. Thus, estimates for construction (fabricative sector), commerce (distributive sector), and service activities where proprietors' income is a significant proportion of the total will be less reliable than those for manufacturing, mining, transport activities, communications, public utilities, and government. In finance, insurance, and real estate activities (services sector), rental income is a significant share of the total and will thus also be less reliable. For the same reasons, agricultural sector estimates, though generally considered more reliable than those of construction, commerce, and service activities, are usually less dependable than those of manufacturing, mining, distribution (commerce excluded), and government [see, for example, U.S. Bureau of the Census (1975, p. 222)].

EMPLOYMENT

The most important source on this variable was the historical statistics provided by U.S. Bureau of the Census (1975, p. 137) for 1900–70 nonagricultural employment, including mining (see Table A–1). These are based on employed persons in establishment payrolls. Data include individuals on sick leave and on paid vacations, and those who were employed during part of the pay period on which information was collected and were unemployed or on strike during the rest of the same pay period. For government employment, only civilian employees are included. Employment estimates also exclude proprietors, the self-employed, unpaid family employees, farmworkers, homemakers, and domestic employees in households.

Agricultural employment data were also obtained from the historical statistics in U.S. Bureau of the Census (1975, pp. 126–27) for 1900–70. These are based on population survey data [see U.S. Bureau of the Census (1975, pp. 121–22) for details]. In these surveys, the employment count included all paid employees in an agricultural activity or on their own farm during the survey week, and unpaid employees who worked fifteen hours or more in a farm or agricultural business operated by a family member. Also included were those unemployed at the time the survey was taken, but who had jobs or were proprietors of businesses from which they were temporarily absent because of illness, vacation, labor disputes, or personal reasons, regardless of whether any remuneration was received for their absence. Employees holding more than one job were counted in the occupation taking the greatest share of their total working time during the survey week.

Employment data for all sectors, including agriculture, for the pre-1900 period were obtained from U.S. Bureau of the Census (1975, p. 138). They are based on estimates of "gainful" employees taken through an occupational count. Differences between data taken through the occupational count, and those obtained from establishment payrolls for 1900 and later years, were not significant enough to warrant concern, whenever data for both of these approaches could be compared [see U.S. Bureau of the Census (1975, pp. 137–38, and 126–127); data based on occupational count were tabulated for several post-1900 years and could therefore be compared with establishment payroll data]. The lack of establishment data for the pre-1900 years made it necessary to combine data taken with both of these approaches in order to complete the time series [see U.S. Bureau of the Census (1975, pp. 121–25) for details on either of these approaches].

Other general sources of data and information that helped this effort, especially for earlier years, were Lebergott (1964) and Fabricant (1949). Post-1970 data were obtained from various sources, as reported in the *Statistical Abstract of the United States*. The general bibliographic listing for all *Statistical Abstract* references is as in U.S. Bureau of the Census (1986).

Regional Sectoral Estimates

The constraints imposed by the unavailability of regional data for some years required the use of different measures for each sector. Thus, for example, the most reliable longitudinal output measures for farming and commerce were gross indicators (sales), while in manufacturing a net measure, value added, was found to be the best available and most reliable longitudinal indicator. In this respect, employment was less of a problem, since greater uniformity between sectors and better consistency in the definition of these data from one year to another could be found.

OUTPUT MEASURES

For farming, Value of Farm Products, a gross measure representing sales, was the best available indicator. Regional data on this variable were available only through the agricultural censuses (see Table B-1 and Figure B-1). Value of Farm Products is a basic measure of farm income, and does not include government payments received by farm operators for participating in any government subsidy programs. Income derived from the provision of recreational services on farms, such as hunting, fishing, camping, boarding, and lodging, was included in the estimates preceding the 1969 censuses. In the 1969 and subsequent estimates, the proportion of total farm income provided by these activities was not important enough to introduce any significant compatibility problems [see U.S. Bureau of the Census (1975 pp. 449–51) for additional details and discussion].

Unfortunately, a sector-wide regional measure of output was not available for all the activities of the agricultural sector. Farming has nevertheless traditionally accounted for the vast proportion of the agricultural sector's contribution to national income. This activity's share, for example, accounted for 96.2 percent of the agricultural sector's total contribution (mining excluded) in 1950, and for 94.3 and 90.6 percent in 1960 and 1970, respectively. Although its share was reduced to 88.1 percent in 1980, it was nevertheless high enough to be a major indicator of agricultural performance.

Table B-1 Agriculture: Regional Farm Employment and Value of Products.

Year	Value of Farm Products							Farm Employment						
	North-east	East North Central	West North Central	South-east	West South Central	Moun-tain	Pacific	North-east	East North Central	West North Central	South-east	West South Central	Moun-tain	Pacific
1889	0.4	0.6	0.5	0.6	0.2	0.04	0.1	1.1	1.7	1.5	3.4	1.0	0.1	0.2
1900	0.7	1.1	1.2	0.9	0.4	0.1	0.2	1.1	1.8	1.7	3.9	1.5	0.2	0.3
1910								1.1	1.9	1.8	—	—	0.4	0.4
1920								0.9	1.6	1.7	4.0	1.8	0.4	0.5
1930	1.0	1.6	2.5	1.6	1.3	0.7	0.9	0.8	1.5	1.7	3.8	1.8	0.4	0.5
1940	1.2	1.3	1.6	1.1	0.8	0.4	0.7	0.9	1.6	1.8	3.9	1.7	0.5	0.6
1945	1.5	2.9	4.1	2.8	1.8	1.1	2.0	0.8	1.5	1.7	3.4	1.4	0.4	0.7
1950	1.9	4.0	5.7	3.5	2.9	1.6	2.4	0.8	1.4	1.7	3.2	1.2	0.4	0.6
1951								0.7	1.4	1.6	3.1	1.1	0.4	0.6
1952								0.7	1.3	1.6	3.0	1.1	0.4	0.6
1953								0.7	1.3	1.5	2.9	1.1	0.4	0.6
1954	2.0	4.6	6.0	4.2	2.8	1.8	3.1	0.7	1.3	1.5	2.9	1.0	0.4	0.6
1955								0.7	1.3	1.4	2.8	1.0	0.4	0.6
1956								0.7	1.2	1.4	2.6	0.9	0.4	0.6
1957								0.6	1.2	1.4	2.5	1.0	0.4	0.6
1958								0.6	1.3	1.4	2.2	1.0	0.3	0.6
1959	2.3	5.2	7.8	5.2	3.7	2.4	3.8	0.6	1.3	1.3	2.2	1.0	0.3	0.6
1960								0.5	1.2	1.3	2.1	1.0	0.3	0.6
1961								0.5	1.2	1.3	2.1	1.0	0.3	0.6
1962								0.5	1.2	1.3	2.0	0.9	0.3	0.5
1963								0.5	1.1	1.3	2.0	0.9	0.3	0.5
1964	2.6	6.1	8.7	6.5	4.1	2.5	4.6	0.4	1.0	1.2	1.8	0.8	0.3	0.5
1965								0.4	1.0	1.1	1.7	0.7	0.3	0.5
1966								0.4	0.9	1.0	1.5	0.7	0.3	0.5
1967								0.3	0.8	1.0	1.4	0.7	0.3	0.4
1968								0.3	0.8	1.0	1.4	0.6	0.2	0.4
1969	2.8	7.5	12.5	7.6	5.7	3.8	5.2	0.3	0.8	0.9	1.3	0.6	0.2	0.4
1970								0.3	0.8	0.9	1.2	0.6	0.2	0.4
1971								0.3	0.8	0.9	1.2	0.5	0.2	0.4
1974	4.3	13.4	23.0	13.1	10.3	6.8	10.1	0.3	0.8	0.8	1.3	0.6	0.2	0.4
1978	6.7	17.5	29.8	16.9	14.3	8.2	12.6	0.3	0.7	0.8	1.2	0.5	0.2	0.4
1982	8.6	22.4	37.0	17.1	15.7	10.5	17.0	0.3	0.6	0.7	1.2	0.4	0.2	0.4

Value of Farm Products estimates in current (billion) dollars. Employment estimates in millions.

Pacific region estimates exclude Alaska and Hawaii.

WEST NORTH CENTRAL

Iowa
Kansas
Minnesota
Missouri
Nebraska
North Dakota
South Dakota

EAST NORTH CENTRAL

Illinois
Indiana
Michigan
Ohio
Wisconsin

NORTHEAST

Connecticut
Maine
Massachusetts
New Hampshire
New Jersey
New York
Pennsylvania
Rhode Island
Vermont

SOUTHEAST

Alabama
Delaware
Florida
Georgia
Kentucky
Maryland
Mississippi
North Carolina
South Carolina
Tennessee
Virginia
West Virginia

WEST SOUTH CENTRAL

Arkansas
Louisiana
Oklahoma
Texas

PACIFIC

California
Oregon
Washington

Arizona
Colorado
Idaho
Montana
Nevada
New Mexico
Utah
Wyoming

Figure B-1 Regional Divisions.

195

Various definitions of farms have been applied over the years. In the 1890 census, the minimum threshold was an output of $500 in sales during the year when the census was taken. Farms of less than 3 acres that did not meet this criterion were excluded. For the 1900 census, there were no acreage or output limits. In the 1910 and 1920 censuses, the minimum output threshold was changed to $250. Farms with output below this figure and of less than 3 acres were included, provided that they required the full-time services of at least one individual. This last exception was then dropped from all censuses taken between 1925 and 1945, although the 3–acre, $250 output minimum was retained. For the 1950 and 1954 censuses, the output minimum was changed to $150; again the 3–acre threshold was retained. For the 1959 and later censuses, farms of less than 10 acres were included if sales amounted at least to $250, while those with more acreage were included only if sales were greater than $50 over the year when the census was taken [see U.S. Bureau of the Census (1975, p. 449) for additional details].

The specific data sources on regional Value of Farm Products were U.S. Bureau of the Census (1904a, pp. 384–85) for 1889 and 1900 data; U.S. Bureau of the Census (1975, p. 464) for 1930–69 data; the *Statistical Abstract* of 1977 (p. 679) for 1974 data [the general bibliographic reference for all statistical abstracts is as in U.S. Bureau of the Census (1986)]; and U.S. Bureau of the Census (1984, pp. 148–54) for 1978 and 1982 data.

Value Added was the most reliable and consistently available indicator of regional manufacturing output (see Table B–2). In all estimates preceding 1958, Value Added was defined as the sale value of manufactured goods plus the value of services rendered, minus expenditures for materials, supplies, fuel, electrical energy, and contract work. This is basically an "unadjusted" measure of Value Added. Starting in 1958, Value Added estimates were adjusted in two ways. First, Value Added by merchandising, or the difference between the sale value and expenditures for any merchandise sold in which no manufacturing was involved, was excluded from enterprise estimates. This adjustment avoids the duplication that would result from the use of outputs of some enterprises as nonmanufacturing materials by others. Second, a modification was made for net change in finished-out and work-in-progress inventories between the beginning and end of the year when the census was taken [see U.S. Bureau of the Census (1975, pp. 652–54) and Easterlin (1957) for additional details and discussion].

It is important to note the difference between Value Added as an indicator of manufacturing output, and the manufacturing sector's contribution to national income. The latter is a more "net" concept of

Value Added than that estimated in the manufacturing censuses. Thus, in an estimation of the sectoral contribution to national income, other costs, in addition to expenditures for materials, are subtracted, such as depreciation, taxes (other than corporate income taxes), costs of bad loans, and cost of services purchased from other firms (such as consultants, marketing and advertising expenses, insurance, royalties, and patent costs).

Data on regional manufacturing Value Added for 1889 were obtained from U.S. Bureau of the Census (1904c, pp. 5–7). Data for 1900 and later years were obtained from various sources, as reported in the *Statistical Abstract* for various years.

Sales volume was the most reliable and consistently available regional output measure for wholesale and retail trade (see Table B–3). Trade was also the only distributive sector activity for which regional data were consistently available over a substantial portion of the period of this study. The wholesale trade estimates exclude sales of corporate manufacturers, as well as sales branches, offices, and the marketing operations of enterprises classified as manufacturers. Retail businesses without paid employees and with sales of less than $100 for the year when the census was taken were excluded from the 1929 and 1939 censuses, even if they operated over the entire year. The minimum sales threshold was $500 in 1948 and $2500 in 1954 and later years. Firms without paid employees were excluded from the wholesale trade data. Starting in 1977, sales tax and finance charges were excluded from all wholesale and retail trade sales estimates.

The specific data sources for wholesale and retail trade sales were obtained from various sources, as reported in the *Statistical Abstract* for various years. National price deflators were uniformly applied to all regional estimates for each sector's output measure. Unfortunately, the lack of data on regional price indexes prevented any adjustment for geographical differences over the time period of this study (see Appendix A for data sources on price deflators).

EMPLOYMENT

Regional farm employment estimates were based on the definition of "gainfully employed," as reported in the various decennial censuses and in estimates provided in the *Statistical Abstract* for various years. Gainful employment data are based on a count of occupations rather than employment status (see Appendix A for a discussion of this definition). Censal reporting on gainful employment through 1930 included all employed individuals 10 years of age or older. Starting in 1940, estimates included only those 14 years old and over. General sources on the gainful employment concept, with detailed

Table B-2 Manufacturing: Regional Employment and Value Added.

Year	Value Added							Employment						
	North-east	East North Central	West North Central	South-east	West South Central	Moun-tain	Pacific	North-east	East North Central	West North Central	South-east	West South Central	Moun-tain	Pacific
1889	2.3	1.0	0.3	0.4	0.1	0.03	0.1	2.8	1.2	0.5	0.7	0.1	0.1	0.2
1900	2.5	1.2	0.3	0.5	0.1	0.1	0.1	3.4	1.6	0.6	0.9	0.2	0.2	0.3
1904	3.2	1.6	0.4	0.6	0.2	0.1	0.2							
1909	4.2	2.2	0.6	0.9	0.2	0.1	0.4	4.8	2.4	0.9	1.4	0.4	0.2	0.5
1910														
1914	4.6	2.8	0.6	1.0	0.3	0.2	0.4							
1919	11.7	7.1	1.4	2.5	0.7	0.3	1.3	5.4	3.2	1.0	1.7	0.6	0.2	0.7
1920														
1921	8.8	4.9	1.1	1.7	0.6	0.2	1.0							
1923	11.7	7.7	1.4	2.5	0.7	0.4	1.4							
1925	11.7	8.3	1.5	2.7	0.8	0.4	1.4							
1927	12.0	8.5	1.6	2.9	0.8	0.3	1.5							
1929	13.4	10.0	1.9	3.4	1.0	0.4	1.9							
1930								5.4	3.6	1.0	2.1	0.8	0.3	0.9
1931	8.6	5.7	1.2	2.5	0.5	0.2	1.1							
1933	6.3	4.1	0.9	1.8	0.5	0.2	0.9							
1935	8.0	6.2	1.1	2.2	0.6	0.2	1.2							
1937	9.8	8.4	1.3	2.9	0.8	0.3	1.6							
1939	9.8	7.8	1.4	3.1	0.8	0.3	1.6	4.2*	2.9*	0.6*	1.8*	0.4*	0.1*	0.6*
1943								6.4	4.9	1.0	2.6	0.8	0.2	—
1947	27.6	23.5	4.1	9.8	3.0	0.8	5.5	5.7	4.5	0.8	2.4	0.6	0.2	1.0
1948								5.6	4.5	0.8	2.2	0.6	0.2	1.0
1949								5.2	4.2	0.8	2.4	0.6	0.1	1.0
1950	30.9	29.8	5.2	11.9	3.8	1.0	7.0	5.5	4.4	0.9	2.4	0.6	0.2	1.1
1951								5.8	4.8	1.0	2.5	0.7	0.2	1.2
1952	37.6	35.5	6.4	13.7	5.2	1.3	9.5	5.7	4.7	1.0	2.5	0.7	0.2	1.3
1953	41.6	39.9	7.0	15.4	5.6	1.5	10.6	6.1	5.1	1.0	2.6	0.8	0.2	1.4
1954	39.5	36.5	7.1	15.4	5.7	1.5	11.2	5.6	4.6	1.0	2.5	0.7	0.2	1.4
1955								5.6	4.8	1.0	2.7	0.8	0.2	1.4
1956								5.7	4.8	1.0	2.7	0.8	0.2	1.6
1957								5.7	4.7	1.0	2.6	0.8	0.2	1.6
1958	45.3	40.9	8.9	20.7	7.8	2.2	15.4	5.2	4.1	0.9	2.6	0.8	0.2	1.5
1959								5.5	4.4	1.0	2.8	0.8	0.2	1.6

	Value Added							Employment						
Year	North-east	East North Central	West North Central	South-east	West South Central	Moun-tain	Pacific	North-east	East North Central	West North Central	South-east	West South Central	Moun-tain	Pacific
1960	51.9	48.3	10.1	24.3	9.0	2.7	17.8	5.6	4.5	1.0	2.9	0.8	0.3	1.7
1961	51.8	47.2	10.2	24.7	9.2	2.9	18.1	5.4	4.2	1.0	2.8	0.8	0.3	1.7
1962	55.2	52.4	11.1	27.4	9.7	3.2	20.2	5.5	4.4	1.0	3.0	0.8	0.3	1.8
1963	57.1	56.3	11.8	30.5	10.9	3.5	21.8	5.4	4.5	1.0	3.1	0.9	0.3	1.8
1964	60.3	60.7	12.9	32.9	12.2	3.5	23.0	5.4	4.6	1.0	3.2	0.9	0.3	1.8
1965	66.9	68.1	13.9	36.7	13.2	3.7	23.9	5.6	4.8	1.1	3.4	1.0	0.3	1.8
1966								5.9	5.2	1.2	3.6	1.0	0.3	2.0
1967	76.2	75.0	16.8	43.0	16.6	4.5	29.2	5.9	5.1	1.2	3.7	1.1	0.3	2.0
1968								5.9	5.2	1.2	3.8	1.2	0.3	2.1
1969	85.9	87.0	19.7	51.1	19.8	5.6	34.8	5.9	5.3	1.3	4.0	1.2	0.4	2.1
1970								5.6	5.0	1.2	3.9	1.2	0.4	2.0
1971								5.2	4.8	1.2	3.9	1.2	0.4	1.9
1972	92.8	100.0	23.6	65.6	24.6	7.4	39.4	5.2	4.9	1.2	4.0	1.2	—	2.2
1973	103.4	114.9	27.6	75.0	28.3	8.7	46.8	5.3	5.2	1.3	4.3	1.3	0.4	2.1
1974								5.3	5.1	1.3	4.3	1.4	0.4	2.1
1975	108.5	118.7	31.4	82.6	38.9	10.4	52.2	4.8	4.6	1.2	3.9	1.3	0.4	2.0
1976	122.8	141.0	35.8	95.6	43.9	12.1	68.8	4.9	4.7	1.2	4.1	1.4	0.4	2.1
1977	138.7	160.2	40.7	108.5	52.0	13.6	70.0	5.0	4.9	1.3	4.2	1.5	0.5	2.2
1978								—	5.0	1.4	4.4	1.5	0.5	2.4
1979								5.2	5.1	1.4	4.5	1.6	0.6	2.5
1980	187.0	185.7	55.1	146.8	73.6	21.0	102.3	5.1	4.7	1.4	4.4	1.7	0.6	2.5
1981								5.0	4.5	1.3	4.4	1.7	0.6	2.5
1982	195.6	184.8	60.4	162.4	81.0	23.1	115.0	4.7	4.1	1.2	4.2	1.6	0.6	2.4
1983								4.5	4.0	1.2	4.2	1.5	0.6	2.4

*1940 estimates.

Value Added estimates in current (billion) dollars. Employment estimates in millions.

Pacific region estimates exclude Alaska and Hawaii.

Table B–3 Distribution: Regional Commercial Sales.

Year	North-east	East North Central	West North Central	South-east	West South Central	Moun-tain	Pacific
1929	43.0	24.6	13.6	13.3	8.4	2.7	9.8
1935	27.9	15.8	8.2	9.7	5.0	1.9	7.1
1939	35.7	20.5	9.9	12.7	6.6	2.5	9.4
1948	103.8	69.2	35.2	45.4	23.9	8.9	32.6
1954	126.0	87.9	39.7	61.1	32.0	12.2	44.8
1958	146.3	101.5	46.3	75.8	40.0	15.8	59.0
1963	175.9	124.0	55.5	97.7	48.9	20.1	78.6
1967	217.9	162.3	69.7	129.7	64.1	24.0	99.1
1972	302.4	224.5	98.3	213.8	102.4	42.1	148.1
1977	480.3	385.2	174.4	365.7	198.5	77.3	267.6
1982	742.6	506.3	251.3	559.6	403.8	129.7	428.6

All estimates in current (billion) dollars. Wholesale and retail combined.

Pacific region estimates exclude Alaska and Hawaii.

Table B–4 Distribution: Regional Employment.

Year	North-east	East North Central	West North Central	South-east	West South Central	Moun-tain	Pacific
1889	1.3	0.7	0.4	0.5	0.1	0.1	0.2
1900	1.9	1.1	0.6	0.7	0.2	0.1	0.2
1910	2.1	1.3	0.8	0.9	0.4	0.2	0.4
1920	2.4	1.6	0.9	1.1	0.6	0.2	0.5
1930	3.2	2.2	1.1	1.5	0.8	0.3	0.9
1940	3.3	2.3	1.1	1.7	0.9	0.5	1.0
1950	4.0	2.9	1.4	2.3	1.2	0.5	1.4
1953	4.2	3.1	1.4	2.6	1.4	0.5	1.6
1954	4.1	3.1	1.4	2.5	1.3	0.5	1.6
1955	4.2	3.2	1.4	2.6	1.4	0.5	1.6
1956	4.3	3.2	1.4	2.8	1.4	0.6	1.7
1957	4.4	3.3	1.4	2.8	1.5	0.6	1.8
1958	4.3	3.1	1.4	2.8	1.5	0.6	1.7
1959	4.1	3.1	1.4	2.8	1.4	0.6	1.8
1960	4.2	3.1	1.4	2.8	1.4	0.6	1.9
1961	4.1	3.1	1.4	2.8	1.4	0.6	1.8
1962	4.2	3.1	1.4	2.8	1.4	0.6	1.9
1963	4.2	3.1	1.4	2.9	1.5	0.6	1.9
1964	4.2	3.2	1.4	3.0	1.5	0.6	2.0
1965	4.4	3.3	1.4	3.1	1.6	0.7	2.1
1966	4.5	3.5	1.5	3.3	1.6	0.7	2.2
1967	4.6	3.6	1.6	3.4	1.7	0.7	2.3
1968	4.7	3.7	1.6	3.5	1.7	0.7	2.4
1969	4.8	3.8	1.6	3.7	1.8	0.8	2.5
1970	4.9	3.8	1.6	3.8	1.8	0.8	2.5
1971	4.9	3.9	1.6	3.9	1.8	0.8	2.5
1972	5.0	3.9	1.7	4.1	2.0	—	2.6
1973	5.1	4.1	1.8	4.4	2.1	1.0	2.8
1974	5.1	4.2	1.8	4.5	2.2	1.0	2.8
1975	5.0	4.1	1.8	4.4	2.2	1.0	2.8
1976	5.0	4.2	1.9	4.6	2.3	1.1	3.0
1977	5.2	4.4	2.0	4.8	2.4	1.1	3.1
1978	—	4.5	2.1	5.0	2.6	1.2	3.4
1979	5.5	4.7	2.2	5.3	2.7	1.3	3.5
1980	5.4	4.6	2.1	5.4	2.8	1.3	3.6
1981	5.4	4.5	2.1	5.5	2.9	1.4	3.7
1982	5.4	4.4	2.1	5.5	3.0	1.4	3.6
1983	5.5	4.4	2.1	5.6	3.0	1.4	3.6

All estimates in millions.

Pacific region estimates exclude Alaska and Hawaii.

200

Table B-5 Services: Regional Employment.

	Services Total							Services, excluding Government						
Year	North-east	East North Central	West North Central	South-east	West South Central	Moun-tain	Pacific	North-east	East North Central	West North Central	South-east	West South Central	Moun-tain	Pacific
1889	2.8	1.5	0.8	1.4	0.5	0.2	0.5	1.8	1.1	0.6	1.0	0.3	0.1	0.2
1900	3.4	1.9	1.0	1.6	0.7	0.3	0.7	2.3	1.5	0.8	1.4	0.4	0.2	0.3
1910	4.6	2.7	1.2	2.1	1.0	0.3	1.1	2.6	1.4	0.8	1.3	0.5	0.2	0.4
1920	3.6	2.1	1.1	2.3	1.0	0.3	1.1	3.1	1.8	0.9	1.4	0.6	0.2	0.6
1930	3.9	2.4	1.1	2.3	1.0	0.5	1.5	4.3	2.6	1.2	2.0	0.9	0.3	1.0
1940	4.2	2.6	1.2	2.6	1.2	0.5	1.7	3.2	1.9	1.0	1.9	0.9	0.3	0.7
1950	4.2	2.6	1.2	2.7	1.2	0.5	1.7	2.3	1.3	0.6	1.0	0.5	0.2	0.8
1953	4.3	2.7	1.2	2.8	1.2	0.6	1.8	2.5	1.4	0.6	1.2	0.6	0.2	0.9
1954	4.5	2.9	1.3	2.9	1.3	0.6	1.9	2.5	1.5	0.6	1.2	0.6	0.3	0.9
1955	4.6	3.0	1.3	3.0	1.4	0.6	2.0	2.6	1.5	0.6	1.2	0.6	0.3	0.9
1956	4.7	3.0	1.3	3.1	1.4	0.7	2.0	2.7	1.6	0.7	1.3	0.6	0.3	1.0
1957	4.8	3.2	1.4	3.3	1.4	0.7	2.1	2.8	1.7	0.7	1.4	0.7	0.3	1.0
1958	5.1	3.3	1.5	3.5	1.5	0.8	2.3	2.8	1.7	0.7	1.5	0.7	0.3	1.0
1959	5.3	3.5	1.6	3.7	1.6	0.8	2.4	2.9	1.7	0.7	1.7	0.7	0.3	1.0
1960	5.4	3.6	1.6	3.8	1.7	0.9	2.5	3.2	1.8	0.8	1.8	0.8	0.4	1.2
1961	4.2	3.7	1.6	4.0	1.7	0.9	2.7	3.2	1.9	0.8	1.8	0.8	0.4	1.2
1962	4.2	3.6	1.7	4.2	1.8	1.0	2.8	3.3	2.0	0.9	1.9	0.8	0.4	1.3
1963	4.4	4.0	1.8	4.4	1.9	1.0	3.0	3.4	2.0	0.9	2.0	0.9	0.4	1.4
1964	4.5	4.2	1.9	4.7	2.0	1.1	3.2	3.5	2.1	0.9	2.1	0.9	0.5	1.4
1965	4.6	4.5	2.0	5.0	2.2	1.1	3.4	3.6	2.2	0.9	2.1	0.9	0.5	1.5
1966	4.7	4.7	2.1	5.2	2.2	1.2	3.5	3.7	2.3	1.0	2.2	1.0	0.5	1.6
1967	4.8	4.9	2.1	5.4	2.4	1.2	3.7	3.9	2.5	1.0	2.4	1.1	0.5	1.7
1968	4.8	4.7	2.1	5.4	2.4	1.2	3.5	4.1	2.6	1.1	2.5	1.1	0.6	1.8
1969	4.9	5.0	2.2	5.6	2.4	1.3	3.9	4.3	2.7	1.1	2.6	1.2	0.6	2.0
1970	4.9	5.0	2.2	5.8	2.4	1.3	3.9	4.4	2.8	1.2	2.8	1.2	0.6	2.0
1971	5.0	5.1	2.3	6.1	2.6	—	4.1	4.5	2.8	1.2	2.9	1.3	0.6	2.2
1972	5.0	5.3	2.4	6.6	2.7	1.5	4.3	4.6	2.9	1.2	3.0	1.4	—	2.2
1973	5.1	5.4	2.4	6.6	2.7	1.6	4.3	4.7	3.1	1.3	3.3	1.4	0.8	2.4
1974	5.1	5.6	2.5	6.9	2.9	1.6	4.4	4.8	3.2	1.3	3.5	1.5	0.8	2.4
1975	5.0	5.8	2.6	7.0	3.0	1.7	4.6	4.9	3.3	1.4	3.6	1.6	0.9	2.5
1976	5.0	5.9	2.6	7.3	3.1	1.7	4.7	5.0	3.4	1.4	3.7	1.7	1.0	2.6
1977	5.2	6.1	2.7	7.5	3.2	1.8	5.0	5.1	3.5	1.5	3.8	1.7	1.0	2.8
1978	—	6.4	2.8	8.0	3.4	2.0	5.4	—	3.7	1.6	4.1	1.8	1.1	3.1
1979	5.5	6.6	3.0	8.3	3.6	2.1	5.5	5.6	3.9	1.7	4.3	2.0	1.2	3.3
1980	5.4	6.8	3.0	8.2	3.8	2.1	5.7	5.8	4.0	1.7	4.0	2.1	1.2	3.4
1981	5.4	6.8	3.0	8.7	3.9	2.2	5.9	6.1	4.1	1.8	4.6	2.2	1.2	3.6
1982	5.4	6.7	3.0	9.0	4.0	2.2	5.8	6.2	4.1	1.8	5.0	2.3	1.3	3.6
1983	5.5	6.8	3.1	9.1	4.1	2.4	5.9	6.4	4.2	1.8	5.1	2.4	1.4	3.7

All estimates in millions.

Pacific region estimates exclude Alaska and Hawaii.

information and discussions, are Durand (1948) and U.S. Bureau of the Census (1975, pp. 123–24). The former was especially useful for earlier year statistics.

The specific data sources on farm employment for the various years were U.S. Bureau of the Census (1904b, pp. lxxxviii–lxxxix) for 1889 and 1900 data; U.S. Bureau of the Census (1923, pp. 45, 48, 50) for 1910 and 1920 data, and U.S. Bureau of the Census (1933b, p. 56) for 1930 data (see Table B–1). Data for other years were obtained from various sources, as reported in the *Statistical Abstract*. Data for 1978 and 1982 were obtained from U.S. Bureau of the Census (1984, pp. 205-11).

Regional manufacturing data were also based on the gainfully employed concept and statistics. The use of this statistic also became necessary in order to maintain comparability with the other sectoral estimates (see Table B–2). The specific data sources were U.S. Bureau of the Census (1904b, pp. lxxxviii, lxxxix) for 1889 and 1900 data; U.S. Bureau of the Census (1923, pp. 45, 48, 50) for 1910 and 1920 data, and U.S. Bureau of the Census (1933b, p. 56) for 1930 data. Data for other years were obtained from various sources, as listed in the *Statistical Abstract*.

The adoption of the gainful employment statistic was essential to the regional estimates for distribution and services, inasmuch as these were the only employment data available for these sectors in earlier years (see Table B–3 and B–4). This also allowed for comparability with the regional estimates of the other economic sectors. Specific data sources for both of these sectors were U.S. Bureau of the Census (1904b, pp. lxxxviii–lxxxix) for 1889 and 1900 data; U.S. Bureau of the Census (1923, pp. 45, 48, 50) for 1910 and 1920 data, and U.S. Bureau of the Census (1933b, p. 56) for 1930 data. Data for other years were obtained from various sources, as reported in the *Statistical Abstract* (data for 1940 excluded those employed in public emergency work).

Population

The national and regional population data were the most accessible and least complicated of all the statistics compiled (see Table C–1 and C–2). The annual estimates of total national resident population for the pre-1900 years were based on linear interpolation between decennial censuses [see U.S. Bureau of the Census (1975, pp. 1–7)]. The 1900–19 estimates were based on the decennial censuses and on interpolations applied to census age data. The 1920 and later annual estimates were based on decennial census statistics and on data on births, deaths, and international migration [U.S. Bureau of the Census (1975, p. 2)].

The definition of urban population used in the various censuses has varied over the years. For 1890, only the population living in places of 4,000 or more inhabitants was considered urban. The 1900 census was the first to establish the minimum urban threshold at 2,500 inhabitants, adopted by every subsequent census. The 1950 census adopted the concept of the "urbanized area" and delineated, in advance, boundaries for unincorporated places. This census also defined urban population as all persons residing in urbanized areas and, outside, in all places, incorporated or not, with 2,500 or more inhabitants [see U.S. Bureau of the Census (1975, p. 2) for additional details].

The specific data sources on national total population were U.S. Bureau of the Census (1975, p. 8) for 1890 and 1900–70 data. Post-1970 data were obtained from various sources, as reported in the *Statistical Abstract*. Data sources on national estimates for the population age 15-64 were obtained from U.S. Bureau of the Census (1975, pp. 10, 15) for 1890–1970. Post-1970 data were obtained from various sources, as reported in the *Statistical Abstract*. Data sources on national estimates of urban and rural population were obtained from U.S. Bureau of the Census (1975, pp. 11–12) for 1890–1970, and from the *Statistical Abstract, 1985* (p. 22), for 1980. Specific data sources for the regional population totals were U.S. Bureau of the Census (1975, pp. 24–37) for 1890–1970 decennial census data. Data for the other years were obtained from various sources, as reported in the *Statistical Abstract*. Data on regional urban population were obtained from U.S. Bureau of the Census (1975, pp. 24–37) for 1890–1970, and from the *Statistical Abstract*, 1986 (p. 10), for 1980. [The general bibliographical reference for all *Statistical Abstract* sources is as in U.S. Bureau of the Census (1986).]

Table C-1 National Population.

Year	Total	15-64 Age Segment	Urban	Rural	Year	Total	15-64 Age Segment	Urban	Rural
1889	61.8				1937	128.8	87.0		
1890	63.1	37.9	22.1	40.8	1938	129.8	88.0		
1891	64.4				1939	130.9	89.0		
1892	65.7				1940	131.9	90.2	74.4	57.2
1893	67.0				1941	133.1	91.2		
1894	68.3				1942	133.9	92.1		
1895	69.6				1943	134.2	93.2		
1896	70.9				1944	132.9	94.2		
1897	72.2				1945	132.5	94.8		
1898	73.5				1946	140.0	95.5		
1899	74.8				1947	143.4	96.3		
1900	76.1	46.9			1948	146.1	97.1		
1901	77.6	47.8			1949	148.7	97.9		
1902	79.2	49.0	30.2	45.8	1950	151.2	98.5	96.5	54.2
1903	80.6	50.2			1951	153.3	99.2		
1904	82.2	51.3			1952	155.7	99.9		
1905	83.8	52.5			1953	158.2	100.6		
1906	85.4	53.8			1954	161.2	101.3		
1907	87.0	54.8			1955	164.3	102.1		
1908	88.7	56.1			1956	167.3	103.0		
1909	90.5	57.5			1957	170.4	104.0		
1910	92.4	58.8			1958	173.3	105.3		
1911	93.9	59.7			1959	176.3	106.4		
1912	95.3	60.8			1960	180.0	107.9	125.3	54.0
1913	97.2	61.9			1961	183.0	109.0		
1914	99.1	63.2			1962	185.8	111.2		
1915	100.5	64.0			1963	188.5	113.0		
1916	102.0	64.9			1964	191.1	114.8		
1917	103.3	65.6			1965	193.5	116.6		
1918	103.5	65.1			1966	195.6	118.5		
1919	104.5	66.2			1967	197.4	120.6		
1920	106.5	67.7	54.2	51.6	1968	199.4	122.7		
1921	108.5	69.0			1969	201.4	124.7		
1922	110.0	70.0			1970	203.8	126.9	149.3	53.9
1923	111.9	71.4			1971	206.2	134.7		
1924	114.1	72.9			1972	209.3	135.3		
1925	115.8	74.1			1973	211.4	137.1		
1926	117.4	75.3			1974	213.3	139.7		
1927	119.0	76.6			1975	215.5	143.2		
1928	120.5	77.9			1976	217.6	145.6		
1929	121.8	79.1			1977	219.8	147.9		
1930	123.1	80.4	69.0	53.8	1978	222.1	150.2		
1931	124.0	81.3			1979	224.6	152.4		
1932	124.8	82.2			1980	227.2	154.4	187.0	59.5
1933	125.6	83.1			1981	229.5	156.0		
1934	126.3	84.1			1982	231.8	157.6		
1935	127.3	85.1			1983	234.0	159.2		
1936	128.0	86.0							

All estimates in millions.

Table C-2 Regional Population.

Year	Northeast Total	Northeast Urban	East North Central Total	East North Central Urban	West North Central Total	West North Central Urban	Southeast Total	Southeast Urban	West South Central Total	West South Central Urban	Mountain Total	Mountain Urban	Pacific Total	Pacific Urban
1890	17.4	10.3	13.5	5.1	8.9	2.3	15.3	2.5	4.7	0.7	1.2	0.3	1.9	0.8
1900	21.0	13.9	16.0	7.2	10.3	2.9	17.7	3.4	6.5	1.1	1.7	0.5	2.2	1.1
1910	25.9	18.6	18.2	9.6	11.6	3.9	20.6	4.7	8.8	2.0	2.6	0.9	4.2	2.4
1920	29.7	22.4	21.5	13.0	12.5	4.7	22.9	6.3	10.2	3.0	3.3	1.2	5.6	3.5
1927	33.1		24.3		13.1		24.9		11.7		3.6		7.5	
1928	33.6		24.6		13.2		25.2		11.8		3.6		7.7	
1929	34.1	26.7	25.0	16.8	13.2	5.6	25.5	8.5	12.0	4.4	3.7	1.5	8.0	5.5
1930	34.4		25.3		13.3		25.7		12.2		3.6		8.2	
1931	34.8		25.4		13.4		26.1		12.3		3.7		8.3	
1932	35.0		25.4		13.5		26.5		12.4		3.7		8.4	
1933	35.3		25.5		13.6		26.8		12.5		3.7		8.5	
1934	35.5		25.6		13.6		27.1		12.6		3.7		8.6	
1935	35.7		25.7		13.7		27.4		12.7		3.8		8.6	
1936	36.0		25.8		13.8		27.7		12.8		3.8		8.7	
1937	36.1		26.2		13.8		28.0		12.9		4.0		8.8	
1938	36.0		26.2		13.5		27.8		12.8		4.1		9.4	
1939	36.0		26.5		13.5		28.3		13.0		4.1		9.6	
1940	36.0	27.6	26.6	17.4	13.5	6.0	28.6	10.1	13.1	5.2	4.2	1.8	9.7	6.3
1941	35.8		26.7		13.4		29.4		13.1		4.3		10.3	
1942	35.6		26.3		13.3		29.8		13.2		4.5		10.9	
1943	34.9		26.2		13.0		29.9		13.7		4.2		11.7	
1944	34.5		26.2		12.7		29.4		13.3		4.1		12.1	
1945	34.5				12.7		28.7		13.1		4.3		12.6	
1946	37.4		28.2		13.5		29.6		13.7		4.4		13.2	
1947	38.4		29.2		13.6		30.1		13.8		4.7		13.7	
1948	38.8		29.8		13.7		31.3		14.1		4.9		13.7	
1949	39.6		30.3		13.8		31.8		14.2		5.1		14.1	
1950	39.5	31.4	30.4	21.2	14.1	7.3	32.7	14.9	14.5	8.1	5.2	2.8	14.5	10.9
1951	39.7		30.8		14.2		33.4		15.0		5.3		15.1	
1952	40.1		31.3		14.2		33.8		15.2		5.5		15.8	
1953	40.8		32.1		14.4		34.1		15.3		5.7		16.2	
1954	41.5		32.9		14.6		34.4		15.3		5.9		16.7	
1955	41.9		33.6		14.8		35.1		15.7		6.1		17.2	
1956	42.6		34.4		14.9		35.3		15.8		6.3		18.1	
1957	43.1		35.0		15.0		36.1		16.2		6.5		18.7	
1958	43.8		35.6		15.0		36.7		16.4		6.7		19.4	
1959	44.4		35.9		15.2		37.4		16.7		6.9		20.0	
1960	44.7	35.8	36.2	26.4	15.4	9.0	38.0	20.7	17.0	11.5	7.2	4.6	20.3	16.6
1961	45.5		36.6		15.5		38.9		17.4		7.4		21.1	
1962	46.0		36.9		15.6		39.6		17.8		7.5		21.7	
1963	46.6		37.2		15.7		40.3		18.0		7.7		22.4	
1964	47.0		37.9		15.8		40.8		18.1		7.7		23.0	
1965	47.4		38.4		15.8		41.4		18.2		7.8		23.5	
1966	47.8		39.0		15.9		41.8		18.4		7.9		23.9	
1967	48.1		39.3				42.2		18.6				24.3	

Year	Northeast Total	Northeast Urban	East North Central Total	East North Central Urban	West North Central Total	West North Central Urban	Southeast Total	Southeast Urban	West South Central Total	West South Central Urban	Mountain Total	Mountain Urban	Pacific Total	Pacific Urban
1968	48.4		39.6		16.0		42.7		18.8		8.0		24.7	
1969	48.7	39.4	39.9		16.2		43.1		19.1		8.2		25.1	
1970	49.0		40.2	30.1	16.3	10.4	43.5	26.5	19.3	14.0	8.3	6.0	25.4	22.0
1971	49.6		40.6		16.5		44.3		19.7		8.6		25.8	
1972	49.7		40.8		16.6		45.1		20.0		8.9		26.0	
1973	49.5		40.8		16.6		45.9		20.1		9.2		26.3	
1974	49.4		40.9		16.6		46.7		20.5		9.4		26.7	
1975	49.5		40.9		16.7		47.2		20.9		9.6		27.0	
1976	49.4		40.9		16.8		47.6		21.6		9.8		27.5	
1977	49.3		41.1		16.9		48.1		21.7		10.1		28.0	
1978	49.2		41.5		17.1		50.2		22.7		10.7		29.2	
1979	49.2		41.6		17.1		51.0		23.3		11.1		29.9	
1980	49.1	38.9	41.7	30.5	17.2	11.0	51.6	33.0	23.8	17.4	11.4	8.7	30.4	26.4
1981	49.3		41.7		17.3		52.6		24.5		11.8		31.1	
1982	49.3		41.6		17.3		53.2		25.3		12.1		31.6	
1983	49.5		41.5		17.4		53.8		25.8		12.3		32.1	

All estimates in millions.

Pacific region estimates exclude Alaska and Hawaii.

Notes

CHAPTER 1

1. The neglect that analytical research on entrepreneurship and related "micro" perspectives have endured over the past five decades is often attributed to the emergence of the Keynesian paradigm. See, for example, Giersch (1984) and Hazlitt (1984) for critiques and historical perspectives on this issue.
2. Conceptual interrelationships in economics usually tend to be specified in terms of their generic properties. In a treatise comparing theory building and methodology in economics and the physical sciences, Northrop (1962) notes that both generic and specific properties are usually specified in the latter.
3. Nelson and Winter (1982, pp. 413–14) summarize some important thoughts on this aspect when they note that "the quest for the 'microeconomic foundations of macroeconomics' has had limited success because the appropriate microeconomics has not existed . . . economists have displayed great reluctance to make contact with the available evidence on microbehavior, probably because that evidence seems riddled with 'arbitrary' features that square imperfectly with maximization-in-equilibrium—and should therefore, according to orthodoxy, be disregarded." In addition to this aspect, the basically static perspectives of the major paradigms are a significant obstacle to their adequate treatment of entrepreneurship.
4. Although, by the complexity of the relationships involved, theory building in the social sciences must necessarily be partial. Since we cannot analyze or know all the influences on the environmental or contextual parameters, it is impossible to determine fully the course of economic history on the basis of economic, or any other single discipline–oriented, theory.
5. Although this perspective has been conspicuously missing in the spatial literature, opinions on its importance have nevertheless been voiced from time to time. Hägerstrand (1969, p.19), for example, years ago called for analysis of the "direct links between the macro and micro realms, links which have been largely unexplored by regional scientists."

CHAPTER 2

1. Leibenstein (1985, p. 7) blames this neglect, first, on the "macro" perspective of much economic development analysis, that relies heavily on various national income accounts, where entrepreneurship cannot be explicitly accounted for. A second obstacle is that most economic development analysis, whether macro or micro, depends heavily on flows, where entrepreneurship can be adequately conceptualized only as a stock variable. This problem has also been reflected in the systems analysis approach as, for example, in Forrester's (1973) simulation of the life cycle of economic development.

2. Years ago, Wilbur Thompson (1965, p. 44) noted that "students of regional economic development are inclined to admit defeat too quickly when faced with the task of quantifying the presumably more qualitative aspects of growth. No one denies that entrepreneurship—inventiveness, promotional artistry, organizational genius, venturesomeness, and so forth—lies at the very heart of industrial development, yet we hurriedly pay our respects to this critical factor and then move on in embarrassed haste to surer, more easily charted grounds, such as the rate of capital formation, capital-to-labor ratios and the like. . . . This is a mistake; we cannot act so cavalierly toward the entrepreneur, least of all in long-term growth analysis."

3. The neglect of entrepreneurship in the spatial economic literature is also obvious in Nijkamp's (1987) significant anthology of regional economic research. Nijkamp's (1985, p. 11) taxonomy of major research topics included (1) location and agglomeration analysis, (2) input-output, spatial interaction, and transportation analysis, (3) efficiency, equity, and distributional analysis, (4) conflict and multiple objective decision analysis, (5) regional planning, (6) local and urban planning, (7) environmental, resource, and energy problems, and (8) spatial changes, technological shifts, and labor market developments. Theoretical and methodological issues, related to all of these topics, were also considered separately.

4. The research topics in Richardson's (1978b) survey were classified under the general headings of Theory (Spatial Price Theory, Location Theory, Regional Growth Theory, Spatial Diffusion of Innovations), Methods (Economic Base Models, Regional Input-Output Models, Regional Econometric Models, Shift-Share Analysis, Gravity Models), Policy (Efficiency vs. Equity, Migration and Regional Development, Capital vs. Labor and Infrastructure Subsidies, Growth Center Theory and Policy, Evaluations of Regional Policy). A less extensive survey of the regional economics literature is that by Kerr and Williamson (1970).

5. Much significant research in economic geography has focused on the study of organizations. Input, product, and information linkages, firm size, and organizational strategies have, for example, been among the most significant research topics in industrial geography over the past three decades. See, for example, Wood (1978), and McDermott and Taylor (1982).

6. Baumol's (1968, p. 66) assertion that, "if we seek to explain the success of those economies which have managed to grow significantly with those that have remained relatively stagnant, we find it difficult to do so without taking into consideration differences in the availability of entrepreneurial talent and in the motivational mechanism which drives them on," is revealing. Significant and more recent discussions on this aspect may also be found in Demsetz (1983) and Kirzner (1983).

7. Significant debates on the scarcity of entrepreneurial talent have appeared in the economic development literature from time to time. For example, Leff (1979, p. 53), an international economist, is selective about the scarcity question, considering entrepreneurial supply for technological development to be the most important bottleneck in less developed economies. On the other hand, Kilby (1983, pp. 108–09), an economic historian, takes a broader view of entrepreneurial scarcity, estimating managerial coordination and production control to be the most important bottlenecks. This view develops earlier assertions by Soltow (1968) and Harbison (1956) that viewed managerial skills, in general, as the most scarce entrepreneurial resource.

8. Orthodox economists have, for example, viewed entrepreneurial supply as being highly elastic, and usually consider its failures to be exogenous to the economic process, or have regarded them as mere market imperfections. Sociologists have focused on societal values and status hierarchies as determinants of entrepreneurial activity, while psychologists have been more concerned with inner, psychic factors as prime causes of entrepreneurial risk bearing. Contrasts in approach have also emerged within the economics literature on entrepreneurship. Schumpeter (1934), for example, on his way to constructing a general theory of economic development, focused on entrepreneurial innovation and viewed it as a critical role in economic expansion. Similarly, Cole (1949) and, later, Cochran (1965) viewed entrepreneurs as the prime motivators of economic growth and change. Some economic historians, such as North (1961) and Habakkuk (1962), have viewed entrepreneurship in more passive roles, performing routine market functions.

9. Similarly, T. S. Ashton's (1948) realistic, multicausal account of industrial entrepreneurship, and Redlich's (1959) concise typology of entrepreneurship. Recent works have also reflected the need to approach this topic from a multidisciplinary perspective; see, for example, the valuable collection of essays in Langlois (1985), Greenfield and Strickon (1986), and a recent article by Hannah (1984).

10. The decision processes employed in arriving at new outcomes or processes may in themselves be innovative. An important question, however, is just how such innovations are to be defined. Here, the spatial context acquires enormous importance. Should an innovation be considered such only if it has never been conceived or applied within a national territory, a region, a local area, an industry, a firm, or the world at large? For the purposes of this research, regions (or geographical areas of a national territory) will serve as the spatial context of reference.

11. Entrepreneurial innovation, though more likely to occur in some activities and roles than in others, is not conceptually restricted here to any given activity or role. The underlying premise is that anyone can be innovative in what he or she does, provided the appropriate motivational environment is functioning.

12. An interesting account of Schumpeterian perspectives and their relationship to von Thünen's spatial division of labor is in Giersch (1984).

13. The Neoclassical focus on profits has a long history; it can be traced back to notions developed by Adam Smith (1776). It attained uppermost preoccupation with Marx (1967), who devoted almost an entire volume of *Das Kapital* to the subject. The exclusive emphasis on hedonic motives in Marx's works nevertheless reveals gaps in his assumptions on entrepreneurial behavior. Rostow (1960, p. 146), for example, notes that "there are a few passages in Marx—and more in Engels—which reveal a perception that human behavior is affected by motives which need not be related to or converge with economic self-interest. This perception, if systematically elaborated, would have altered radically the whole flow of Marxist argument and its conclusions."

14. A significant and recent critique of the application of Neoclassical assumptions to organizational analysis is in Teece and Winter (1984); interesting discussions comparing the Neoclassical and Marxian perspectives on this point may also be found in Leibenstein (1978, p. 161). More recently,

Mirowski (1986), critical of both the Neoclassical and Marxian paradigms, anthologizes various contributions to a possible "third stream" of modern economic theory.

15. The mythical assumptions of both Neoclassical and Marxian orthodoxy are discussed in Simon (1977, pp. 100–01); for a more detailed critique of Neoclassical assumptions on decision making and production, also applicable to the Marxian approach, see Simon (1979). Leibenstein's (1976) work on the X-Efficiency paradigm and Nelson and Winter's (1974, 1982a) perspectives on evolutionary economic change also provide significant critiques. In an eloquent critique of the orthodox paradigm's static underpinnings, Nordhaus and Tobin (1972, p. 2) note that "Neoclassical theory conceals, either through the aggregate or through the abstract generality of multi-sectoral models, all of the drama of events—the rise and fall of products, technologies and industries, and the accompanying transformation of the spatial and occupational distributions of the population." Equally troublesome is the pervasive reliance on equilibrium theory. Although the best technical work in economics has dealt with equilibrium analysis, it is obvious that the study of equilibrium alone is of little help in understanding economic change. In his presidential address to the Econometric Society, Hahn (1970, pp. 11–12), for example, noted that "perhaps the time has now come to see whether [equilibrium theory] can serve in an analysis of how economies behave." Equilibrium analysis is unfortunately no closer to explaining how economies actually behave now than at the time of Hahn's notable address.

16. Although a questioning of the assumed inevitability of social inequality in capitalist economic expansion has occurred in recent years; see J. G. Williamson (1986).

17. Significant critiques of the shortcomings of Marxian centrally planned economies on this and other points may be found in Kornai (1986) and Rydenfelt (1986). A broader critique of the Marxian ethos may be found in the less well-known, earlier twentieth-century work of Sorel (1986); a more recent critique, based on a comparison of the works of Marx and Nietzche, is in Love (1986).

18. A major and recent contribution by Stahl (1986) relates these three major typologies to organizational and managerial action, finding significant predictive power.

19. Social psychologists have frequently observed that material rewards are not, for their own sake, a primary goal in entrepreneurial action; see, for example, McClelland et al. (1953) and McClelland (1955, 1961) for seminal findings on this aspect. Schumpeter (1934) had much earlier observed that entrepreneurs usually retire from their activities when their strength is spent rather than when profits or their capital declines; this view has been supported by much empirical analysis in the behavioral science literature. The assumption of purely hedonic, material rewards for their own sake has nevertheless been implicit in most of the major historical works in the field of economics. Years ago, for example, Evans (1949, pp. 339–40), in a review of major economic works, found Adam Smith's, like Marx's, views to be completely biased in favor of purely hedonic, materialistic motivations. Curiously, Evans found that J. S. Mill related hedonic motives to enterprise size; smaller entrepreneurs were not assumed to be motivated by purely hedonic or materialistic motives, while entrepreneurs associated with large firms were

assumed to be so motivated. A recent review of the historical debate on the legitimacy of self-interest as a major motivator of economic action and entrepreneurship, from the time of Thomas Hobbes to Adam Smith's, is in Myers (1983).

20. Significant and more recent contributions developing McClelland's work may be found in Vanneman (1973), Rosen (1982), and Nicholls (1984). Two significant earlier articles linking "n-Achievement" to entrepreneurship and economic growth are in McClelland (1965, 1966).

21. McClelland's stress on childhood experiences reflects the importance placed on this phase of the life cycle for adult development and achievement throughout the psychological literature. An interesting account of the importance of childhood experiences in major American entrepreneurial figures is in Sarachek (1978). A case study of Japanese schooling and its impact on subsequent socioeconomic performance that reflects McClelland's assumptions is in Duke (1986). McClelland's contribution undoubtedly had a significant impact on the human capital approach in economics; see, for example, Denison (1962). Unfortunately, this linkage is seldom acknowledged in the economics literature.

22. McClelland therefore does appear to extend Max Weber's (1985) causal sequence by introducing an intermediating motive: the need for economic achievement. This has been observed by Kilby (1971), among others.

23. Freeman's (1976) test with cross-sectional data from 21 nations, taken from McClelland's original sample, measured the contribution of the achievement variable to economic growth. The inclusion of the achievement variable reduced the variance of the other coefficients in a production function specification, and increased the measure of the economy-wide returns to scale, thereby providing significant evidence of this variable's importance.

24. Shultz (1980, 1981) has repeatedly emphasized mainstream economics' tendency to undervalue education. Reports and publications on other, more recent achievement motivation learning experiments are in Nicholls (1984), Durand (1975, 1983), and Pandey and Tewary (1979).

25. A substantial review of major contributions to this approach up to the 1960s is in Kilby (1971, pp. 6–26). The works of Cochran (1965) and Kunkel (1965) are often considered most representative of this approach; to a great extent, they follow in the Weberian-Parsonian tradition.

26. This view is most often associated with Hagen's (1962) work. See also Hoselitz (1963) for compatible approaches. A more recent and significant account of the importance of such ethnic groups and the role of immigration in economic development is in Glade (1983). Most recently, Frank (1985) explores the implications of status search, deprivation, and the role of reference groups in promoting social inequalities.

27. Bauer (1984), for example, claims that more static societies result whenever governments limit human action by monopolizing entrepreneurial roles, and provides examples based on historical research and personal experience from Asia and Western Africa. Berger (1986a) endorses a limited welfare state, and empirically compares five types of socioeconomic systems (Western capitalist democracies, capitalist and socialist less developed nations, East Asian capitalism, and Soviet Bloc nations) by looking at their impact on material well-being, equality and upward mobility, economic development, political liberties, and personal liberation. From another perspective, Rosenberg and Birdzell (1987) argue that political pluralism and

institutional flexibility in Western societies, rather than corporate organization and mass production technology, explain their unparalleled wealth and prosperity. For a synthetic discussion of the relationship between the international diffusion of entrepreneurial innovations and the role of the major global socioeconomic systems, see Suarez-Villa (1987a). The relationship among the diffusion of innovations in electronics, the performance of the major producers, and the national industrialization strategies is explored in Suarez-Villa and Han (1989).

28. For significant treatments of entrepreneurial supply issues related to this aspect, see Alexander (1967), Glade (1967), Dahmén (1970), Harris (1973), Kilby (1983), Baumol (1983), and Leibenstein (1985). All of these contributions discuss variables and issues deserving empirical evaluation.

29. This is akin to what Leibenstein (1978, p. 47) refers to as "owning a lottery ticket," or the expectation that unforeseen, positive events may eventually occur. An interesting alternative to orthodox models of rational choice that can be related to this discussion is provided in Margolis (1984). A more general discussion on both pecuniary and nonpecuniary advantages, based on interviews, is in Ronen (1983).

30. See, for example, Okun (1974). Bauer (1981) and Berger (1986b) focus on equity issues from the viewpoint of less developed nations.

31. See, for example, Berliner (1976), Levine (1983), and Nelson (1984).

32. To a great extent, the neglect of entrepreneurship has prevented the orthodox paradigm from dealing realistically with the process of long-term economic change. With respect to the very substantial residual found in Solow's (1957) well-known production function test, to be discussed later in this chapter, Baumol (1968, p. 65), for example, states that "by ignoring the entrepreneur we are prevented from accounting fully for a very substantial proportion of our historical growth."

33. Although the use of a production function specification need not necessarily be subordinated to Neoclassical assumptions. A test of the effect of changes in the allocation of labor and capital, or any other variables, on output could, for example, be considered analogous to a "recipe" that can be helpful in understanding their interaction with output change. Similar thoughts on this aspect have been expressed by Stigler (1949, p. 109) and Boulding (1955, p. 585). Georgescu-Roegen (1971, p. 244), in particular, states that "as Samuelson views it, the production function is a catalog of all recipes found in the cookbook of the prevailing state of arts for obtaining a *given* product out of *given* factors. . . . The only role the production function has . . . is to enable us to know what factors, and in what amounts, enter into the cost of every possible factory process." Leibenstein (1978, p. 115) then takes this thought further by stating that "one can visualize the production function as a set of 'recipes.' Each recipe indicates most of the essential elements that enter into the production function, but like a real recipe, or a real blueprint, it does not truly indicate all of them. A given recipe may be carried out slowly or quickly, or with careful or sloppy workmanship. . . ." An application of this approach to the analysis of spatial phenomena, including a modified production function specification that considers managerial entrepreneurship, is in Suarez-Villa (1984).

34. Other studies, completed about the same time as Solow's, showed that the unexplained residual, not covered by the allocation of either labor or capital, accounted for from 50 to 80 percent of economic growth in advanced nations.

See, for example, Abramovitz (1956), Aukrust (1959), Fabricant (1959), Niitamo (1958), and Denison (1974). In a longitudinal study of technological adoptions in 4,000 Massachusetts plants, Shen (1973) found that most output differences could not be accounted for by capital or labor substitution.

35. Perhaps one of the best accounts of Cantillon's contribution is in Schumpeter (1954); see also Kilby (1971, pp. 2–3) and Casson (1982, p. 37).

36. The roots of this view are thought to date back to the thirteenth century and the rise of mercantilism, epitomized by the Venetian "societas maris," which required cooperation between the "stans," who provided the capital and assumed the financial risk, and the "tractator," who actually undertook the venture and risked his own personal well-being; see Redlich (1966, p. 712).

37. This distinction becomes most obvious in Schumpeter (1954, p. 556): "It should be obvious, so soon as we have realized that the entrepreneur's function is distinct from the capitalist's function, that an entrepreneur, when he employs his own capital in an unsuccessful enterprise, loses as a capitalist and not as an entrepreneur." This point is analyzed in Kanbur (1980); for a comparison of Schumpeter's and Max Weber's views on this and other points, see Macdonald (1971).

38. Many of these models are reviewed in Walters (1963), Jorgenson and Siebert (1968), Jorgenson (1971), and Clark (1979). Jorgenson and Siebert (1968) classify models of investment behavior into four groups: Neoclassical, including two types: those where desired capital is proportional to the value of output divided by the price of capital services, including capital gains, and those where capital gains are excluded; accelerator models, where desired capital is assumed to be proportional to output; liquidity models, where desired capital is assumed to be proportional to liquidity; and expected profits models, where desired capital is proportional to the firm's market value.

39. A detailed discussion of these specific shortcomings is in Cyert, DeGroot, and Holt (1979).

40. See, for example, Bower (1970), and Baumol and Stewart (1964). Of major significance in this respect is the behavioral school's attempt to embed the decision-making process in a theory of the firm; efforts on this date from Cyert and March's (1963) contribution. It has often been argued that the use of behavioral rules leads to the same outcomes as profit maximization. Cyert and Simon (1983, pp. 105–6), however, note that this argument is false and ignores the main reason for an entrepreneur's recourse to such rules in the first place.

41. For an exhaustive review of this literature, see Lichtenstein, Fischhoff, and Phillips (1982).

42. Greenhut (1970) explicitly considered this role in his spatial theory of the firm and its microeconomic context. His definition was essentially Smithian, viewing entrepreneurship as the provision of capital, but was expanded to consider the role of risk-sharing institutions. The flows and spatial effects of capital movements and investment have been most notably treated in Borts (1971). More recently, Thrall and Erol (1983) developed a dynamic equilibrium model of regional investment, while Persky and Klein (1975) have provided insights on regional capital growth and change.

43. See, for example, Grossman (1984) on the development of local entrepreneurship in less developed nations, and Rostow's (1956) earlier

views on the significance of supply characteristics for sustained, long-term growth.

44. Schmenner's (1982) research has provided significant insights on this point.
45. Leff (1978) discusses this aspect, applied to the case of less developed nations but also applicable to less developed regions, finding monopolies to be more likely. A recent and significant contribution that applies spatial analysis to imperfect competition and related policies is Greenhut, Hung, and Norman (1986).
46. See, for example, Leff (1979, pp. 57–58).
47. See, for example, Morawetz (1974); an extensive survey revealed the undistinguished performance of such enterprises in promoting economic growth and social objectives.
48. See also Isard and Longford (1971) on the first application to a metropolitan region in the United States (Philadelphia area). Significant contributions in the spatial application of this technique were also Miernyk's (1965), Tiebout's (1967), and Richardson's (1972). Polenske (1980) provided a multiregional matrix of the United States based on 1963 data. Most recently, Hewings, Sonis, and Jensen (1988) apply the input-output framework to measure the effects of technological change over the long term.
49. See, for example, Hansen (1967) and Thomas (1972).
50. A review of many of the various studies and topics is in Scott (1983). Beyers (1981) presents a comprehensive overview of spatial linkage structures. Townroe (1970), Lever (1972), and Goddard (1978), among others, explored different aspects of industrial linkages; more recently, McDermott and Taylor (1982) related linkage structures to internal organizational structure conceptually and with an extensive empirical analysis. A collection of significant articles in this area can be found in Hamilton (1974).
51. Mintzberg's (1973) review of the literature and empirical analyses, based on survey research, provide substantive details on managerial work that can be closely related to the definition of this role.
52. Although significant efforts have been made in the spatial literature to consider aspects of decision making that can be related to this role; see Isard and Reiner (1962), Wolpert (1964), Pred (1967), Isard (1969), Townroe (1971), and Webber (1972). The relationship between this and other entrepreneurial roles in spatial decision making is also considered in Suarez-Villa (1987b).
53. This and related views are most capably argued by Teece and Winter (1984), Teece (1980), and Simon (1979).
54. Chandler (1977, pp. 240–83) provides an excellent account of the early experiences with mass production; see also Taylor (1895, 1911) on his approach to factory operation, and Nevins and Hill (1954) on Henry Ford's experience.
55. This view was later confirmed by Coase (1937). His transactions cost approach would later on be extended by Penrose (1959) and Williamson (1970, 1981). See also Vernon (1970).
56. A more recent and significant contribution that compares the organizational history and development of industrial enterprises in various advanced economies is in Chandler and Daems (1980).
57. See, for example, Kendrick (1986) and Hoenack (1983) for the conceptual underpinnings. Mowday, Porter, and Steers (1981) summarize much theory and research on employee-organization linkages; syntheses of research in organizational structuring over the 1960s and 1970s can be found, for ex-

ample, in Mintzberg (1979) and Aldrich (1979). The studies of the Aston group are also of particular interest, because of their measurement of organizational structure, which effectively replaced unitary measures of organizations that were typical of early organizational theory, with four major dimensions (work standardization, task formality and specificity, centralization of authority, and the extent of control over the workflow) that can be applied to evaluate management's performance; see Pugh et al. (1968, 1969).

58. Among the most significant research on firms are the Hawthorne studies, which pioneered research on the effect of managerial techniques on productivity; see Roethlisberger and Dickson (1939), and Landsberger (1958). Davison et al. (1958) found incentives to be crucial in effecting productivity change; Johnston (1963) found that raising managerial expertise through consultants' advice significantly increased plant productivity. In Prais (1981), four out of seven major factors (vocational training, strikes, competition, shift working, plant size, enterprise finances, and control) that are significant in explaining productivity differences can be directly related to the coordinative role. Other major studies on firms are, for example, the International Labor Organization's (1951) study of the effects of "payment by results" methods on productivity change, its (1957a, 1957b) studies on the effect of improvements of management-labor relations on productivity, its (1979) studies on new forms of work organization, their costs and benefits, and effects on productivity change in various nations, and its (1982) study on improvements in work environments in three key Japanese industries: autos, electrical machinery, and shipbuilding. Various ILO case studies up to the 1960s were reviewed in Kilby (1962); other evidence may be found in Leibenstein (1976, pp. 34–40).

59. See, for example, McDermott and Taylor's (1982) very significant application of contingency theory. Reviews and critiques of efforts to relate internal organizational questions to spatial phenomena may be found in Marshall (1982) and Massey (1979).

60. It has often been observed that capital intensive production processes require more skilled managerial capability, while labor intensive production requires less; some evidence on this is reviewed in Suarez-Villa (1984). Clearly, cost reduction through labor and managerial skill reduction must offset any increases in any other factor costs.

61. See, for example, Galbraith (1967), Chandler (1968), Vernon (1974, 1983), and Gilder (1984). The emergence of the multinational corporation kindled much interest in this topic; see Vernon (1977), Caves (1983), and readings in Kindleberger and Audretsch (1986).

62. Thus, for example, the orientation of advertising and promotional strategies and, internally, the adoption of new technologies to meet competition, and the preparation of the enterprise's budget, would be important activities under its control.

63. A "function" would, in this sense, be production, service, research and development, or any other unit that can be significantly differentiated. Eighteenth-century weaving mills, whose only function was production, could be considered an example of the first type; locomotive manufacturers whose operations included repair services and the production of what was basically one type of propulsion equipment, would be an example of the second. The modern electronics firm incorporating various units (produc-

tion, repair, research and development, for example) and product lines (computers, appliances, aerospace equipment) would be an appropriate example of the third type.

64. Thomas (1980) provides a view of growth and change in the multiregional enterprise based on behavioral and managerial perspectives. Earlier views on locational decision making based on the behavioral approach, applicable to multiregional enterprises, are in Walker (1975) and Dicken (1971); see also Krumme (1969), Aydalot (1978), and Harrington (1986) for significant insights on aspects of corporate structure and locational decision making.

65. A discussion on the connection between von Thünen's model and Schumpeter's contribution may be found in Giersch (1984, p. 107).

66. To a great extent, an appreciation of this outcome led to much interest in research on "leading" industries and sectors in the process of development. See, for example, Chinitz (1961) for an early study of metropolitan leading industries; more recently, Swales (1979) relates some aspects of this approach to regional policy issues dealing with economic growth.

67. A significant account of the relationship between such pressures and the different market institutions as they affect industrial organization is in Plott (1982).

68. This is consonant with Caves' (1980) view of the organization as an adaptive organism.

69. The longitudinal aggregate of all locational decision making in this role is of paramount importance for long-term spatial economic change. Decision making and decision theory have unfortunately been much neglected in the spatial literature. Some of the exceptions are Isard (1969), who made the first major attempt to link uncertainty with classical location theory, and Isard and Reiner (1962). Webber's (1972) contribution to the application of risk and uncertainty considerations to location decisions is also noteworthy. For a discussion of the locational implications of satisficing as a decision-making heuristic, see Richardson (1969, pp. 99–100).

70. Analyzing the results of location changes of manufacturing plants by Fortune 500 companies, Schmenner (1982, p. 104) notes that "what is striking about these [empirical] results is that the typical mover plant is characterized so much by managerial considerations and not by more factor-related items such as rising labor costs or transportation costs."

71. Rubin and Huber (1986) provide a significant account of the importance of education, R&D, and information in the U.S. economy between 1960 and 1980; an earlier and significant study on this subject is in Machlup (1962). A very interesting account of the development of the steam engine, and studies exploring the relationship between firm size and innovative output are in Scherer (1986). Significant case studies on the relationship between entrepreneurship and technological and organizational innovation, from a historical perspective, are in Libecap (1986).

72. An early survey of the economics literature by Nelson (1959) is very revealing in this respect.

73. Substantial evidence has accumulated over the years that documents the existence of, and major differences between, individual entrepreneurs and firms in purpose and calculation in the inventive process, in contradiction with the Neoclassical assumptions. The works of economic historians, such as Usher (1954), Habakkuk (1962), Landes (1969), Rosenberg (1972, 1986) and David (1974), and of specialists in organizations and technological change,

such as Griliches (1957, 1984), Jewkes, Sawers, and Stillerman (1961), Peck (1962), Schmookler (1966), Mansfield (1968), Freeman (1974), Davies (1979), and Donaldson and Lorsch (1986), have provided important insights on these aspects. A synthesis and review of some of these works is in Nelson and Winter (1982a, pp. 195–205).

74. The existence of major R&D operations in firms with oligopolistic market power has, to some extent, confirmed the Schumpeterian tradeoff principle, where only monopolistic and oligopolistic firms were assumed to have the resources to produce major inventions. A significant discussion on this question is in Nelson and Winter (1982b). Important studies on various aspects of corporate R&D and productivity may be found in Mansfield (1971) and Griliches (1984); an early study that reflects the state of knowledge in this area up to the 1940s is in Hertz (1950).

75. A very significant and timely discussion on the role of government and other institutions in supporting inventive entrepreneurship is in Nelson (1984).

76. Nelson and Winter (1982a, pp. 250–54) provide an excellent discussion of the various decision rules guiding the inventive effort.

77. Among the more significant earlier works on this process, Schmookler (1966) assumed market size to influence the amount of inventive search. A related spatial assumption would then be that more inventive effort may be expected, the larger the potential market area of the new invention.

78. Rosenberg (1974) has noted that the success rate of inventiveness is better in enterprises and activities that are more related to science.

79. See, for example, Brown (1981), Boulianne and Maillat (1983), Thomas (1986b), and Andersson (1986). An earlier consideration of the relationship between inventiveness, using patent data, city size, and industry mix is Thompson's (1965, p. 50). A broad review of the literature is in Malecki (1983).

80. Thomas and LeHeron (1975) provided one of earliest studies focusing on the manufacturing sector; see also Feller (1975) on the relationship between invention and industrial location. More recent contributions are, for example, in Malecki (1980), Molle (1983), Thomas (1986a), Stöhr (1986), and Sweeney (1987). Nijkamp and Rietveld (1986) explore the relationship between technological development and regional labor markets.

81. These characteristics are typical of those economies that Giersch (1984) classifies as "Schumpeterian"; a global typology of economic systems based on their potential for entrepreneurial innovation and diffusion may be found in Suarez-Villa (1987a).

82. A recent study by Nelson (1986) may have significant implications for the study of the spatial linkages between inventive activities and supportive institutions, and may help explain the concentration of those activities in areas with major research universities and institutions. Nelson's survey of 130 industries found that university research alone accounted for 72 percent of their R&D intensity, while the joint contribution of university research and technical societies accounted for 82 percent of their materials suppliers' R&D (the "upstream" or backwardly linked industries). He then concluded (pp. 188–89) that "university research rarely in itself generates new technology; rather it enhances technological opportunities and the productivity of private research and development . . . [while] the contribution of technical societies was strongly correlated with, and can be interpreted as facilitating, the contributions of upstream firms."

83. The case of small regions and nations, with no significant natural resource endowments and major disadvantages related to market size and transport or labor costs, that have nevertheless become major actors in the global economy due to entrepreneurial resourcefulness can be related to this point.

84. See Nelson and Winter (1982b) for a general account and simulation of the Schumpeterian tradeoff; significant discussions may also be found in Futia (1980) and Scherer (1980). For an earlier treatment of some policy aspects of this question see Nelson, Peck, and Kalachek (1967). Unfortunately, the lack of substantial research on this topic makes it difficult to provide any conclusive answers.

85. Thus, for example, the inventive role can be most commonly associated with R&D units, while the coordinative role's main operational concern is in production and service components. Strategic planning is usually found in the top policy-making echelons, and in marketing and budgeting units, while intermarket linkage can be found both in the top policy-making groups and in purchasing units. Increasingly, large corporate organizations have assumed greater responsibility for the investment role in many industries, though the sphere of activity of this role is still primarily external to most enterprises.

CHAPTER 3

1. Despite the neglect of the long-term view, reflections on its importance have not been lacking in the mainstream economic literature. Years ago, Viner (1958, pp. 112–13), for example, noted that "no matter how refined and elaborate the analysis, if it rests solely on the short view it will still be . . . a structure built on shifting sands." More recently, Baumol (1986, p. 1084), reflecting on long-term changes in the U.S. economy, noted that "the long run is important because it is not sensible for economists and policymakers to attempt to discern long-run trends and their outcomes from the flow of short-run developments, which may be dominated by transient conditions."

2. Three major, all-encompassing macroeconomic sectors will be considered in this chapter: agriculture, manufacturing, and services (including government and distributive activities). This classification therefore follows the established taxonomy of economic activities.

3. Steuart's work, and that of the other historical contributions reviewed in this section up to and including Alfred Weber's, are systematically analyzed and discussed in Jones (1961), in what is undoubtedly one of the best, though unpublished, historical accounts of the evolution of urban and regional economic theory from the seventeenth to the early twentieth century.

4. See Steuart (1767, pp. 46–52).

5. See Smith (1776, pp. 356–96).

6. For an expanded discussion of these aspects and their relationship to Smith's early contribution to a location theory of economic activities, see Jones (1961, pp. 38–43).

7. Henry Charles Carey (1871, p. 205), an early nineteenth-century American economist, would later modify and stylize Smith's focus on trade by postulating four phases of development: "appropriation," or a subsistence stage of extraction and some cultivation; a second stage of "changes of place," where agricultural market towns begin to form; a third stage where "chemical and mechanical changes of form" occur, meaning the establishment of

urban services and manufactures; followed by a fourth and final stage where "vital changes of form" appear, referring to the growth of larger cities and the rise of significant interregional trade flows. Jones (1961, p. 72) believes Carey attempted to shift the emphasis in international trade found in the mainstream literature of his time to interregional and intraregional trade, following Smith's assumptions on the latter's greater relative importance. Undoubtedly, the emphasis on interregional trade of the early theoreticians influenced Ohlin's (1933) attention to this aspect in his well-known contribution.

8. The concentric ring scheme would again draw considerable attention a century later, through the work of intraurban location and land use filtering theorists. See, for example, Burgess (1925) and Hoyt (1939).

9. Giersch (1984, p. 107) provides an interesting, though much too brief, extension and linkage of von Thünen's spatial division of labor with a Schumpeterian perspective on international and global innovation diffusion. His typology of economic systems and their potential for significant innovation diffusion could also be applied at a subnational level, where significant differences in regional levels of development exist.

10. Gray's arguments and insights would later on be expanded upon by other anti-Malthusian scholars; see, for example, Boserup's (1965) significant contribution.

11. Among the many interesting insights, Gray's (1819, p. 40) statistical analyses show a very positive correlation between urban population size and income. In what amounts to an early and rudimentary discussion on the optimality and limits of urban population concentration, Gray concludes that this is reached whenever the population of the large cities (defined as those with 5,000 inhabitants or more) equals the population of the rest of the country. Going further, Gray then attempts to estimate the maximum population that England could support, based on analyses of density, agricultural land, and urban population distribution. Interestingly, in his review of Gray's work, Jones (1961, p. 49) found Gray's estimate (320 inhabitants per square mile) to be significantly close to the population size when England's population began to level off.

12. See Gray (1819, pp. 92–94).

13. By the end of the nineteenth century, the significance of the spatial dimension of long-term economic change had been acknowledged by almost every major stages framework. The one exception was Marx's, which virtually regarded the spatial dimension as irrelevant. Thus, Marx's four "macro" stages: feudalism, capitalism, socialism, and communism (along with the central assumptions of historical materialism) provide no indication of their impact on such phenomena as regional population distributions, processes of urban agglomeration and dispersion, or the urban and regional implications of sectoral change. This neglect has undoubtedly hampered Marxist spatial scholarship greatly over the years.

14. Almost a decade before Adna Weber, one of the first spatial scholars to introduce the concept of natural selection as a biological analogy was the French statistician and demographer Pierre Emile Levasseur (1889). Among Levasseur's many insights on this topic was the notion that only those industries that adopt the best possible locations are the ones most likely to survive and prosper over the long term. The natural selection paradigm would again inspire other spatial scholars and economists more than a

century and a half later; see, for example, Tiebout (1957), Alchian (1950), Winter (1964), and Nelson and Winter (1982a).

15. See Weber (1899, pp. 156–94). These simple definitions are discussed and illustrated with examples from the natural sciences in Herbert Spencer's (1890) significant contribution. The consideration of differentiation as a biological analogy, so eloquently described by Weber, had previously been introduced by the American economist Edward Ross (1896) in his analysis of industrial location. Ross assumed, as most evolutionary biologists do, a progression from homogeneity to heterogeneity, assuming a tendency for natural resource location-oriented industries to become more specialized over time, as new kinds of raw materials and techniques are discovered, and substitutions or new uses become feasible. Analogies from the biological and physical sciences would again play a central part, over half a century later, in Nisbet's (1969), Dunn's (1971), Georgescu-Roegen's (1971), and Boulding's (1981) contributions. An interesting systems simulation of a life cycle analogy applied to the process of economic development is that by N. B. Forrester (1973). An earlier critique of biological analogies in managerial science and microeconomic theory is in Penrose (1952).

16. Jones (1961, p. 102) notes that Weber's four-level classification of economic activities, as extractive (including agriculture), manufacturing, distributive (including transportation, communications and commerce), and services, is a significant early attempt to provide a universal economic taxonomy.

17. Apparently, concerns with the relatively unexplored, and important, static analyses of topics such as market areas and technological influences on location, led Lösch and Hoover to forego consideration of broader, long-term perspectives on spatial change.

18. Schumpeter's (1950) contribution on very long-term societal evolution was also significant during this period. Significant analyses and extensions of Schumpeter's work on this aspect are Perroux (1965) and Sylos-Labini (1984). Much conceptual and empirical interest in stages frameworks would also be generated by Rostow's (1956, 1960) significant contributions on long-term economic development. To a great extent, his stages framework both echoed and expanded upon previous eighteenth- and nineteenth-century conceptualizations. In Rostow's first stage, "traditional society," the main obstacles to further advance were the limitations placed on per capita output by a lack of technological development. A second, "pre-takeoff" transitional stage would have investment increasing substantially in transport, communications, and raw materials development, while "internal" (domestic) and "external" trade grew rapidly. The third, "takeoff" stage would then see a surge in technological applications, the buildup of social overhead capital, and the emergence of greater political power and income (to be saved and invested at a higher rate than that of the general population) for an entrepreneurial elite. Substantial increases in agricultural productivity would be essential to the success of this stage. A fourth, "drive to maturity" stage of sustained but fluctuating growth would see technological advances extend over all the economic sectors, with international trade becoming an important component of economic performance. The fifth and final, "high mass consumption" stage would then feature a major shift toward the production of durable consumer goods and services, made possible by higher per capita incomes. This stage would also exhibit the highest proportion of urban to rural population.

19. In contrast with much of mainstream economics' theory-building efforts of the nineteenth, eighteenth, and early twentieth centuries, where spatial perspectives and applications were an integral part of the mainstream literature, an increasing separation between spatial and mainstream theory building would now be found. This may have been due primarily to the emphasis placed on Keynesian economics in the mainstream literature since the 1930s, and to the erroneously perceived irrelevance of spatial questions to that approach.

20. Excellent reviews and critiques of the urban export base theory developed in these and subsequent studies may be found in Tiebout (1962) and Hirsch (1973). Significant specific applications of economic base and urban life cycle stages on the New York metropolitan area were made by Vernon (1960), Chinitz (1960), and Lichtenberg (1960). Forrester's (1969) application of systems theory to simulate metropolitan change was also very significant in exploring the interrelationships between the economic and demographic processes affecting the urban economy; a more recent modeling effort in this area is Nijkamp's (1984b). For broader regional perspectives on export base theory and statistical analyses see Isard (1960), Perloff et al. (1960), and North (1961).

21. See, for example, von Böventer's (1978) application of product cycle assumptions to the development of urban infrastructure, such as the housing stock, to explain metropolitan land use changes.

22. Norton's zonal analysis was based on data from the Cleveland metropolitan area. Two relatively recent European studies, by Hall and Hay (1980) and van den Berg et al. (1982), have further extended the intraurban focus explored by Norton. Very similar stages frameworks are proposed in each of these works: "urbanization" (van den Berg et al.) or "centralization" (Hall and Hay) as the initial stage; "suburbanization" (van den Berg et al.) or "decentralization" (Hall and Hay) as a second stage; a third stage of migration to the adjacent metropolitan periphery, and a fourth one of relative metropolitan area decline. These stages frameworks were generally verified with very similar methods and data from samples of various European nations for the period 1950–75. An important difference between the two frameworks arises with respect to the definition of "decline" in the final stage. Van den Berg et al. define that stage as "reurbanization," implying an eventual turnaround, or at least a preservation of metropolitan size over the long term, thereby coinciding with a conclusion implicit in Norton's work. Hall and Hay, on the other hand, define the final stage as "decentralization during loss," projecting total decline, thereby implying a bell-shaped life cycle function over the long term. This view has so far not been borne out by the empirical analyses of long-term metropolitan fluctuations.

23. The significant contributions of Perloff et al. (1960) and North (1961) provided much impetus to this interest.

24. This point was more extensively discussed, with regard to the urban economic base, in Richardson (1978a).

25. The elaboration of growth pole theory, by exploring its interrelationships with other concepts and policy issues, would provide fertile ground for many significant contributions. Among the earliest was Hansen's (1967, 1975) consideration of regional economic development theory and policy, and urban size issues (1971). Subsequently, Parr (1973, 1981) related the concept to central place theory, while Thomas (1972, 1975) explored its

relationship with technological and manufacturing change. Important extensions and applications were also Berry's (1972), exploring the concept's relationship with the spatial diffusion of economic activities, and Alonso and Medrich's (1972) and Leven's (1980), relating metropolitan growth trends to changes in the U.S. urban system and its interregional differences

26. The enormous interest generated by growth theory in the economic development literature of the 1950s and 1960s was undoubtedly a major force behind the formal spatial interest in this topic; see, for example, Lewis (1955) and North (1955).

27. Obviously, Richardson's concern with the relationship between the processes of agglomeration and economic growth was made significant by the fact that his general model provided a non-Neoclassical perspective on regional growth.

28. The processes associated with regional growth theory also sparked interest in techniques, such as catastrophe theory, that could be applied to study major long-term changes. See, for example, Casetti (1981).

29. As before, a recent strong parallel interest in the mainstream economics literature, though nonspatial, on this topic, can be assumed to have influenced much of the spatial interest. See, for example, Maddison's (1982) important international comparative study on long-term economic trends and stages in sixteen nations from 1820 through the 1980s, finding a significant degree of long-term convergence in all cases; Ratner, Soltow, and Sylla's (1979) elaboration of four macrohistorical stages of U.S. economic change that relate to some of the broader eighteenth- and nineteenth-century stages frameworks discussed in this chapter; also, the collection of readings in Kindleberger and di Tella (1982), with a retrospective on Rostow's contributions and their impact.

30. Alonso (1980), for example, has attempted a synthesis of long-term development issues based on demographic trends, social and regional inequalities, and urban concentration and dispersion, based on a two-stage framework of rapid economic growth and slowdown; see also Miyao (1983) for a development of some of Alonso's ideas and a mathematical model. Coffey and Polese (1984) have developed a regional macroeconomic stages model of endogenous growth that focuses on the role of local firms and entrepreneurship; see also Burns (1987) and the significant collection of articles in van den Berg et al. (1987). Andersson (1986) develops a macrohistorical model covering four stages from 1100 A.D. through the 1980s, outlining the effects of trade, specialization, transaction costs, and information on urban growth and the global hierarchy of cities. The relationship among metropolitan long-term stages, the city size distribution, and the dispersion of manufacturing activities is explored in Suarez-Villa (1988a, 1989), while Lakshmanan and Chatterjee (1986) explore the relationship among "long waves," technological change, and metropolitan maturity.

31. And, irrespective of who the actual agent of entrepreneurship turns out to be (e.g., individuals, corporations, nonprofit institutions, or government).

32. Braudel (1981, chs. 2–4) provides a revealing account of the evolution of daily necessities from the fifteenth through the eighteenth centuries.

33. Schumpeter's (1954, p. 961) discussion of Engel's law provides significant insights on its relationship with entrepreneurship and the processes leading to long-term macroeconomic change.

34. Astounding increases in the long-term aggregate productivity of many market economies is testimony to this possibility. Maddison (1982), for example, found that U.S. output per work-hour increased by 1,100 percent since 1870, yet this was somewhat lower than the average of fifteen other advanced nations. Japan's, in contrast, increased by over 2,500 percent, while the United Kingdom's rose by 600 percent. In light of these advances, it is curious to note that Marx (1967, vol. I, p. 835) thought the possibilities for raising capitalist productivity to have been pretty much exhausted by the 1860s [see Baumol (1985a, p. 28; 1986, pp. 1073–74) for comments on some of Marx's views regarding productivity]. Such a gross miscalculation of long-term entrepreneurial potentialities can be attributed primarily to Marx's own very limited insights on human behavior, and his essentially static view of human wants and needs. To a great extent, this shortsightedness is derived from his central assumption of conflict as the driving force of long-term change. The legacy of Marxism's mistaken reliance on conflict and crises as the major determinants of socioeconomic change, rather than on the vastly more important "pull" of human initiative and inventiveness, is still being reproduced by many Marxist and Neo-Marxist contributions.

35. A significant empirical analysis of these trends during the postwar decades is in Jones (1984); earlier, Simon (1947, 1982) explored these relationships through a two-sector (agricultural, manufacturing), spatially dichotomous (urban, rural) model of the national economy.

36. Although attaining competitive productivity levels has often been billed as the ultimate measure of success for lagging regions. Attaining more competitive productivity will, in fact, probably require a reallocation of labor toward the more dynamic sectors, resulting in local and regional unemployment or outmigration.

37. It should therefore come as no surprise that the periods outlined in this stages framework differ from those of other historical stages conceptualizations. Ratner, Soltow, and Sylla (1979), for example, identify four major periods in their study of American macroeconomic evolution: a colonial stage (1492–1790), agricultural and emerging industrialism (1790–1860), a transformation period (1860–1914), and a final stage of super industrialization (1914–onward). Maddison's (1982) empirically derived stages consider four periods (1820–1913, 1913–50, 1950–73, 1973–onward), greatly influenced by international trade patterns among sixteen Western nations Earlier, Rostow (1960) identified five major stages, punctuated by a "takeoff", occurring around the 1850s for the United States, "maturity" (1910s), and "high mass consumption" (post-1920s). Kondratieff's (1935) cyclical periods, (1789–1849, 1849–1896, 1896–1938, 1938–onward) also deserve to be mentioned, based on American, British, and French wholesale price trends. On the latter, the temporal parameters of two Kondratieff cycles ("Industrial Revolution Kondratieff" through the 1840s, and "Bourgeois Kondratieff" through the 1890s) identified in Kuznets (1953) do coincide with the temporal parameters of the first two stages in Table 3.1. The historical underpinnings of these trends, and their relationship with entrepreneurship and organizational change, were unfortunately never explored by Kondratieff or Kuznets. An enlightening comparison of Kondratieff's, Kuznets', and Schumpeter's views on the long waves is in Rostow (1975).

38. A comprehensive discussion of American industrialization up to the middle of the nineteenth century may be found in V. S. Clark (1916); see also Ratner, Soltow, and Sylla (1979, pp. 182–207). Broader perspectives on the sources of economic growth and their relationship to the historical process are in Engerman and Gallman (1987), North (1981), and the numerous contributions in Uselding (1986). An excellent treatment of stages analysis of business developments in the early times of the industrial era is in Gras (1939); Landes (1969) provides an insightful discussion of European industrial stages. The locational impacts of industrialization throughout the nineteenth century are conceptually treated in Pred (1966).

39. This is not to say that the preindustrial era was devoid of important inventions. The commercial revolution, advancing over the previous centuries, had introduced major inventions in, for example, the design of ships, agricultural cultivation methods, architectural technology, and bookkeeping methods in commerce. Baumol (1985a, p. 4) and de Roover (1953), among others, provide accounts of these developments.

40. Chandler (1977) refers to this period as "prefactory production," and locates it roughly between 1790 and 1840. Other insightful accounts and analyses of this general period are in Braudel (1982), on Europe; and in Berg (1985), who focuses on the early industrial workshops and their organization. Significant also is Hohenberg and Lee's (1986) analysis of European urban industrial history through the first three general stages outlined in Table 3–1.

41. See Chandler (1977, p. 53)

42. See, for example, the collection of articles in Fogel and Engerman (1971), and Chandler (1977, pp. 75–76). The metal-working industries were the first to expand output on the basis of increased coal supplies.

43. For a significant account of the preponderance of iron and iron manufactures during the nineteenth century, see Temin (1964) and Ratner, Soltow, and Sylla (1979, p. 186).

44. For a discussion of these trends in textile industries see, for example, McGouldrick (1968); Chandler (1977, pp. 67–75) discusses cases from both the textile and armory industries.

45. Significant and informative accounts of post-Civil War frontier expansion are those by Billington (1974) and Fite (1966). A regional perspective on resource changes, including agriculture, is in Perloff et al. (1960).

46. Chandler (1977, p. 272) traces the origins of the scientific management movement in America to the 1870s, when a prolonged drop in demand and the resulting unutilized capacity began to turn some manufacturers' attention from technology toward organization. This movement was relatively insignificant until the 1890s, however, when Frederick Taylor (1895) delivered his first treatise on what he called "scientific management." Taylor's views on a modified piece-rate system attempted to determine output and time standards, and made it essential to have what he called "functional foremen"; these would be very specialized shop bosses in charge of line and middle management. On these views, Chandler (1977, p. 281) notes that "as the fate of Taylor's functional foreman emphasizes, specialization without coordination was unproductive. This challenge of coordination and control that led to the development of modern factory management initially appeared in those industries where high velocity of throughput required careful control to assure steady use of a plant's equipment and working force and where, at the same time, such effective coordination could

not be assured by the careful designing of plants and works." Productive coordination would be especially critical in the metalworking and metal manufacturing industries of the day.

47. Henry Ford's introduction of mass production in automobile manufacturing in 1913 was actually based on the combination of organizational advances developed over previous decades, such as the standardization of products and interchangeable parts, initially started in firearms manufacturing almost a century earlier. Similarly, the concept of a moving assembly line had already been employed in grain mills in the late eighteenth century, while Taylor's ideas on work organization and scheduling had appeared almost two decades before. See Rosenberg (1972, pp. 112–13) and Ratner, Soltow, and Sylla (1979, p. 284) for some insightful discussions on this issue.

48. See Ratner, Soltow, and Sylla (1979, p. 277) and Rosenberg (1972).

49. A concern over excessive vertical integration and the development of trusts in some industries led, in 1890, to the passing of the Sherman Antitrust Act in Congress. Efforts at increasing vertical integration nevertheless continued at a rapid pace. Indeed, the vagueness of the act did not have an immediate impact on this phenomenon, except in the most extreme cases where cartels or pooling arrangements were formed. See Letwin (1965) for an historical treatment of this issue; in two major contributions, Cochran (1972, 1977) relates this issue to the emergence of big business.

50. The establishment or consolidation of agricultural extension programs in many Southeastern and Southwestern states by the turn of the century, supported by earlier federal land grant programs, was a reflection of this concern.

51. Many recent authors have noted the importance of this role for long-term, future economic growth. See, for example, Denison's (1985) conclusions in his study of 1929–82 trends in American economic growth and the importance of services.

52. Broad treatments of the role of technological innovation in long-term growth may be found in Rosenberg (1972) and, more recently, in the various articles in Freeman (1987). The relationship between long-term technological innovation and enterprise size in manufacturing is explored in Suarez-Villa (1988b).

53. For an excellent documentary history of American agriculture for 1914–73, see the collection of articles in Rasmussen (1975); one of the most comprehensive histories of American agriculture covering the period 1914–50 is that by Benedict (1953).

54. The importance of the sectoral approach in long-term spatial analysis was, for example, revealed by Garnick and Friedenberg (1982), who observed that the vast proportion of the decrease in U.S. interregional inequalities in per capita income over a fifty-year period (1929–79) could be explained by interregional convergences in sectoral composition and employment. Borts and Stein (1964) provided the most important Neoclassical contribution on the factor costs approach. Their model, grounded in the Neoclassical production function, assumes a fixed production capability based on the available stock of technological innovations, to arrive at a spatial economic structure. In line with Neoclassical assumptions, the roles of the entrepreneur were completely ignored. Indeed, the standard assumptions of perfect foresight, optimization, and equilibrium were a central component of this model. Adopting a short/medium-term outlook and applying a

Neomarxist perspective, Clark, Gertler, and Whiteman (1986) disputed Borts and Stein's assumptions and conclusions. Their Marxian supply-side perspective of the firm offers what is basically a "black box" model, with assumptions that are similar to those of the Neoclassical approach, insofar as the role of the entrepreneur is concerned. An empirical component analyzes the relationship between capital supply, output, and employment, with data for three industries (Printing and Publishing, Textiles and Apparel, Electrical and Electronic Equipment) in selected cities for 1972–80. Short- and medium-term capital availability is emphasized, while the importance of deeper and more crucial variables, such as technological and organizational innovations and the role of expectations on product demand (based on projections of consumers' wants and preferences), as major determinants of the supply of capital to producers, is basically ignored. This becomes obvious in the authors' findings (p. 99) when they state that, when output is taken into account, "neither real profit nor real output is a significant determinant of the demand for labor." Instead, the real causes of *what* drives the supply of capital to producers, which is assumed to determine labor demand, are not explored. Needless to say, the assumptions of the Marxian model would make it impossible to consider such causes in a realistic way. Only by disowning the Marxian approach could such an analysis have possibly arrived at an adequate consideration of the entrepreneurial function. Using the findings noted above to cast doubts on the economic base concept, their assertion ironically and inadvertently also casts serious doubts on the central assumptions of another Marxian model, the profit cycle [see Markusen (1985) and footnote 69, this chapter].

55. This point is developed in various recent contributions, such as Abernathy, Clark, and Kantrow (1986) and Cohen and Zysman (1987). The latter, in particular, attack the notion of a "post-industrial" society, pinpointing the importance of manufacturing for long-term national economic welfare.

56. The spatial dimensions of this linkage are usually found in what are considered "creative" regions. Andersson (1985), for example, researches this aspect by relating the micro aspects of knowledge creation with the importance of R&D in some regions. Stöhr (1986) believes synergetic regional interaction between innovative high technology industries to be essential to an explanation of why these industries agglomerate in some regions more than others.

57. Chandler (1977, pp. 240–41) defines technological change as "innovations in materials, power sources, machinery, and other artifacts." He defines organizational change as "innovation in the way such artifacts are arranged and the ways in which the movements and activities of workers and managers are coordinated and controlled." Technological output growth for a given input of capital, labor, and materials is achieved, according to Chandler (p. 241), through "the development of more efficient machinery and equipment, the use of higher quality raw materials, and an intensified application of energy." Organizational output growth is, on the other hand, expanded through "improved design of manufacturing or processing plants and by innovations in managerial practices and procedures required to synchronize flows and supervise the work force."

58. See, for example, Chandler (1977, chapters 1 and 2). Some accounts of these interrelationships in the development of Western European industrialization may be found in Landes (1969).

59. The opening up of new raw material supply sources in the hinterland would also be a major cause of the canal and railroad building boom of the early nineteenth century, which in turn helped diffuse many industrial, commercial, and agricultural innovations to the hinterland.

60. Although it is impossible to specify to what extent manufacturing innovations were diffused and applied to improve input linkages and backwardly linked activities, indications are that these were quite substantial. Some evidence on this is in Habakkuk's (1962) insightful comparative study of nineteenth-century British and American manufacturing technology; see also Kemp (1969) on nineteenth-century European industrialization.

61. See, for example, Porter and Livesay (1971) on the development of nineteenth-century marketing techniques and strategies, and the interrelationships between manufacturing and commerce. Barras (1976) and Roehrich (1984) provide additional perspectives on innovation in service activities that can be related to innovation in manufacturing.

62. Chandler (1977, chs. 3–6) provides an excellent account of the development of American railroads during the nineteenth century, their organization, and their innovation adoption and diffusion impacts on other sectors.

63. Goodman, Sorj, and Wilkinson (1987) provide an original interpretation of the "industrialization" of agriculture since the middle of the nineteenth century, and the impact of industrial innovations on this sector.

64. The proliferation of department stores, the first form of mass retailing, in the late nineteenth century was an important factor in this respect. Two other forms of mass retailing, mail-order houses and chain stores, would appear later on, in the 1870s and around the turn of the century, respectively. These would benefit substantially from the organizational innovations developed in manufacturing and in department store mass retailing, Chandler (1977, pp. 240–41 and ch. 7) refers to these innovations as "mass distribution," and compares them with mass production in manufacturing by noting that "mass distribution came primarily through organizational innovation and improvement. . . . Mass production, on the other hand, normally called for technological as well as organizational innovation." A significant historical account of the role of these innovations, and of commercial activities in American economic change since the 1870s is in Barger (1955).

65. See, for example, Schlebecker (1975), for an historical account of American agricultural technology from the seventeenth century to the 1970s.

66. The proliferation of retail chain stores is a case in point. By the 1920s, chain stores had become the fastest growing type of mass retailing; less than a decade later they would become the standard vehicle for mass retailing in America. See Chandler (1977, pp. 233–35).

67. An early and significant discussion of conceptual perspectives on spatial filtering, and its relationship to growth pole theory and to product cycle changes within manufacturing, is that by Thomas (1975). Erickson (1976) and Erickson and Leinbach (1979) found branch plant creation to be the major vehicle of industrial filtering toward the hinterland, especially in nonmetropolitan industrial growth. Applications of shift-share analysis to study interregional industrial filtering are Norton and Rees' (1979), which also related this phenomenon to product cycle dynamics in manufacturing, assuming the spatial filtering of production to occur whenever an industry's product reaches maturity, and Dunn's (1983) on changes in urban manufacturing during the postwar decades. Perspectives on spatial filtering were

also much enriched by Hansen's (1979) work relating this phenomenon to broader changes in international industrial trends, Miernyk's (1980) study of U.S. regional economic base shifts between 1940–70, and Moriarty's (1983) research on industrial filtering through the urban hierarchy. Industry studies, also related to the spatial filtering and international diffusion of manufacturing, have focused more on internal organizational and product cycle dynamics. Thus, for example, Vernon (1974) related industrial location to product cycles and oligopoly formation, while Krumme and Hayter (1975) and Taylor (1986) have focused more on internal industrial firm strategies and decisions related to product cycle changes. Seninger (1985) has provided a general model of regional cyclical employment change based on technological adjustments linked to product cycles, while Hekman's (1980) empirical analysis of a major industry (textiles) in an impacted region (New England) has helped us understand the local impacts of product cycle changes. Norton's (1986) extensive and significant review related industrial policy issues, U.S. industrial change, and regional economic trends to product cycle dynamics.

68. Among the more significant applications of the product cycle dealing with innovation diffusion, Magee (1977) provides a variant, the industry technology cycle, that relates industry-based inventions (patents) to industry age, using a logistic function. Kurth (1979) analyzes the international political impacts of product cycles in textiles, steel, and automobiles by focusing on the international diffusion of these industries. Nelson and Norman (1977) provide a model of diffusion focusing on international comparative advantages, factor substitution, and profit levels over the product cycle stages. Earlier and significant contributions relating the product cycle concept to international trade and innovation diffusion were Vernon's (1966) seminal article on the product cycle and international trade, Hirsch's (1967) on the international diffusion of manufacturing, and the valuable collection of articles on the same topic in Wells (1972). More recent general works that may be related to this topic are those by Lewis (1978a) and Grunwald and Flamm (1985) on international economic and industrial change. It may not be fully realized how much the biological analogy implicit in this concept owes to the early popularity of Darwin's ideas in the social sciences. Shortly after the turn of the century, for example, the idea of life cycle–type changes in industries was evident in Chapman and Ashton's (1914) statistical study of industrial firm sizes. An early conceptual elaboration related to economics is in Boulding (1950); this prompted Penrose (1952) to express serious conceptual objections to the application of biological analogies in the study of business processes. Despite all the objections raised over time, however, it is hard to find other concepts in the social sciences that have enjoyed greater longevity.

69. Although it could be logically expected that the rates of return might be highest for any given product during this stage, the evidence is not at all clear on this point. At the root of it is the question of whether profit levels can be expected to represent secular trends, with life cycle functions of their own, or whether they are primarily cyclical phenomena occurring in a product's life span. Even when a secular trajectory is assumed, major shortcomings are found. One of these is the fact that profits are only a "bottom line" measure of enterprise performance, and as such are less than adequate for understanding the internal workings, adjustments, and

decisions made within the organization. In this sense, profits, when utilized as a major indicator of performance on products or any other aspect, usually deal with the enterprise as a "black box," masking its internal dynamics. Profit maximization, whether Neoclassical or Marxian, has furthermore been widely questioned as a viable behavioral assumption. Equally questionable, as discussed in a previous chapter, is whether profits can be considered to be the sole, or main, motivation of entrepreneurial action. Also, the production process and internal organizational structuring have been shown, in the organizational literature, to be more important than profit levels in determining internal decision making. Important bits and pieces of evidence have contributed some knowledge on these aspects. Stigler (1968, p. 145), for example, found profit levels to be insignificantly determined by industry concentration, yielding variances of 20 percent and, in the best of cases, no greater than 50 percent. Other doubtful conclusions on this aspect were voiced early on by Bain (1951), Fuchs (1961), and Stigler (1963), among others. These doubts have, to some extent, been contradicted by Mueller's (1986) study, which found that companies with consistently high profitability have larger market shares and sell differentiated products. From a regional perspective, industrial profitability in a sample of the largest U.S. corporations tested by Schmenner (1982, pp. 158–62) was not found to be a significant determinant of Sunbelt-Frostbelt manufacturing change. From a Marxian perspective, evidence on the significance and performance of profit rates has been quite inconclusive. In an extensive study of Italian manufacturing, Reati's (1980) results contradicted the well-known Marxian assumptions on long-term falling profit rates, and found industry profit levels to be better explained by international competitive pressures and technology, rather than by monopoly or oligopoly power. Earlier empirical analyses of profitability by Lovell (1978) were also quite inconclusive on the question of any decline in profit rates. A regional perspective on "profit cycles," as a variant and spatial adaptation of the product cycle concept, is Markusen's (1985), combining Marxian and Mandellian perspectives on long-run profits performance with a product cycle-type industrial dynamic. This study nevertheless mostly tested industrial employment and relative concentration, rather than profits per se. An earlier, non-Marxian formulation of a profit cycle industrial dynamic may be found in Nelson and Norman (1977, pp. 10–13). Marshall's (1987) regional critique of the Mandellian perspective on profit rates, on the other hand, mostly views long-run profit changes as cyclical phenomena, relating them to Kondratieff's "long cycles."

70. Clearly, not all entrepreneurial roles will be equally important in every product cycle phase. If four product cycle phases are assumed, for example, invention and capital investment can be expected to be most important during the first phase, strategic planning and intermarket linkage during the second, while productive coordination will be crucial during the mature and declining phases, because of greater competition, market saturation, and the need to increase labor productivity. For a detailed discussion of these interrelations, see Suarez-Villa (1987a). Among the various significant studies on corporate strategy over the product cycle that can be related to the strategic planning role, Wasson's (1974) contribution is one of the most detailed, while Hofer's (1975) linkage of organizational contingency theory to this concept revealed some unexplored aspects.

71. For a discussion of the interrelationships between product and process cycles, see Suarez-Villa (1987a). Any given process cycle can accommodate more than one, and in many cases numerous, product cycles. The development and formulation of a "process cycle" conceptualization of industrial change were originally grounded in organizational theory, and on the interrelations found between organizational structuring and technology. A major early study was that by Woodward (1958), on the relationship between technology and organizational structure. In the 1970s, Abernathy and Townsend (1975), Abernathy (1976), and Abernathy and Utterback (1978) provided the basic structure and empirical evidence on a life cycle framework of productive process development and innovation, based on a case study of the automobile industry. This was later expanded upon by Hayes and Wheelwright (1979a, 1979b), who related four typologies of production process structure (job shop, batch production, assembly line, continuous flow) to the most representative output volumes and level of standardization of each product cycle stage. Mensch's (1979, pp. 73–79) "metamorphosis model" of industrial evolution linked long-term Kondratieff-like cyclical changes in manufacturing with innovation adoptions in industrial products and processes, believing basic innovations to "bunch up" in time rather than to appear randomly. In a similar vein, the relationship between product and process innovation was placed in historical perspective by Kleinknecht (1987, pp. 129–46), who showed that a shift from product to process innovations occurs during "long-wave" upswings, based on a study of eight high growth industries during the post–World War II era. Significant studies on the diffusion of process innovations in manufacturing and other activities are Davies (1979), Mansfield et al. (1977), Freeman (1974), Schmookler (1972), and an insightful collection of articles in Nabseth and Ray (1974). Most studies have emphasized the technological aspects of process innovation and development, however. Kimberly and Miles (1980) and Cameron and Whetten (1981) have, on the other hand, focused on the organizational aspect, referring to an "organizational life cycle." In the spatial literature, Oakey, Thwaites, and Nash (1982) have considered the regional impacts of product and process innovation, while Camagni (1985) provided a dynamic simulation model of process innovation. Suarez-Villa (1984) formalized a broad process cycle conceptualization that considers organizational environments (managerial skills, strategy, marketing, organizational scale), labor (skills, costs), technology (R&D, capital equipment, financing, raw materials), and the spatial impacts of major changes in these variables, with special reference to labor and managerial skills.

72. The attraction and massive migration of much entrepreneurial talent to the Western United States over the past forty years and the emergence of major, internationally competitive high technology industries in that region are examples of this tendency.

CHAPTER 4

1. An early model of rural-urban population redistribution, based on sectoral growth and productivity shifts, was Simon's (1947). Insightful empirical analyses of this model with U.S. data are in Jones (1984) and Jones and Shepherd (1985).

2. In this respect, the U.S. Census Bureau's (1975) historical statistics series proved to be extremely helpful. Earlier national studies such as Kuznets' (1930), which analyzed data starting with the mid-nineteenth century, provided insights on the basis of selected industries and activities rather than on broad, aggregate sectoral estimates. Virtually all of these previous studies were more concerned with measuring cyclical fluctuations rather than providing any historical explanations for the changes they observed. As such, their perspective was usually *ahistorical*. Limited historical perspectives were usually invoked only to support the empirical evidence. Thus, an overarching conceptual framework was missing from these works, where concepts, if they were at all present, usually followed the evidence. The historical conception of long-term change adopted here is best suited to consider relative changes among the different sectors. To a great extent, therefore, the concept of this study has determined the approach and method that are used. Data limitations have unfortunately restricted the possibility of applying more sophisticated statistical techniques. Thus, the most suitable measure of change applied to evaluate the various indicators was the average rate of increase or decline over the various periods considered (see Table 4–7). Coincidentally, this measure was regarded by Kuznets (1930) to be most appropriate in his analysis of long-term trends for various subsectors and activities.

3. National income is defined here as gross national product minus capital consumption allowances (with capital adjustments).

4. For a substantially broader and significant treatment of growth trends for 1929–82, with eight output measures, see Denison (1985). A significant statistical compilation, starting in 1860, is the U.S. Department of Commerce's (1973) study of long-term growth.

5. An informative discussion on continental expansion and frontier agriculture related to this point may be found in Ratner, Soltow, and Sylla (1979, pp. 255–74); more extensive discussions on post-Civil War agriculture and frontier expansion are in Fite (1966).

6. For a broader perspective on the international importance of services in the post-World War II economy, with data from 77 countries at various levels of development, see Riddle (1986). Other significant works on the emergence of services are Fuchs (1968) and Stanback et al. (1981); the collection of readings in Faulhaber, Noam, and Talsey (1986) provide various perspectives on more recent changes within the services sector, while Bailly et al. (1987) explore the interaction between services and manufacturing, providing a new typology for regional analysis.

7. Such as, for example, the expansion of the interstate highway system, and of air transport.

8. Data for additional years may be found in the Appendixes. The selection of intervals was based on an analysis of the most commonly important years, based on shifting trends, for all the various sectors.

9. A significant decline in the services' total for 1946–50 was due to post-war demobilization.

10. The sharp 1980–83 decline is quite misleading, because of the onset of the recession during that period, and the subsequent turnaround of the mid-1980s.

11. Because of constraints on data availability for the earlier periods, and the need for uniformity, the 15–64 age group has been defined as the "working

age" population. This categorization will no doubt overestimate the size of this population segment, especially after periods of increasing birth rates.

12. Standardized estimates for employment shares per working age population (15–64 age group) were insignificantly different from the estimates for total population shown in Table 4-6.

13. Excellent insights on U.S. productivity change, well above and beyond the treatment provided in this section, may be found in Kendrick and Grossman (1980). Broader perspectives on U.S. productivity and international competitiveness, including policy recommendations, are in the collection of readings in Baumol and McLennan (1985). Fuchs and Wilburn (1969) provide an excellent analysis of productivity differences in services between 1939 and 1963; other aspects of productivity in services related to policy are in Baumol (1985b).

14. Sectoral contribution to national income per employee was used as the main indicator of productivity. Other, more potentially accurate variables to measure labor participation, such as man-hours worked, could not be obtained for all of the sectors over the full period of this study. For a discussion of alternative approaches to productivity measurement, including those used in this chapter, see the contributions in Dogramaci (1986).

15. See, for example, Rasmussen (1975) for a documentary account of changes in U.S. agriculture.

16. The "differential application" and unequal impact of the various entrepreneurial roles mean that, for example, in the "new frontier" sector, strategic planning and intermarket linkage will very likely be in greater demand, while in the less favored sectors productive coordination will be essential to achieving greater productivity.

17. The pioneering tabulations in Leontief (1941) and subsequent efforts such as the U.S. Department of Commerce's (1984) Interindustry Economics Division publication of the 1977 input-output matrix were extremely helpful. Another important source of related data is the U.S. Department of Commerce's (1986) Bureau of Economic Analysis publication on the national income and product accounts for 1929–82.

18. All of these changes are relative, however. Thus, for example, although a decline in the input rank and shares of Motor Vehicle inputs may have occurred between 1939 and 1977, the purchases of such inputs may have actually increased substantially, but not enough to offset the greater value of, or expenditures for, other inputs.

19. Complete input-output data for distributive sector activities were unavailable for 1919 and 1939.

20. Jones' (1984) empirical test of Simon's (1947, 1982) model reveals how the U.S. rural-urban population balance has shifted over the years. The relationship between the assumptions of Simon's model and changes in the distribution of income is explored in Varaiya, Artle, and Humes (1979).

21. A dip in total population during the mid-1940s reflects the human toll of World War II.

22. Of particular interest during the 1970s was a noticeable shift toward greater nonmetropolitan (non-S.M.S.A.) area growth, as a reversal of previous trends. See, for example, Garnick (1984) for a discussion and analysis of this phenomenon. More recently, Berry (1988) provides evidence on 55-year "long waves" of urbanward migration, that are significantly influenced by sustained national economic expansions and recessions.

CHAPTER 5

1. A listing of the various states included in these regional divisions may be found in U.S. Bureau of the Census (1986). The Northeast and Southeast classifications include the New England and Middle Atlantic, and the South Atlantic and East South Central regions, respectively. Alaska and Hawaii have been excluded from the Pacific region's estimates; the regional analysis of this study is therefore limited to the continental United States.
2. Value added, rather than gross output, for example, turned out to be a more reliable regional measure of value for the manufacturing sector, especially in the earlier years.
3. Unfortunately, the lack of sufficiently reliable data for the earlier years made it impossible to consider these activities. Farming nevertheless accounts for the largest proportion of agricultural output.
4. The agricultural sector's least favored position since the 1930s became obvious in the analysis of national trends of the previous chapter; see, for example, Table 4–7 on the magnitude sequences for sectoral contribution to national income.
5. The value-added indicator has a clear advantage over total output in that it is less affected by variations in product mix.
6. Such diffusion has been greatly encouraged by lower relative production costs and significant amenities in some Sunbelt states, especially in the Pacific, West South Central, and Southeastern regions.
7. In a simulation model that projects regional trends through 1995, Stevens and Treyz (1986) conclude that the shift from the "Frostbelt" to the "Sunbelt" can be only partially explained by objective and measurable economic factors. A "long-wave" approach providing complementary perspectives on U.S. interregional change and disparities is in Booth (1987), while, in an earlier monograph, Nijkamp (1984a) explores the relationship between long waves, innovation, and spatial economic change through a basic model. Interesting discussions on the diffusion of manufacturing toward the Sunbelt regions may be found in the collection of readings in Wheaton (1979); an early study on changes in the location of manufacturing since 1929 is that by Fuchs (1962).
8. For a significant perspective on this point, and its relationship to U.S. industrial change and the policy debates, see Norton (1986). Contributions in Rees (1986) explore the relationship between public policy making, regional development, and high technology industrialization; an earlier and broader, perspective on regional policy with a historical dimension is in Rostow (1978). A concise overview of U.S. "macro" regional changes in 1900, 1950, and 1980 is in Chinitz (1986).
9. In an interesting study, Wheat (1986) analyzes regional differences in manufacturing employment growth from 1963–77 in the continental United States, finding that markets alone explain 55 percent of the variance, climate 15 percent, "rural state attraction" 11 percent, unionization 5 percent, and amenities 5 percent. Resources, taxes, and business climate are found to lack significance. The major regional contrasts, caused largely by markets, are between the "Manufacturing Belt" (6 percent), a bordering "Transition Zone" (35 percent), and the combined South and West (58 percent).
10. Several recent studies have explored regional productivity performances in manufacturing. Hulten and Schwab (1984) link national productivity change

to regional performances, applying a Hicks–neutral production function, and conclude that productivity slowed down broadly across regions. Furthermore, these authors find that interregional productivity differences are largely a result of differential growth in capital and labor inputs. Little support is found for differences in productivity between "Snowbelt" and "Sunbelt" as a cause for manufacturing decline in the former, and the authors assume their evidence to support Olson's (1982) argument on the growth-inhibiting role of special interest groups in the Northeast and Midwest. The latter, in fact, assumed that such groups would reduce growth in these regions by encouraging out-migration of capital and labor, but with little effect on productivity itself. For a review of empirical analyses of spatial productivity variations, see Moomaw (1983); this study concluded that urbanization and localization economies influence labor productivity variations across regions and city sizes. A third study is Casetti's (1984) test of Verdoorn's Law, which assumes productivity to grow faster in expanding economic sectors. Using 1958–76 data, his study confirmed Verdoorn's assumptions. Clearly, the assumptions of that study contradict the findings of this section, and the national analyses of the previous chapter. Important questions here are whether indeed Verdoorn's assumptions can be confirmed with longer term data, which clearly do not support its assumptions in this study, and whether the productivity of the new sectors is being compared with that of older sectors or with plants of the same sector in different regions. As Casetti noted, the level of aggregation may have much influence on the outcome of those tests.

11. The abbreviated intervals exclude the Depression and World War II periods.
12. An interesting study of regional trends since 1960, and projections to 1990, is Jackson et al's (1981) analysis of the relationships among population growth, employment, and income.
13. Although, advances in communications and transportation technology were no doubt extremely important.
14. Distribution was included in the services sector in the conceptual framework of Chapter 3. It was considered separately in this and the previous chapters, however, in order to make the services estimates more representative. This approach was especially important, for example, whenever the effect of governmental activities on the services totals were evaluated.
15. Though there are obvious exceptions to this situation, such as the case of small nations without much agricultural activity that nevertheless become important centers of manufacturing, commerce, and services. Most nations in this situation originally developed through commerce, however, including trade in agricultural products.
16. The interval corresponding to World War II (1939–47) has been excluded primarily because of the very temporary distortions it introduced in the national and regional industrial structures. In the vast majority of cases, however, the consideration of this interval actually bolsters the conceptual assumptions.
17. These assumptions were verified for the national estimates in Chapter 4.
18. The "spatial economic context" includes, for example, the advantages of larger spatial market shares, due to a lower level of spatial competition, and more favorable demand for some consumer durable and nondurable goods. The lower level of Hinterland development can be expected to be a major cause of the latter, as the population's preferences raise the regional income

elastic characteristics of some manufactured goods. A growing Hinterland population also enhances these advantages.

19. Data for nongovernmental services during 1940–50 were unavailable.

Bibliography

Abernathy, W. J. 1976. "Production Process Structure and Technological Change." *Decision Sciences* 7:607–19.

——, and P. L. Townsend. 1975. "Technology, Productivity and Process Change." *Technological Forecasting and Social Change* 7:379–96.

——, and J. M. Utterback. 1978. "Patterns of Industrial Innovation." *Technology Review* 80:40–47.

——, K. B. Clark, and A. M. Kantrow. 1986. *Industrial Renaissance*. New York: Basic Books.

Abramovitz, M. 1956. "Resources and Output Trends in the U.S. Since 1870." *American Economic Review* 46:5–23.

Alchian, A. A. 1950. "Uncertainty, Evolution and Economic Theory." *Journal of Political Economy* 58:211–22.

Aldrich, H. 1979. *Organizations and Environments*. Englewood Cliffs, N.J.: Prentice-Hall.

Alexander, A. P. 1967. "The Supply of Industrial Entrepreneurship." *Explorations in Entrepreneurial History* (2d series) 4:136–49.

Alonso, W. 1980. "Five Bell Shapes in Development." *Papers of the Regional Science Association* 45:5–16.

——, and E. Medrich. 1972. "Spontaneous Growth Centers in Twentieth Century American Urbanization." In *Growth Centers in Regional Economic Development*, ed. N. M. Hansen. New York: Free Press.

Andersson, Å. E., and B. Johansson. 1985. "Creativity and Regional Development." *Papers of the Regional Science Association* 56:5–20.

——. 1986. "The Four Logistical Revolutions." *Papers of the Regional Science Association* 59:1–12.

Ashton, T. S. 1948. *The Industrial Revolution, 1760–1830*. New York: Oxford University Press.

Aukrust, O. 1959. "Investment and Economic Growth." *Productivity Measures Review* 16:35–53.

Aydalot, P. 1978. "The Regional Policy and Spatial Strategy of Large Organizations." In *Polarized Development and Regional Policy: Tribute to Jacques Boudeville*, ed. A. Kuklinski. The Hague: Mouton.

Bailly, A., L. Boulianne, D. Maillat, M. Rey, and L. Thevoz. 1987. "Services and Production: For a Reassessment of Economic Sectors." *Annals of Regional Science* 21:45–59.

Bain, J. S. 1951. "Relation of Profit Rate to Industry Concentration: American Manufacturing, 1936–1940." *Quarterly Journal of Economics* 65:293–324.

Barger, H. 1955. *Distribution's Place in the American Economy Since 1869*. Princeton, N.J.: Princeton University Press.

Barras, R. 1976. "Towards a Theory of Innovation in Services." *Research Policy* 5:161–73.

Bauer, P. T. 1981. *Equality, the Third World, and Economic Delusion*. Cambridge, Mass.: Harvard University Press.

———. 1984. *Reality and Rhetoric: Studies in the Economics of Development*. Cambridge, Mass.: Harvard University Press.

Baumol, W. J. 1968. "Entrepreneurship in Economic Theory." *American Economic Review* 58:64–71.

———. 1983. "Toward Operational Models of Entrepreneurship." In *Entrepreneurship*, ed. J. Ronen. Lexington, Mass.: Lexington Books.

———. 1985a. *Entrepreneurship and the Long Run Productivity Record*. Research Report 86–04. New York: C. V. Starr Center for Applied Economics, New York University.

———. 1985b. "Productivity Policy and the Service Sector." In *Managing the Service Economy: Prospects and Problems*, ed. R. P. Inman. London: Cambridge University Press.

———. 1986. "Productivity Growth, Convergence, and Welfare: What the Long-Run Data Show." *American Economic Review* 76:1072–85.

———, and K. McLennan. 1985. *Productivity Growth and U.S. Competitiveness*. New York: Oxford University Press.

———, and M. Stewart. 1964. "Rules of Thumb and Optimally Imperfect Decisions." *American Economic Review* 54:23–46.

Benedict, M. R. 1953. *Farm Policies of the United States, 1790–1950*. New York: Twentieth Century Fund.

Berg, M. 1985. *The Age of Manufactures: 1700–1820*. Totowa, N.J.: Barnes and Noble.

van den Berg, L., L. S. Burns, and L. H. Klaassen, eds. 1987. *Spatial Cycles*. Aldershot, England: Gower.

———, L., R. Drewett, L. H. Klaassen, A. Rossi, and C. H. T. Vijverberg. 1982. *Urban Europe: A Study of Growth and Decline*. Oxford, England: Pergamon.

Berger, P. L. 1986a. *The Capitalist Revolution: Fifty Propositions about Prosperity, Equality and Liberty*. New York: Basic Books.

———, ed. 1986b. *Capitalism and Equality in the Third World: Modern Capitalism*. Vol. 2. Lanham, Md.: University Press of America.

Berliner, J. S. 1976. *The Innovation Decision in Soviet Industry*. Cambridge, Mass.: Harvard University Press.

Berry, B. J. L. 1972. "Hierarchical Diffusion: The Basis of Developmental Filtering and Spread in a System of Growth Centers." In *Growth Centers in Regional Economic Development*, ed. N. M. Hansen. New York: Free Press.

———1988. "Migration Reversals in Perspective: The Long-Wave Evidence." *International Regional Science Review* 11: 245–51.

Beyers, W. B. 1981. "Alternative Spatial Linkage Structures in Multiregional Economic Systems." In *Industrial Location and Regional Systems*, ed. J. Rees, G. J. D. Hewings, and H. A. Stafford. New York: Bergin.

Billington, R. A. 1974. *Westward Expansion: A History of the American Frontier*. 4th ed. New York: Macmillan.

Booth, D. E. 1987. *Regional Long Waves, Uneven Growth, and the Cooperative Alternative.* New York: Praeger.

Borts, G. H. 1971. "Growth and Capital Movements Among U.S. Regions in the Postwar Period." In *Essays in Regional Economics*, ed. J. F. Kain and J. R. Meyer. Cambridge, Mass.: Harvard University Press.

————, and J. L. Stein. 1964. *Economic Growth in a Free Market.* New York: Columbia University Press.

Boserup, E. 1965. *The Conditions of Agricultural Growth.* London: Allen and Unwin.

Boulding, K. E. 1950. *A Reconstruction of Economics.* New York: Wiley.

————. 1955. *Economic Analysis.* New York: Harper & Row.

————. 1981. *Evolutionary Economics.* Beverly Hills, Calif.: Sage.

Boulianne, L., and D. Maillat. 1983. *Technologie, Entreprises et Régions.* St. Saphorin, Switzerland: Georgi.

von Böventer, E. 1975. "Regional Growth Theory." *Urban Studies* 12:1–29.

————. 1978. "Bandwagon Effects and Product Cycles in Urban Dynamics." *Urban Studies* 15:261–72.

Bower, J. L. 1970. *Managing the Resource Allocation Process: A Study of Corporate Planning and Investment.* Cambridge, Mass.: Graduate School of Business Administration, Harvard University.

Braudel, F. 1981. *Civilization and Capitalism: 15th–18th Century; The Structures of Everyday Life.* Vol. 1. New York: Harper & Row.

————. 1982. *Civilization and Capitalism: 15th–18th Century; Perspective of the World.* Vol. 3. New York: Harper & Row.

Brown, L. 1981. *Innovation Diffusion: A New Perspective.* New York: Methuen.

Burgess, E. W. 1925. "The Growth of the City: An Introduction to a Research Project." In *The City*, ed. R. E. Park, E. W. Burgess, and R. D. McKenzie. Chicago: University of Chicago Press.

Burns, L. S. 1987. "Cyclical Patterns in U.S. Regional Development." In *Spatial Cycles*, ed. J. van den Berg, L. S. Burns, and L. H. Klaassen. Aldershot, England: Gower.

Camagni, R. P. 1985. "Spatial Diffusion of Pervasive Process Innovation." *Papers of the Regional Science Association* 58:83–95.

Cameron, K. S. and P. A. Whetten. 1981. "Perceptions of Organizational Effectiveness over Organizational Life Cycles." *Administrative Science Quarterly* 26:525–44.

Cantillon, R. 1931. *Essai sur la Nature du Commerce en Général*, ed. H. Higgs. London: Macmillan (orig. publ. 1755; London: Gyles).

Carey, H. C. 1871. *Principles of Social Science.* 3 vols. Philadelphia: Lippincott.

Casetti, E. 1981. "A Catastrophe Model of Regional Dynamics." *Annals of the Association of American Geographers* 71:572–79.

————. 1984. "Manufacturing Productivity and Snowbelt-Sunbelt Shifts." *Economic Geography* 60:313–24.

Casson, M. 1982. *The Entrepreneur: An Economic Theory.* Totowa, N.J.: Barnes and Noble.

Caves, R. E. 1966. "Industrial Organization, Corporate Strategy, and Structure." *Journal of Economic Literature* 18:64–92.

———. 1980. "Corporate Strategy and Structure." *Journal of Economic Literature* 18:64-92.

———. 1983. *Multinational Enterprise and Economic Analysis.* New York: Cambridge University Press.

Chandler, A. D. 1962. *Strategy and Structure: Chapters in the History of the Industrial Enterprise.* Cambridge, Mass.: M.I.T. Press.

———. 1968. "The Coming of Big Business." In *The Changing Economic Order,* ed. A. D. Chandler, S. Bruchey, and L. Galambos. New York: Harcourt, Brace & World.

———. 1977. *The Visible Hand: The Managerial Revolution in American Business.* Cambridge, Mass.: Harvard University Press.

———, and H. Daems, eds. 1980. *Managerial Hierarchies: Comparative Perspectives on the Rise of the Modern Industrial Enterprise.* Cambridge, Mass.: Harvard University Press.

———, and F. Redlich. 1961. "Recent Developments in American Business Administration and their Conceptualization." *Business History Review* 35:1–27.

Chapman, S. J., and T. S. Ashton. 1914. "The Sizes of Businesses, Mainly in the Textile Industries." *Journal of the Royal Statistical Society* 77:510–47.

Chinitz, B. 1960. *Freight in the Metropolis.* Cambridge, Mass.: Harvard University Press.

———. 1961. "Contrasts in Agglomeration: New York and Pittsburgh." *American Economic Review* 51:279–89.

———. 1986. "The Regional Transformation of the American Economy." *American Economic Review* 76:300–03.

Christaller, W. 1966. *Central Places in Southern Germany.* Trans. C. W. Baskin. Englewood Cliffs, N.J.: Prentice-Hall.

Clark, C. 1940. *The Conditions of Economic Progress.* London: Macmillan.

Clark, G. L., M. S. Gertler, and J. E. M. Whiteman. 1986. *Regional Dynamics: Studies in Adjustment Theory.* Boston: Allen & Unwin.

Clark, P. K. 1979. "Investment in the 1970s: Theory, Performance, and Prediction." *Brookings Papers on Economic Activity* 1:73–113.

Clark, V. S. 1916. *History of Manufacture in the United States, 1607–1860.* Washington, D.C.: Carnegie Institution.

Coase, R. H. 1937. "The Nature of the Firm." *Economica* 4:386–405.

Cochran, T. C. 1965. "The Entrepreneur in Economic Change." *Explorations in Entrepreneurial History* (2d series) 3:25–38.

———. 1972. *American Business in the Twentieth Century.* Cambridge, Mass.: Harvard University Press.

———. 1977. *Two Hundred Years of American Business.* New York: Basic Books.

Coffey, W. J., and M. Polese. 1984. "The Concept of Local Development: A Stages Model of Endogenous Regional Growth." *Papers of the Regional Science Association* 55:1–12.

Cohen, S. S., and J. Zysman. 1987. *Manufacturing Matters: The Myth of the Post-Industrial Economy.* New York: Basic Books.

Cole, A. H. 1949. *Change and the Entrepreneur: Postulates and Patterns for Entrepreneurial History.* Cambridge, Mass.: Harvard University Press.

Cyert, R. M., and J. G. March. 1963. *A Behavioral Theory of the Firm*. Englewood Cliffs, N.J.: Prentice-Hall.

—————, and H. A. Simon. 1983. "The Behavioral Approach: With Emphasis on Economics." *Behavioral Science* 28:95–108.

—————, M. H. DeGroot, and C. A. Holt. 1979. "Capital Allocation within a Firm." *Behavioral Science* 24:287–95.

Dahmén, E. 1970. *Entrepreneurial Activity and the Development of Swedish Industry, 1919-1939*. Trans. A. Leijonhufvud. Homewood, Ill.: Irwin.

David, P. A. 1974. *Technical Change, Innovation and Economic Growth*. London: Cambridge University Press.

Davies, S. 1979. *The Diffusion of Process Innovations*. Cambridge, England: Cambridge University Press.

Davison, J. P., P. S. Florence, B. Gray, and N. Ross. 1958. *Productivity and Economic Incentives*. London: Allen & Unwin.

Demsetz, H. 1983. "The Neglect of the Entrepreneur." In *Entrepreneurship*, ed. J. Ronen. Lexington, Mass.: Lexington Books.

Denison, E. F. 1962. *The Sources of Economic Growth in the United States and the Alternatives Before Us*. New York: Committee for Economic Development.

—————. 1974. *Accounting for United States Economic Growth, 1929–1969*. Washington, D.C.: Brookings Institution.

—————. 1985. *Trends in American Economic Growth, 1929–1982*. Washington, D.C.: Brookings Institution.

Dicken, P. 1971. "Some Aspects of the Decision Making Behavior of Business Organizations." *Economic Geography* 47:426–37.

Dogramaci, A., ed. 1986. *Measurement Issues and Behavior of Productivity Variables*. Hingham, Mass.: Kluwer-Nijhoff.

Donaldson, G., and J. W. Lorsch. 1986. *Decision Making at the Top: The Shaping of Strategic Decisions*. New York: Basic Books.

Duke, B. 1986. *The Japanese School: Lessons for Industrial America*. New York: Praeger.

Dunn, E. S. 1971. *Economic and Social Development*. Baltimore, Md.: Johns Hopkins University Press.

—————. 1983. *The Development of the U.S. Urban System*. Vol. II, *Industrial Shifts, Implications*. Baltimore, Md.: Johns Hopkins University Press.

Durand, D. E. 1975. "Effects of Achievement Motivation and Skill Training on the Entrepreneurial Behavior of Black Businessmen." *Organizational Behavior and Human Performance* 14:76–90.

—————. 1983. "Modified Achievement Motivation Training: A Longitudinal Study of the Effects of a Condensed Training Design for Entrepreneurs." *Psychological Reports* 52:907–11.

Durand, J. D. 1948. *The Labor Force in the United States, 1890-1940*. New York: Social Science Research Council.

Easterlin, R. A. 1957. "Estimate of Manufacturing Activity." In *Population Redistribution and Economic Growth, United States, 1870-1950*, Vol. I, ed. E. S. Lee, A. Ratner, C. P. Brainerd, and R. A. Easterlin. Philadelphia: American Philosophical Society.

Engerman, S. L., and R. E. Gallman, eds. 1987. *Long-Term Factors in American Economic Growth.* Chicago: University of Chicago Press.
Erickson, R. A. 1972. "The 'Lead Firm' Concept: An Analysis of Theoretical Elements." *Tijdschrift voor Economische en Sociale Geografie* 63:426–37.
———. 1976. "Nonmetropolitan Industrial Expansion: Emerging Implications for Regional Development." *Review of Regional Studies* 6:35–48.
———, and T. R. Leinbach. 1979. "Characteristics of Branch Plants Attracted to Nonmetropolitan Areas." In *Nonmetropolitan Industrialization,* ed. R. E. Lonsdale and H. L. Seyler. New York: Wiley.
Evans, G. H. 1949. "The Entrepreneur and Economic Theory: A Historical and Analytical Approach." *American Economic Review* 39:336–48.
Fabricant, S. 1949. "The Changing Industrial Distribution of Gainful Workers: Some Comments on the American Decennial Statistics for 1820–1940." In *Studies in Income and Wealth,* Vol. 11, ed. National Bureau of Economic Research. New York: National Bureau of Economic Research.
———. 1959. *Basic Facts on Productivity.* New York: National Bureau of Economic Research.
Faulhaber, G., E. Noam, and R. Talsey, eds. 1986. *Services in Transition.* Cambridge, Mass.: Ballinger.
Feller, I. 1975. "Invention, Diffusion and Industrial Location." In *Locational Dynamics of Manufacturing Activity,* ed. L. Collins and D. F. Walker. London: Wiley.
Fisher, A. G. B. 1933. "Capital and the Growth of Knowledge." *Economic Journal* 43:379–89.
———. 1939. "Production: Primary, Secondary and Tertiary." *Economic Journal* 49:24–38.
Fite, G. C. 1966. *The Farmer's Frontier, 1865–1900.* New York: Holt, Rinehart & Winston.
Fogel, R. W., and S. L. Engerman, eds. 1971. *The Reinterpretation of American Economic History.* New York: Harper & Row.
Forrester, J. W. 1969. *Urban Dynamics.* Cambridge, Mass.: M.I.T. Press.
Forrester, N. B. 1973. *The Life Cycle of Economic Development.* Cambridge, Mass.: Wright-Allen.
Frank, R. H. 1985. *Choosing the Right Pond: Human Behavior and the Quest for Status.* New York: Oxford University Press.
Freeman, C. 1974. *The Economics of Industrial Innovation.* Harmondsworth, England: Penguin.
———, ed. 1987. *Design, Innovation and Long Cycles in Economic Development.* London: Frances Pinter.
Freeman, K. B. 1976. "The Significance of McClelland's Achievement Variable in the Aggregate Production Function." *Economic Development and Cultural Change* 24:815–24.
Fuchs, V. 1961. "Integration, Concentration, and Profits in Manufacturing Industries." *Quarterly Journal of Economics* 75:282–305.
———. 1962. *Changes in the Location of Manufacturing in the United States Since 1929.* New Haven, Conn.: Yale University Press.

———. 1968. *The Services Economy*. New York: National Bureau of Economic Research and Columbia University Press.

———, and J. A. Wilburn. 1967. *Productivity Differences Within the Service Sector*. New York: National Bureau of Economic Research and Columbia University Press.

Futia, C. 1980. "Schumpeterian Competition." *Quarterly Journal of Economics* 94:675–95.

Galbraith, J. K. 1967. *The New Industrial State*. New York: New American Library.

Garnick, D. H. 1984. "Shifting Balances in U.S. Metropolitan and Nonmetropolitan Area Growth." *International Regional Science Review* 9:257–73.

———, and H. L. Friedenberg. 1982. "Accounting for Regional Differences in Per Capita Personal Income Growth, 1929–1979." *Survey of Current Business* 62:24–34.

Georgescu-Roegen, N. 1971. *The Entropy Law and the Economic Process*. Cambridge, Mass.: Harvard University Press.

Giersch, H. 1984. "The Age of Schumpeter." *American Economic Review* 74:103–09.

Gilder, G. 1984. *The Spirit of Enterprise*. New York: Simon & Schuster.

Glade, W. P. 1967. "Approaches to a Theory of Entrepreneurial Formation." *Explorations in Entrepreneurial History* (2d series) 4:245–59.

———. 1983. "The Levantines in Latin America." *American Economic Review* 73:118–22.

Goddard, J. B. 1978. "The Location of Non-Manufacturing Activities within Manufacturing Industries." In *Contemporary Industrialization*, ed. F. E. I. Hamilton. London: Longman.

Goodman, D., B. Sorj, and J. Wilkinson. 1987. *From Farming to Biotechnology*. New York: Basil Blackwell.

Gras, N. S. B. 1922. *An Introduction to Economic History*. New York: Harper.

———. 1939. *Business and Capitalism: An Introduction to Business History*. New York: Crofts.

Gray, S. 1819. *The Happieness of States*. London: Hatchard.

Greenfield, S. M., and A. Strickon, eds. 1986. *Entrepreneurship and Social Change: Monographs in Economic Anthropology*. Lanham, Md.: University Press of America.

Greenhut, M. L. 1970. *A Theory of the Firm in Economic Space*. New York: Appleton-Century-Crofts.

———, C. S. Hung, and G. Norman. 1986. *The Economics of Imperfect Competition: A Spatial Approach*. New York: Cambridge University Press.

Griliches, Z. 1957. "Hybrid Corn: An Exploration in the Economics of Technological Change." *Econometrica* 25:501–22.

———, ed. 1984. *R & D, Patents, and Productivity*. Chicago: University of Chicago Press.

Grossman, G. M. 1984. "International Trade, Foreign Investment, and the Formation of the Entrepreneurial Class." *American EconomicReview* 74:605–14.

Grunwald, J., and K. Flamm. 1985. *The Global Factory: Foreign Assembly in International Trade.* Washington, D.C.: Brookings Institution.

Habakkuk, H. J. 1962. *American and British Technology in the Nineteenth Century.* Cambridge, England: Cambridge University Press.

Hagen, E. E. 1962. *On the Theory of Social Change: How Economic Growth Begins.* Homewood, Ill.: Irwin.

Hägerstrand, T. 1967. *Innovation Diffusion as a Spatial Process.* Trans. A. Pred. Chicago: University of Chicago Press.

————. 1969. "What About People in Regional Science?" *Papers of the Regional Science Association* 24:7–21.

Hahn, F. H. 1970. "Some Adjustment Problems." *Econometrica* 38:1–17.

Haig, R. M. 1926. "Toward an Understanding of the Metropolis: I. Some Speculations Regarding the Economic Base of Urban Concentration." *Quarterly Journal of Economics* 40:179–208.

Hall, P., and D. Hay. 1980. *Growth Centers in the European Urban System.* Berkeley: University of California Press.

Hamilton, F. E. I., ed. 1974. *Spatial Perspectives on Industrial Organization and Decision Making.* London: Wiley.

Hannah, L. 1984. "Entrepreneurs in the Social Sciences." *Economica* 51:219–34.

Hansen, N. M. 1967. "Development Pole Theory in a Regional Context." *Kyklos* 20:709–25.

————. 1971. *Intermediate Size Cities as Growth Centers.* New York: Praeger.

————. 1975. "An Evaluation of Growth Center Theory and Practice." *Environment and Planning A* 7:821–32.

————. 1979. "The New International Division of Labor and Manufacturing Decentralization in the United States." *Review of Regional Studies* 9:1–11.

————. 1980. "Dualism, Capital-Labor Ratios and the Regions of the U. S.: A Comment." *Journal of Regional Science* 20:401–03.

Harbison, F. H. 1956. "Entrepreneurial Organization as a Factor in Economic Development." *Quarterly Journal of Economics* 70:364–79.

Harrington, J. W. 1986. "Strategy Formulation, Organizational Learning, and Location." In *New Technology and Regional Development*, ed. G. A. van der Knaap and E. Wever. Beckenham, England.: Croom Helm.

Harris, J. R. 1973. "Entrepreneurship and Economic Development." In *Business Enterprise and Economic Change: Essays in Honor of Harold F. Williamson*, ed. L. P. Cain and P. J. Uselding. Kent, Ohio: Kent State University Press.

von Hayek, F. A. 1945. "The Use of Knowledge in Society." *American Economic Review* 35:519–30.

Hayes, R. H., and S. C. Wheelwright. 1979a. "Link Manufacturing Process and Product Life Cycles." *Harvard Business Review* 57:133–40.

————., 1979b. "The Dynamics of Process-Product Life Cycles." *Harvard Business Review* 57:127–36.

Hazlitt, H. 1984. *The Failure of the "New Economics": An Analysis of the Keynesian Fallacies.* Lanham, Md.: University Press of America (orig. publ. 1959; New York: Arlington House).

Hekman, J. S. 1980. "The Product Cycle and New England Textiles." *Quarterly Journal of Economics* 94:697–717.

Hertz, D. B. 1950. *The Theory and Practice of Industrial Research*. New York: McGraw-Hill.

Hewings, G. J. D., M. Sonis, and R. C. Jensen, 1988. "Fields of Influence of Technological Change in Input-Output Models." *Papers of the Regional Science Association* 64:25–36.

Hirsch, S. 1967. *Location of Industry and International Competitiveness*. London: Oxford University Press.

Hirsch, W. Z. 1973. *Urban Economic Analysis*. New York: McGraw-Hill.

Hirschman, A. O. 1958. *The Strategy of Economic Development*. New Haven, Conn.: Yale University Press.

Hoenack, S. A. 1983. *Economic Behavior Within Organizations*. New York: Cambridge University Press.

Hofer, C. W. 1975. "Toward a Contingency Theory of Business Strategy." *Academy of Management Journal* 18:784–810.

Hohenberg, P. M., and L. H. Lees. 1986. *The Making of Urban Europe, 1000–1950*. Cambridge, Mass.: Harvard University Press.

Hoover, E. M. 1948. *The Location of Economic Activity*. New York: McGraw-Hill.

Hoselitz, B. F. 1963. "Entrepreneurship and Traditional Elites." *Explorations in Entrepreneurial History* (2d series) 1:36–49.

Hoyt, H. 1939. *The Structure and Growth of Residential Neighborhoods in American Cities*. Washington, D.C.: Federal Housing Administration.

———. 1941. "Economic Background of Cities." *Journal of Land and Public Utility Economics* 17:188–195.

Hulten, C. R., and R. M. Schwab. 1984. "Regional Productivity Growth in U.S. Manufacturing: 1951–78." *American Economic Review* 74:152–62.

International Labor Organization. 1951. *Payment by Results*. ILO Studies and Reports, no. 27. Geneva: ILO.

———. 1957a. "ILO Productivity Missions to Underdeveloped Countries, Part I." *International Labor Review* 76:1–29.

———. 1957b. "ILO Productivity Missions to Underdeveloped Countries, Part II." *International Labor Review* 76:139–66.

———. 1979. *New Forms of Work Organization*. Vols. 1, 2. Geneva: ILO.

———. 1982. *Improvements in the Quality of Working Life in Three Japanese Industries*. Geneva: ILO.

Isard, W. 1951. "Interregional and Regional Input-Output Analysis: A Model of a Space Economy." *Review of Economics and Statistics* 33:318–28.

———. 1953. "Some Empirical Results and Problems of Regional Input-Output Analysis." In *Studies in the Structure of the American Economy*, ed. W. W. Leontief. New York: Oxford University Press.

———. 1960. *Methods of Regional Analysis*. Cambridge, Mass.: M.I.T. Press.

———. 1969. *General Theory: Social, Political, Economic, and Regional*. Cambridge, Mass.: M.I.T. Press.

———, and T. W. Longford. 1971. *Regional Input-Output Study: Recollections, Reflections, and Diverse Notes on the Philadelphia Experience.* Cambridge, Mass.: M.I.T. Press.

———, and T. A. Reiner. 1962. "Aspects of Decision-Making Theory and Regional Science." *Papers and Proceedings of the Regional Science Association* 9:25–33.

Jackson, G., G. Masnick, R. Bolton, S. Bartlett, and J. Pitkin. 1981. *Regional Diversity: Growth in the United States, 1960–1990.* Boston: Auburn House.

Jewkes, J., D. Sawers, and R. Stillerman. 1961. *The Sources of Invention.* New York: Norton.

Johnston, J. 1963. "The Productivity of Management Consultants." *Journal of the Royal Statistical Society, series A,* 126:248–73.

Jones, B. G. 1961. "The Theory of the Urban Economy: Origins and Development with Emphasis on Intraurban Distribution of Population and Economic Activity." Unpublished Ph.D. dissertation. Chapel Hill, NC: Department of Economics, University of North Carolina.

———. 1984. "Productivity and the Spatial Implications of Structural Change: Empirical Evidence for Simon's Model." *Papers of the Regional Science Association* 54:1–11.

———, and W. F. Shepherd. 1985. "Economic Growth and Structural Change: Manufacturing in the United States, 1954–1977." Mimeo. Ithaca, N.Y.: Department of City and Regional Planning, Cornell University.

Jorgenson, D. W. 1971. "Econometric Studies of Investment Behavior: A Survey." *Journal of Economic Literature* 9:1111–47.

———, and C.D. Siebert. 1968. "A Comparison of Alternative Theories of Corporate Investment Behavior." *American Economic Review* 58:681–712.

Kanbur, S. M. 1980. "A Note on Risk Taking, Entrepreneurship and Schumpeter." *History of Political Economy* 12:489–98.

Kemp, T. 1969. *Industrialization in Nineteenth Century Europe.* London: Longman.

Kendrick, J. W. 1961. *Productivity Trends in the United States.* National Bureau of Economic Research. Princeton, N.J.: Princeton University Press.

———. 1986. *Improving Company Productivity.* Baltimore, Md.: Johns Hopkins University Press.

———, and E. S. Grossman. 1980. *Productivity in the United States: Trends and Cycles.* Baltimore, Md: Johns Hopkins University Press.

Kerr, A., and R. B. Williamson. 1970. "Regional Economics in the U.S.: A Review Essay." *Growth and Change* 1:5–19.

Kilby, P. 1962. "Organization and Productivity in Backward Economies." *Quarterly Journal of Economics* 76:303–10.

———. 1971. "Hunting the Heffalump." In *Entrepreneurship and Economic Development,* ed. P. Kilby. New York: Free Press.

———. 1983. "An Entrepreneurial Problem." *American Economic Review* 73:107–11.

Kimberly, J. R., and R. H. Miles. 1980. *The Organizational Life Cycle.* San Francisco: Jossey-Bass.

Kindleberger, C. P., and D. B. Audretsch, eds. 1986. *The Multinational Corporation in the 1980s*. Cambridge, Mass.: M.I.T. Press.

————, and G. diTella, eds. 1982. *Economics in the Long View: Essays in Honor of W. W. Rostow*. New York: New York University Press.

Kirzner, I. M. 1979. *Perception, Opportunity and Profit: Studies in the Theory of Entrepreneurship*. Chicago: University of Chicago Press.

————. 1983. "Entrepreneurs and the Entrepreneurial Function: A Commentary." In *Entrepreneurship*, ed. J. Ronen. Lexington, Mass.: Lexington Books.

Kleinknecht, A. 1987. *Innovation Patterns in Crisis and Prosperity*. London: Macmillan.

Knight, F. H. 1921. *Risk, Uncertainty and Profit*. Boston: Houghton Mifflin.

Kondratieff, N. D. 1935. "The Long Waves in Economic Life." *Review of Economics and Statistics* 17:105–15.

Kornai, J. 1986. *Contradictions and Dilemmas: Studies on the Socialist Economy and Society*. Cambridge, Mass.: M.I.T. Press.

Krumme, G. 1969. "Toward a Geography of Enterprise." *Economic Geography* 45:30–40.

————, and R. Hayter. 1975. "Implications of Corporate Strategies and Product Cycle Adjustments for Regional Employment Changes." In *Locational Dynamics of Manufacturing Activity*, ed. L. Collins and D. F. Walker. London: Wiley.

Kunkel, J. H. 1965. "Values and Behavior in Economic Development." *Economic Development and Cultural Change* 13:257–77.

Kurth, J. R. 1979. "The Political Consequences of the Product Cycle: Industrial History and Political Outcomes." *International Organization* 33:1–35.

Kuznets, S. 1930. *Secular Movements in Production and Prices*. Boston: Houghton Mifflin.

————. 1953. *Economic Change*. New York: Norton.

————. 1961. *Capital in the American Economy: Its Formation and Financing*. New York: National Bureau of Economic Research.

Lakshmanan, T. R., and L. Chatterjee. 1986. "Technical Change and Metropolitan Adjustments: Some Policy and Analytical Implications." *Regional Science and Urban Economics*, 16:7–30.

Landes, D. 1969. *The Unbound Prometheus*. London: Cambridge University Press.

Landsberger, H. A. 1958. *Hawthorne Revisited*. Cornell Studies in Industrial and Labor Relations, vol. 9. Ithaca, N.Y.: New York State School of Industrial and Labor Relations, Cornell University.

Langlois, R. N., ed. 1985. *Economics as a Process*. New York: Cambridge University Press.

Lebergott, S. 1964. *Manpower in Economic Growth: The American Record Since 1800*. New York: McGraw-Hill.

Leff, N. 1978. "Industrial Organization and Entrepreneurship in the Developing Countries: The Economic Groups." *Economic Development and Cultural Change* 26:661–75.

————. 1979. "Entrepreneurship and Economic Development: The Problem Revisited." *Journal of Economic Literature* 17:46–64.

Leibenstein, H. 1966. "Allocative Efficiency vs. 'X-Efficiency.'" *American Economic Review* 56:392–415.

————. 1968. "Entrepreneurship and Development." *American Economic Review* 58:72–83.

————. 1976. *Beyond Economic Man: A New Foundation for Microeconomics.* Cambridge, Mass.: Harvard University Press.

————. 1978. *General X-Efficiency Theory and Economic Development.* New York: Oxford University Press.

————. 1979a. "The General X-Efficiency Paradigm and the Role of the Entrepreneur." In *Time, Uncertainty, and Disequilibrium,* ed. M. J. Rizzio. Lexington, Mass.: Heath.

————. 1979b. "A Branch of Economics is Missing: Micro-Micro Theory." *Journal of Economic Literature* 17:477–502.

————. 1985. "Entrepreneurship, Entrepreneurship Training, and Economics: The Case of the Missing Inputs." Mimeo. Cambridge, Mass: Department of Economics, Harvard University.

————. 1987. *Inside the Firm: The Inefficiencies of Hierarchy.* Cambridge, Mass.: Harvard University Press.

Leontief, W. W. 1936. "Quantitative Input and Output Relations in the Economic System of the United States." *Review of Economics and Statistics* 18:105–25.

————. 1941. *The Structure of the American Economy, 1919–1939.* New York: Oxford University Press.

Letwin, W. 1965. *Law and Economic Policy in America.* New York: Random House.

Levasseur, P. E. 1889. *La Population Française.* Vol. 1. Paris: Arthur Rousseau.

Leven, C. L. 1980. "Regional Variations in Metropolitan Growth and Development." In *Alternatives to Confrontation: A National Policy toward Regional Change,* ed. V. L. Arnold. Lexington, Mass.: Lexington Books.

Lever, W. F. 1972. "Industrial Movement, Spatial Association and Fundamental Linkages." *Regional Studies* 6:371–84.

Levine, H. S. 1983. "On the Nature and Location of Entrepreneurial Activity in Centrally Planned Economies: The Soviet Case." In *Entrepreneurship,* ed. J. Ronen. Lexington, Mass: Lexington Books.

Lewis, W. A. 1955. *The Theory of Economic Growth.* London: Allen & Unwin.

————. 1978a. *The Evolution of the International Economic Order.* Princeton, N.J.: Princeton University Press.

————. 1978b. *Growth and Fluctuations, 1870–1913.* London: Allen & Unwin.

Libecap, G., ed. 1986. *Advances in the Study of Entrepreneurship, Innovation and Economic Growth.* Vols. I, II. Greenwich, Conn.: J. A. I. Press.

Lichtenberg, R. 1960. *One Tenth of a Nation: National Forces in the Economic Growth of the New York Region.* Cambridge, Mass.: Harvard University Press.

Lichtenstein, S., B. Fischhoff, and L. D. Phillips. 1982. "Calibration and Probabilities: The State of the Art to 1980." In *Judgment underUncertainties:*

Heuristics and Biases, ed. D. Kahneman, P. Slovic, and A. Tversky. New York: Cambridge University Press.

Lösch, A. 1954. *The Economics of Location.* Trans. W. H. Woglom and W. F. Stolper. New Haven, Conn.: Yale University Press.

Love, N. S. 1986. *Marx, Nietzche, and Modernity.* New York: Columbia University Press.

Lovell, M. C. 1978. "The Profit Picture: Trends and Cycles." *Brookings Papers on Economic Activity* 3:769–789.

Macdonald, R. 1971. "Schumpeter and Max Weber: Central Visions and Social Theories." In *Entrepreneurship and Economic Development*, ed. P. Kilby. New York: Free Press.

Machlup, F. 1962. *The Production and Distribution of Knowledge in the United States.* Princeton, N.J.: Princeton University Press.

Maddison, A. 1982. *Phases of Capitalist Development.* New York: Oxford University Press.

Magee, S. P. 1977. "Multinational Corporations, the Industry Technology Cycle and Development." *Journal of World Trade Law* 11:297–321.

Malecki, E. J. 1980."Corporate Organization of R&D and the Location of Technological Activities." *Regional Studies* 14:219–34.

———. 1983. "Technology and Regional Development: A Survey." *International Regional Science Review* 8:89–125.

Mansfield, E. 1968. *Industrial Research and Technological Innovation.* New York: Norton.

———. 1971. *Research and Innovation in the Modern Corporation.* New York: Norton.

———, J. Rapaport, A. Romeo, E. Villani, S. Wagner, and F. Husic. 1977. *The Production and Application of New Industrial Technology.* New York: Norton.

Margolis, H. 1984. *Selfishness, Altruism, and Rationality: A Theory of Social Choice.* Chicago: University of Chicago Press.

Markusen, A. R. 1985. *Profit Cycles, Oligopoly, and Regional Development.* Cambridge, Mass.: M.I.T. Press.

Marshall, A. 1961. *Principles of Economics*, ed. G. W. Guilleband. London: Macmillan (orig. publ. 1890).

Marshall, J. N. 1982. "Organizational Theory and Industrial Location." *Environment and Planning A* 14:1667–83.

Marshall, M. 1987. *Long Waves of Regional Development.* London: Macmillan.

Martin, R. F. 1939. *National Income in the United States, 1799–1938.* New York: National Industrial Conference Board.

Marx, K. 1967. *Capital.* Vols. 1 and 3, ed. F. Engels. New York: International Publishers [orig. publ. as *Das Kapital* in 1867 (vol. 1), 1894 (vol. 3); Hamburg: Meissner].

Massey, D. 1979. "A Critical Evaluation of Industrial Location Theory." In *Spatial Analysis, Industry and the Industrial Environment.* Vol. 1, *Industrial Systems*, ed. F. E. I. Hamilton, and G. J. R. Linge. New York: Wiley.

McClelland, D. C., ed. 1955. *Studies in Motivation.* New York: Appleton-Century-Crofts.

———. 1961. *The Achieving Society.* Princeton, N.J.: Van Nostrand.

————. 1965. "N-Achievement and Entrepreneurship: A Longitudinal Study." *Journal of Personality and Social Psychology–* 1:389–92.

————. 1966. "Does Education Accelerate Economic Growth?" *Economic Development and Cultural Change* 14:257–78.

————, and E. Steel. 1972. *Motivation Workshops.* New York: General Learning Press.

————, and D. G. Winter. 1969. *Motivating Economic Achievement.* New York: Free Press.

————, J. W. Atkinson, R. A. Clark, and E. L. Lowell. 1953. *The Achievement Motive.* New York: Appleton-Century-Crofts.

McDermott, P., and M. Taylor. 1982. *Industrial Organisation and Location.* New York: Cambridge University Press.

McGouldrick, P. F. 1968. *New England Textiles in the Nineteenth Century.* Cambridge, Mass.: Harvard University Press.

Mensch, G. O. 1979. *Stalemate in Technology.* Cambridge, Mass.: Ballinger.

Meyer, J. R. 1963. "Regional Economics: A Survey." *American Economic Review* 53:19–54.

Miernyk, W. H. 1965. *The Elements of Input-Output Analysis.* New York: Random House.

————. 1980. "Regional Shifts in Economic Base and Structure in the United States Since 1940." In *Alternatives to Confrontation: A National Policy toward Regional Change,* ed. V. L. Arnold. Lexington, Mass.: Lexington Books.

Mill, J. S. 1848. *Principles of Political Economy.* Boston: Little and Brown.

Mintzberg, H. 1973. *The Nature of Managerial Work.* New York: Harper & Row.

————. 1979. *The Structuring of Organizations: A Synthesis of Research.* Englewood Cliffs, N.J.: Prentice-Hall.

Miron, D., and D. C. McClelland. 1979. "The Impact of Achievement Motivation Training on Small Businesses." *California Management Review* 21:13–28.

Mirowski, P., ed. 1986. *The Reconstruction of Economic Theory.* Hingham, Mass.: Kluwer-Nijhoff.

Miyao, T. 1983. "Rural and Urban Population Changes and the Stages of Economic Development: A Unified Approach." *Environment and Planning A* 15:1161–1174.

Molle, W. 1983. *Industrial Change, Innovation and Location.* Paris: Organization for Economic Cooperation and Development.

Moomaw, R. L. 1983. "Spatial Productivity Variations in Manufacturing: A Critical Survey of Cross-Sectional Analyses." *International Regional Science Review* 8:1–22.

Morawetz, D. 1974. "Employment Implications of Industrialization in Developing Countries: A Survey." *Economic Journal* 84:491–542.

Moriarty, B. M. 1983. "Hierarchies of Cities and the Spatial Filtering of Industrial Development." *Papers of the Regional Science Association* 53:59–82.

Mowday, R. T., L. W. Porter, and R. M. Steers. 1981. *Employee-Organization Linkages.* Orlando, Fla.: Academic Press.

Mueller, D. C. 1986. *Profits in the Long Run.* New York: Cambridge University Press.

Myers, M. L. 1983. *The Soul of Modern Economic Man: Ideas of Self Interest, Thomas Hobbes to Adam Smith*. Chicago: University of Chicago Press.

Nabseth, L., and G. F. Ray, eds. 1974. *The Diffusion of New Industrial Processes*. Cambridge, England: Cambridge University Press.

Nelson, R. R. 1959. "The Economics of Invention: A Survey of the Literature." *Journal of Business* 32:101–27.

———. 1984. "Incentives for Entrepreneurship and Supporting Institutions." *Weltwirtschaftliches Archiv* 120:646–61.

———. 1986. "Institutions Supporting Technical Advance in Industry." *American Economic Review* 76:186–89.

———, and V. D. Norman. 1977. "Technological Change and Factor Mix over the Product Cycle: A Model of Dynamic Comparative Advantage." *Journal of Development Economics* 4:3–24.

———, and S. G. Winter. 1974. "Neoclassical vs. Evolutionary Theories of Economic Growth: Critique and Prospectus." *Economic Journal* 84:886–905.

———. 1982a. *An Evolutionary Theory of Economic Change*. Cambridge, Mass.: Belknap.

———. 1982b. "The Schumpeterian Tradeoff Revisited." *American Economic Review* 72:114–32.

———, M. J. Peck, and E. Kalachek. 1967. *Technology, Economic Growth, and Public Policy*. Washington, D.C.: Brookings Institution.

Nevins, A., and F. E. Hill. 1954. *Ford: The Times, the Men, and the Company*. New York: Scribner.

Nicholls, J. G., ed. 1984. *The Development of Achievement Motivation*. Greenwich, Conn.: J.A.I. Press.

Niitamo, O. 1958. "Development of Productivity in Finnish Industry, 1925-1952." *Productivity Measures Review* 15:30–41.

Nijkamp, P. 1984a. *Long-Term Economic Fluctuations: A Spatial View*. Working Paper 1984–2. Amsterdam: Department of Economics, Free University.

———. 1984b. *Analysis of Episodes in Urban Event Histories*. Working Paper 84-75. Laxenburg, Austria: International Institute of Applied Systems Analysis.

———. 1985. "Twenty Five Years of Regional Science: Retrospect and Prospect." Paper presented at the 25th European Congress, Regional Science Association, Budapest.

———, ed. 1987. *Handbook of Regional Economics*. Amsterdam: North-Holland.

———, and P. Rietveld. 1986. "Technological Development and Regional Labour Markets." In *Regional Labour Market Analysis*, ed. M. M. Fischer and P. Nijkamp. Amsterdam: North-Holland.

Nisbet, R. 1969. *Social Change and History*. London: Oxford University Press.

Nordhaus, W., and J. Tobin. 1972. "Is Growth Obsolete?" In *Economic Research: Retrospect and Prospect, Economic Growth*, ed. R. A. Gordon. New York: National Bureau of Economic Research.

North, D. C. 1955. "Location Theory and Regional Economic Growth." *Journal of Political Economy* 63:243–58.

———. 1961. *The Economic Growth of the United States, 1790–1860.* Englewood Cliffs, N.J.: Prentice-Hall.

———. 1981. *Structure and Change in Economic History.* New York: Norton.

Northrop, F. S. C. 1962. "The Methodology and Limited Predictive Power of Classical Economic Science." In *The Logic of the Sciences and the Humanities,* ed. Meridian. Cleveland: World Publishing.

Norton, R. D. 1979. *City Life-Cycles and American Urban Policy.* New York: Academic Press.

———. 1986. "Industrial Policy and American Renewal." *Journal of Economic Literature* 24:1–40.

———, and J. Rees. 1979. "The Product Cycle and the Spatial Decentralization of American Manufacturing." *Regional Studies* 13:141–51.

Nussbaum, F. L. 1933. *A History of the Economic Institutions of Modern Europe.* New York: Crofts.

Oakey, R. P., A. T. Thwaites, and P. A. Nash. 1982. "Technological Change and Regional Development: Some Evidence on Regional Variations in Product and Process Innovation." *Environment and Planning A* 14:1073–86.

Ohlin, B. 1933. *Interregional and International Trade.* Cambridge, Mass.: Harvard University Press.

Okun, A. M. 1974. *Equality and Efficiency: The Big Tradeoff.* Washington, D.C.: Brookings Institution.

Olson, M. 1982. *The Rise and Decline of Nations: Economic Growth, Stagflation, and Social Rigidities.* New Haven, Conn.: Yale University Press.

Pandey, J., and N. B. Tewary. 1979. "Locus of Control and Achievement in Entrepreneurial Personalities." *Journal of Occupational Psychology* 52:107–11.

Parr, J. B. 1973. "Growth Poles, Regional Development, and Central Place Theory." *Papers of the Regional Science Association* 31:173–202.

———. 1981. "Temporal Change in a Central-Place System." *Environment and Planning A* 13:97–118.

Peck, M. J. 1962. "Inventions in the Postwar American Aluminum Industry." In *The Rate and Direction of Inventive Activity,* ed. National Bureau of Economic Research. Princeton, N.J.: Princeton University Press.

Penrose, E. T. 1952. "Biological Analogies in the Theory of the Firm." *American Economic Review* 41:804–19.

———. 1959. *The Theory of the Growth of the Firm.* New York: Wiley.

Perloff, H. S., E. S. Dunn, E. E. Lampard, and R. F. Muth. 1960. *Regions, Resources and Economic Growth.* Baltimore, Md.: Johns Hopkins University Press and Resources for the Future.

Perroux, F. 1955. "Note sur la Notion de 'Pole de Croissance.'" *Economie Appliquée* 8:307–20.

———. 1965. *La Pensée Economique de Joseph Schumpeter: Les Dynamiques du Capitalisme.* Geneva, Switzerland: Droz.

Persky, J., and W. Klein. 1975. "Regional Capital Growth and Some of those Other Things We Never Talk About." *Papers of the Regional Science Association* 35:181–190.

Plott, C. R. 1982. "Industrial Organization Theory and Experimental Economics." *Journal of Economic Literature* 20:1485–1527.

Polenske, K. R. 1980. *The U.S. Multiregional Input-Output Accounts and Model.* Lexington, Mass.: Lexington Books.

Porter, G., and H. C. Livesay. 1971. *Merchants and Manufacturers: Studies in the Changing Structure of Nineteenth Century Marketing.* Baltimore, Md.: Johns Hopkins University Press.

Prais, S. J. 1981. *Productivity and Industrial Structure.* New York: Cambridge University Press.

Pred, A. R. 1966. *The Spatial Dynamics of U.S. Urban Industrial Growth, 1800–1914.* Cambridge, Mass.: M.I.T. Press.

————. 1967. *Behavior and Location: Foundations for a Geographic and Dynamic Location Theory.* Lund Studies in Geography, ser. B, nos. 27, 28, parts I, II. Lund, Sweden: University of Lund.

Pugh, D. S., D. J. Hickson, C. R. Hinings, and C. Turner. 1968. "Dimensions of Organization Structure." *Administrative Science Quarterly* 13:65–105.

————. 1969. "The Context of Organization Structures." *Administrative Science Quarterly* 14:91–114.

Rasmussen, W. D., ed. 1975. *Agriculture in the United States.* Vols. 3, 4. New York: Random House.

Ratner, S., J. H. Soltow, and R. Sylla. 1979. *The Evolution of the American Economy.* New York: Basic Books.

Reati, A. 1980. "A Propos de la Baisse Tendancielle du Taux de Profit: Analyse Désagregée de l'Industrie Italienne, 1951–71; Premiére Partie." *Cahiers Economiques de Bruxelles* 88:507–46.

Redlich, F. 1959. "Entrepreneurial Typology." *Weltwirtschaftliches Archiv* 82:150–168.

————. 1966. "Toward the Understanding of an Unfortunate Legacy." *Kyklos* 19:709–16.

Rees, J., ed. 1986. *Technology, Regions and Policy.* Totowa, N.J.: Rowman & Littlefield.

Richardson, H. W. 1969. *Regional Economics.* New York: Praeger.

————. 1972. *Input-Output and Regional Economics.* London: Weidenfeld & Nicolson.

————. 1973. *Regional Growth Theory.* New York: Wiley.

————. 1978a. "'Basic Economic Activities in Metropolis." In *The Mature Metropolis,* ed. C. L. Leven. Lexington, Mass.: Heath.

————. 1978b. "The State of Regional Economics: A Survey Article." *International Regional Science Review* 3:1–48.

Riddle, D. I. 1986. *Service-Led Growth: The Role of the Service Sector in World Development.* New York: Praeger.

Robinson, A. 1934. "The Problem of Management and the Size of Firms." *Economic Journal* 44:242–57.

Roehrich, R. L. 1984. "The Relationship Between Technological and Business Innovation." *Journal of Business Strategy* 5:60–73.

Roethlisberger, R. T. and W. J. Dickson. 1939. *Management and the Worker.* Cambridge, Mass.: Harvard University Press.

de Roover, R. 1953. "The Commercial Revolution of the Thirteenth Century." In *Enterprise and Secular Change*, ed. F. Lane and S. Riemersa. London: Allen & Unwin.

Ronen, J. 1983. "Some Insights into the Entrepreneurial Process." In *Entrepreneurship*, ed. J. Ronen. Lexington, Mass.: Lexington Books.

Rosen, B. C. 1982. *The Industrial Connection: Achievement and the Family in Developing Societies*. Hawthorne, N.Y.: Aldine.

Rosenberg, N. 1972. *Technology and American Economic Growth*. New York: Harper & Row.

———. 1974. "Science, Invention, and Economic Growth." *Economic Journal* 84:90–108.

———. 1986. *Inside the Black Box: Technology and Economics*. New York: Cambridge University Press.

———, and L. E. Birdzell. 1987. *How the West Grew Rich: The Economic Transformation of the Industrial World*. New York: Basic Books.

Ross, E. A. 1896. "The Location of Industries." *Quarterly Journal of Economics* 10:247–68.

Rostow, W. W. 1956. "The Take-Off into Self-Sustained Growth." *Economic Journal* 66:25–48.

———. 1960. *The Stages of Economic Growth*. New York: Cambridge University Press.

———. 1975. "Kondratieff, Schumpeter, and Kuznets: Trend Periods Revisited." *Journal of Economic History* 35:719–53.

———. 1978. "A National Policy Towards Regional Change." In *Revitalizing the Northeast: Prelude to an Agenda*, ed. G. Sternlieb, and J. W. Hughes. New Brunswick, N.J.: Center for Urban Policy Research, Rutgers University.

Rubin, M. R., and M. T. Huber. 1986. *The Knowledge Industry in the United States, 1960–80*. Princeton, N.J.: Princeton University Press.

Rydenfelt, S. 1986. *A Pattern for Failure: Socialist Economies in Crisis*. Orlando, Fla.: Harcourt Brace Jovanovich.

Sarachek, B. 1978. "American Entrepreneurs and the Horatio Alger Myth." *Journal of Economic History* 38:439–56.

Say, J. B. 1803. *Traité de Economie Politique*. Paris: Deterville.

Scherer, F. M. 1980. *Industrial Market Structure and Economic Performance*. 2d ed. Chicago: Rand McNally.

———. 1986. *Innovation and Growth: Schumpeterian Perspectives*. Cambridge, Mass.: M.I.T. Press.

Schlebecker, J. T. 1975. *Whereby We Thrive: A History of American Farming, 1607–1972*. Ames: Iowa State University Press.

Schmenner, R. W. 1982. *Making Business Location Decisions*. Englewood Cliffs, N.J.: Prentice-Hall.

Schmookler, J. 1966. *Invention and Economic Growth*. Cambridge, Mass.: Harvard University Press.

———. 1972. *Patents, Invention and Economic Change*. Cambridge, Mass.: Harvard University Press.

Schumpeter, J. A. 1934. *The Theory of Economic Development: An Inquiry into Profits, Capital, Credit, Interest, and the Business Cycle.* Cambridge, Mass.: Harvard University Press (orig. publ. 1912; Leipzig: Duncker & Humblot).

———. 1950. *Capitalism, Socialism, and Democracy.* 3d ed. New York: Harper & Row.

———. 1954. *History of Economic Analysis,* ed. E. B. Schumpeter. New York: Oxford University Press.

Scott, A. J. 1983. "Location and Linkage Systems: A Survey and Reassessment." *Annals of Regional Science* 17:1–39.

Seninger, S. F. 1985. "Employment Cycles and Process Innovation in Regional Structural Change." *Journal of Regional Science* 25:259–72.

Shen, T. Y. 1973. "Technology Diffusion, Substitution, and X-Efficiency." *Econometrica* 41:263–84.

Shultz, T. W. 1980. "Investment in Entrepreneurial Ability." *Scandinavian Journal of Economics* 82:437–48.

———. 1981. *Investing in People: The Economics of Population Quality.* Berkeley: University of California Press.

Simon, H. A. 1947. "Effects of Increased Productivity upon the Ratio of Urban to Rural Population." *Econometrica* 15:31–42.

———. 1955a. "On a Class of Skew Distribution Functions." *Biometrika* 42:425–40.

———. 1955b. "A Behavioral Model of Rational Choice." *Quarterly Journal of Economics* 69:99–118.

———. 1977. *The New Science of Management Decision.* Englewood Cliffs, N.J.: Prentice-Hall.

———. 1979. "On Parsimonious Explanations of Production Relations." *Scandinavian Journal of Economics* 81:459–74.

———. 1982. "The Rural-Urban Population Balance Again." *Regional Science and Urban Economics* 12:599–606.

Smith, A. 1776. *An Inquiry into the Nature and Causes of the Wealth of Nations.* London: Strahan & Cadell.

Solow, R. M. 1957. "Technological Change and the Aggregate Production Function." *Review of Economics and Statistics* 39:312–30.

Soltow, J. H. 1968. "The Entrepreneur in Economic History." *American Economic Review* 58:84–92.

Sorel, G. 1986. *Essays on Socialism and Philosophy.* Vol. 1. New Brunswick, N.J.: Transaction Books.

Spencer, H. 1890. *First Principles.* New York: Appleton.

Stahl, M. J. 1986. *Managerial and Technical Motivation: Assessing Needs for Achievement, Power and Affiliation.* New York: Praeger.

Stanback, T. M., P. J. Bearse, T. J. Noyelle, and R. A. Karased. 1981. *Services: The New Economy.* Totowa, N.J.: Allanheld & Osmun.

Steuart, J. 1767. *An Inquiry into the Principles of Political Oeconomy.* London: Millar & Cadell.

Stevens, B., and G. I. Treyz. 1986. "A Multiregional Model Forecast for the United States Through 1995." *American Economic Review* 76:304–07.

Stigler, G. J. 1949. *The Theory of Price.* New York: Macmillan.

———. 1963. *Capital and Rates of Return in Manufacturing Industries*. Princeton, N.J.: Princeton University Press and National Bureau of Economic Research.

———. 1968. *The Organization of Industry*. Chicago: University of Chicago Press.

Stöhr, W. B. 1986. "Regional Innovation Complexes." *Papers of the Regional Science Association* 59:29–44.

Strauss, F., and L. H. Bean. 1940. *Gross Farm Income and Indices of Farm Production and Prices in the United States, 1929–1974*. Technical Bulletin 703, U.S. Department of Agriculture. Washington, D.C.: Government Printing Office.

Suarez-Villa, L. 1984. "Industrial Export Enclaves and Manufacturing Change." *Papers of the Regional Science Association* 54:89–111.

———. 1987a. "Entrepreneurship and the International Diffusion of Innovations in Manufacturing: A General Approach." *Rivista Internazionale di Scienze Economiche e Commerciali* 34:369–91.

———. 1987b. "Entrepreneurship in the Space-Economy." *Revue d'Economie Régionale et Urbaine* 28:59–79.

———. 1988a. "Metropolitan Evolution, Sectoral Economic Change, and the City Size Distribution." *Urban Studies* 25:1–20.

———. 1988b. "Innovation, Entrepreneurship, and the Role of Small and Medium Size Industries: A Long Term View." In *Small and Medium Size Enterprises in Regional Development*, ed. M. Giaoutzi, P. Nijkamp, and D. Storey. London: Routledge.

———. 1989. "Policentric Restructuring, Metropolitan Evolution, and the Decentralization of Manufacturing." *Tijdschrift voor Economische en Sociale Geografie* 80, in press.

———, and P. H. Han. 1989. "International Trends in Electronics Manufacturing and the Strategy of Industrialization." *Rivista Internazionale di Scienze Economiche e Commerciali* 36, in press.

Swales, J. K. 1979. "Entrepreneurship and Regional Development: Implications for Regional Policy." In *Regional Policy: Past Experience and New Directions*, ed. D. Maclennan and J. B. Parr. Oxford, Engl.: Martin Robertson.

Sweeney, G. P. 1987. *Innovation, Entrepreneurs and Regional Development*. London: Frances Pinter.

Sylos-Labini, P. 1984. *The Forces of Economic Growth and Decline*. Cambridge, Mass.: M.I.T. Press.

Taylor, F. W. 1895. "A Piece-Rate System, Being a Step toward Partial Solution of the Labor Problem." *Transactions, American Society of Mechanical Engineers* 16:856–83.

———. 1911. *Shop Management*. New York: McGraw-Hill.

Taylor, M. 1986. "Enterprises and the Product Cycle Model: Conceptual Ambiguities." In *New Technology and Regional Development*, ed. G. A. van der Knaap, and E. Wever. Beckenham, England: Croom Helm.

Teece, D. J. 1980. "Economies of Scope and the Scope of the Enterprise." *Journal of Economic Behavior and Organization* 1:223–47.

————, and S. G. Winter. 1984. "The Limits of Neoclassical Theory in Management Education." *American Economic Review* 74:116–121.

Temin, P. 1964. *Iron and Steel in Nineteenth Century America: An Economic Inquiry.* Cambridge, Mass.: M.I.T. Press.

Thomas, M. D. 1964. "The Export Base and Development Stages Theories of Regional Economic Growth: An Appraisal." *Land Economics* 40:421–32.

————. 1972. "Growth Pole Theory: An Examination of Some of its Basic Concepts." In *Growth Centers in Regional Economic Development,* ed. N. M. Hansen. New York: Free Press.

————. 1975. "Growth Pole Theory, Technological Change, and Regional Economic Growth." *Papers of the Regional Science Association* 34:3–25.

————. 1980. "Explanatory Frameworks for Growth and Change in Multi-regional Firms." *Economic Geography* 56:1–17.

————. 1986a. "The Innovation Factor in the Process of Regional Microeconomic Industrial Change: Conceptual Explorations." In *New Technology and Regional Development,* ed. G. A. van der Knaap, and E. Wever. Beckenham, England: Croom Helm.

————. 1986b. "Growth and Structural Change: The Role of Technical Innovation." In *Technological Change, Industrial Restructuring and Regional Development,* ed. A. Amin, and J. B. Goddard. Boston: Allen & Unwin.

————, and R. B. LeHeron. 1975. "Perspectives on Technological Change and the Process of Diffusion in the Manufacturing Sector." *Economic Geography* 51:231–51.

Thompson, W. R. 1965. *A Preface to Urban Economics.* Baltimore, Md.: Johns Hopkins University Press.

Thrall, G. I., and C. Erol. 1983. "A Dynamic Equilibrium Model of Regional Capital Investment with Supporting Evidence from Canada and the United States." *Economic Geography* 53:272–81.

von Thünen, J. H. 1826. *Der isolierte Staat in Beziehung auf Landwirtschaft und Nationalökonomie.* Hamburg: Derthes.

Tiebout, C. M. 1957. "Location Theory, Empirical Evidence, and Economic Evolution." *Papers and Proceedings of the Regional Science Association* 3:74–86.

————. 1962. *The Community Economic Base Study.* Supplementary Paper no. 16. New York: Committee for Economic Development.

————. 1967. "Input-Output and the Firm: A Technique for Using National and Regional Tables." *Review of Economics and Statistics* 49:206–62.

Tinbergen, J. 1939. *Business Cycles in the United States of America, 1919–1932.* Geneva: League of Nations.

Townroe, P. M. 1970. "Industrial Linkage, Agglomeration, and External Economies." *Journal of the Town Planning Institute* 56:18–20.

————. 1971. *Industrial Location Decisions: A Study of Management Behavior.* Occasional Paper no. 15. Birmingham, England: Centre for Urban and Regional Studies, University of Birmingham.

Tversky, A., and D. Kahneman. 1982. "Judgment under Uncertainty: Heuristics and Biases." In *Judgment under Uncertainty: Heuristics and Biases,* ed. D.

Kahneman, P. Slovic, and A. Tversky. New York: Cambridge University Press.

U. S. Bureau of the Census. 1904a. *Abstract of the Twelfth Census of the United States, 1900*. Washington, D.C.: Government Printing Office.

———. 1904b. *Occupations at the Twelfth Census, 1900*. Special Report. Washington, D.C.: Government Printing Office.

———. 1904c. *Report on Manufacturing Industries in the United States at the Eleventh Census, 1890*. Part I. Washington, D.C.: Government Printing Office.

———. 1913. *Thirteenth Census of the United States, 1910*. Washington, D.C.: Government Printing Office.

———. 1923. *Fourteenth Census of the United States, 1920; Occupations*. Washington, D.C.: Government Printing Office.

———. 1933a. *Fifteenth Census of the United States, 1930*. Washington, D.C.: Government Printing Office.

———. 1933b. *General Report on Occupations; Fifteenth Census of the United States, 1930*. Vol. 5. Washington, D.C.: Government Printing Office.

———. 1975. *Historical Statistics of the United States, Colonial Times to 1970*. Parts 1, 2. Washington, D.C.: Government Printing Office.

———. 1978. *Census of Agriculture, 1974*. Washington, D.C.: Government Printing Office.

———. 1984. *Census of Agriculture, 1982*. Washington, D.C.: Government Printing Office.

———. 1986. *Statistical Abstract of the United States, 1987*. Washington, D.C.: Government Printing Office.

U. S. Department of Commerce. 1973. *Long Term Economic Growth, 1860–1970*. Washington, D.C.: Government Printing Office.

———. 1984. "The Input-Output Structure of the U.S. Economy, 1977." *Survey of Current Business* 64:42–84. .

———. 1986. *The National Income and Product Accounts of the United States, 1929–1982*. Washington, D.C.: Government Printing Office.

Uselding, P., ed. 1986. *Research in Economic History*. Vols. 1–10. Greenwich, Conn.: J.A.I. Press.

Usher, A. P. 1954. *A History of Mechanical Inventions*. Cambridge, Mass.: Harvard University Press.

Vanneman, R. D. 1973. "Dominance and Achievement in Entrepreneurial Personalities." In *Micro Aspects of Development*, ed. E. B. Ayal. New York: Praeger.

Varaiya, P., R. Artle, and C. Humes. 1979. "Division of Labor and the Distribution of Income." *Regional Science and Urban Economics* 9:71–82.

Vernon, R. A. 1960. *Metropolis 1985*. Cambridge, Mass.: Harvard University Press.

———. 1966. "International Investment and International Trade in the Product Cycle." *Quarterly Journal of Economics* 80:190–207.

———. 1970. "Organization as a Scale Factor in the Growth of Firms." In *Industrial Organization and Economic Development*, ed. J. W. Markham, and G. F. Papanek. Boston: Houghton Mifflin.

———. 1974. "The Location of Economic Activity." In *Economic Analysis and the Multinational Enterprise*, ed. J. H. Dunning. London: Allen & Unwin.

———. 1977. *Storm over the Multinationals*. Cambridge, Mass.: Harvard University Press.

———. 1983. "Organizational and Institutional Responses to International Risk." In *Managing International Risk*, ed. R. J. Herring. New York: Cambridge University Press.

Viner, J. 1958. *The Long View and the Short*. Glencoe, Ill.: Free Press.

Walker, D. F. 1975. "A Behavioural Approach to Industrial Location." In *Locational Dynamics of Manufacturing Activity*, ed. L. Collins, and D. F. Walker. London: Wiley.

Walters, A. A. 1963. "Production and Cost Functions: An Econometric Survey." *Econometrica* 31:1–66.

Wasson, C. R. 1974. *Dynamic Competitive Strategy and Product Life Cycles*. St. Charles, Ill.: Challenge Books.

Webber, M. J. 1972. *Impact of Uncertainty on Location*. Cambridge, Mass.: M.I.T. Press.

Weber, A. F. 1899. *The Growth of Cities in the Nineteenth Century: A Study in Statistics*. New York: Macmillan.

Weber, A. 1929. *Theory of the Location of Industries*. Trans. C. J. Friedrich. Chicago: University of Chicago Press (orig. publ. 1909).

Weber, M. 1985. *The Protestant Ethic and the Spirit of Capitalism*. Trans. T. Parsons. Winchester, Mass.: Allen & Unwin (orig. publ. 1904).

Wells, L., ed. 1972. *The Product Life Cycle and International Trade*. Cambridge, Mass.: Harvard University Press.

Wheat, L. F. 1986. "The Determinants of 1963-77 Regional Manufacturing Growth: Why the South and West Grow." *Journal of Regional Science* 26:635–59.

Wheaton, W. C., ed. 1979. *Interregional Movements and Regional Growth*. Washington, D.C.: Urban Institute.

Williamson, J. G. 1986. "Is Inequality Inevitable under Capitalism?" In *Capitalism and Equality in America: Modern Capitalism*, ed. P. L. Berger. Vol. 1. Lanham, Md.: University Press of America.

Williamson, O. E. 1970. *Corporate Control and Business Behavior*. Englewood Cliffs, N.J.: Prentice-Hall.

———. 1981. "The Modern Corporation: Origins, Evolution, Attributes." *Journal of Economic Literature* 19:1537–68.

Winter, S. G. 1964. "Economic 'Natural Selection' and the Theory of the Firm." *Yale Economic Essays* 4:225–72.

Wolpert, J. 1964. "The Decision Process in Spatial Context." *Annals of the Association of American Geographers* 54:537–58.

Wood, P. A., ed. 1978. *Priorities in Industrial Location Research*. Report to the Human Geography Committee. London: Social Science Research Council.

Woodward, J. 1958. *Management and Technology*. London: H. M. Stationery Office.

Index

About the Author

LUIS SUAREZ-VILLA is associate professor of social ecology at the University of California at Irvine, where he teaches urban and regional analysis, regional science, and urban planning and policy studies. His work has appeared in a wide range of academic journals in North America, Europe, Latin America, and Asia, including *Urban Studies,* the *Journal of Regional Science,* the *Papers of The Regional Science Association, Revue d'Economie Régionale et Urbaine,* and the *Annals of Regional Science.*

Dr. Suarez-Villa holds a Ph.D. with specializations in city and regional planning and economics from Cornell University.